JOKES
FOR
BLOKES

JOKES
FOR
BLOKES

THE ULTIMATE BOOK OF JOKES
NOT SUITABLE FOR MIXED COMPANY

Llewellyn Dowd & Phil McCracken

EBURY
PRESS

5 7 9 10 8 6 4

First published in 2011 by Ebury Press, an imprint of Ebury Publishing

A Random House Group company

The Random House Group Limited Reg. No. 954009

Addresses for companies within the Random House Group can be found at
www.randomhouse.co.uk

A CIP catalogue record for this book is available from the British Library

The Random House Group Limited supports The Forest Stewardship Council (FSC®), the leading international forest certification organisation. Our books carrying the FSC label are printed on FSC® certified paper. FSC is the only forest certification scheme endorsed by the leading environmental organisations, including Greenpeace. Our paper procurement policy can be found at www.randomhouse.co.uk/environment

To buy books by your favourite authors and register for offers visit
www.randomhouse.co.uk

Cover designed by Two Associates
Interior by seagulls.net

ISBN 9780091940447

Printed and bound by CPI Group (UK) Ltd, Croydon, CR0 4YY

CONTENTS

CONTENTS

CONTENTS

CONTENTS

CONTENTS

CONTENTS

ACCIDENTS

▶ A man woke up in the hospital and the doctor said, 'I've got some good news and some bad news.'

'What's the bad news?' the man asked.

'You've been in a car crash and you're paralysed from the waist down, your girlfriend died on impact and your son is in a coma showing no response.'

'Bloody hell, that *is* bad news!' he said. 'What's the good?'

'You're favourite to win *X Factor* next year.'

▶ You should always unplug appliances before going to bed at night. There are two exceptions to this rule: fridges and life-support machines. Otherwise you could end up wasting a lot of vegetables.

▶ What's the last thing that goes through a fly's mind when it hits a windscreen? Its arse!

▶ The TV presenter Ulrika Jonsson suffered an accident at home yesterday. Apparently after having showered, she walked over the marble hallway to her bedroom, slipped and ended up with a mobile phone stuck in her rectum.

Doctors at the hospital where she is being treated are unconcerned, however, and anticipate she'll make a full recovery.

As one of them said, 'It's not the first time she's had an Eriksson up her arse.'

▶ Why did Humpty Dumpty push his girlfriend off the wall? To see her crack.

▶ A man was explaining to the A&E nurse how the accident happened:
'I fitted a mirror to our bedroom ceiling but it came crashing down when
the wife and I were shagging.'

The nurse asked, 'Who was on top?'

'She was,' he replied.

'I see,' said the nurse. 'She has several lacerations to her head, back and
legs, but could you explain how she managed to dislocate her jaw?'

'Nobody criticises my DIY.'

▶ I was in my car, driving along, and my boss rang up and said, 'You've
been promoted.' And I swerved. And then he rang up a second time and
said, 'You've been promoted again.' And I swerved again. He rang up a
third time and said, 'You're managing director.' And I went into a tree.
And a policeman came up and said, 'What happened to you?' And I said,
'I careered off the road.'

▶ I got stopped by a woman in the street today.

She said, 'Excuse me, sir, have you had an accident in the last three
years that wasn't your fault?'

I said, 'Yes, she's nearly two now.'

▶ When I left school, I wanted to take all my birthday money and buy
myself a motorcycle, but my mum said no. She had a brother who died in
a horrible motorcycle accident when he was 18. So she said I could just
have his.

▶ I saw a poor old lady fall unconscious in the snow today. Well, I'm
assuming she was poor – she only had 24 pence in her purse.

▶ A woman purchased a piece of a forest. There was a large tree on one of the highest points in the woods. She wanted a good view of the natural splendour of her recently acquired land so she started to climb the big tree. As she neared the top, she encountered a savage owl that attacked her. In her haste to escape, the woman slid down the tree to the ground and got many splinters in her crotch. In considerable pain, she hurried to the nearest doctor. She told him how she came to get all the splinters. The doctor listened to her story with great patience and then told her to go into the examining room and he would see if he could help her.

She sat and waited three hours before the doctor reappeared. The angry woman demanded, 'What took you so long?'

He smiled and then told her, 'Well, I had to get permits from the Department for the Environment, the Forestry Commission Service and the local council before I could remove old-growth timber from your recreational area. I'm sorry, but they turned me down.'

▶ Did you hear about the terrible accident at Spaghetti Junction? Twelve people were injured, and three pasta way.

▶ A guy calls his wife from the hospital. He tells her that his finger got cut off at the building site where he works.

'Oh my God!' cries the woman. 'The whole finger?'

'No,' replies the guy. 'The one next to it!'

▶ A man working at a timber merchant accidentally sheared off all ten of his fingers. At the hospital, the surgeon said, 'Give me the fingers and I'll see what I can do.'

'I haven't got them,' said the man.

'Why not?' asked the surgeon. 'This is 2011, we've got microsurgery and all kinds of amazing techniques. I could have put them back on and made you like new. So why didn't you bring the fingers?'

The man replied, 'I couldn't pick them up.'

▶ Driving his date down a country lane one night, a man pretended to run out of petrol in the hope of being able to have sex with his date in the back seat. But she wasn't falling for such an old trick, and said that she had a £50 note in her purse.

'I'll walk with you into town,' she said. 'You can use the money to buy petrol.'

He said he had to pee first. But while he was peeing, she decided to light a match near the petrol tank to see if there was any petrol in it. There was a big explosion, scattering things far and wide. As the bang subsided, she called out, 'Help me find my purse. It's got £50 in it.'

'Never mind that,' he yelled. 'Help me find my right hand, it's got my dick in it.'

▶ A police officer arrived at the scene of a horrific road accident with several fatalities. Body parts were strewn everywhere. He was making notes of where everything was, when he suddenly came across a decapitated human head. He wrote in his notebook, 'Head on bullevard', but couldn't spell it. He tried 'bouelevard' and 'boolevard' but still couldn't get it right. So when no one was looking, he kicked the head and wrote, 'Head on kerb'.

▶ What's the difference between a guy falling from the first floor and one falling from the 16th floor? The guy falling from the first floor goes, 'Splat, aaaargh!' and the one falling from the 16th floor goes, 'Aaaargh, splat!'

▶ Did you hear about the man who fell asleep at the wheel? There was a terrible mess – clay everywhere.

▶ The M25 was blocked for an hour yesterday after a car driven by a hunchback crashed into a car driven by a bearded lady. Police are describing it as a freak accident.

▶ A policeman arrived at the scene of a car crash. He rushed over and asked the driver, 'Are you seriously hurt?'

'I don't know,' said the driver. 'I haven't spoken to my lawyer yet.'

▶ Have you heard about the new Australian range of sunblock called Irwin? Protects against harmful rays.

▶ Two guys were sitting in a bar. One said, 'Did you hear the news? Dave is dead.'

'How?' gasped the other. 'What happened to him?'

'Well, he was on his way over to my house the other day and when he pulled up outside, he didn't brake properly and – bang – he hit the pavement. The car flipped over and he went crashing through the sunroof. He went flying through the air and smashed through my upstairs bedroom window.'

'Wow! What a horrible way to die!'

'No, no, he survived that. That didn't kill him. So, after landing in my upstairs bedroom, he was lying on the floor covered in broken glass. Then he spotted the big antique wardrobe we have in the room and reached for the handle to try and pull himself up. He was just dragging himself up when – bang – this massive wardrobe came crashing down on top of him, crushing him and breaking most of his bones.'

'What a way to go! That's terrible!'

'No, no, that didn't kill him, he survived that. He managed to get the wardrobe off him and crawled out onto the landing. There, he tried to pull himself up on the banister, but under his weight the banister broke and he fell down to the first floor. In mid-air, all the broken banister poles spun and fell on him, pinning him to the floor, sticking right through him.'

'Gee! That is an awful way to go!'

'No, no, that didn't kill him, he even survived that. So he was on the downstairs landing, just beside the kitchen. He crawled into the kitchen, tried to pull himself up by the cooker, but accidentally reached for a big pot of boiling water. Whoosh! The whole thing came down on him and burned off most of his skin.'

'Man! What a way to go!'

'No, no, he survived that. He was lying on the ground, covered in boiling water, and he spotted the phone. He thought he'd reach for the phone to call for help but instead he grabbed the light switch and pulled the whole thing off the wall. Well, water and electricity don't mix, so he got electrocuted – boom – 10,000 volts shot through him.'

'Now that is one horrible way to go!'

'No, no, that didn't kill him. He survived that, he...'

'Hold on now, just how the hell did Dave die?'

'I shot him!'

'You shot him? What the hell did you shoot him for?'

'He was wrecking my house!'

▶ A man fell out of an 11th-storey window. He was lying on the ground with a crowd gathered around him when a cop walked over and said, 'What happened?'

The guy said, 'I don't know. I just got here.'

▶ A woman was drying herself after taking a shower when she slipped and landed on the floor with her legs spread wide apart. Worse still, her pussy created a vacuum so that she was unable to move. She called her husband to help but, hard though he tried, he couldn't prise her pussy away from the floor tiles.

In desperation, he then summoned a neighbour, who also tried unsuccessfully to shift her. Finally the neighbour suggested, 'Why don't we get a hammer and break the tiles around her legs and lift her that way?'

'Great idea,' said the husband, 'but let me just rub her tits a little so I can push her over to the kitchen. The tiles are cheaper in there.'

ACCOUNTANTS

▶ An accountant is walking down the street when he comes across a tramp.

'Spare some loose change?' asks the tramp.

'And why should I do that?' asks the accountant.

'Because I'm skint. Haven't got a penny to my name and nothing to eat,' says the tramp.

'I see,' says the accountant. 'And how does this compare to the same quarter last year?'

▶ How do accountants liven up their office parties? They invite an undertaker.

▶ Two accountants go to the cemetery to pay their respects at the grave of a colleague. However, they search and search and can't find his tombstone anywhere. Eventually one turns to the other and says, 'Perhaps he put it in the name of his last wife?'

▶ What's an accountant's idea of trashing his hotel room? Refusing to fill out the guest comment card.

ACTORS

▶ Have you seen the Harry Potter games? They're a quid each.

▶ 'Did you hear on the news today about that American actress who got stabbed? Reese somebody or other.'
  'Witherspoon?'
  'No. With a knife.'

▶ Actor to fellow thespian: 'At the end of my last recitation it took the audience 45 minutes to leave the theatre.'
  Thespian: 'Goodness, was it very well attended?'
  Actor: 'No, he was on crutches.'

▶ An actor is on stage doing a terrible version of *Hamlet.* He's so bad, the audience start booing. Finally the actor stops, looks at the audience and says, 'Don't blame me! I didn't write this rubbish!'

▶ Sean Connery has fallen on hard times. All work has dried up and he's just sat at home twiddling his thumbs. Suddenly the phone rings and Sean answers it. It's his agent and Sean gets very excited.
  The agent says, 'Sean, I've got a job for you. Starts tomorrow, but you've got to get there early, for 10ish.'
  Sean frowns and replies, '10ish? But I haven't even got a racket.'

▶ A man walks into a bar and goes up to the hottest girl he sees.
'Hi, the name's Bond,' he says.
'Let me guess, James Bond,' replies the girl.
'No,' he says. 'Unibond. I'm here to fill your crack.'

▶ How does James Bond like his pussy? Shaven, not furred.

▶ Did you hear about the man who was sacked from his job as a theatre designer? He tried to leave without making a scene.

▶ *Famous altered egos:*

- Bruise Lee: inept martial-arts student

- Merlyn Streep: professional magician

- Sean Cannery: manager, fish-packing plant

- Splint Eastwood: respected osteopath

- Bette Fidler: skilled symphony musician

- Marlon Brandy: maker of fine liqueurs

- Jackie Masonry: journeyman bricklayer

- Draw Barrymore: portrait artist

- Leonardo de Cappuccino: founder, coffee-shop chain

▶ My sister wanted to be an actress but she never made it. She does live in a trailer. She got halfway. She's an actress, she just never gets called to the set.

▶ The famous stage magician had a great climax to his act: he would fill a large bowl with shit and proceed to slurp it down, to the amazement and delight of the audience. One evening he had just begun the wow finish to his act when he stopped dead in his tracks.

'Go ahead,' murmured the stage manager. 'Eat the shit! Eat it!'

'Can't do it,' said the magician. 'There's a hair in it.'

AEROPLANES

▶ An aeroplane is about to crash, when a female passenger jumps up frantically and announces, 'If I'm going to die, I want to die feeling like a woman.' She removes all her clothing and asks, 'Is there someone on this plane who is man enough to make me feel like a woman?'

A man stands up, removes his shirt and says, 'Here, iron this!'

▶ I glanced under the seat of the aircraft I was on and saw a life jacket, and thought, 'Bugger, the ferries must have the parachutes!'

▶ Air controller to pilot: 'What height are you?'

Pilot: 'Six foot.'

▶ 'Flight 1234, turn right 45 degrees for noise abatement,' advised the control tower.

'Roger,' the pilot responded, 'but we're flying at 35,000 feet. How much noise can we make up here?'

'Sir,' replied the control tower, 'have you ever heard the noise a 727 makes when it hits a 747?'

▶ A passenger was sitting on an aeroplane, sweating profusely and chewing his nails. The air hostess said, 'Sir, can I get you something from the bar to calm you down?'

She got him a whisky and he knocked it back, but 20 minutes later she noticed that he was shaking like a leaf. 'Would another drink help?' she asked sympathetically. He nodded feverishly. So she fetched him another whisky, and he gulped it down. But a quarter of an hour later, there was no improvement. In fact, he was worse than ever, and was sobbing audibly. The air hostess remarked, 'I've never seen anyone so afraid of flying.'

'I'm not afraid of flying,' said the man. 'I'm trying to give up drinking!'

▶ As an aeroplane prepared for takeoff, the air hostess concluded her announcement by saying, 'And on behalf of your captain, Diane Jones, we wish you all a pleasant journey.' A male passenger in row nine was appalled to hear that the plane had a woman pilot. When the air hostess came around to make the last-minute checks, he said, 'Is that right? This plane is being flown by a woman?'

'Yes,' replied the air hostess politely. 'In fact, the entire crew is female.'

'In that case,' he grumbled, 'I'll need a stiff drink once we get under way. I don't know what to think of all those women up there in the cockpit.'

'That's another thing,' said the air hostess. 'We no longer call it the cockpit. Now it's the box office.'

▶ With a plane about to crash, the captain asked the passengers, 'Does anyone on board believe in the power of prayer?' A priest immediately put his hand up. 'Good,' said the captain. 'We're one parachute short.'

▶ The aeroplane was just taking off when the pilot, making a routine announcement, suddenly screamed, 'Oh, my God!' A few minutes later, he came back on the intercom and apologised if he had scared any of the passengers. He explained, 'While I was talking, the flight attendant brought me a cup of hot coffee and spilled it in my lap. You should see the front of my trousers!'

One of the passengers said, 'That's nothing. He should see the back of mine!'

▶ Three women were on a flight when the captain suddenly announced, 'Please prepare for a crash-landing!' The first woman immediately began putting on all her jewellery.

'Why are you doing that?' asked the other two.

'Well, when they come to rescue us, they will see that I am rich and will rescue me first.'

The second woman, not wishing to be outdone, began removing her top and bra.

'Why are you doing that?' asked her two friends.

'Well, when they come to rescue us, they will see what great tits I have and will pick me up first.'

Not wishing to be outdone, the third woman, who was West Indian, started taking off her skirt and panties.

'Why are you doing that?' asked the other two. 'Well, they always search for the black box first!'

▶ A small plane crashed in the middle of the desert. The pilot and co-pilot wandered around for days in search of food, but could find nothing. Finally the co-pilot announced, 'I'm so hungry, I'm going to chop off my dick and eat it.'

'Before you do,' said the pilot, 'think of your girlfriend.'

'What's the point? At this rate I will never see her again anyway.'

'I know, but if you think of her first, hopefully there will be enough for both of us.'

AFFAIRS

▶ A professor of mathematics sent a fax to his wife. It read: 'Dear wife, you must realise that you are 54 years old and I have certain needs which you are no longer able to satisfy. I am otherwise happy with you as a wife, and I sincerely hope you will not be hurt or offended to learn that by the time you receive this letter, I will be at the Grand Hotel with my 18-year-old teaching assistant. I'll be home before midnight. Your husband.'

When he arrived at the hotel, there was a faxed letter waiting for him that read as follows: 'Dear husband. You too are 54 years old, and by the time you receive this, I will be at the Ritz Hotel with the 18-year-old pool boy. Being the brilliant mathematician that you are, you can easily appreciate the fact that 18 goes into 54 a lot more times than 54 goes into 18. Don't wait up.'

▶ Married men have two ages. When they want to remain faithful but don't, and when they want to be unfaithful but can't.

▶ I always call out my wife's name during sex. Just to make sure she's not around.

▶ Keith and Malcolm are drinking, when Keith leans over and starts stroking Malcolm's beard.

Keith says, 'Your face feels just like my wife's pussy.'

Malcolm strokes it himself and says, 'You're right.'

▶ A woman was at home one afternoon, when she heard a knock at the door. She answered it and it was a man who said, 'Do you have a vagina?' She screamed and slammed the door in his face. The next day she heard another knock on the door and when she opened it the same man said, 'Do you have a vagina?' So she slammed the door in his face again. She told her husband about this and they came up with an idea. The husband decided to take the day off work and if the man knocked on the door, his wife would keep the man talking so that he could be confronted. Sure enough the next day there was a knock on the door and the same man said, 'Do you have a vagina?'

'Yes, I do,' replied the woman.

'Good,' said the man. 'Then tell your husband to stop screwing my wife.'

▶ A man had worked his whole life in a pickle factory. One day he came home and told his wife that he had been fired from his job. She began to scream and yell, 'You have given them 20 years of devoted service. Why did they fire you?'

'For 20 years I've wanted to stick my pecker in the pickle slicer,' he explained, 'and today I finally did it!'

The wife ran over and pulled his pants down to see what damage had been done. 'You look OK,' she said with a sigh of relief. 'So what happened to the pickle slicer?'

'They fired her, too.'

▶ How do you make your girlfriend scream when you're having sex?
Ring her and tell her what you're doing.

▶ A woman goes to the doctor and says, 'Doctor, I've got a bit of a problem. I'll have to take my clothes off to show you.'

The doctor tells her to go behind the screen and disrobe. She does so, and the doctor goes round to see her when she is ready.

'Well, what is it?' he asks.

'It's a bit embarrassing,' she replies. 'These two green circles have appeared on the inside of my thighs.'

The doctor examines her and finally admits he has no idea what the cause is. Then he suddenly asks, 'Have you been having an affair with a gypsy lately?'

The woman blushes and says, 'Well, actually I have.'

'That's the problem,' the doctor says. 'Tell him his earrings aren't made of gold!'

▶ A man came home and found his wife in bed with another man. So he dragged the man down the stairs to the garage and put his cock in a vice. He secured it tightly and removed the handle. Then he picked up a hacksaw.

The man, terrified, screamed, 'Stop! Stop! You're not going to cut it off, are you?'

'Oh no,' the husband replied. 'You are. I'm going to set the garage on fire!'

▶ When a man steals your wife, there is no better revenge than to let him keep her.

▶ A woman was in bed with her lover when she heard her husband opening the front door. 'Hurry!' she said. 'Stand in the corner.' She quickly rubbed baby oil all over him and then she dusted him with talcum powder. 'Don't move until I tell you to,' she whispered. 'Just pretend you're a statue.'

'What's this, honey?' the husband enquired as he entered the room.

'Oh, it's just a statue,' she replied nonchalantly. 'The Smiths bought one for their bedroom. I liked it so much, I got one for us, too.'

No more was said about the statue, not even later that night when they went to sleep.

Around two in the morning the husband got out of bed, went to the kitchen and returned a while later with a sandwich and a glass of milk. 'Here,' he said to the 'statue'. 'Eat something. I stood like an idiot at the Smiths' for three days and nobody offered me as much as a glass of water.'

▶ Arriving home from a shopping trip, a wife was horrified to find her husband in bed with a pretty girl. Just as the wife was about to storm out of the house, her husband called out, 'Before you go, I want you to hear how all this came about. Driving home, I saw this young girl, looking poor and tired. I offered her a ride. She was hungry, so I brought her home and fed her some of the roast you had forgotten about in the refrigerator. Her shoes were worn out, so I gave her a pair of your shoes that you don't wear because they are out of fashion. She was cold, so I gave her the new birthday sweater you never wear because the colour doesn't suit you. Her trousers had holes in them, so I gave her a pair of yours that don't fit you anymore. Then, as this poor girl was about to leave the house, she paused and asked, "Is there anything else that your wife doesn't use anymore?" So here we are!'

▶ A married couple invited a male friend over to their house for the evening, but when a sudden blizzard blew up, the friend was prevented from travelling home. Since the couple didn't have a guest room, he said he would book into a nearby hotel, but the wife wouldn't hear of it.

'Nonsense,' she insisted. 'Our bed is plenty big enough for all three of us, and we're all friends here.'

The husband agreed, so they settled down in bed together. The husband was in the middle, the wife on his left and the friend on his right. Soon the husband began snoring loudly, and the wife sneaked over to the friend's side of the bed and invited him to have sex with her.

'Look, I'd really like to,' said the friend. 'You know I've always fancied you. But it wouldn't be right, not in the same bed as your husband. Anyway, he'll wake up, and then he'll kill me!'

'Don't worry about him,' said the wife. 'He's such a heavy sleeper, he'll never notice. If you don't believe me, just yank a hair out of his arse. He won't even wake up.'

So the friend pulled a hair from the husband's arse, and sure enough he didn't even flinch. Reassured, he proceeded to have sex with the wife, who then returned to her side of the bed.

But she was restless, and 30 minutes later she was back on the friend's side of the bed, pleading for more sex. The friend was sure the husband would wake up this time, but once more the wife persuaded him to yank a hair from the husband's arse. And when the husband failed to stir, they had sex again. They carried on like this for the next four hours, always first making sure that it was safe by yanking a hair from the husband's arse. Finally, after about the seventh bout of sex, the wife returned to her side of the bed.

The husband then rolled over and whispered to his friend, 'Listen, I don't care if you screw my wife, but could you please stop using my arse for a scoreboard!'

▶ A few guys always used to meet up on Fridays after work for a drink. One Friday, Dave showed up late, sat down forlornly at the bar and knocked back his first beer in one gulp.

'You OK?' asked Phil, another of the gang.

'Not really,' sighed Dave. 'This morning my wife told me that she's rationing our sex life – she's cutting me back to just once a week. I can't believe it.'

Phil put a consoling arm around Dave's shoulder. 'You think you've got it bad – she's cut some guys out altogether!'

▶ When her husband had to cancel his vacation to the Caribbean because of business commitments, a wife decided to go alone. Making the most of her freedom, she allowed herself to be seduced by a Jamaican man. After a passionate night of sex, she asked him his name.

'I'm not going to tell you,' he said, 'because you'll laugh.'

'No, I won't,' she said.

'You will.'

'I won't – I promise.'

'OK, my first name is Snow.'

The woman immediately started laughing.

'I knew you'd make fun of it!' he said.

'No, it's just that my husband won't believe me when I tell him that I had ten inches of snow every day in the Caribbean!'

▶ Two Irishmen were talking. Joe says to Paddy, 'Close your curtains the next time you're shagging your wife. The whole street was watching and laughing at you yesterday.'

Paddy says, 'Well, the joke's on them because I wasn't even at home yesterday.'

▶ A man got home from work only to find his wife in bed screwing a strange man.

'What the hell's going on here?' he shouted.

'See,' said the wife to the stranger, 'I told you he was stupid.'

▶ A man told his wife he'd be late home from the office. Instead he went to a hotel, where he had wild sex with his secretary. Driving home afterwards, he looked in the mirror and was horrified to see a huge love bite on his neck. Worried that his wife would notice, he opened the front door to be greeted by his excited dog. Thinking quickly, he pretended to wrestle with his pet, then went into the kitchen holding his neck. 'Look what the dog did to my neck,' he said to his wife.

His wife turned round and ripped open her shirt. 'That's nothing. Look what he did to my tits!'

▶ Although scheduled for all-night duty at the station, a police officer was allowed to go home early. Creeping into the house at two o'clock in the morning, he took great pains not to wake his wife. He undressed in the dark, crept into the bedroom and began climbing gingerly into bed. But just as he pulled back the sheet, his wife sat up sleepily and said, 'Darling, would you go down to the all-night chemist and get some aspirin? I've got a splitting headache.'

'Sure, honey,' he said and, feeling his way across the room, he got dressed again in the dark and walked to the chemist.

As he entered, the pharmacist looked up in surprise and asked, 'Aren't you a policeman?'

'Yes, that's right,' replied the officer.

'Then why on earth are you wearing a fireman's uniform?'

▶ A husband staggered home at two o'clock in the morning. He opened the bedroom door to find another man in bed with his wife. The wife pushed the man off her and demanded to know why her husband was so late home.

The husband yelled, 'Who the hell is this guy, and what's he doing in bed with you?'

The wife shouted back, 'Don't go changing the subject! Where the hell have you been till this time of night?'

▶ A man walked into a bar, ordered a double Scotch and moaned to the barman, 'An irate husband has written to me, threatening to have me killed unless I stop screwing his wife.'

'So why don't you just stop?' said the barman.

'It's not as easy as that,' replied the man. 'He didn't sign his name.'

▶ Three men were in heaven discussing how they died.

The first man said, 'I died of cancer.'

The second man said, 'I died of tuberculosis.'

The third man said, 'I died of seenus.'

The first two men asked, 'Do you mean sinus?'

'No, I mean seenus. I was out with my best friend's wife and he seen us!'

▶ A lord returned home to his country manor early from a grouse shoot to find his wife having sex in bed with his best friend, the local MP.

'How could you, Cynthia?' he cried. 'After everything I've done for you. I've given you this beautiful house, I've always provided you with the most expensive clothes and jewels and I bought you a Ferrari for your birthday. I've tried to be a good husband and this is how you repay me!'

Hearing this, his wife burst into tears.

The lord then turned to the MP. 'And as for you, Geoffrey, you could at least have the decency to stop while I'm talking!'

▶ Two men were chatting over a beer. One said, 'Do you like women with bad body odour and bad breath?'

'No way,' replied his friend.

'Do you like pussies you could hide a watermelon in?'
'No way!'
'Then what the hell are you doing messing around with my wife?'

ALIMONY

▶A woman was telling her friend: 'It is I who made my husband a millionaire.'
'And what was he before you married him?' asked the friend.
The woman replied, 'A billionaire.'

▶ The definition of alimony: The screwing you get for the screwing you got.

▶ 'Alimony, a Latin term for removing a man's wallet through his genitals' – Robin Williams

▶ 'Mr Smith, I have reviewed this case very carefully,' the divorce court judge said, 'and I've decided to give your wife £275 a week.'
'That's very fair, your honour,' the husband said. 'And every now and then I'll try to send her a few pounds myself.'

▶ Why are cyclones/tornadoes usually named after women? Because what starts off as a small blow ends up taking half your house.

ALLIGATORS

▶ What do you get when you cross an alligator and a railway track?
Three pieces of alligator.

▶ A guy walks into a bar with his dog on a leash.

The barman says, 'Geez, that's a weird dog: he's stumpy-legged, pink and doesn't have a tail. I bet my Rottweiler would beat the hell out of it.'

Fifty quid is laid down. Out in the yard the Rottweiler gets mauled to pieces. Another drinker comes over and says his pit bull can take this strange-looking dog on, but the bet is now £100.

Another trip to the yard and when it's finished, there are bits of pit bull terrier all over the place.

The drinker pays up and says, 'Say, what breed is that anyway?'

The owner says, 'Until I cut his tail off and painted it pink it was the same breed as every other alligator.'

ALZHEIMER'S

▶ What's a Catholic Alzheimer's disease? When you forget everything but the guilt.

▶ An old man walks up to a lady at a dinner dance and says 'I *say*, do I come here often?'

▶ What's the best thing about having children with Alzheimer's? You can give them the same presents year after year.

▶ Three friends with Alzheimer's were chatting together at a train station. They were so engrossed in their conversation that they didn't hear the guard blow his whistle to signal the train's departure. Just as the train began to pull away, two of the men managed to scramble aboard, but the third didn't make it.

The guard came over to console him. 'Never mind,' he said. 'Two of you made it, and there's another train in an hour.'

'No, you don't understand,' said the man. 'They came to see *me* off.'

▶ What was the name of Ronald Reagan's last movie? *Partial Recall.*

▶ What's the best thing about Alzheimer's? You never have to watch any repeats.

▶ Did you hear about the Easter egg hunt for Alzheimer's patients? They hid their own eggs.

▶ My uncle came out of the closet yesterday. He's not gay. He has Alzheimer's and thought it was the car.

▶ Chant at the Alzheimer's protest march:
  'What do we want?'
  'I don't know!'
  'When do we want it?'
  'Want what?'

▶ My mother just rang me – she's worried she may be getting Alzheimer's. I told her to forget about it.

▶ This year's Alzheimer's Society annual dinner will be an evening to remember.

▶ A group of 40-year-old women had a reunion and agreed to meet at the Ocean View Restaurant because the male waiters had tight pants and nice bums.

Ten years later the 50-year-olds again held their reunion, agreeing to meet at the Ocean View Restaurant because the food was very good.

Ten years later the 60-year-olds again held their reunion, agreeing to meet at the Ocean View Restaurant because they could eat there in peace and quiet, and the restaurant had a lovely view of the ocean.

Ten years later the 70-year-olds again held their reunion, agreeing to meet at the Ocean View Restaurant because it was wheelchair accessible.

Ten years later the 80-year-olds again held their reunion, agreeing to meet at the Ocean View Restaurant because they wanted to see what it was like, as none of them had been there before.

▶ According to studies, every five minutes someone is diagnosed with Alzheimer's. His name is Barry.

AMERICANS

▶ A Swiss man, looking for directions, pulled up at a bus stop, where two Americans were waiting. *'Entschuldigung, koennen Sie Deutsch sprechen?'* he asked. The two Americans just stared at him. He tried again. *'Excusez-moi, parlez-vous français?'* The two Americans continued to stare. *'Parlare italiano?'* asked the Swiss. No response. *'Hablan ustedes español?'* he ventured. Still nothing. The Swiss man then drove off, disgusted.

The first American turned to the other and said, 'Y'know, maybe we should learn a foreign language.'

'Why?' said the other. 'That guy knew four languages, and it didn't do him any good.'

AMISH

▶ What do you call an Amish guy with his hand up a horse's arse?
A mechanic.

▶ An Amish boy was sitting on his bed reading the Bible. All of a sudden, his father storms in, grabs him and drags him out into the pasture. In the pasture is one sheep chewing grass. The father points to the sheep and says, 'Thou hast had sexual relations with yon sheep!'

The boy kneels and says, 'Father, forgive me, for I did indeed spill my seed in yon lowly beast.'

Saddened, the father says, 'Thou are forgiven, my son. But know this... there will fire and brimstone if I taste it again!'

▶ *Signs that your Amish teen is in trouble:*

• He sometimes stays in bed until after 6.00 a.m.

• Under his bed, you find pictures of women without bonnets.

• He defiantly says, 'If I had a radio, I'd listen to rap.'

• When you criticise him, he yells, 'Thou suck!'

• His name is Jebediah but he prefers to be known as 'Jeb Daddy'.

• You discover his secret stash of colourful socks.

• He uses the slang expression, 'Talk to the hand cos the beard ain't listening.'

• He was recently pulled over for driving under the influence of cottage cheese.

- He has taken to wearing his big black hat backwards.

▶ What goes clippity-clop, clippity-clop, clippity-clop, bang, bang, bang? An Amish drive-by shooting.

▶ A young Amish girl was going out on her first date. As it was a bitterly cold night, she put on some gloves, only to be chastised by her mother, who thought gloves were unbecoming of a lady. The girl protested, 'What am I supposed to do with my hands if they get cold from riding in the buggy?' The mother advised, 'Just stick your hands between your legs and they will get warm.'

The girl obeyed her mother's wishes and went off on her date. On their way home, her hands got cold, so she placed them between her legs. Her young escort looked across and asked, 'Why on earth have you got your hands between your legs?'

She replied, 'My mother told me that if my hands got cold, I should stick them between my legs to get them warm.'

Her date said, 'Well, my dick is frozen solid. So would you mind if I stick it between your legs to get it warm?' The girl could see no harm in the idea and allowed him to stick his dick between her legs.

When she arrived home, she asked her mother, 'What do you know about dicks?'

Her mother was startled. 'Why, what do you know about dicks?'

The girl said, 'All I know is that when they thaw out, they make an awful mess!'

▶ Two Amish women were picking potatoes one day. Holding two potatoes in her hand, the first Amish woman turned to the other and said, 'These potatoes remind me of my husband's testicles.'

The second woman said, 'Are his testicles that big?'

'No, they're that dirty.'

▶ An Amish boy and his father made their first visit to a big city shopping mall. They were amazed by everything they saw, especially the two shiny silver walls that could move apart and then slide back together again.

'What is it?' asked the boy.

The father, never having seen an elevator before, said, 'I don't know.'

They watched intently as an old lady went over to the moving walls and pressed a button. They saw the walls open and the old lady went into a small room. Then the walls closed, and the boy and his father were transfixed as the small numbers above the walls lit up in sequence. The pair continued to gaze in awe until the light reached the last number, and then the numbers began to light in reverse order.

Finally the walls opened again and out stepped a beautiful young woman. The father turned to the boy and said, 'Go get your mother.'

ANIMALS

▶ A farmer and his wife were lying in bed one evening. She was knitting; he was reading the latest issue of *Animal Husbandry*. He looks up from the page and says to her, 'Did you know that humans are the only species in which the female achieves orgasm?'

She looks at him wistfully, smiles and replies, 'Oh yeah? Prove it.'

He frowns for a moment, then says, 'OK.' He then gets up and walks out, leaving his wife with a confused look on her face.

About half an hour later he returns all tired and sweaty and proclaims, 'Well, I'm sure the cow and sheep didn't, but the way that pig's always squealing, how can I tell?'

▶ What do you get if you insert human DNA into a goat? Banned from the petting zoo.

▶ How do you titillate an ocelot? Oscillate its titalot.

▶ How does an elephant hide in a cherry tree? He climbs to the top and paints his nuts red.

▶ What's the loudest noise in the jungle? A giraffe eating cherries.

▶ A vampire bat comes flapping into its cave, covered in fresh blood.
All the other bats smell the blood and begin hassling him about where he got it.
   'OK, follow me,' he says and flies out of the cave with hundreds of bats behind him.
   Down through a valley they go, across a river and into a forest. Finally he slows down and all the other bats excitedly mill around him.
   'Now, do you see that tree over there?' he asks.
   'Yes, yes, yes!' scream the bats.
   'Good!' says the first bat. 'Because I didn't!'

▶ Why do polar bears have fur coats? Because they would look silly in anoraks.

▶ A chicken and an egg are lying in bed next to each other. The chicken is smoking a cigarette and the egg is looking annoyed.
   'Well,' says the egg, 'I guess that answers that question!'

▶ What do you call a camel with four humps? A Saudi quattro.

▶ What's cold, white and unstable? A bi-polar bear.

▶ How many hamsters does it take to screw in a lightbulb? Only two, but they've got to be in the mood.

▶ A fellow was walking through a cemetery one dark and stormy night. As he got well into the cemetery, he heard a voice say, 'Mark! Mark!' Pretending not to let it bother him, he pulled his coat a little tighter and kept walking. Again the voice said, 'Mark! Mark!'

That did it. He took off full speed and didn't stop till he was well outside the gates. As he stopped to catch his breath, the moon broke through the clouds enough so he could see what had been following him. It was a dog with a hare lip.

▶ The Pedigree Dog Food company has gone bust. They've called in the retrievers.

▶ What do you call a meerkat with acne? Pimples.

▶ Some of the animals went to see God in order to complain about their lot in life. The elephant moaned, 'I really hate this long trunk – it's always getting in the way. It makes me so clumsy and if I'm not careful I trip over it.'

'Maybe,' said God, 'but your trunk makes you useful to humans. It allows you to lift huge weights that they cannot manage. Without it, you would serve no purpose.'

While the elephant thought about what God had said, the giraffe butted in. 'I hate my long neck,' said the giraffe. 'It's such a nuisance in high winds. Why can't I have something more normal?'

God replied, 'But your long neck enables you to reach succulent leaves at the very tops of trees – places no other animal can get to. It gives you a tremendous advantage. Without your long neck, you would always have to battle with shorter creatures for food.'

While the giraffe digested God's words, the hen interrupted, 'Either let me have a bigger arse or smaller eggs... '

▶ Two crocodiles were sitting at the side of the Thames at Westminster. The smaller one turned to the bigger one and said, 'I can't understand how you can be so much bigger than me. We're the same age. We were the same size as kids. I just don't get it.'

'Well,' said the big croc, 'what have you been eating?'

'Politicians, same as you,' replied the small croc.

'Hmm. Well, where do you catch them?'

'Down the other side of the river by Parliament.'

'Same here. Hmm... How do you catch them?'

'Well, I crawl up under one of their cars and wait for one to unlock the car door. Then I jump out, grab them by the leg, shake the shit out of them and eat 'em!'

'Ah!' said the big crocodile. 'I think I see your problem. You're not getting any real nourishment. See, by the time you finish shaking the shit out of a politician, there's nothing left but an arsehole and a briefcase.'

▶ I was recently on safari in the Serengeti and witnessed two male lions shagging each other. I thought, 'Blimey, have they got no pride?'

▶ One morning, the daddy mole reached his head out of the hole and said, 'Mmmmm, I smell sausage.'

The mummy mole reached her head outside of the hole and said, 'Mmmmm, I smell bacon.'

As the baby mole repeatedly tried to stick his head out of the hole to get a whiff, he became frustrated because the two bigger moles were in the way. Unable to take it any longer, the baby mole grumbled, 'The only thing I can smell is molasses.'

▶ Three elderly gentlemen were sitting on a park bench discussing what the meanest animal in the world was.

The first said, 'The meanest animal in the world is a hippopotamus cos it's got such big jowls. One bite and you're gone.'

The second shook his head and said, 'Nah, hippo may be mean, but ain't nothing meaner than an alligator. He got a big mouth and all them teeth, snap, one bite, ha, one swallow, you gone.'

The third gentleman sat for a moment, and finally he spoke and said, 'No, sir, the meanest animal in the world is a hippagator.'

The other two enquired as to what in the world was a hippagator, believing there was no such animal.

The gentleman slowly began to explain. 'A hippagator got a hippo head on one end, and a gator head on the other.'

'WAIT!' interrupted the others. 'If he has a head on both ends, how does he shit?'

The reply was simply: 'He don't – that's what makes him so mean.'

▶ Feeling horrible, an alligator goes to the veterinarian.

'What seems to be the problem?' the vet asks.

'I just don't have the drive I used to, Doc,' the gator says. 'Used to be, I could swim underwater for miles and catch any animal I wanted. Now all I can do is let them swim by.'

Concerned, the vet gives him a thorough examination and hands him a few pills.

'What are these?' the gator asks.

'It's a pill very similar to Viagra,' the vet answers.

'Hold on, I don't have that kind of problem,' the alligator protests. 'What exactly is wrong with me?'

'Well,' the vet says, 'you have a reptile dysfunction.'

▶ A New York boy goes to the countryside to visit his uncle in the South. After the sun goes down, the boy hears strange howling. He gets frightened and runs to his uncle. 'Uncle, uncle, there are werewolves!'

'That's rubbish, boy, ain't no such thing.'

'Then there must be man-eating wolves.'

'No, we haven't got those critters, either.'

'What is this sound, then?' the boy asks.

'They coyotes, boy.'

'Coyotes? What are those?'

'They look a lot like dogs. In fact, ya'll can consider them a kind of dog.'

The boy wants to find out more. 'Why are they making that frightening noise?'

'See, nephew, we ain't got many trees around here. We got cactuses!'

▶ A young lion was talking to an older lion just before they were to be let into the coliseum for a showdown with the Christians.

'This is the first time for me, I'm not sure what I should do,' said the younger lion.

The older lion said, 'It's easy: you run up to the Christians and roar as load as you can and take a swipe at them with your paw, just before you eat them!'

'Why all the theatrics?' said the younger lion. 'Shouldn't we just eat them?'

The older lion shook his head. 'No, it's better to scare the shit out of them first – they taste better that way!'

▶ What do you call an aardvark that's just been beaten up? Vark.

▶ What is the most stupid animal in the jungle? A polar bear.

▶ 'What's the difference between the North American porcupine and the African porcupine?' the society matron asked the zookeeper.

'The principal difference is the North American species has a longer prick.'

This, as you might suspect, distressed the prim and proper matron, who stormed immediately to the zoo manager's office to protest.

The zoo manager said, 'Ma'am, I do apologise for my staff's uncouth choice of terms. What the keeper should have said is that the North American species has a long "quill". In fact, their pricks are just about the same size.'

▶ There was an elephant, a snake and a gorilla in the jungle. The snake suggested, 'Shall we have a game of snooker?'

The elephant replied, 'How can we play snooker when we haven't got a table?'

So the snake said, 'We can pretend. Instead of hitting the ball, we'll each do a trick. Whoever does the best trick will get the most points.'

The gorilla said, 'OK, I'll go first. I'll climb up that tree, swing around that branch three times, do a double somersault and land on my feet. That's got to be worth the black ball and that's seven points.'

The elephant said, 'No it's not worth seven points because you're good at climbing trees. We'll give you the blue and that's worth five points.'

The gorilla agreed and off he went up the tree. He swung round the branch three times, did a double somersault and landed on his feet.

The elephant said, 'I'll climb up the tree, swing around the branch twice, do a single somersault and land on my feet. That's got to be worth seven points because I can't climb trees very well.'

So the snake and the gorilla agreed, 'OK, if you can do that we'll give you seven points.'

The elephant went up the tree, swung round the branch twice, did the somersault and landed on his feet with an almighty bang.

The snake said, 'That was brilliant.'

'So what are you going to do, Snake?' the gorilla asked.

'Well, I'll go up the elephant's bum through his intestine and out of his trunk. That's got to be worth seven points,' said the snake.

The gorilla said, 'If you can do that we'll give you seven points.' So off went the snake up the elephant's bum. The gorilla got hold of the elephant's trunk and stuck it up his bum and said, 'That's got him snookered!'

▶ A little rabbit is happily running through the forest, when he stumbles upon a giraffe rolling a joint.

The rabbit looks at her and says, 'Giraffe, my friend, think about what you're doing to yourself! Come with me running through the forest. You'll see, you'll feel so much better!' The giraffe looks at him, looks at the joint, tosses it away and goes off running with the rabbit.

Then they come across an elephant doing coke. So the rabbit again says, 'Elephant, my friend, why do you do this? Think about what you're doing to yourself! Come running with us through the pretty forest. You'll see, you'll feel so good!' The elephant looks at them, looks at his razor, mirror and all, then tosses them away and starts running with the rabbit and giraffe.

The three animals then come across a lion about to shoot up. 'Lion, my friend, why do you do this? Think about what you're doing to yourself!

Come running with us through the sunny forest. You'll see, you will feel so good!' The lion looks at him, puts down his needle and starts to beat the crap out of the little rabbit.

The giraffe and elephant watch in horror, then finally obtain the presence of mind to pull the lion off the rabbit. 'Lion,' they reprimand, 'why did you do this? He was merely trying to help us all!'

The lion answers, 'That little bastard has me running around the forest like an idiot for hours every time he's on Ecstasy!'

▶ A group of bats is hanging around, upside down, as usual, mostly sleeping. Suddenly one notices that Charlie is on the floor, standing upright and looking around.

'Hey, Charlie,' he calls out. 'What are you doing down there?'

Charlie looks up and says, 'Yoga!'

▶ A monkey is sitting in a tree smoking a joint, when a lizard walks past, looks up and says to the monkey, 'Hey, what're you doing?'

The monkey replies, 'Smokin' a joint. Come up and have some.'

So the lizard climbs up and sits next to the monkey and they smoke a few joints.

After a while the lizard says his mouth is dry and he's going to get a drink from the river.

The lizard is so stoned that he leans over too far and falls into the river.

A crocodile sees this and swims over to the lizard and helps him to the side, then asks the lizard, 'What's the matter with you?'

The lizard explains to the crocodile that he was sitting up in a tree with a monkey smoking pot, got too stoned and then fell into the river while taking a drink.

The crocodile says he has to check this out and wanders into the jungle. He finds the tree where the monkey is sitting finishing up a joint.

The crocodile yells up to the monkey and says, 'Hey!'

The monkey looks down and says, 'Damn... How much water did you drink?!'

▶ *How animals think...*

- Camel: 'Who's dumped that on my back?'

- Giraffe: 'Hope I don't get a sore throat.'

- Hyena: 'That is so damn funny.'

- Monkey: 'Want to buy a car aerial or wing mirror?'

- Crocodile: 'I'm just a log, nothing to worry about.'

- Elephant: 'Does my bum look big in this?'

- Cheetah: 'These new trainers are brilliant.'

- Polar bear: 'This is bloody mint.'

- Snake: 'I won't put student fees up. Trust me.'

ARM LESS

▶ I have a butler with a missing left arm. Serves 'em right.

▶ Did you hear about the man with no arm who entered a national masturbation competition? Poor sod didn't come anywhere.

▶ A jogger is running along one morning, when he hears crying. He slows down and sees an armless, legless woman sitting at a table bawling. Heart heavy, he walks over and asks her what the problem is.

Sniffling, she says, 'I've never been hugged before.'

The jogger leans over, hugs her and smiles as he takes off.

The next day the cripple is still there, crying again. The jogger slows down and asks her what the matter is this time. She leans over and wipes her snotty nose on the table and says, 'I've never been kissed before.'

The man leans over and lays a wet one on her cheek. He jogs off, waving bye to her smiling face.

The next day, he jogs up and she's crying her eyes out yet again. The jogger runs over and asks her, 'What now?'

The bleary-eyed woman looks up and says, 'I've never been fucked before.'

The man bends over, picks her up, chucks her into a pool and calls, 'Now you're fucked!'

▶ Local news: 'Amputee robber evaded police for 15 days.' That's amazing, considering he wasn't armed.

ARMY

▶ *Army bumper stickers:*

- US Army – travel agents to Allah

- Stop global whining

- What do I feel when I kill a terrorist? A little recoil

- Happiness is a belt-fed weapon

- It's God's job to forgive Bin Laden – it's our job to arrange the meeting

- Artillery brings dignity to what would otherwise be just a brawl

- Do draft dodgers have reunions? If so, what do they talk about?

- Machine gunners – accuracy by volume

▶ The commanding officer at the Russian military academy gave a lecture on Potential Problems and Military Strategy. At the end of the lecture, he asked if there were any questions.

An officer stood up and asked, 'Will there be a third world war? And will Russia take part in it?'

The general answered both questions in the affirmative.

Another officer asked, 'Who will be the enemy?'

The general replied, 'All indications point to China.'

Everyone in the audience was shocked. A third officer remarked, 'General, we are a nation of only 150 million, compared to the 1.5 billion Chinese. Can we win at all, or even survive?'

The general answered, 'Just think about this for a moment: in modern warfare, it is not the quantity of soldiers that matters but the quality of an army's capabilities. For example, in the Middle East we have had a few wars recently where five million Jews fought against 150 million Arabs, and Israel was always victorious.'

After a small pause, yet another officer from the back of the auditorium asked, 'Do we have enough Jews?'

▶ A British general had sent some of his men off to fight for their country in the Falkland Islands crisis. Upon returning to Britain from the South Atlantic island, three soldiers that had distinguished themselves in battle were summoned to the general's office. 'Since we weren't actually at war,' the general began, 'I can't give out any medals. We did, however, want to let each of you know your efforts were appreciated. What we've decided to do is to let each of you choose two points on your body. You will be given £2 sterling for each inch of distance between those parts. We'll start on the left, boys, so what'll it be?'

Soldier 1: 'The tip of me head to me toes, sahr!'

General: 'Very good, son, that's 70 inches, which comes to £140.'

Soldier 2: 'The tip of the finger on one outstretched hand to the tip of the other, sir!'

General: 'Even better, son, that's 72 inches, which comes to £144.'

Soldier 3: 'The tip of me dick to me balls, sahr!'

General: 'That's a strange request, but drop your trousers, son!' He begins the measurement. 'My God, son, where are your balls?'

Soldier 3: 'Falkland Islands, sahr!'

ART

▶ A man goes to an art gallery and sees a painting that is a violent, incoherent swirl of clashing colours. The artist happens to be in the gallery, so the man asks him where he got the idea for the painting.

'I had no idea,' replies the artist. 'I merely painted to expel what was inside of me.'

'Really?' replies the man. 'Well, next time try some indigestion tablets.'

▶ At an art exhibition, two women were staring at a painting entitled 'Home for Lunch'. The painting was of three very naked and very black men, sitting on a park bench. What was unusual was that the men on either end of the bench had black penises, but the man in the middle had a pink penis. The two women were standing there, staring at the picture, scratching their heads and trying to figure this out.

Then the artist walked by and, noticing the women's confusion, asked, 'Can I help you at all?'

'Well, yes,' said one of the women. 'We were curious about the picture of the black men on the bench. Why does the man in the middle have a pink penis?'

'Oh,' said the artist. 'I'm afraid you've misunderstood the painting. The three men are not African-Americans, they're coal miners, and the fellow in the middle went home for lunch.'

▶ After much careful research, it has been discovered that the artist Vincent Van Gogh had many relatives. Among them were:

• His obnoxious brother: Please Gogh

• His dizzy aunt: Verti Gogh

• The brother who ate prunes: Gotta Gogh

• The brother who worked on traffic lights: Stoppen Gogh

• His magician uncle: Wherediddy Gogh

• His Mexican cousin: Amee Gogh

• The Mexican cousin's American half-brother: Grin Gogh

• The nephew who drove a stagecoach: Wellsfar Gogh

• The constipated uncle: Cant Gogh

• The ballroom dancing aunt: Tang Gogh

• The bird-lover uncle: Phlamin Gogh

- His nephew psychoanalyst: E Gogh

- The greengrocer cousin: Man Gogh

- The aunt who taught positive thinking: Wayto Gogh

- The little bouncy nephew: Poe Gogh

- A sister who loved disco: Go Gogh

- And his niece who travels the country in a van: Winnie Bay Gogh

ASSASSINS

▶ Assassins do it from behind.

AUSTRALIA

▶ An Aborigine was fishing in Queensland, Australia, when a crocodile suddenly leaped from the water and grabbed him by the legs. The crocodile was halfway through devouring the man when a boatload of American tourists passed by. One woman said, 'I thought Aborigines were meant to be poor. Well, there's one over there with a Lacoste sleeping bag.'

▶ What's the definition of Australian aristocracy? A man who can trace his lineage back to his father.

▶ How do you know when an Australian woman is having her period? She's only wearing one sock.

▶ An Australian had been wandering through the outback for months, when he came to an isolated farm with a pretty girl standing at the gate. 'D'ya shag?' he asked.

'No, but you've talked me into it, you silver-tongued bastard!'

▶ An Englishman wanted to become an Irishman, so he visited a doctor to find out how to go about it. The doctor said, 'This is a very delicate and dangerous operation. You see, in order to make you Irish, I'll have to remove half your brain. Are you happy with that?'

'Yes, that's OK,' said the Englishman. 'I've always wanted to be Irish, and I'm prepared to take the risk.'

The operation went ahead, but the Englishman woke to find a look of horror on the doctor's face. 'I'm so terribly sorry,' said the doctor. 'Instead of removing half the brain, I've taken the whole brain out.'

The patient replied, 'No worries, mate.'

▶ An Australian ends up next to a British soldier in the trenches during World War I. The British soldier turns to him and says, 'Good to see you, old boy, have you come here to die?'

To which the Australian replies, 'No, mate, I came here yesterday!'

▶ Why do so many Australian men divorce their wives? They like to know there's a ball and chain they can get rid of.

AUTISM

▶ Did you know that if you counted up all the pies bought at football matches every weekend in the UK, the chances are... you're autistic.

▶ This little kid said to me, 'You've got autism!'

I replied, 'That's a big word for someone who can't be more than 2,861 days old.'

BABIES AND BIRTH

▶ A man was having an affair with his secretary. Inevitably, she fell pregnant, and to avoid his wife finding out, he decided to send the secretary abroad to have the baby.

'How will I let you know when it's born?' she asked.

'Just send me a postcard with the word "spaghetti" on it,' he replied. 'Then I'll know the baby has been born.'

A few months later the man went to pick up his mail after the postman had been. He picked up a postcard, turned it over to read it, went white and fell down dead from a massive heart attack. His distraught wife ran to his side. Wondering what could have brought on the fatal shock, she picked up the postcard. On it was written, 'Spaghetti, spaghetti, spaghetti. Two with meatballs, one without.'

▶ Why do babies have soft bits in the middle of their heads? So nurses can pick up five on each hand.

▶ A man went to a bar and got talking to a less than attractive woman. 'What's your name?' he asked.

'Tuesday,' she replied.

He said, 'That's a strange name.'

She said, 'Yeah, when I was born my mum and dad looked in the cot and said, "I think we'd better call it a day."'

▶ A nervous young man was pacing up and down the waiting room at a maternity hospital. Eventually he asked another guy, who seemed more experienced in these matters, 'How long after the baby is born can you have sex with the mother?'

The older guy replied, 'Hmmm, it depends whether she's in a public ward or a private one.'

▶ Nine months to the day following their wedding, a young couple had a baby. Unfortunately it was born without arms or legs – without even a torso. It was just a head, but they still loved and cared for their child, spoiling and indulging it.

Finally, after 20 years, the couple took a much-needed vacation, and who should they meet but a European doctor who had recently achieved a medical breakthrough. 'I know,' he said, 'how to attach arms and legs to your child, how to make him whole.'

The excited couple cut their trip short and rushed home to where the head lay in its crib. 'Honey, Mum and Dad have the most wonderful surprise for you!'

'No,' shrieked the head. 'Not another fucking hat!'

▶ My wife's pregnant and my doctor asked me if I had ever been present at a childbirth before.

I replied, 'Yes, just once.'

The doctor asked, 'What was it like?'

I said, 'It was dark, then suddenly very light.'

▶ A Catholic couple were becoming increasingly desperate for a baby. Eventually they asked their priest to pray for them. The priest said, 'I'm going to Rome on a long sabbatical and, while I'm there, I'll light a candle for you at the altar of St Peter.'

When the priest returned to his parish ten months later, he discovered that the woman had given birth to sextuplets.

'It's a miracle!' exclaimed the priest. 'But I understand your husband has left the country?'

'So he has, Father. He's flown to Rome to blow your bloody candle out.'

▶ A woman went to her doctor and said, 'Doctor, I can't sleep at night. When I'm in the next room, I have this terrible fear that I won't hear the baby if he falls out of his cot at night. What should I do?'

'Easy,' said the doctor. 'Just take the carpet off the floor.'

▶ A woman and a baby were in the doctor's examining room, waiting for the doctor to come in. The doctor arrived, examined the baby, checked his weight, found it somewhat below normal and asked if the baby was breast- or bottle-fed.

'Breast-fed,' she replied.

'Well, strip down to your waist,' the doctor ordered. She did. He pressed, kneaded, rolled, cupped and pinched both breasts for a while in a detailed, rigorously thorough examination. Motioning to her to get dressed, he said, 'No wonder this baby is underweight. You don't have any milk.'

'I know,' she said. 'I'm his grandmother but I'm really pleased I brought him in!'

▶ A guest lecturer to the medical college stopped by the bulletin board. Listed for the day was the topic, 'Surprises in obstetrics'. Scrawled under it in pencil were the words: 'Mary had a little lamb'.

▶ Minutes after a woman gives birth, the doctor comes in and says, 'Mrs Jones, I have to tell you something about your baby.'

The woman, terrified, sits up in bed and says, 'What's wrong with my baby, Doctor? What's wrong?'

'Well,' says the doctor, 'your baby is a hermaphrodite.'

'A hermaphrodite? What's that?'

'It means your baby has the... er... features... of both the male and the female.'

'Oh my God!' sighs the woman with relief. 'You mean, Doctor, my baby has a penis... and a brain?'

▶ While waiting for a train, a man was holding two babies, one in each arm. A woman came up to him and said, 'Aren't they cute? What are their names?'

'I don't know,' said the guy, irritated.

'Are they boys or girls?' continued the woman.

'I don't know,' snapped the man.

'What kind of a father are you?' she said.

'I'm not their father,' he answered, 'I'm a condom salesman. And these are the two complaints I'm taking back to my company!'

▶ What's the difference between a seagull and a baby? A seagull flits along the shore.

▶ Two storks – father stork and baby stork – were sitting on the nest. Baby stork was crying incessantly, and father stork was trying to calm him down. 'Don't worry, your mother will come back. She's only bringing people babies and making them happy.'

The following night it was the father's turn to do the rounds. So as mother and baby stork sat on the nest, she told him, 'Don't worry, your father will be back as soon as possible. But for now he's bringing joy to new mummies and daddies.'

A few days later, mother and father stork were sick with worry. Baby stork had been gone from the nest all night. When he finally returned the next morning, they said, 'Where on earth have you been?'

'Oh,' he said, 'just scaring the shit out of students!'

▶ What's the bad news about being a test tube baby? You know for sure that your dad is a wanker.

▶ It was the talk of the town when an 80-year-old man married a 20-year-old girl, particularly when a year later she went into hospital to give birth. The nurse came out to congratulate the proud father. 'This is amazing. How do you do it at your age?'

He answered, 'You've got to keep that old motor running.'

The following year his young wife gave birth again. The same nurse said, 'You really are amazing. How do you do it?'

He replied knowingly, 'You've got to keep that old motor running.'

The same thing happened the next year. The nurse said, 'You must be quite a man.'

He laughed, 'You've got to keep that old motor running.'

The nurse said, 'Well, you had better change the oil. This one's black.'

▶ A married couple had to rent their first two homes, so when they finally saved up enough money to be able to buy a house, they were absolutely thrilled. So was the husband's brother, who bought them a bottle of champagne to mark the occasion.

In the hustle and bustle of settling into the first home that they actually owned, the gift was tucked away and temporarily forgotten. Then three months later, the couple held a christening party for their third child. Champagne flowed in celebration until, running short, the wife remembered her brother-in-law's housewarming gift. In front of her guests, she opened the attached card and read it aloud, 'Bill, take good care of this one – it's yours!'

▶ A couple were trying for a baby, with no luck. The man went to the doctor, who told him of a radical new treatment which would increase his virility by transplanting monkey glands into his body. The man agreed and went ahead with the operation and, sure enough, he managed to get his wife pregnant the next week.

Nine months passed and they had a baby. The man went to see the doctor again to get a birth certificate.

'What did you have, a boy or girl?' asked the doctor.

'We're not sure yet,' replied the man. 'We're still waiting for it to come down off the chandelier.'

BAD LUCK

▶ I inherited a painting and a violin, which turned out to be a Rembrandt and a Stradivarius. Unfortunately, Rembrandt made lousy violins and Stradivarius was a terrible painter.

▶ When you're having a really bad day and it seems like people are trying to piss you off, remember it takes 42 muscles to frown and only four to extend your finger and tell them to fuck off.

BALDNESS

▶ Why did the bald man cut holes in his pockets? So he could run his fingers through his hair.

▶ Did you hear about the man who spent years trying to find a cure for his bad breath and baldness, only to find out people didn't like him anyway?

▶ A man with a bald head and a wooden leg gets invited to a Halloween party. He doesn't know what costume to wear to hide his head and his leg, so he writes to a fancy dress company to explain the problem.

A few days later he receives a parcel with a note. 'Dear sir, please find enclosed a pirate's outfit. The spotted handkerchief will cover your bald head and, with your wooden leg, you will look really good as a pirate.'

The man thinks this is terrible because they have just emphasised his wooden leg so he writes a letter of complaint. A week passes and he receives another parcel and a note, which says, 'Dear sir, please find enclosed a monk's habit. The long robe will cover your wooden leg, and with your bald head, you will really look the part.'

Now the man is really annoyed since they have gone from emphasising his wooden leg to emphasising his bald head so he writes the company another letter of complaint. The next day he receives a small parcel and a note, which reads, 'Dear sir, please find enclosed a bottle of molasses. Pour the molasses over your bald head, stick your wooden leg up your arse and go as a toffee apple!'

▶ Are you really that bald, or is your neck just blowing a bubble?

▶ Karen: 'Have you noticed that Daddy is getting taller?'

Sharon: 'No, why?'

Karen: 'His head is sticking through his hair.'

▶ Who never gets his hair wet in the shower? A bald man.

BALLS

▶ What is the cheapest meat? Deer balls – they're under a buck.

BATHS

▶ Prince Charles arrives in Iran on an official visit. He asks the president, 'Where is the Shah?'

'What do you mean?' says the president. 'There is no Shah. We got rid of the Shah years ago.'

'In that case,' says Charles, 'I'll have a bath.'

▶ Why do men take showers instead of baths? Because pissing in the bath is disgusting.

▶ *Signs that you don't take enough baths:*

• The dirt on your body can be seen from 100 yards away.

• The manager at the sewage works greets you with the words, 'What's that smell?'

• On Christmas morning you find several bars of soap in your stocking.

- You stick to everything.

- Two or more people have choked to death in your presence.

- Whenever you walk down the street, it seems like it's raining flies.

- Old people are offended by your odour.

- Jehovah's Witnesses call at every house except yours.

▶ Just seen a sign outside a kitchen furniture shop: 'Stainless steel sinks'. 'Bit obvious,' I thought.

▶ What do you find in a clean nose? Fingerprints!

BATTLE OF THE SEXES

▶ *Reasons why beer is better than women:*

1. You can enjoy a beer all month long.

2. Beer stains wash out.

3. You don't have to wine and dine a beer.

4. Your beer will always wait patiently for you in the car while you play football.

5. When your beer goes flat, you toss it out and get another one.

6. Beer is never late.

7. A beer doesn't get jealous when you grab another beer.

8. Hangovers go away.

9. When you go to a bar, you know you can always pick up a beer.

10. Beer never has a headache.

11. After you're finished with a beer, the bottle is still worth five pence.

12. A beer won't get upset if you come home with another beer.

13. If you pour a beer right you'll always get good head.

14. A beer always goes down easy.

15. You can always share a beer with friends.

16. You know you're always the first one to pop a beer.

17. Beer is always wet.

18. Beer doesn't demand equality.

19. You can have a beer in public.

20. A beer doesn't care what time you come home.

21. A frigid beer is a good beer.

22. You don't have to wash a beer before it tastes good.

23. If you change beers you don't have to pay maintenance.

▶ What should you give a woman who has everything? A man to show her how to work it.

▶ Why did God create woman? To carry semen from the bedroom to the toilet.

▶ A blonde, a brunette and a redhead just bought a car. Which one drives it first? None, they're all in the kitchen.

▶ If your wife comes out of the kitchen to shout at you, what have you usually done wrong? Made her chain too long.

▶ Why are women poor skiers? There's not much snow between the kitchen and the bedroom.

▶ Why did God make women? You think *he's* going to wash the dishes?

▶ How do you know when it's time to get a new dishwasher? When the old one expects you to 'do your share'.

▶ What is the difference between a woman and a washing machine? You can bung your load in a washing machine and it won't call you a week later.

▶ How many men does it take to change a lightbulb in the kitchen? Why bother? Can't the bitch cook in the dark?

▶ Got an e-mail today from a 'Bored housewife, 32, looking for some action!' I sent her my ironing – that'll keep the bitch busy.

▶ Touch it gently...
Put two fingers inside. If it's big, put three fingers in...
Make sure it's wet...
Rub it up and down...
Yeah...
That's how you wash a cup.

Apple will be releasing a new gadget exclusively for women later this year. It's called the iRon.

▶ What's the difference between a wife and a wheelie bin? You only have to take out a wheelie bin once a week.

How do men sort out their laundry? Filthy, and filthy but wearable.

▶ Why don't women wear watches? Because there's a clock on the cooker.

Why do women have arms? Have you any idea how long it would take to LICK a bathroom clean?

Why do women have small feet? So they can stand closer to the kitchen sink.

Why did the woman cross the road? Never mind that, what the fuck is she doing out of the kitchen?

▶ I got one of those Dyson Ball Cleaners for Christmas. Unfortunately, I misunderstood what it was, which is why I'm now in casualty.

What's the difference between men and women? A woman wants one man to satisfy her every need. A man wants every woman to satisfy his one need.

How many men does it take to tile a bathroom? Two. If you slice them very thinly.

▶ What do you instantly know about a well-dressed man? His wife is good at picking out clothes.

▶ What makes a man think about a candle-lit dinner? A power failure.

▶ What's the difference between a golf ball and a G-spot? A man will spend 20 or 30 minutes looking for a golf ball.

▶ What's the difference between a man and a condom? Condoms have changed. They're no longer thick and insensitive.

▶ What's the one thing that all men at singles' bars have in common? They're married.

▶ There are three types of women: the intelligent, the beautiful and the majority.

▶ Why are middle-aged women like MTV? They get turned on about once a month, and you've had enough after about 15 minutes.

▶ Many women believe that a man's ultimate fantasy is to have two women at once. This is true, but one woman is cooking and the other is cleaning.

▶ How many men does it take to fix a vacuum cleaner? Why the hell should we fix it? We don't use the damn thing.

▶ How many men does it take to open a can of beer? None, it should be open when she brings it to you.

▶ Being sexist doesn't bother me at all. The only people that will call me sexist are women, and their opinion doesn't matter.

▶ Scientists have discovered that there is intelligent DNA in some women. Unfortunately, 95 per cent of them spat it out!

▶ The BBC have decided to air a television programme entitled *Why Men Aren't Sexist*. It's aimed at feminists and women in general who are frustrated with the way in which men see them in society. After careful planning, it has been scheduled to begin at 8.00 p.m. This allows women plenty of time to cook the dinner and wash up before the programme starts.

▶ My wife came to me and asked for my advice on what she should wear out tonight. I told her, 'The carpets between the kitchen and the bedroom.'

▶ I like my women how I like my coffee – ground up and in the freezer.

▶ **Her side of the story:**
He was in an odd mood Sunday night. We planned to meet at a bar for a drink. I spent the afternoon shopping with the girls and I thought it might have been my fault because I was a bit later than I promised. He didn't say anything about it. The conversation was very slow, so I thought we should go somewhere more intimate and talk privately. We went to a restaurant and he was STILL acting a bit funny. I tried to cheer him up. I started to wonder whether it was me, or something else. I asked him, and he said no. I wasn't really sure. In the car, on the way back home, I said that I loved him deeply. He just put his arm around me. I didn't know what the hell that meant because he didn't say it back. We finally got home and I was

wondering if he was going to leave me! So, I tried to get him to talk, but he just switched on the TV. Reluctantly, I said I was going to bed. After about ten minutes, he joined me. To my surprise, we made love. He still seemed really distracted. Afterwards, I just wanted to confront him, but I cried myself to sleep. I just don't know what to do anymore. I really think he is seeing someone else.

His side of the story:
Arsenal lost. Got laid, though.

▶ A recent survey asked 100 sexually active women if their twat twitched after sex. Ninety-eight per cent replied, 'No, he just rolls over and goes to sleep.'

▶ Why do doctors spank babies when they are born? To knock the dicks off the stupid ones.

BIGAMY

▶ 'Bigamy is having one wife too many. Monogamy is the same.'
– Oscar Wilde

BINGO

▶ What has a whole load of little balls and screws old ladies? A bingo machine.

▶ How do you get 200 cows into a barn? Put up a BINGO sign.

BIRTH CONTROL

▶ What's the best form of birth control after 50? Nudity.

▶ What's a diaphragm? A trampoline for dickheads.

▶ Three women were discussing birth control.
The first said, 'We're Catholic so we don't practise birth control.'
The second said, 'I am, too, but we use the rhythm method.'
The third said, 'We use the bucket and saucer method.'
'What's that?' asked the others.
'Well,' she said, 'I'm five foot eleven inches tall and my husband is five foot two inches. We make love standing up, with him standing on a bucket, and when his eyes get as big as saucers, I kick the bucket out from under him.'

▶ A bus driver was sitting in the canteen, when an inspector asked him, 'What time did you pull out this morning?'
'I didn't,' said the driver. 'And it's been worrying me all day.'

▶ Four young women spent the afternoon on a clothes-shopping spree but as they made their way back to the car, one of them realised that she had forgotten to stop at the pharmacy for her contraceptive pills. So she ran to the nearest store, rushed in with a prescription and said to the pharmacist, 'Please fill this immediately. I've got people waiting in my car.'

▶ An old man complained to the doctor of feeling tired. The doctor asked him if he had done anything.

The old man said, 'Wednesday night, I picked up a 20-year-old secretary and nailed her three times; Thursday, I hit on a 19-year-old waitress; Friday, I made out with an 18-year-old friend of my granddaughter; and Saturday, I was lured to a motel by 17-year-old twins.'

The doctor said, 'I hope you took precautions.'

'Sure,' replied the old man. 'I gave them all a false name.'

▶ What did the penis say to the condom? 'Cover me, I'm going in!'

▶ A chav and his girlfriend are waiting for a bus to go to town to do some shoplifting in Primark. With them are their eight children. A blind man joins them in the queue after a few minutes. When the bus arrives, they find it overloaded and only Waynetta and the eight children are able to fit in the bus, so the chav and the blind man decide to walk.

After a while the chav gets irritated by the ticking of the stick of the blind man and says to him, 'Oi! Why don't you put a piece of rubber at the end of your stick – that ticking sound is driving me nuts!'

The blind man replies, 'If you'd put a rubber on the end of YOUR stick, we'd both be sitting in the bus! So shut up and keep walking!'

▶ Have you heard about the new super-sensitive condoms? They hang around after the man leaves and talk to the woman.

▶ I went into a chemist yesterday and said to the pharmacist, 'Excuse me, mate, I'm after some condoms.'

'Just a minute,' he replied.

I said, 'Yes, that's my brand.'

▶ A travelling salesman was passing through a small country town, when he decided to stop for the night. He stopped by a farmer's house to see if he could get a room. The farmer agreed to let the stranger stay but warned him to keep away from his young daughter.

The salesman agreed but to make sure he kept his word, the farmer quietly placed three fresh eggs above his daughter's bedroom door. If the eggs fell and broke, then the farmer would know the salesman had indulged in hanky-panky with her.

Temptation got the better of the salesman and he snuck into the girl's room that night and they did the deed. Of course he broke all the eggs, so he and the girl spent the rest of the night cleaning up the mess, gluing the shells back together, then placing them back on the top of the door. The farmer got up the next morning and checked his daughter's room. All three eggs appeared to be in place.

He felt good about his daughter and the salesman and decided to make them breakfast with the eggs he'd used. He cracked the first one. Nothing inside. It was the same with the second and third eggs.

The farmer thought, 'Hang on!'

He angrily stormed out of the house, stood on his porch and shouted, 'OK, I want to know the truth! Which one of you roosters is wearing a condom?!'

▶ A guy walks into a chemists and says, 'I want 144 condoms!'

The assistant behind the counter replies, 'How come you need so many?'

The guy answers, 'I want to commit a gross indecency.'

BIKES AND BIKERS

▶ Why do Hell's Angels wear leather? Because chiffon wrinkles too easily.

▶ What's the difference between a Harley and a Hoover? The location of the dirtbag.

▶ A guy riding a motorbike was wearing a leather jacket with a broken zip. After a mile or so, he stopped the bike and said to his pillion passenger, 'I can't ride anymore with the wind hitting my chest. I'm gonna put my jacket on backwards to keep the cold out.' A couple of miles further on, he took a bend too fast and smashed the bike into a tree. A farmer living nearby immediately called the police.

When the policeman arrived on the scene, he asked the farmer, 'Are either of them showing signs of life?'

'One of them was,' replied the farmer, 'until I turned his head round the right way.'

▶ 'Help, send someone over quickly,' yelled a middle-aged spinster into the phone. 'Two hairy bikers are climbing up to my bedroom window.'

'This is the fire brigade, madam. I'll have to transfer you to the police.'

'No, no,' she shouted, 'it's you I want – they need a longer ladder.'

BILL GATES

▶ How did Bill Gates get rich? By never spending more than $3 on a haircut.

BIRDS

▶ A man was in court charged with killing a tawny owl, an endangered and protected species. After listening to the evidence in what appeared to be an open and shut case, the judge asked the defendant if he had anything to say.

The defendant stood up and said, 'It was a life or death situation. I had broken my leg while out hiking and it was pouring with rain, so I took refuge in a barn. Days passed without seeing a single person. I was starving and needed to eat, so I killed the bird and ate it. I really had no choice.'

Impressed by the speech, the judge decided to grant him his freedom. Before the court adjourned, the judge asked out of curiosity what a tawny owl tasted like.

The man thought for a second and replied, 'A bit like golden eagle.'

▶ Why did the turkey cross the road? To prove it was no chicken.

▶ Eagles mate for life, so this nearsighted eagle goes out to look for a mate. He finds a dove. They go back to his nest and they make love. It was fantastic sex but all night long this dove says, 'I'm a dove, let's make love. I'm a dove, let's make love.' Well, the eagle just can't take this for the rest of his life so next morning he kicks her out of his nest.

Then he returns to the quest for a mate. He runs into a wren. He takes her back to his nest and makes love to her. Again fantastic sex but all night long this wren says, 'I'm a wren, let's do it again. I'm a wren, let's do it again.' Well, the eagle is getting really irritated so next morning he kicks her out of the nest.

Being very cautious he goes out to look for another mate and finds the perfect one – a duck! So again he takes her to his nest and makes love to her. You'll never guess what this duck said all night long.

'I'm a drake, you made a mistake. I'm a drake, you made a mistake.'

▶ For decades two heroic statues, one male and one female, faced each other in a city park until, one day, an angel came down from heaven and approached the statues. 'You've been such exemplary statues,' the angel announced to them, 'that I'm going to give you a special gift. I'm going to bring you both to life for 30 minutes, in which you can do anything you want.' And with a clap of his hands, the angel brought the statues to life.

The two approached each other a bit shyly, but soon dashed for the bushes, from which shortly could be heard a good deal of giggling, laughter and shaking of branches. Fifteen minutes later, the two statues emerged from the bushes, wide grins on their faces.

'You still have 15 more minutes,' said the angel, winking at them.

Grinning widely, the female statue turned to the male statue and said, 'Great! Only this time you hold the pigeon down and I'll crap on its head!'

▶ Each evening bird-lover Keith stood in his backyard, hooting like an owl, and one night an owl finally called back to him. For a year, the man and his feathered friend hooted back and forth. He even kept a log of their 'conversations'.

Just as he thought he was on the verge of a breakthrough in interspecies communication, his wife had a chat with her next-door neighbour. 'My husband spends his nights calling out to owls,' she said.

'That's odd,' the neighbour replied. 'So does mine.'

▶ What do you call a duck that's been dead for a week? A humming bird.

▶ What do you call a woodpecker with no beak? A headbanger.

▶ What's Afghanistan's national bird? Duck.

▶ When your pet bird sees you reading the newspaper, does he wonder why you're sitting there, staring at carpeting?

▶ Which side of the chicken has the most feathers? The outside.

▶ Why do birds fly south in the winter? Because it's too far to walk.

▶ Why do chicken coops have two doors? Because if it had four doors, it'd be a chicken sedan.

▶ I've just had my first tit wank. It wasn't very successful; one of them flew away and the other just kept pecking away at my scrotum.

▶ A woman had started a new job collecting the sperm from turkeys to use for artificial insemination. On day one, as she went up to a turkey, which went, 'Gobble, gobble,' she replied, 'Quieten down! You'll settle for a hand job like the rest!'

▶ Winter is here and our native birds are finding food scarce. Please go to the pet shop and buy a hanging mesh container of nuts for our feathered friends. There is no finer sight on a winter's morning than a pair of tits around your nut bag!

▶ There are these two ducks hanging around beside a lake, a lady duck and a gentleman duck, and it's the mating season. The man duck starts prodding her with his beak, and she says, 'Here, what do you think you're doing? Haven't you any subtlety?'

He says, 'Oh, don't you want to, then?'

She says, 'Well, not here, there's people watching. Let's go to a hotel for the afternoon, like everyone else.'

He says, 'Where's a hotel, then?'

She says, 'There's one on the other side of the lake. Don't you know anything?'

So they fly across the lake and plod into the hotel and she says, 'Go on, ask him for a room.'

So the man duck says to the receptionist, 'Quack! We want a room for the afternoon, please. We're on our honeymoon.'

The receptionist says, 'Certainly, sir; room 22, here's your key.'

So the ducks get in the lift and go up to the second floor and let themselves into their room. No sooner have they got in there than he starts prodding her with his beak again. After a while she says, 'Hang on a minute. You got a condom?'

'What?' he says.

'A condom! I'm not going to do it without a condom.'

'Oh. Well, er, where are we going to get one?'

'Haven't you had any education?' she says. 'Ring room service and ask them to send one up.'

'How do I ring room service?'

'For crying out loud! Dial 0 and ask for room service.'

So he knocks the receiver off the hook, prods the 0 on the phone with his beak and asks for room service, and when they answer, he says, 'Quack! I'd like a pot of tea for two, some bread, a couple of slices of cake, the evening paper and, er, a condom.'

'Certainly, sir,' says room service. 'That'll be with you in ten minutes.'

So the ducks hang around for a few minutes looking out at the lake, and then there's a knock and the lackey comes in with the tray. He puts the tray down on the table, fishes something out of his pocket and says, 'There's your tea, sir, and here's your condom. Shall I put it on your bill?'

'Certainly not,' says the duck. 'What do you think I am, a pervert?'

▶ 'Mummy, Mummy. There's a man at the door with a bill.'

'Don't be silly, darling. It's a duck with a hat on... '

▶ Two eagles are soaring along, when suddenly a passenger jet screams past them.

One eagle says to the other, 'Wow, did you see how fast that thing was moving?'

The other replies, 'Yeah. You'd move fast, too, if you had three arseholes and they were all on fire!'

▶ An old lady took a stroll through the woods one Sunday after church. Suddenly a little white duck, all covered with shit, crossed her path. 'Oh, dear,' the lady said, 'come on, I'll clean you!' She took a Kleenex from her purse and wiped the duck clean. After finishing, she urged the duck away, saying, 'Be careful next time!' She walked on and suddenly another duck, with shit all over it, crossed her way. Again she took out a Kleenex and cleaned the little duck. She warned this one as well and the duck took off. Soon after, she encountered a third duck with the same problem. 'Now I've had it!' she complained. 'What have you all been doing?' And for the third time she cleaned the duck.

She continued her stroll, when suddenly she heard a voice from the bushes. 'Hey, excuse me, lady!' sounded a male voice in distress.

'Yes?' she replied.

'Do you have a Kleenex?'

'No, not anymore,' she answered.

'Too bad. I'll just have to use another duck.'

▶ An elderly woman said to her friend, 'Last week I bought two budgerigars – a male and a female – but the trouble is, I don't know which is which.'

'Can't you tell by the colour above their beak?' said the friend.

'No, not when they're young.'

'Well, why don't you wait until they're "doing the business", as it were, then put a collar on the bird on top, because that will be the male?'

'That's an excellent idea,' said the woman.

So she waited for the birds to start mating and put a collar on the male budgerigar. A week later, the vicar came round for tea. The budgie took one look at him and squawked, 'Caught you, too, did they, mate?'

▶ A Mississippi woodpecker and a Texas woodpecker were in Mississippi arguing about which state had the toughest trees to peck. The Mississippi woodpecker said his state had a tree that no woodpecker had ever been able to peck and challenged the Texas woodpecker to try it. To the amazement of the Mississippi woodpecker, the Texas woodpecker pecked a hole in the tree with no problem. Now it was the Texas woodpecker's turn to try and prove that his state had the most impenetrable trees. He told the Mississippi woodpecker that in Texas there was a tree with a bark so hard that no bird had managed to get his beak into it. The Mississippi woodpecker took up the challenge of driving his beak into the tree and, to the dismay of the Texas woodpecker, succeeded easily. Both woodpeckers were puzzled as to why they were more successful with trees in states other than their own. In the end they concluded that your pecker is always harder when you're away from home.

BLINDNESS

▶ Why don't blind people skydive? Because it scares the dog.

▶ I was asked to run a marathon and I said no chance. Then I was told it was for blind kids and I thought, 'Damn it. I could win that!'

▶ Children at a blind school set off on their annual day trip to the coast and pulled into a motorway service station for lunch. So that the children could stretch their legs while their lunch orders were being taken, one of the teachers took out a special ball with a bell in it and suggested they had a game of football on a nearby strip of grass. The teachers started the game off and then went to collect the food.

While the teachers were waiting at the restaurant, the coach driver came running in. 'Quick!' he yelled. 'Your kids are kicking the shit out of a group of Morris dancers!'

▶ What goes, 'CLICK – is that it? CLICK – is that it? CLICK– is that it?'
A blind person with a Rubik's Cube.

▶ A blind man was travelling in his private jet, when he detected something was wrong. He made his way to the cockpit but got no response from the pilot. The blind guy then found the radio and started calling the tower. 'Help! Help!' he shouted.

The tower came back and asked, 'What's the problem?'

The blind guy yelled, 'Help me! I'm blind. The pilot is dead, and we're flying upside down!'

The tower said, 'How do you know you're upside down?'

'Because the shit is running down my back!' he replied.

▶ How do you recognise a blind man in a nudist colony? It's not hard.

▶ A little old lady was nearly blind. Her three sons doted on her and each wanted to prove that he was the kindest. The first son, who was very wealthy, bought her a mansion; the second son, who was fairly wealthy, bought her a Mercedes with a chauffeur. The third son, who was much poorer than the other two, spent all his savings on a parrot, which, by virtue of 15 years' dedicated training, could recite the entire Bible. Knowing that she was such a devoted churchgoer, he thought it would be an ideal and unique gift for her.

The old lady told the first son, 'The house is lovely, but it is too big for me, so I don't really want it.' Then she told the second son, 'The car is beautiful, but I don't drive and I don't care for the driver, so please return the car.' However, turning to the third son, she said gratefully, 'Your gift was by far the most thoughtful. That chicken was delicious.'

▶ Mike, an experienced skydiver, was getting ready for a jump one day, when he spotted another man preparing to dive wearing dark glasses, carrying a white stick and holding a guide dog by the lead. Shocked that a blind man was also going to jump, Mike struck up conversation, expressing admiration for the man's bravery. Puzzled, he asked, 'How do you know when the ground is getting close?'

'Easy,' replied the blind man. 'The lead goes slack.'

Did you hear about the blind circumciser? He got the sack.

A blind man was at the optician's with his guide dog. Man and dog were facing the eye chart on the wall. Then the optician took the guide dog away, replaced it with another guide dog and asked the man, 'There, is that better or worse?'

▶ A man was sitting on a park bench having a lunch of Ryvita crackers. A blind man came and sat next to him. Feeling neighbourly, the man handed the blind fellow a cracker.

The blind man sat and fingered it for a while before turning and saying 'Who wrote this shit?'

How do you confuse a blind lesbian? Take her to a fish market.

I'm going on a blind date tonight. I hope our dogs get on.

▶ A blind man is walking down the street with his guide dog, when it leads him to smack into a post. Once he's recovered, the blind man reaches into his pocket and fetches out a treat to feed the dog.

A passer-by remarks, 'That's marvellous! Even after he's made a mistake like that, you're giving him a treat.'

'Not really,' says the blind man. 'I'm just trying to find which end is which so I can kick him in the bollocks!'

▶ A blind bloke was bragging in the pub that because of his disability, his sense of smell had improved to such a degree that he could tell any type of wood purely by smell alone. As a challenge for every piece of wood he can name, the other drinkers should buy him a drink. People agree and start bringing in bits of wood and twigs. The first bloke holds a drawer close to him to sniff.

'That's easy, it's oak. I guess about 30 years old.'

Next a woman holds a twig.

'Another easy one, that's larch.'

Somebody comes in with a black piano key.

'Slightly harder, that one. It's ebony, but it's disguised quite well by the sweat off the pianist's fingers and the fact that it's been sat in between the ivory keys for so long.'

The onlookers are becoming a little disgruntled by his prowess and the bar manager decides he's had enough so he gets his wife to take off her knickers and stand in front of the blind man in an effort to confuse him.

He sniffs and sniffs again.

'This one's a little harder; can you turn it over, please.'

The woman turns around and presents her arse quite close to him.

'Oh, I've got it now. That's the shithouse door off a Grimsby fish trawler!'

▶ Little Sally came home from school and gave her daddy her school report. He opened it with pride and read out aloud.

'Ninety-four per cent in French. Well done, Sally, that is brilliant. You are going to be a top ambassador for the British government.'

He continued, 'Ninety-seven per cent in Geography. Sally, this is unbelievable. You are going to be a famous explorer like Christopher Columbus.'

He was now welling up with pride. 'Ninety-eight per cent in History. My God, Sally you are a little genius. You are going to work in the world's top museums. Maybe even be Tony Robinson's partner on *Time Team*!'

The list continued in the same excellent vein with exceptionally high percentages in all subjects – until he turned to Reading.

'Five per cent! Five pathetic per cent. Sally, you are a useless child. I spend all this money on your education and you repay me with five bloody per cent. A disgrace!'

He then clipped her around the ear and locked her in a dark, cold cupboard without any tea or sweets.

Sally started sobbing and protested, 'Daddy, Daddy. You know it's hard to read Braille with my hook.'

▶ I bought a guide dog the other day. How he got the job I will never know. Took him to the museum and he didn't explain anything to me.

▶ Eyesight was getting a bit bad so I decided to go to an optician to get my eyes tested.

'You should have gone to Specsavers!' came a voice from behind the counter.

Amazed by the man's honesty, I asked, 'Is it cheaper there?'

'No, it's next door, this is a hardware shop.'

▶ What goes 'thud', 'YELP', 'thud', 'WOOF!' and 'thud', 'YELP'? David Blunkett playing darts.

▶ A secretary calls her boss one morning and tells him that she is staying at home because she is not feeling well.

'So, what's the matter?' he asks.

'I have a case of anal blindness,' she says in a weak voice.

'And what the hell is anal blindness?'

'I just can't see my arse coming into work today.'

▶ My mum warned me that masturbation would make me blind and in a way she was right – my arm's too tired to pick up my glasses.

▶ My friend has been on so many blind dates, he should get a free dog.

▶ I had to end my relationship with a blind girl I was seeing. She was way too touchy-feely.

BLONDES

▶ Two men bump into each other in the supermarket.

'Sorry,' says the first one, 'I'm a bit confused. I lost my wife – can't find her anywhere.'

Second bloke replies, 'You know, I can't find mine, either. How about we go and look for them together?'

'Sure,' says the first one, 'what does your wife look like?'

'Well, she's blonde, long hair, tall slim body, well tanned, large breasts and she's wearing a tight-fitting, low-cut black dress. What does your wife look like?'

'Forget about my wife,' says the other bloke, 'let's go and look for yours!'

▶ A blonde entered a store that sold curtains and told the salesman she wanted to buy a pair of pink curtains. He showed her several patterns but the blonde was struggling to make a choice. Eventually she selected a pink floral print.

'What size curtains do you need?' asked the salesman.

'Fifteen inches,' replied the blonde.

'That sounds very small. What room are they for?'

'They're not for a room,' said the blonde. 'They're for my computer monitor.'

The salesman was baffled. 'But, miss, computers do not need curtains!'

The blonde said, 'Helloooo! Haven't they got Windoooows!'

▶ Ten blondes and a brunette were on a rock-climbing expedition, when some of the grappling hooks suddenly gave way, leaving the entire party clinging precariously to the rope 200 feet above the ground. The situation was so desperate that as a group they decided that one of their number should let go to ease the weight on the rope. No one volunteered until eventually the brunette gave a truly moving speech saying that she would sacrifice her own life to save the lives of the others. All of the blondes applauded.

▶ A blonde walks into a doctor's office. 'Doc, I hurt all over,' complains the blonde. She touches herself on her leg and winces. 'Ouch! I hurt there!' She touches her earlobe. 'Ouch! I hurt there, too!' She touches her hair. 'Ouch! Even my hair hurts!'

The doctor says, 'You've got a broken finger.'

▶ A ventriloquist is telling blonde jokes in a bar, when one of his audience, a young blonde lady, stands up and complains. 'I've heard just about enough of your lousy blonde jokes!' she shouts. 'What makes you think you can stereotype women this way? What does a person's hair colour have to do with their worth as a human being?'

The ventriloquist is very embarrassed and starts to apologise.

The blonde interrupts, 'Stay out of it, mister! I'm talking to the little bastard on your knee!'

▶ How did the blonde break her leg raking leaves? She fell out of the tree.

▶ What do blondes put behind their ears to attract men? Their knees.

▶ What's the difference between a blonde and a 747? Not everyone's been in a 747.

▶ What's the difference between a blonde and the *Titanic*? They know how many men went down on the *Titanic*.

▶ What's the difference between butter and a blonde? Butter is difficult to spread.

▶ Why did the blonde like the car with a sunroof? More leg room!

▶ Why do blondes have bruised belly buttons? Because they have blond boyfriends.

▶ Why do blondes wear hoop earrings? So they have a place to rest their ankles.

▶ A blonde was speeding, when a cop pulled her over. The officer, who also happened to be blonde, asked for her driver's licence. The blonde driver searched in her purse, then said, 'What does a driver's licence look like?'

The blonde cop said, 'You dummy, it's got your picture on it!'

The blonde driver finally found a small rectangular mirror at the bottom of her purse. Holding it up to her face, she said, 'Aha, this must be my driver's licence,' and handed it to the blonde cop.

The blonde policewoman looked in the mirror, handed it back to the driver and said, 'You're free to go. And if I had known you were a police officer, too, we could have avoided all of this.'

▶ Did you hear about the blonde who put lipstick on her forehead because she wanted to make up her mind?

▶ Did you hear about the blonde who didn't like breast-feeding her children because it hurt when she boiled her nipples?

▶ Did you hear about the blonde who, at the bottom of the application form where it said 'sign here', put 'Sagittarius'?

▶ A man is in the waiting room at a sperm donor clinic anxiously awaiting his turn, when in walks a beautiful blonde woman who smiles and sits next to him. Feeling a little confused, he turns to her and says, 'I'm sorry. I thought this was the sperm donor place. What are you doing here?'

'Mmmgghmh mmmgmhpghmm mmmmgh.'

▶ What's the difference between a blonde and a pair of sunglasses? The sunglasses sit higher on your face.

▶ What's the similarity between blondes and carpenters? They both have saws in their boxes.

▶ What did the blonde say to her swimming instructor? 'Will I really drown if you take your finger out?'

▶ Why do blondes use tampons with long strings? So the crabs can go bungee jumping.

▶ A blonde decided to redecorate her bedroom. She wasn't sure how many rolls of wallpaper she'd need but she knew her blonde friend Sharon from next door had recently done the same job and the two rooms were identical in size.

'Shaz,' she said, 'how many rolls of wallpaper did you buy for your bedroom?'

'Ten,' answered Sharon.

So the blonde bought ten rolls of wallpaper and did the job, but at the end she had two rolls left over.

'Shaz,' she said, 'I bought ten rolls of wallpaper for the bedroom, but I've got two left over.'

'Yeah,' said Sharon. 'So did I.'

▶ One night a blonde nun was praying in her room, when God appeared before her.

'My daughter,' said God, 'you have pleased me greatly. Your heart is full of love for your fellow creatures, and your actions and prayers are always for the benefit of others. I have come to you, not only to thank and commend you, but also to grant you anything you wish.'

'Dear Heavenly Father,' she replied, 'I am blissfully happy. I am a bride of Christ. I am doing what I love. I lack for nothing material since the Church supports me. I am content in all ways.'

'There must be something you would have of me?' asked God.

'Well, I suppose there is one thing,' she replied.

'Just name it,' said God.

'It's those blonde jokes,' she said. 'They are so demeaning to blondes everywhere, not just to me. I would wish for blonde jokes to stop.'

'Consider it done,' said God. 'Blonde jokes shall be stricken from the minds of humans everywhere. But there you go again, always thinking of others. Surely there is something that I can do just for you.'

'There is one thing,' she said hesitantly. 'But it's really small, and simply not worth your time.'

'Name it, please,' said God.

'It's M&Ms,' she said. 'They're so hard to peel!'

▶ What do a blonde and an instant lottery ticket have in common? All you have to do is scratch the box to win.

▶ What's the difference between a blonde and an inflatable doll? About two cans of hairspray.

▶ An executive interviewed a blonde for a job. Wanting to find out something about her personality, he asked her, 'If you could have a conversation with someone, living or dead, who would it be?'

The blonde gave the question careful consideration before answering, 'The living one.'

▶ A blonde holding a baby walked into a chemist and asked to use their baby scale.

'Sorry,' said the clerk, 'but our baby scale is broken. However, we can work out the baby's weight if we weigh mother and baby together on the adult scale, then weigh the mother alone and subtract the second number from the first.'

'That won't work,' said the blonde.

'Why not?' the clerk asked, mystified.

'Because,' said the blonde, 'I'm not the mother – I'm the aunt.'

▶ Did you hear about the blonde who got a pair of water skis? She's still looking for a lake with a slope.

▶ What did the blonde say when she got a book for her birthday? 'Thanks, but I've already got one.'

▶ A blonde motorist pulled out sharply from a side road, causing a truck driver to slam on his brakes. The furious trucker stormed over to the blonde's car and ordered her out. Then he drew a circle on the roadside and told her, 'Lady, don't step out of that circle.'

Overflowing with road rage, he ripped off her wing mirrors, but as he did so, the blonde began laughing. This further infuriated him and, taking a sledgehammer from his truck, he proceeded to smash every window on her car. Still, the blonde roared with laughter. So he picked up the sledgehammer again and, with a violent blow, punctured a gaping hole in her car's bodywork. Still she laughed hysterically. With steam almost coming from his ears, he marched over to her and roared, 'Lady, I just wrecked your car. What's so funny?'

The blonde giggled, 'Every time you turned around, I stepped out of the circle.'

▶ A blonde came home from her first day of commuting into the city. Her mother saw that she was looking tired and asked, 'Honey, are you feeling OK?'

'Not really,' replied the blonde. 'I'm nauseous from sitting backwards on the train.'

'Oh, you poor love,' said the mother. 'Why didn't you ask the person sitting opposite you to switch seats?'

'I couldn't,' said the blonde. 'There was no one there.'

▶ Did you hear about the blonde who faked an orgasm with her vibrator?

▶ A blonde went to a seafood restaurant and saw the tank where they kept the lobsters. Taking pity on them, she hid them in her handbag. Later she went to the woods and set the poor animals free.

▶ As a trucker stopped for a red light, a blonde caught up with him. She jumped from her car, ran up to his truck and knocked on the door. When he wound down the window, she said, 'Hi, I'm Kelly. You're losing some of your load!' He ignored her and drove on. At the next red light, the blonde caught up with him again. Jumping from her car, she ran to his truck and knocked on the door. As if she had never met him before, she shouted, 'Hi, I'm Kelly. You're losing some of your load!' He shook his head at her and drove off. At the next red light, the blonde again jumped from her car, ran to the truck and knocked on the door. 'Hi, I'm Kelly,' she shouted. 'You're losing some of your load!' The trucker waved his arms at her angrily and drove off.

At the next red light, the trucker quickly jumped from his cab and ran back to the blonde's car. As she wound down the window, he said, 'Hi, I'm George, it's winter and I'm driving the gritting lorry!'

▶ A blonde in a headscarf decided to take up the accordion, so she went into a music shop and asked to see the accordions. 'They're over there,' said the shop owner.

'Right, I'll have the big red one in the corner.'

The shop owner looked at her quizzically. 'You're a blonde, aren't you?'

'Yes, how did you know?'

'That big red accordion is a radiator.'

▶ A young businessman picked up a blonde in a bar and took her back to his place. When she saw the bedroom, she exclaimed, 'Wow! A waterbed! I've never had sex on a waterbed before!' As they lay down on the bed, things soon got hot. She said, 'Before we go any further, don't you think we should put on some protection?'

'Good idea,' he said.

So the blonde jumped up from the waterbed and went into the next room. When she returned, she was wearing a life jacket.

▶ A blonde called the police to report that she had been assaulted.

'When did this happen?' asked the officer.

'Ten days ago,' she replied.

'Why did you wait until now to report it?' he enquired.

'Well, I didn't know I was assaulted till the cheque bounced.'

▶ A blonde went out of her house and checked her mailbox. Seeing nothing, she closed the mailbox and went back into the house. Ten minutes later, she came out again to check for mail, but, finding nothing, closed the mailbox and returned indoors.

When she did this for a third time in quick succession, her nosey neighbour called out, 'You must be waiting for a very important letter?'

'No,' said the blonde. 'But I'm working on my computer and it keeps telling me I've got new mail.'

▶ Two blondes were strolling along Australia's Bondi Beach by moonlight. One turned to the other and said, 'Which do you think is closer? The moon or New York?'

The other blonde replied, 'Wow! Can you see New York?'

▶ A blonde rang down to hotel reception to complain that she was trapped in her room. 'I can't get out!' she wailed.

'Why not?' asked the reception clerk. 'Have you tried the door?'

The blonde said, 'But there are only three doors in here. One is the bathroom, one is the closet and one has a sign on it that says "Do Not Disturb".'

▶ Desperate for money, a blonde decided to kidnap a small boy and hold him for ransom. Having snatched her victim, she wrote a note, saying, 'I've kidnapped your son. Tomorrow evening put £100,000 in a bag and leave it by the fountain in the park.' And she signed it mysteriously, 'A blonde'. She then pinned the note to the boy's jacket and sent him home.

The following evening, she went to the fountain in the park and found the boy standing there with the bag full of money. He handed the blonde a note that read, 'How could you do this to a fellow blonde?'

▶ Why do blondes get confused in the ladies' room? Because they have to pull their own pants down.

▶ Did you hear about the blonde who thought Eartha Kitt was a set of garden tools?

▶ A blonde in a cab suddenly realised that she didn't have any money for the fare. So she said to the driver, 'You'd better stop. I can't pay you, and it's £10 already.'

The driver checked her out in the rear-view mirror and said, 'That's OK. I'll turn down the next dark street and I can get in the back seat and take off your bra.'

'You'd be cheating yourself,' said the blonde. 'This bra is only worth £5.'

▶ What is the difference between Bigfoot and an intelligent blonde? There have actually been sightings of Bigfoot.

▶ A brunette, a redhead and a blonde escaped a burning building by climbing to the roof. On the street below, firemen were waiting, holding a blanket for them to jump into.

The firemen yelled to the brunette, 'Jump! Jump! It's your only chance of survival.'

The brunette jumped, but suddenly the firemen yanked the blanket away, and she slammed onto the pavement like a tomato. 'Jump! Jump!' the firemen yelled to the redhead. 'You've got to jump!'

'No!' shouted the redhead. 'You're going to pull the blanket away!'

'No,' replied the firemen. 'It's only brunettes we hate, we're OK with redheads.' So the redhead jumped but halfway down the firemen whipped the blanket away, and she was flattened on the pavement like a pancake.

Finally the blonde stepped to the edge of the roof. Again the firemen yelled, 'Jump! You have to jump! It's your only hope!'

'No way!' shouted the blonde. 'You're just going to pull the blanket away!'

'We promise we won't,' replied the firemen. 'You have to jump. We won't pull the blanket away this time.'

'Listen,' said the blonde. 'Nothing you can say will convince me that you're not going to pull the blanket away! So what I want you to do is, put the blanket down and back away from it... '

▶ What did the blonde name her pet zebra? Spot.

▶ A young man wanted to get his beautiful blonde wife something nice for their first wedding anniversary. So he decided to buy her a mobile phone. After he had explained to her all the features on the phone, she was absolutely thrilled with the present. The next day the blonde was out shopping when her phone rang. It was her husband.

'Hi, honey,' he said. 'How do you like your new phone?'

'I just love it,' she replied. 'It's so compact, and your voice is as clear as a bell. And I love all the different features. There's just one thing I don't understand, though.'

'What's that, baby?' asked the husband.

'How did you know I was in Sainsbury's?'

▶ Why are blondes only allowed 30-minute lunch breaks? It takes too long to retrain them if they take an hour.

▶ Why did the blonde girl scale the glass wall? To see what was on the other side.

▶ Joe is sitting on a train across from a busty blonde wearing a tiny miniskirt. Despite his efforts, he is unable to stop staring at the top of her thighs. To his delight, he realises she has gone without underwear.

The blonde realises he is staring and enquires, 'Are you looking at my pussy?'

'Yes, I'm sorry,' says Joe and promises to avert his eyes.

'It's quite all right,' replies the woman. 'It's very talented. Watch this, I'll make it blow a kiss to you.'

Sure enough, the pussy blows him a kiss. Joe, who is completely absorbed, wonders what else the wonder pussy can do.

'I can also make it wink,' says the woman. Joe stares in amazement as the pussy winks at him. 'Come and sit next to me,' suggests the woman, patting the seat. Joe moves over and she asks, 'Would you like to stick a couple of fingers in?'

Stunned, Joe replies, 'Good grief! Can it whistle, too?'

▶ What did the blonde girl say after the guy blew her in the ear? Thanks for the refill.

▶ Why was the blonde so pleased to complete a jigsaw puzzle in 18 months? Because the box said: 'From two to five years'.

▶ Why is it good to have a blonde passenger? You can park in the handicapped spots.

▶ Why do blondes wear so much hairspray? So they can catch all the things going over their heads.

▶ What do you call a blonde with an IQ of 50? Cheat!

▶ Why do blondes wear green lipstick? Red means stop.

▶ What do you do if a blonde throws a grenade at you? Catch it, pull out the pin and throw it back.

▶ How do blonde girls pierce their ears? They put tacks in their shoulder pads.

▶ Why did the blonde stop using the pill? It kept falling out.

▶ What do you call a brunette girl between two blondes? An interpreter.

▶ How do you describe a blonde surrounded by drooling idiots? Flattered.

▶ Why did the blonde go halfway to Norway, then turn around and come home? It took her that long to figure out a 14-inch Viking was a TV set.

▶ What did the blonde customer say to the buxom waitress (reading her nametag)? 'Stephanie… that's cute. What did you name the other one?'

▶ What do you call a blonde with a whole brain? A golden retriever!

▶ Why do blondes have one more brain cell than a cow? So when you pull their tits, they don't shit on the floor.

▶ Hired as a secretary at an office, a blonde's first job was to go out for coffee. Eager to impress on her first day, she grabbed a large thermos and hurried to a nearby coffee shop. She held up the thermos, and the coffee-shop assistant quickly came over to take her order. The blonde asked, 'Is this big enough to hold six cups of coffee?'

The assistant looked at the thermos for a few seconds before replying, 'Yeah. It looks like about six cups to me.'

'Oh, good!' sighed the blonde in relief. 'Then give me two regular, two black and two decaf.'

▶ Why do blondes wear underwear? They make good ankle warmers.

▶ How can you tell if a blonde has been in your refrigerator? By the lipstick on the cucumber.

▶ Did you hear about the blonde who was treated in A&E for concussion and serious head wounds? She had tried to commit suicide by hanging herself with a bungee cord.

▶ What can strike a blonde without her even knowing it? A thought.

▶ A blonde went to a restaurant, bought a coffee and sat down to drink it. She looked on the side of her cup and found a peel-off prize. Then she pulled off the tab and yelled excitedly, 'I won! I won! I won a motor home! I won a motor home!'

The waitress ran over and said, 'That's impossible. The biggest prize given away was a DVD player!'

The blonde insisted, 'No. I won a motor home, I won a motor home!'

Hearing the commotion, the manager made his way over to the table and said, 'You couldn't possibly have won a motor home because we didn't have that as a prize!'

Again the blonde said, 'There's no mistake. I won a motor home, I won a motor home! Look, here's the ticket if you don't believe me.'

She handed the prize ticket to the manager, and he read out loud, 'WIN A BAGEL.'

▶ A blonde playing Trivial Pursuit threw the dice and landed on a Science and Nature question. The question was, 'If you are in a vacuum and someone calls your name, can you hear it?'

After a moment's thought she asked, 'Is the vacuum on or off?'

▶ What's the first thing a blonde learns when she takes driving lessons? You can sit upright in a car.

▶ What's the difference between a chorus line of blondes and a magician? A magician has a cunning array of stunts.

▶ When a surgeon came to see his blonde patient on the day after her operation, she asked him just how long it would be before she could resume her sex life.

'Uh, I hadn't really thought about it,' replied the surgeon. 'You're the first one ever to ask that after a tonsillectomy.'

▶ A blonde walks into the local dry cleaners. She places a garment on the counter. 'I'll be back tomorrow afternoon to pick up my dress,' she says.

'Come again?' says the clerk, cupping his ear.

'No,' she replies. 'This time it's mayonnaise.'

▶ How does a blonde turn on the light after sex? She opens the car door.

▶ Visiting a blonde's house, her friend asked, 'Why do you have that huge picture of yourself above the bathroom sink?'

The blonde said, 'My bathroom mirror broke, and I didn't want to buy a new one!'

BODYBUILDING

▶ Dear sirs,

Since taking your bodybuilding course, I now have a 44-inch chest, a 32-inch waist, 17-inch biceps and an 18-inch neck. I feel absolutely marvellous but, at the same time, I do feel that my chances of marriage are spoiled.

Yours faithfully,

Mary Smith

▶ My sister took up bodybuilding recently. She's really good at it; in fact, she's so good, she's now my brother.

BOOKS

▶ From the bestseller lists...

● *50 Years in the Saddle* by Major Asburn

● *And the Other People* by Allan Sundry

● *I'm God's Gift to Women* by P Rick

- *Drinking Problems* by Imorf Mihead

- *One Night Stands* by Amanda Use

- *The Reproductive and Sexual Organs* by Jenna Talia

- *Becoming a Woman* by Paul Mcokof

- *Donating Your Body* by Ivan A Bolokk

- *Become a Better Lover* by Roger Ring

- *Overcoming Impotence* by Eric Shon

- *Dealing with Constipation* by Erma Roid

- *Memoirs of a Porn Star* by Mike Oxlong

BOSSES

▶ I texted my boss, 'What's the difference between this morning and your daughter?'

He answered, 'I don't know.'

I replied, 'I'm not coming in this morning.'

▶ I hear that the credit crunch is even affecting fairgrounds. My friend's a dodgems operator and he lost his job this morning. He's suing for funfair dismissal.

▶ The boss told four of his employees, 'We made a heavy loss last quarter, and I'm afraid I'm going to have to let one of you go.'

The first, a black man, said, 'I'm a protected minority, you can't fire me.'

The second said, 'And I'm a woman. You can't get rid of me.'

The third, an old man, said, 'And if you fire me, I'll hit you with an age discrimination suit so fast, it'll make your head spin!'

All eyes turned on the young, white, male employee who thought for a second before suggesting meekly, 'I think I might be gay.'

BOYS WILL BE BOYS

▶ *What men say and what they actually mean:*

- 'I'M GOING FISHING' means: 'I'm going to drink myself dangerously stupid and stand by a stream with a stick in my hand, while the fish swim by in complete safety.'

- 'IT'S A GUY THING' means: 'There is no rational thought pattern connected with it, and you have no chance at all of making it logical.'

- 'CAN I HELP WITH DINNER?' means: 'Why isn't it already on the table?'

- 'UH HUH,' 'SURE, DARLING' OR 'YES, DEAR... ' means: Absolutely nothing. It's a conditioned response.

- 'IT WOULD TAKE TOO LONG TO EXPLAIN' means: 'I have no idea how it works.'

- 'I WAS LISTENING TO YOU. IT'S JUST THAT I HAVE THINGS ON MY MIND' means: 'I was wondering if that blonde over there is wearing a bra.'

- 'TAKE A BREAK, DEAR, YOU'RE WORKING TOO HARD' means: 'I can't hear the football over the vacuum cleaner.'

- 'THAT'S INTERESTING, DEAR' means: 'Are you still talking?'

- 'YOU KNOW HOW BAD MY MEMORY IS' means: 'I remember the theme song to *Tomorrow's World*, the address of the first girl I ever kissed and the registration numbers of every car I've ever owned, but I forgot your birthday.'

- 'I WAS JUST THINKING ABOUT YOU, AND GOT YOU THESE ROSES' means: 'The girl selling them on the corner was a real babe.'

- 'OH, DON'T FUSS, I JUST CUT MYSELF, IT'S NO BIG DEAL' means: 'I have actually severed a limb, but will bleed to death before I admit that I'm hurt.'

- 'HEY, I'VE GOT MY REASONS FOR WHAT I'M DOING' means: 'And I sure hope I think of some pretty soon.'

- 'I CAN'T FIND IT' means: 'It didn't fall into my outstretched hands, so I'm completely clueless.'

- 'WHAT DID I DO THIS TIME?' means: 'What did you catch me at?'

- 'I HEARD YOU' means: 'I haven't the foggiest clue what you just said and am hoping desperately that I can fake it well enough so that you don't spend the next three days yelling at me.'

- 'YOU KNOW I COULD NEVER LOVE ANYONE ELSE' means: 'I am used to the way you yell at me and realise it could be worse.'

- 'YOU LOOK TERRIFIC' means: 'Please don't try on one more outfit, I'm starving.'

- 'I'M NOT LOST. I KNOW EXACTLY WHERE WE ARE' means: 'No one will ever see us alive again.'

- 'WE SHARE THE HOUSEWORK' means: 'I make the messes, she cleans them up.'

▶ This political correctness has gone mad. I can't even refer to my child as 'my disabled son'.

Apparently the correct term these days is 'daughter'.

BREASTS

▶ I'm as confused as a baby in a topless bar.

▶ A guy goes to buy a train ticket, and the girl selling tickets has an incredible set of jugs. He says, 'Give me two pickets to Titsburgh... umm... I mean, two tickets to Pittsburgh.' He's really embarrassed.

The guy in line behind him says, 'Relax, pal. We all make Freudian slips. Just the other day at breakfast I meant to say to my wife, "Please pass the sugar," but I accidentally said, "You fucking bitch, you wrecked my life."'

▶ What did one saggy tit say to the other saggy tit? 'If we don't get some support soon, people will think we're nuts!'

▶ Once upon a time there lived a beautiful queen with large breasts. Nick the Dragon Slayer obsessed over the queen for this reason. He knew that the penalty for his desire would be death should he try to touch them, but he had to try. One day Nick revealed his secret desire to his colleague, Horatio the Physician, the king's chief doctor. Horatio thought about this and said that he could arrange for Nick to more than satisfy his desire, but it would cost him 1,000 gold coins to arrange it. Without pause, Nick readily agreed to the scheme. The next day, Horatio made a batch of itching powder and poured a little bit into the queen's bra while she bathed. Soon after she dressed, the itching commenced and grew intense. Upon being summoned to the Royal Chambers to address this incident, Horatio informed the king and queen that only a special saliva, if applied for four hours, would cure this type of itch, and that tests had shown that only the saliva of Nick would work as the antidote to cure the itch. The king, eager to help his queen, quickly summoned Nick to their chambers. Horatio then slipped Nick the antidote for the itching powder, which he put into his mouth, and for the next four hours, Nick worked passionately on the queen's large and magnificent breasts.

The queen's itching was eventually relieved, and Nick left satisfied and hailed as a hero. Upon returning to his chamber, Nick found Horatio demanding his payment of 1,000 gold coins. With his obsession now satisfied, Nick couldn't have cared less, knowing that Horatio could never report this matter to the king, and with a laugh told him to get lost. The next day, Horatio slipped a massive dose of the same itching powder into the king's underwear. The king immediately summoned Nick.

The moral of the story – pay your bloody bills!

▶ What does an old woman have between her breasts that a young woman doesn't? A navel.

▶ What's the difference between a sewing machine and a girl jogging? A sewing machine only has one bobbin.

▶ What's worse than a cardboard box? Paper tits.

▶ Why is the space between a woman's breasts and her hips called a waist? Because you could easily fit another pair of tits in there.

▶ What are the small bumps around a woman's nipples for? It's Braille for 'Suck here'.

▶ Why do men find it difficult to make eye contact? Because breasts don't have eyes.

▶ The other day, while I was seeing my shrink, he asked me what I looked for in a woman.

Naturally I replied, 'Big tits.'

He said, 'No, I meant for a serious relationship.'

So I said, 'Oh, seriously big tits.'

'No, no, no. I mean what do you look for in the one woman you want to spend the rest of your life with?'

He looked at me kind of worried as I just sat there on his couch laughing until my gut hurt. 'Spend the rest of my life with one woman? No woman's tits are that big.'

▶ How do you make five pounds of fat look great? Put a nipple on it.

▶ A biker and his wife were celebrating their 50th wedding anniversary. That night, she entered the bedroom wearing the same sexy little negligee that she had worn on their wedding night.

She said, 'Honey, do you remember this?'

'Yeah,' he said. 'You were wearing that on the night we married.'

'That's right,' she smiled. 'And do you remember what you said to me that night?'

'Yeah, I said, "Baby, I'm going to suck the life out of those big tits and screw your brains out."'

She giggled and said, 'That's exactly what you said. So now it's 50 years later, and I'm in the same negligee I wore that night. What do you have to say tonight?'

He looked her up and down and said, 'Mission accomplished.'

BROTHELS

▶ A man went to a brothel and enquired how much it would be for a good time.

'£150 for full sex,' answered the madam.

'£150! You're putting me on,' cried the man.

'That'll be another £10,' said the madam.

▶ Why does a one-storey brothel make more money than a two-storey brothel? Because there's no fucking overhead.

▶ A new mortuary in a tough town decided to advertise in an unorthodox fashion, and so draped a banner on the front of their building that read: 'Our staff will stuff your stiff.'

Not to be outdone, the madam across the street had her girls respond with a banner, too: 'Our stuff will stiff your staff.'

▶ What do you call kids born in whorehouses? Brothel sprouts.

▶ A man was walking one day, when he came to this big house in a nice neighbourhood. Suddenly he realised there was a couple making love out on the lawn. Then he noticed another couple over behind a tree. Then another couple behind some bushes by the house. He walked up to the door of the house, and knocked. A well-dressed woman answered the door, and the man asked what kind of a place this was.

'This is a brothel,' replied the madam.

'Well, what's all this out on the lawn?' queried the man.

'Oh, we're having a yard sale today.'

▶ The madam of a brothel answered the ring of the bell and, on opening the door, she found standing there on the threshold an ancient, bearded gentleman.

'May I come in?' asked the old man in an aged, quavering voice.

Feeling a little confused, the madam said, 'But, sir, surely you must be in the wrong place. Here is where we—'

'I know what you do here,' interrupted the old man. 'You don't think I came here for my tea, do you? Bring on the girls.'

Still confused, but understanding her professional duties, the madam had several of her girls line up for the pensioner. The old man tottered from one girl to another until he reached Rosie, a large redhead with enormous breasts. He looked at her with appreciation and pointed. 'Good! I'll take those.'

He paid out the necessary money and Rosie led him upstairs. She helped him off with his coat and hung it up carefully on the nail on the door. Then she helped him off with the rest of his clothes and got into bed. There, to Rosie's astonishment, the old man performed with vigour skill that was unbelievable. In fact, Rosie, a hardened professional, found herself enjoying it!

As they lay in bed a few minutes afterwards, relaxing, Rosie said, 'How old are you?'

The old man said, 'God has been good to me. I am 98 years old.'

'That is certainly amazing. Listen, if you're ever in the neighbourhood again and if you should feel in the mood, please ask for me – Rosie. I would be delighted to oblige you.'

The old man replied, irritated, 'What do you mean, if I should be in the mood again? Let me sleep for five minutes right now and, believe me, I will be in the mood again.'

'Really?' replied Rosie eagerly. 'Then please have a nap.'

The old man adjusted himself into a relaxed position, face up, placed his arms across his chest and then said, 'Wait one minute. This is important. While I'm asleep, scoop up my testicles with your right hand and hold them an inch above the sheet, without moving them. Keep them absolutely motionless.'

'Of course,' said Rosie, and did as she was told, holding the old man's testicles free of the sheet for five minutes as he slept. Then he woke with a start and said, 'I'm ready.' And away he went again, even better the second time than the first.

As she lay panting, Rosie said, 'It was wonderful, but one thing I don't understand. Why was it necessary to hold your testicles motionless above the sheet while you were sleeping?'

'Oh that,' said the old man. 'Well, you are a nice girl and I like you very much. Still, the truth is I don't know you very well, and over there, in my coat, hanging on the hook on the door, is £1,000 in cash.'

▶ A man was feeling really horny but was broke. He went to a brothel with £5 and begged the madam to give him whatever she could for that price.

'I'm sorry,' she said, 'but £5 will only cover the rent of a room for ten minutes. And none of my girls work for free.' Nevertheless he paid up and was shown to the room, but there was nothing to screw. In desperation, he spotted a pigeon on the window ledge. He gently opened the window, grabbed the pigeon and fucked the hell out of it. Satisfied, he then went home.

The following week he returned to the brothel, this time with a wallet full of cash from payday. He said to the madam, 'I've got lots of money now, so give me a hooker.'

She replied, 'All of my girls are busy right now. Why don't you go to the peepshow and get yourself in the mood?'

So he went to the peepshow and was enjoying it so much that he turned to the man next to him and said, 'These girls are really hot, aren't they?'

'Yeah,' he responded, 'but you should've been here last week. There was this guy fucking a pigeon!'

BUMPER STICKERS

▶ *Bumper stickers and slogans to live by:*

- Porn: it's cheaper than dating

- Snatch a kiss, or vice versa

- Good girls get fat, bad girls get eaten

- Impotence: Nature's way of saying 'No hard feelings'

- If you don't believe in oral sex, keep your mouth shut!

- Dial 999 – Make a cop come

- Be kind to donkeys... kiss my ass!

- My karma ran over your dogma

BUSINESS TRIPS

▶ A salesman was on a business trip in Birmingham. One evening he began chatting to a woman in a bar and eventually he realised she was a prostitute.

'I'll give you £100 for a crap blowjob,' he said.

'Darling,' she replied. 'For £100 I'll give you the best blowjob of your life.'

'You don't understand,' he said. 'I'm not horny, just homesick.'

CAMELS

▶ A mother and baby camel are talking one day, when the baby camel asks, 'Mum, why have I got these huge three-toed feet?'

The mother replies, 'Well, son, when we trek across the desert your toes will help you to stay on top of the soft sand.'

'OK,' said the son. A few minutes later the son asks, 'Mum, why have I got these great long eyelashes?'

'They are there to keep the sand out of your eyes on the trips through the desert.'

'Thanks, Mum,' replies the son. After a short while, the son returns and asks, 'Mum, why have I got these great big humps on my back?'

The mother, now a little impatient with the boy, replies, 'They are there to help us store water for our long treks across the desert, so we can go without drinking for long periods.'

'That's great, Mum, so we have huge feet to stop us sinking, and long eyelashes to keep the sand from our eyes and these humps to store water, but Mum... '

'Yes, son?'

'Why are we in London Zoo?'

▶ A bloke buys a camel from some guy on a street corner, and he proudly rides it into the pub car park, causing a bit of a stir with the local drinkers.

'Nice camel, mate,' one of his drinking partners commented. 'Is it male or female?'

'Female!' the bloke beamed.

'How do you know?' his mate enquired.

'Well,' the bloke explained, 'on the way here today, at least 20 people yelled out: "Hey – look at the twat on that camel!"'

▶ Ali goes to the used camel dealer. He wants a cheap camel to take him on only one trip across the desert.

The dealer says, 'I have a good used camel for you. It hasn't done many miles, only had one owner but has a small fault. Because of the fault, I'm willing to let him go cheap.'

'What's the fault?' asks Ali.

'The camel will go for many miles and then stop. The only way to get him to walk again is to jerk off the camel.'

'That's disgusting!' says Ali.

'Yeah, but he's very cheap!' adds the dealer.

After some massive internal discussions with himself, Ali thinks, 'What the hell, it's a cheap camel and no one will see me wanking the camel off in the desert.'

'OK, I'll take him,' says Ali to the dealer. After packing his bags on the camel's back, he mounts up and sets off across the desert.

After 50 miles the camel stops. Ali dismounts and tries to persuade the camel to walk. But to no avail.

He then remembers the fault. Gingerly he takes hold of the camel's dick and slowly jerks him off. When the camel comes, Ali mounts up and away they go. Ali thinks, 'That wasn't so bad!'

Fifty miles later, the same thing happens. This time Ali jerks the camel off faster, finishes, wipes his hands and mounts up to continue the trip.

This happens four more times: stop, jerk off, continue. Then after a short walk, the camel comes to a sudden stop. Ali gets off and prepares to jerk off the camel but then the camel shakes his head, pouts his lips and makes sucking sounds.

CANADIANS

▶ There are two seasons in Canada – six months of cold followed by six months of poor snowmobiling.

▶ Two Canadians are sitting in a bar and getting bored. They decide to play 20 questions. The first Canadian tries to think of a word and after a little pondering comes up with the word: moosecock.

The second Canadian tries his first question: 'Is it something good to eat?'

The first guy thinks a moment, then laughs and replies, 'Sure, I suppose you could eat it.'

The second Canadian says, 'Is it a moosecock?'

▶ Why don't Canadians have group sex? Too many thank-you letters to write afterwards.

▶ A study was being conducted by the US to determine why the head of a man's penis is larger than the shaft. The study took two years and cost $1.5 million. The results of the study concluded that the head of the penis is larger than the shaft to provide the man with more pleasure during sex.

When the results were published, Germany, not convinced by the results of the American study, decided that they needed to do their own study. Three years later, and at a cost of 3.6 million Euros, they concluded that the head of a man's penis is larger than the shaft to provide the woman with more pleasure during sex.

Hearing of these results, a group of scientists in Newfoundland decided to conduct their own study since they didn't trust either the American or German studies. After three weeks of intense research and a cost of $75, the Newfoundland study reached a conclusion: the head of a man's penis is larger than the shaft to prevent the man's hand from flying off and hitting him in the forehead.

▶ A Canadian man was having coffee and croissants with butter and jam in a Toronto diner, when an American guy, chewing gum, sat down next to him. The Canadian ignored the American, who nevertheless started up a conversation. The American snapped his gum and said, 'You Canadian folk eat the whole bread?'

Annoyed at having his leisurely breakfast interrupted, the Canadian frowned and replied, 'Of course.'

The American blew a huge bubble and grinned. 'We don't. In the States, we only eat what's inside. We collect the crusts in a container, recycle them, transform them into croissants and sell them to Canada.'

The Canadian listened in silence, but the American persisted. 'D'ya eat jelly with the bread?'

The Canadian sighed. 'Of course.' Cracking his gum between his teeth, the American said, 'We don't. In the States, we eat fresh fruit for breakfast, then we put all the peels, seeds and leftovers in containers, recycle them, transform them into jelly and sell it to Canada.'

The Canadian then asked, 'Do you have sex in the States?'

The American smiled and said, 'Of course we do.'

The Canadian leaned closer and asked, 'And what do you do with the condoms once you've used them?'

'We throw them away, of course.'

Now it was the Canadian's turn to smile. 'We don't. In Canada, we put them in a container, recycle them, melt them down into chewing gum and sell them to the United States.'

CANNIBALISM

▶ Two missionaries were captured by fearsome cannibals. They were tied up and thrown in a huge pot, which was filled with water. The cannibals placed the pot on a huge pile of firewood and set it ablaze. One of the missionaries started to pray, while the cannibals danced round the fire. Then he heard his companion laughing uncontrollably.

'What's wrong with you?' shouted the first missionary. 'Why are you laughing? Don't you see, we're going to die a horrible, painful death. What's so funny?'

'I know,' gasped the other missionary, 'but I've just done a huge turd in the pot!'

▶ A tribe of cannibals captured a missionary, chucked him into a huge pot with water, started the fire and asked the missionary, 'What's your name?'

The surprised missionary said, 'Why do want to know my name? What for?'

The chief said, 'What do you mean what for? For the menu, of course.'

▶ What is the definition of trust? Two cannibals giving each other a blowjob.

CARD GAMES

▶ My wife made me join a bridge club. I jump off next Tuesday.

CAR MECHANICS

▶ How can you tell when a car mechanic just had sex? One of his fingers is clean.

▶ Saw an advert that said, 'Need help, call Jesus. 0800 123 4567.' Out of curiosity I did. A Mexican showed up with a tow truck.

▶ How did the octogenarian car mechanic make love? He attached leads to his nipples and got a jump start from a younger man.

CARS

▶ If it's got tits or wheels, sooner or later you're gonna have problems with it.

▶ What gets longer when pulled, fits between breasts, inserts neatly in a hole and works best when jerked? A seatbelt.

▶ What occupies the last six pages of Lada user's manual? The bus and train timetables.

▶ What do you call a Lada on a hill? A bloody miracle.

▶ Finding a woman sobbing that she had locked her keys in her car, a man assures her that he can help. She looks on amazed as he removes his trousers, rolls them into a tight ball and rubs them against the car door.

Magically it opens. 'That's so clever,' the woman gasps. 'How did you do it?'

'Easy,' replies the man. 'These are my khakis.'

▶ How do you know when petrol prices are at their highest? London taxi drivers start to take the shortest route.

▶ On his way home from work, a man stopped off at the petrol station to put some air in his tyres as they were a bit flat. He put the air in and went inside to pay.

The cashier said, '£2, please.'

'£2!' he said. 'It's air, for crying out loud, it shouldn't be that expensive!'

'Well', the cashier replied, 'that's inflation for you.'

▶ What do a man and a car have in common? They both have the ability to misfire.

▶ A blonde was trying to sell her old car but was having trouble attracting a buyer because the car had almost 250,000 miles on the clock. One day she was pouring out her problems to a brunette workmate who confided, 'There is a way of making the car easier to sell, but it's not legal.'

'I don't mind whether or not it's legal,' said the blonde. 'I just want to sell that damned car.'

'OK,' said the brunette. 'Here is the address of a friend of mine who owns a car repair shop. Tell him I sent you and he'll sort it out. After that, you shouldn't have any difficulty selling your car.'

The next day, the blonde went to see the mechanic.

A few weeks later, she bumped into the brunette at work. 'Did you sell your car?' asked the brunette.

'No,' replied the blonde. 'Why should I? It only has 40,000 miles on the clock!'

▶ Why do schools in Essex only have driving classes two days a week? Because they need their cars for sex education the other three days a week!

▶ I was driving around the other day and started feeling really horny. So I decided to swing by this well-known dogging spot that was close by. There were a few other cars there so I pulled up and joined in.

I had a great time, but I think I failed my driving test.

▶ My mate was addicted to brake fluid. But he said he could stop any time.

▶ My mate Dirk gets around quickly on his hands and knees by fastening springs to them. It's called four-sprung Dirk technique.

▶ Did you hear about the new device that makes your car run 95 per cent quieter? It fits right over her mouth.

▶ A 90-year-old man was caught doing 8 miles per hour in his mobility scooter on the inside lane of the M1. His life was in serious danger – particularly on the three occasions he pulled into the middle lane to overtake women drivers.

▶ I know a lot about cars. I can look at a car's headlights and tell you exactly which way it's coming.

▶ A wealthy lady was being driven by her chauffeur, when their car got a flat tyre. The chauffeur got out and began trying to remove the hubcap.

After watching him struggle for five minutes, she leaned out of the window and asked, 'Would you like a screwdriver?'

'We might as well,' he said. 'I can't get this bloody wheel off!'

▶ Having just bought a small sports car, a young guy was keen to show it off to his girlfriend. So they went for a drive in the country, where she began to feel decidedly amorous. As he stopped the car in a quiet lane, she said, 'There's no room in here; let's go and screw behind that grassy bank. Hurry up and get out of the car before I get out of the mood!'

The guy struggled for a minute, then said dejectedly, 'Until I get out of the mood, I can't get out of the car!'

▶ A speeding car smashed through a guardrail, rolled down a cliff, bounced off a tree and landed upside down, wheels spinning frantically.

As the driver climbed slowly back up to the road, a passing motorist said, 'Are you drunk?'

'Of course,' he said. 'What do you think I am, a stunt driver?'

▶ Out on a date, a young couple went for a drive in the countryside. Starting to feel randy, they looked for a quiet lane and tried to have sex in the back seat. However the car was too small and instead they decided to carry on underneath the vehicle where there was more legroom.

A few minutes later, a police officer happened to be passing. He immediately announced that he was arresting the couple for indecent exposure.

'But I'm not doing anything illegal,' protested the man. 'I'm just fixing my car.'

'You're having sex,' replied the officer coldly. 'And I know that to be a fact for three reasons. Firstly, you have no tools out. Secondly, I can see a second pair of legs in addition to yours. And thirdly, your car's been stolen.'

▶ How can an American be certain that the car he's just bought is actually new? When it's recalled by the factory.

▶ Andy was driving around town in a Rolls-Royce, when he saw his friend Bob waving to him.

'Hey, where did you get the car?' asked Bob.

'Well,' explained Andy, 'I was walking down the road to the general store when a beautiful blonde pulled up in this car and offered me a ride. I got in, but instead of going into town, she drove up to the lane by the lake and removed all of her clothes except her black lacy knickers. She then lay back in the seat, spread her legs and said, "Take anything you want from me." Well, I could see her underwear would never fit me, so I took the car!'

CATHOLICS

▶ Two Irishmen were sitting in a pub opposite a brothel. A Baptist minister went into the brothel and one of the Irishmen said, 'Ah 'tis a shame to see a man of the cloth going bad.' A few minutes later a rabbi went in and the Irishman shook his head sadly and remarked, ''Tis a shame to see that the Jews are also falling victim to temptation.' Ten minutes later a Catholic priest went in. 'Ah, what a terrible shame,' said the Irishman. 'One of the girls must be ill!'

▶ Did you hear they're coming out with a new Catholic edition of *Playboy*? It has the same centrefold as the regular edition, but you have to pull it out at just the right moment.

▶ What's the difference between a Catholic wife and a Jewish wife?
The Catholic wife has real orgasms and fake jewellery.

▶ Old Andrze was a minister in a small Polish town. He had always been a good man and lived by the Bible. One day God decided to reward him, with the answer to any three questions Andrze would like to ask.

Old Andrze did not need much time to consider, and the first question was: 'Will there ever be married Catholic priests?'

God promptly replied: 'Not in your lifetime.'

Andrze thought for a while, and then came up with the second question: 'What about female priests, then? Will we have them one day?'

Again God had to disappoint old Andrze. 'Not in your lifetime, I'm afraid.'

Andrze was sorry to hear that, and he decided to drop the subject. After having thought for a while, he asked the last question: 'Will there ever be another Polish pope?'

God answered quickly and with a firm voice: 'Not in my lifetime.'

▶ The Pope calls his mother right after being elected Pope. 'Hi Mum, I've got some good news and some bad news.'

His mother asks, 'What's the good news?'

'I've just been elected Pope.'

'What's the bad news?'

'I have to move into an Italian neighbourhood.'

▶ In a small town in the south of Ireland, there were two churches, as there always are in small towns in the south of Ireland: a small, modest Protestant church and a large, fancy Catholic church. On a certain Saturday, the Catholic priest came down with the flu and he called and asked the Protestant pastor to substitute for him at Mass on the following Sunday. The pastor told the priest that he would like to help, but he knew nothing of the Catholic faith or the rituals of the Mass. The priest responded that there were several altar boys and priests in training who would help him through the rough spots, but he really needed the pastor, because a rousing sermon was the thing his congregation needed the most. Somewhat reluctantly, the pastor agreed.

The priest then asked him to do the confession after the Mass. At this, the pastor drew the line and said that confession was the one thing he would not do, first, because it was in conflict with his own faith and, second, he was certain that he could not get all of the various penances right. The priest responded that he too sometimes had difficulty remembering all of the various punishments, but he had written them all down in a small book, which he had hidden under the seat. If a person said, 'Forgive me Father, I have sinned. I have done this, that and the other thing,' he simply had to look them up and give the person his or her punishment. Still feeling somewhat uneasy about it, the pastor finally agreed.

On the next day, the Mass went surprisingly well. The helpers helped him at all of the right times and the congregation responded to his sermon very well. He had chosen 'The Ten Commandments' because it always goes over well. With slightly sweating palms, he finished the Mass and slowly made his way into the confessional booth.

The first person, a young woman, said, 'Forgive me Father, I have sinned. I have done A, B and C,' and sure enough he found all of the sins and their individual punishments clearly written out in the priest's neat handwriting. It went the same way for each and every person that followed and he found that he rather enjoyed listening in on all of these people's private lives. Up to the last person, that is.

An older man came into the booth, sat down and began. 'Forgive me, Father, I have sinned. I know that I should not have done it but I have had anal intercourse once again.' The pastor looked up 'anal intercourse' in the book. It wasn't there! He fervently tried 'sodomy', 'butt fucking', 'rectal sex' and everything else he could think of but none of them were in the book! He excused himself and ran into the priest's small office and called him on the telephone.

When the priest answered, he said, 'Quick, tell me, what do you give for "anal sex"?'

The priest thought about it and responded, slowly, 'Well, it all depends. Sometimes a candy bar. Sometimes an ice-cream cone. But usually not money.'

▶ A young Irish boy falls in love with a girl and takes her home to meet his family. The boy, his lady-friend and his family gather around the dining room table and his mother asks the girlfriend what she does. The girl hesitates, then says, 'I'm a prostitute.'

The mother screams, faints and has to have water splashed in her face to bring her round. 'Forgive me, my dear. But I don't think I heard you correctly. Did you say you were a prostitute?'

'Yes,' says the girl.

The mother laughs and says, 'Thank goodness. For a moment I thought you said you were a Protestant.'

▶ Why do Catholic women stop having kids at 35? Because they think 36 is just too many.

CATS

▶ How do you know when your cat's finished cleaning himself? He's smoking a cigarette.

▶ An old lady went to the bus stop to get to the vet with her very ill cat. As she boarded the bus, she whispered to the driver, 'Can I get on, I think have a dead pussy?'

The driver pointed to the woman in the seat behind him and said, 'Sit with my wife. You two have a lot in common. '

▶ Three female cats were bragging about their kittens.

The first cat said, 'My kittens are part Persian. Their father was a pure Persian cat.'

The third cat said nothing.

The second cat said, 'Well, that is nothing. My kittens are part Siamese. Their father was a pure-bred Siamese.'

The third cat still said nothing.

Then the first two cats asked her, 'What are your kittens?'

She replied, 'Oh, I don't know. I had my head stuck in the tuna can at the time.'

▶ Large cats can be dangerous, but a little pussy never hurt anyone.

▶ What do you call a septic cat? Pus.

▶ It's never good when your cat thinks outside the box.

CHAT-UP LINES

▶ A rather confident man walks into a bar and takes a seat next to a very attractive woman. He gives her a quick glance, then casually looks at his watch for a moment.

The woman notices this and asks, 'Is your date running late?'

'No,' he replies, 'I just bought this state-of-the-art watch and was testing it.'

Intrigued, the woman says, 'A state-of-the-art watch? What's so special about it?'

'It uses alpha waves to telepathically talk to me,' he explains.

'What's it telling you now?' she asks.

'Well, it says you're not wearing any panties,' he says.

The woman giggles and replies, 'Well, it must be broken then because I am wearing panties!'

The man explains, 'Damn thing must be an hour fast.'

CHAVS

▶ Two chavs are in a car, and no music is playing. Who's driving?
The police.

▶ What is the difference between the Holy Grail and a chav's father?
We may one day find the Grail.

CHICKENS

▶ A chicken and an egg walk into a bar. The barman says, 'Right, who's first?'

▶ Why doesn't a chicken wear pants? Because his pecker is on his head!

▶ Why did the pervert cross the road? Because he was stuck in the chicken.

▶ What do you call a chicken in a shell suit? An egg.

▶ What's the difference between erotic and kinky?
Erotic = using a feather
Kinky = using the whole chicken

▶ Medical Association researchers have made a remarkable discovery.
It seems that some patients needing blood transfusions may benefit from
receiving chicken blood rather than human blood.
It tends to make the men cocky and the women lay better.

▶ What do you get when you cross a rooster with a jar of peanut butter?
A cock that sticks to the roof of your mouth!

▶ If I had a rooster and you had a donkey and your donkey ate my rooster,
what would you have? My cock in your ass.

▶ A chicken laid a five-kilogram egg. Newspaper and TV reporters raced to
the scene and asked her how she'd managed it. The chicken replied,
'That's a secret!'
The reporters asked, 'And what are your plans for the future?'
'To lay a ten-kilogram egg,' the chicken said.
The reporters went to the rooster and asked, 'How did it happen?' and
the rooster replied, 'That's a secret!'
'Any plans for the future?' they asked, and the rooster said, 'To find the
bloody ostrich and beat him up real good!'

▶ A man was driving down a quiet country lane, when a cockerel strayed into the road. Whack! The cockerel disappeared under his car in a cloud of feathers. Shaken, the man pulled over at the farmhouse and rang the doorbell. A farmer appeared.

The man, somewhat nervously, said, 'I think I killed your cockerel, please allow me to replace him.'

'Suit yourself,' the farmer replied, 'the chickens are round the back.'

▶ After the Easter Sunday egg hunt, a farmer's son played a prank by going into the chicken house and replacing every egg with a brightly coloured one. A few minutes later, the cockerel walked in, saw all the coloured eggs, then stormed outside and beat up the peacock.

▶ A farmer goes out one day and buys a brand new stud rooster for his chicken coop. The rooster struts over to the old rooster and says, 'OK, old fart, time to retire.'

The old rooster replies, 'Come on, you can't handle ALL these chickens. Look what it's done to me. Can't you just let me have the two old hens over in the corner?'

The young rooster says, 'Beat it! You're washed up and I'm taking over.'

The old rooster says, 'I'll tell you what, young stud, I'll race you around the farmhouse. Whoever wins gets exclusive domain over the entire chicken coop.'

The young rooster laughs, 'You know you don't stand a chance, old man, so just to be fair, I'll give you a head start.'

The old rooster takes off running. About 15 seconds later, the young rooster takes off after him. They round the front of the farmhouse and the young rooster has closed the gap. He's already about five inches behind the old rooster and gaining fast.

The farmer, meanwhile, is sitting on the front porch when he sees the roosters running by. He grabs up his shotgun and – BOOM! – he blows the young rooster to bits.

'Damn!' he says. 'That's the third queer rooster I bought this month.'

CHILDREN

▶ A little boy goes up to his father and asks, 'Dad, what's the difference between hypothetical and reality?'

The father replies, 'Well, son, I could give you the book definitions, but I feel it would be best to show you by example. Go upstairs and ask your mother if she'd have sex with the postman for £500,000.'

The boy goes and asks his mother, 'Mum, would you have sex with the postman for £500,000?'

The mother replies, 'Hell, yes I would!'

The little boy returns to his father. 'Dad, she said, "Hell, yes I would!"'

The father then says, 'OK, now go and ask your older sister if she'd have sex with her teacher for £500,000.'

The boy asks his sister, 'Would you have sex with your teacher for £500,000?'

The sister replies, 'Hell, yes I would!'

He returns to his father. 'Dad, she said, "Hell, yes I would!"'

The father answers, 'OK, son, here's the deal. Hypothetically, we're millionaires, but in reality, we're just living with a couple of whores.'

▶ A woman sees a very small boy sitting on the swings drinking a bottle of Scotch and smoking a cigarette. 'Shouldn't you be at school, young man?'

'Fuck off, granny. I'm only four.'

▶ Three young kids are smoking behind the barn. 'My dad can blow smoke through his nose,' says the first boy.

'That's nothing,' says the second. 'Mine can blow smoke through his ears.'

'You think that's good,' says the third. 'Mine can blow smoke through his arse. And I've seen the nicotine stains in his pants to prove it.'

▶ I was walking in the park one bright sunny Sunday afternoon, when I noticed a cute little girl out walking her dog. As she approached me on the path, she looked about nine years old, all dressed up in her Sunday best, and her freshly scrubbed face was just gleaming with cutsiness. Tugging on her leash was a well-groomed terrier. As we met on the path, I greeted her, 'Hi there! My, aren't you pretty today and what a fine-looking dog you have.'

'Thank you, sir,' she said. 'And what a nice day this is, isn't it?'

'Yes it is,' I answered. 'My, what a polite little girl you are, and what a pretty dress you're wearing.'

'Oh, thank you, sir. My mother taught me to always be polite and she made this dress for me. Isn't it pretty?' she said with a beaming smile.

'Yes, very pretty,' I answered. 'By the way, what's your dog's name?'

'Oh, sir, my dog's name is Porky. Isn't that cute?'

'Well, it certainly is an unusual name for a dog. Why do you call him Porky?'

'Because he fucks pigs!'

▶ A little boy hurts his finger so runs into the house and calls out to his mother.

'Oh,' she says, 'let me get a plaster for that.'

'No!' cries the boy. 'Cider!'

'Cider?' the mother exclaims. 'What on earth do you want cider for?'

'Because,' he explains, 'Sis says whenever she gets a prick in her hand, she likes to put it in cider.'

▶ Why did the boy fall off the swing? He didn't have any arms.

▶ My neighbours bought their little boy a drum kit a week ago. I went round there to see him earlier. What a noise he makes! You'd think he'd never had a drumstick shoved up his arse before!

▶ Quasimodo is running along a street being chased by a pack of children. He stops, turns around and shouts, 'Will you all get lost! I haven't got your bloody ball!'

CHILDREN'S BOOKS

▶ *Kid's books you'll never see:*

- *How to Dress Sexy for Grown-ups*

- *Bi-curious George*

- *Some Kittens Can Fly!*

- *Dad's New Wife Timothy*

- *The Hardy Boys, the Barbie Twins and the Vice Squad*

- *Why Mummy Has So Many Boyfriends*

- *The Tickling Babysitter*

- *A Pictorial History of Circus Geek Suicides*

- *Charles Manson Bedtime Stories*

- *The Cat that Shat in the Hat: A Kid's Guide to Scatology*

- *Jacking and Jilling: The Dummy's Guide to Masturbation*

- *How to Write with Your Wee-wee*

- *What's that Bag for, Grandpa?*

- *Horton Hires a Ho*

- *Where the Curly Red Fur Grows*

CHINESE JOKES

▶ Man, to waitress in Chinese restaurant: 'Excuse me, but this chicken is rubbery.'

   Waitress: 'Thank you, sir.'

▶ Since Mr Chang can't cook and there's no Chinese restaurant nearby, he's forced to go to Paddy's Café for his meals. Mr Chang loves fried rice but is always annoyed when Paddy sniggers at the way he says, 'flied rice'. Eventually Mr Chang has elocution lessons to learn how to say 'fried rice' properly, then goes to the café to give Paddy a surprise. He sits down and says, 'Hello, Paddy. I'll have a plate of fried rice, please.'

   'What was that?' says Paddy.

   Mr Chang replies, 'I say "fried rice", you stupid Ilish plick!'

▶ *Learn Chinese in five minutes...*

- That's not right... *Sum Ting Wong*

- Are you harbouring a fugitive?... *Hu Yu Hai Ding*

- See me ASAP... *Kum Hia Nao*

- Stupid man... *Dum Fuk*

- Small horse... *Tai Ni Po Ni*

- Did you go to the beach?... *Wai Yu So Tan*

- I bumped into a coffee table... *Ai Bang Mai Fa Kin Ni*

- I think you need a facelift... *Chin Tu Fat*

- It's very dark in here... *Wao So Dim*

- I thought you were on a diet... *Wai Yu Mun Ching?*

- This is a tow-away zone... *No Pah King*

- Our meeting is scheduled for next week... *Wai Yu Kum Nao?*

- Staying out of sight... *Lei Ying Lo*

- He's cleaning his automobile... *Wa Shing Ka*

- Your body odour is offensive... *Yu Stin Ki Pu*

- Great... *Fa Kin Su Pah*

▶ What do you call a Chinese 69? *Two Can Chew!*

▶ Why would the world have been a better place if Adam and Eve had been Chinese? Because they would have eaten the snake instead of the apple!

▶ Have you heard about the new Chinese cookbook? One hundred ways to wok your dog!

▶ Confucius say, 'Blonde who fly upside down have crack up!'

▶ A Chinese man arranges for a hooker to come to his room for the evening. Once in the room they undress, climb into bed and go at it.

When finished, the Chinese man jumps up, runs over to the window, takes a deep breath, dives under the bed, climbs out of the other side, jumps back into bed with the hooker and commences a repeat performance.

The hooker is impressed with the gusto of the second encounter. When finished, the Chinese man jumps up, runs over to the window, takes a deep breath, dives under the bed, climbs out the other side, jumps back into bed with the hooker and begins to fuck her again.

The hooker is amazed as this sequence is repeated four more times. During the fifth encore, she decides to try it herself. So when they are done, she jumps up, goes to the window, takes a deep breath, dives under the bed... and finds four Chinese men hiding!

▶ A Jew and a Chinese man were in a bar together. The Jew brought up the subject of Pearl Harbor, reprimanding the Chinese man for the disgraceful role his country had played. He protested vehemently, pointing out that the raid had been made by the Japanese.

'Japanese, Chinese, they are all the same to me!' said the Jew.

Pretty soon the Chinese man started talking about the tragic sinking of the *Titanic*, asking the Jew if he didn't feel guilty about sinking it.

'Hey, wait a minute,' replied the Jew. 'The Jews didn't have anything to do with the *Titanic* sinking, it was an iceberg!'

'Iceberg, Goldberg,' said the Chinese man, 'they're all the same to me!'

▶ What do you call a Chinese homosexual? *Chew Man Chew!*

▶ What do you call a fat Chinaman? A chunk!

▶ The most common surname in China is Chang; correct me if you think that's Wong.

CHRISTMAS

▶ A TV station in the USA rings up the British ambassador and asks him what he'd like for Christmas. 'I couldn't possibly accept gifts in my position,' says the ambassador. The TV station insists and says he can have anything he wants, no matter how big or small. 'Well,' says the ambassador. 'If you insist, I suppose I could accept a small box of chocolates.'

A month later the ambassador is watching TV when the news presenter says, 'A while back we asked a number of ambassadors what they'd like for Christmas. The French ambassador said he'd like universal peace. The German ambassador said he'd like prosperity for the world's poor. And the British ambassador said he'd like a small box of candy.'

CHUCK NORRIS

▶ Superman wears Chuck Norris underpants.

▶ Chuck Norris was once put on the adverts for a toilet paper company. The company field tested it but it didn't work because Chuck Norris doesn't take crap from nobody.

▶ When Chuck Norris does push-ups, he doesn't push himself up; he pushes the world down.

▶ Chuck Norris doesn't read books, he just stares them down until he gets the information he wants out of them.

▶ If Chuck Norris is late, time better slow the fuck down.

▶ There is no chin behind Chuck Norris's beard. There is only another fist.

▶ Chuck Norris built a time machine and went back in time to stop the JFK assassination. As Oswald shot, Chuck Norris met all three bullets with his beard, deflecting them. JFK's head exploded out of sheer amazement.

▶ Chuck Norris counted to infinity – twice.

▶ The chief export of Chuck Norris is pain.

▶ China was once bordering the United States, until Chuck Norris roundhouse-kicked it all the way through the earth.

▶ When Chuck Norris had surgery, the anaesthesia was applied to the doctors.

▶ Some kids piss their names in the snow. Chuck Norris can piss his name in concrete.

▶ Monsters check under their bed for Chuck Norris before they go to sleep.

A disabled parking sign does not signify that this spot is for handicapped people. It is in fact a warning that the spot belongs to Chuck Norris and that you will be handicapped if you park there.

Chuck Norris drinks napalm to quell his heartburn.

Chuck Norris doesn't sleep, he waits.

Chuck Norris can slam a revolving door.

Chuck Norris recently had the idea to sell his urine as a canned beverage. We know this beverage as Red Bull.

Chuck Norris can sneeze with his eyes open.

Chuck Norris wears a live rattlesnake as a condom.

There is no 'Ctrl' button on Chuck Norris's computer. Chuck Norris is always in control.

Chuck Norris died 20 years ago. Death just never had the guts to tell him.

Chuck Norris destroyed the periodic table, because the only element he understands is the element of surprise.

Chuck Norris didn't wet his bed as a child. The bed wet itself out of fear.

Chuck Norris doesn't step away from the vehicle. The vehicle steps away from Chuck Norris.

▶ Chuck Norris is not politically correct. He is just correct. Always.

▶ Chuck Norris can whistle in German.

CIRCUMCISION

▶ How do you circumcise a hillbilly? Kick his sister in the jaw.

▶ A surgeon retires from his long career as a specialist in circumcision. Throughout his career he has saved hundreds of foreskins as mementoes and now wishes to turn them into a souvenir. He takes his specimens to a leathersmith and asks him to make something out of them. A week later the surgeon returns and the leathersmith presents him with a wallet.

'All those foreskins and you only made me a wallet?' exclaims the surgeon.

The leathersmith replies, 'Yes, but if you stroke it, it becomes a briefcase.'

▶ A Texan bought a round of drinks for everyone in the bar, explaining that his wife had just produced 'a typical Texas baby' weighing 20 pounds.

Two weeks later he returned to the bar. The barman recognised him and asked, 'Aren't you the father of the typical Texas baby that weighed 20 pounds at birth?'

'Yes, I sure am!' said the man.

'How much does he weigh now?' asked the barman.

'Ten pounds,' the proud father answered.

'What happened?' the barman asked. 'He weighed 20 pounds before.'

'Well,' the proud Texas father said, 'I just had him circumcised!'

▶ A man had just picked up his girlfriend in his new convertible and was driving by a hospital. At that time a baby was being circumcised, and the doctor did not have a receptacle handy to put the removed foreskin in, so he just chucked it out the window. It landed in the woman's lap as the convertible passed by.

She screamed and shrieked, 'Arghhhhh... what's that?!'

The man replied, 'Taste it, and if you like it I'll give you a bigger piece.'

CLOWN'S POCKET

▶ A man goes to see his doctor and says, 'Doc, I'm not getting full enjoyment from my sex life and I think it would help if my willy was bigger.'

The doctor asks, 'What do you normally drink?'

'Lager,' is the reply.

'Oh dear,' says the doc. 'That tends to shrink things. Try switching to Guinness.'

The man comes back the following week, shakes the doctor's hand and says, 'Thanks for the advice.'

The doc says, 'You switched to Guinness, then?'

'No,' says the man. 'I've put the wife on lager.'

▶ An explorer is searching in the Amazon jungle for this lost tribe whose women are reputed to have vaginas that are three inches wide and 12 inches long. Finally he finds the tribe and is invited to sit down with the chief.

'Is it correct,' he says to the chief, 'that your women have vaginas that are three inches wide and 12 inches long?'

'That correct, man,' says the chief.

'However do you manage to have sex with women with vaginas that are three inches wide and 12 inches long?' enquires the explorer.

The chief looks at him as if he were an idiot and says, 'They stretch, man. They stretch!'

▶ A man was on a date with a woman. They had returned to her place and were sitting on the sofa. Nibbling her earlobe, the man whispered, 'You know, I'd like a little soft wet pussy.'

She said, 'Oh, me too, mine's like an enamel bucket.'

▶ A woman went to her new gynaecologist for her first check-up. The doctor got her in the stirrups and spread her legs. He took a glance and said, 'Oh my God! In all of my career, I have never seen such a huge vagina... huge vagina!'

She said, 'Doctor, I know it and I'm very self-conscious about it. But you didn't have to repeat yourself.'

The doctor replied, 'I didn't. It was an echo!'

▶ After her fifth child, a woman decided that she should have some cosmetic surgery 'down below' to restore herself to her former youthful glory. Time and childbirth had taken its toll and she reckoned that, with five children now being the limit, she'd tidy things with a nip here and a tuck there. Following the operation, she awoke from her anaesthetic to find three roses at the end of the bed.

'Who are these from?' she asked the nurse. 'They're very nice but I'm a bit confused as to why I've received them.'

'Well,' said the nurse. 'The first is from the surgeon – the operation went so well and you were such a model patient that he wanted to say thanks.'

'Ahhh, that's really nice,' said the woman.

'The second is from your husband – he's delighted the operation was such a success that he can't wait to get you home. Apparently it'll be the first time he's touched the sides for years and he's very excited!'

'Brilliant!' said the woman. 'And the third?'

'That's from Keith in the burns unit,' said the nurse. 'He just wanted to say thanks for his new ears.'

COOKERY

▶ When a man volunteers to do some cooking, the following chain of events is put into motion:

• The woman goes to the supermarket.

• The woman fixes the salad, vegetables and dessert.

• The woman prepares the meat for cooking, places it on a tray along with the necessary cooking utensils and takes it to the man, who is lounging beside the BBQ, drinking a beer.

• The man places the meat on the BBQ.

• The woman goes inside to set the table and check the vegetables.

• The woman comes out to tell the man that the meat is burning.

• The man takes the meat off the BBQ and hands it to the woman.

• The woman prepares the plates and brings them to the table.

• After eating, the woman clears the table and does the dishes.

- The man asks the woman how she enjoyed her 'night off'. And, upon seeing her annoyed reaction, concludes that there's just no pleasing some women.

▶ War was on and the captain was attempting to rally the infantry on the eve of a big offensive.

'Out there,' said the captain, 'is your enemy. The man who has made your life miserable, who is working to destroy you; the man who has been trying to kill you day after day throughout this war.'

Private Johnson jumped to his feet. 'My God! The cook's working for the other side!'

▶ What is the difference between pussy and apple pie? You can eat your mum's apple pie.

CONSTIPATION

▶ Did you hear about the constipated mathematician? He worked it out with a pencil.

COWBOYS AND INDIANS

▶ Two cowboys are having a chat about their favourite sexual positions, when one of them says, 'I like the rodeo rider best.'

'The rodeo rider?' the other cowboy asks. 'What is that? '

'Well,' says the first cowboy, 'when you're doing it doggy style you lean forwards, get a firm hold of your wife's boobs and then you whisper in her ear, "Hey, they feel exactly the same as your sister's." And then you try to stay on for another ten seconds!'

▶ *Ten phrases from cowboy movies ruined by* Brokeback Mountain*:*

- 'I'm gonna pump you fulla lead!'

- 'Give me a stiff one, barkeep!'

- 'Don't fret – I've been in tight spots before.'

- 'Howdy, pardner.'

- 'You stay here while I sneak around from behind.'

- Two words: saddle sore.

- 'Hold it right there! Now, move your hand, reeeal slow-like.'

- 'Let's mount up!'

- 'Nice spread ya got there!'

- 'Ride 'em, cowboy!'

▶ A young Native American woman went to a doctor for her first-ever physical exam. After checking all of her vitals and running the usual tests, the doctor said, 'Well, Running Doe, you are in fine health. I could find no problems. I did notice one anomaly, however.'

'Oh, what is that, Doctor?'

'Well, you have no nipples.'

'None of the people in my tribe have nipples,' she replied.

'That is amazing,' said the doctor. 'I'd like to write this up for *The Journal of Medicine*, if you don't mind.'

She said, 'OK.'

'First of all,' asked the doctor, 'how many people are in your tribe?'

She answered, 'Approximately 500.'

'And what is the name of your tribe?' asked the doctor.

Running Doe replied, 'We're called the Indiannippleless Five Hundred.'

▶ An attractive woman from New York was driving through a remote part of New Mexico, when her car broke down. A Native American on horseback came along and offered her a ride to a nearby town. She climbed up behind him on the horse and they rode off. The ride was uneventful except that every few minutes the Native American would let out a whoop so loud that it would echo from the surrounding hills. When they arrived in town, he let her off at the local petrol station, yelled one final 'Yahoo!' and rode off.

'What did you do to get that Indian so excited?' asked the service station attendant.

'Nothing,' she said. 'I just sat behind him on the horse, put my arms around his waist and held onto his saddle horn so I wouldn't fall off.'

'Lady,' the attendant said, 'Indians ride bareback.'

▶ A cowboy was riding in the desert, when he came across an Indian lying on his back with his dick out. The cowboy asked him what he was doing.

'Me telling time. Penis act as sundial,' replied the Indian.

'Really! What time do you make it?' asked the cowboy.

'Me say it is 2.33 p.m.,' said the Indian.

The cowboy checked his own watch. 'Me, too. That's amazing.'

Riding on for a few miles, he came across another Indian lying with his dick out.

'I know what you're doing,' said the cowboy. 'What time do you say it is?'

'2.47 p.m.,' replied the Indian.

'That's right,' said the cowboy. 'Incredible.'

Riding on a while longer, he came across another Indian, lying on his back and vigorously wanking.

'What the hell are you doing?' asked the cowboy.

'Me winding clock.'

▶ A Native American boy was talking to his mother one day.

Boy: 'Mom, why is my brother named Mighty Storm?'

Mom: 'Because he was conceived during a mighty storm.'

Boy: 'Well, then why is my sister named Cornfield?'

Mom: 'Well, your father and I were in a cornfield when we made her.'

Boy: 'And why is my other sister called Moonchild?'

Mom: 'We were watching the moon landing while she was conceived. Tell me, why are you so curious about their names, Two Dogs Fucking?'

▶ A beautiful woman is sitting on a train with an empty seat next to her. A cowboy dressed in a Stetson hat and fancy boots saunters over and says, 'Pardon me, ma'am, do you mind if I sit here?'

The woman looks up at him and says, 'I most certainly do! Cowboys are disgusting! I hate cowboys! Cowboys are mean, crude, vile and uncouth! I'll tell you something else I know about cowboys. Cowboys will screw anything! Cowboys will fuck sheep, they'll fuck cattle, they'll fuck dogs, they'll fuck lizards, they'll fuck chickens.'

Suddenly the incredulous cowboy asks, 'Chickens?'

COWS

▶ Two bulls are in a field as night falls. One turns to the other and says, 'It's getting cold, isn't it?'

'Yes,' replies the other bull, 'I think I might slip into a warm Jersey.'

▶ Two cows were chatting in a field.

'I was artificially inseminated this morning.'

'I don't believe you!'

'It's true, no bull.'

▶ Elsie the Cow and Ferdinand the Bull were on either side of a fence. Elsie the Cow gave him a wink and he leaped over the fence to her side.

'Aren't you Ferdinand the Bull?' she asked.

'Just call me Ferdinand. The fence was a lot higher than I thought.'

▶ I was in a field full of cattle yesterday, when one of the bulls suddenly exploded, littering the entire area with blood and gore, leaving it a horrible red mess, with nothing left of the poor animal but a set of flaming stumps where its legs were.

I stood there in horror, wondering what could have caused such a thing.

It was abominable.

▶ A female reporter was interviewing a farmer concerning mad cow disease.

'Farmer Giles, have you any ideas as to what might be causing this disease?' asked the reporter.

'I sure do,' the farmer stated. 'Do you know the bulls only screw the cows once a year?'

'Well, sir, that's new information to me, but what is the relationship between that and mad cow?' enquired the reporter.

'In addition to that,' continued the farmer, 'did you know we milk the cows twice a day?'

'That's very interesting, Farmer Giles, but what's your point?' demanded the reporter.

'The point is this, lady,' the farmer replied. 'If I played with your tits twice a day but only screwed you once a year, wouldn't you go mad, too?'

▶ A city slicker was spending some time with his country cousins. The first morning the farmer said, 'We need some help today. I'd sure appreciate it if you could take the bull to pasture three to breed with the cow there.'

The city slicker agreed. Six hours later, he staggered back to the farmhouse, his clothing all torn and dishevelled.

The farmer took a look, then asked, 'The bull give you a problem?'

'Hell, no, the bull was eager and raring to go.'

'Then why did it take you all day?'

'Because,' the city slicker replied, 'the cow fought me for hours before she'd roll over on her back.'

▶ A bunch of cows and bulls are standing in a field. A huge gust of wind comes along and all the cows fall over, but the bulls just stand there, bracing themselves against the gale.

All the cows stand up and go back to their chewing.

Pretty soon, an even stronger wind blows through and all of the cows are knocked to the ground, but the bulls just munch on the grass.

Next, a bona fide tornado comes through and all the cows are knocked clean into the next pasture. The bulls just say, 'Mooo... '

Finally, one of the cows walks up to one of the bulls and says, 'Moo? Is that all you can say? How come the wind always knocks us right over and you just stand there?'

'Isn't it obvious?' the bull replies. 'We bulls wobble but we don't fall down.'

▶ The only cow in a small Cheshire town stopped giving milk. The people did some research and found that they could buy a cow just across the county line in Staffordshire for £200. They bought the cow from Staffordshire and the cow was wonderful. It produced lots of milk all of the time, and the people were very happy.

They decided to acquire a bull to mate with the cow to produce more cows like it. They would never have to worry about their milk supply again. They bought the bull and put it in the pasture with their beloved cow. However, whenever the bull came close to the cow, the cow would move away. No matter what approach the bull tried, the cow would move away from the bull and he could not succeed in his quest.

The people were very upset and decided to ask the vet, who was very wise, what to do. They told the vet what was happening. 'Whenever the bull approaches our cow, she moves away. If he approaches from the back, she moves forwards. When he approaches her from the front, she backs off. An approach from the side, she walks away to the other side.'

The vet thought about this for a minute and asked, 'Did you by chance buy this cow in Staffordshire?' The people were dumbfounded, since no one had ever mentioned where they bought the cow.

'You are truly a wise vet,' they said. 'How did you know we got the cow in Staffordshire?'

The vet replied with a distant look in his eye, 'My wife is from Staffordshire.'

▶ Three bulls heard that the farmer was introducing a new bull. The three were reluctant to give up any of their cows to the newcomer.

The first bull said proudly, 'I've been here five years, I've got 100 cows, and I'm keeping them.'

The second bull announced, 'I've been here five years, I've got 50 cows, and I intend on keeping them.'

The third bull, the youngest of the three, warned, 'I've been here a year and although I only have ten cows, I'm going to keep them.'

A few minutes after their shows of bravado, a lorry pulled up to the farm and out stepped the biggest bull they had ever seen – a truly awesome creature. The first two bulls immediately backed down and said the newcomer could have as many of their cows as he wanted. Meanwhile, the third bull began pawing the dirt, shaking his horns and snorting.

The first bull went over to him and said, 'Son, let me give you some advice real quick. Let him have some of your cows and live to tell the tale.'

The third bull said, 'Hey, as far as I'm concerned, he can have all my cows. I'm just making sure he knows I'm a bull!'

▶ What's the difference between a hamster and a cow? Cows survive the branding.

CRAP JOKES (LITERALLY)

▶ Two naturalists were observing wildlife in the forests of Canada. One said, 'Did you see that bear over there?'

'No,' replied the second, 'I didn't.'

A few minutes later the first naturalist said, 'Did you just see that eagle flying overheard?'

'No, I missed that,' said the second, dejected.

Five minutes later, the first naturalist said, 'Did you see that moose go behind those trees?'

'Damn!' said the second. 'I missed that, too!'

'You really ought to keep your eyes open,' said the first. 'That way you won't keep missing things.'

A few minutes later, the first naturalist said, 'Hey, did you see that?'

'As a matter of fact I did,' snapped the second man, determined not to be ridiculed further. 'Indeed, I probably spotted it before you!'

'Oh, yes?' said the first naturalist. 'So why did you step in it?'

▶ Two strangers were seated next to each other on a plane, when the guy turned to the blonde girl and made his move by saying, 'Let's talk. I've heard that flights will go quicker if you strike up a conversation with your fellow passenger.'

The blonde, who had just opened her book, closed it slowly and said to the guy, 'What would you like to discuss?'

'Oh, I don't know,' said the player. 'How about nuclear power?'

'OK,' said the blonde. 'That could be an interesting topic. But let me ask you a question first. A horse, a cow and a deer all eat grass. The same stuff. Yet a deer excretes little pellets while a cow turns out a flat patty, and a horse produces clumps of dried grass. Why do you suppose that is?'

'Oh, brother,' said the guy. 'I have no idea.'

'Well, then,' said the blonde. 'How is it that you feel qualified to discuss nuclear power when you don't know shit?'

▶ When I wake up in the morning, I just can't get started until I've had that first, piping hot pot of coffee. Oh, I've tried other enemas...

▶ A bear and a bunny are sitting in a forest taking a dump. The bear leans over to the bunny and says, 'Do you ever have the problem of shit sticking to your fur?'

The bunny says no.

So the bear grabs the bunny and wipes his arse with it.

▶ Two men are approaching each other on the pavement. Both are dragging their right foot as they walk.

As they meet, one man looks at the other knowingly, points at his foot and says, 'Vietnam, 1969.'

The other points behind him and says, 'Dog shit, 20 feet back.'

▶ What's ten inches long, two inches thick and starts with a P? A really good crap.

▶ A guy walks into an optician's with a 12-inch turd in a carrier bag. The optician says, 'I am an eye specialist not a gastric doctor.'

The guy replies, 'I know that, but every time I drop one of these, my eyes water!'

▶ There were two rats living in a sewer. One rat turns to the other and says, 'I'm sick of this!'

'Sick of what?' responds the other rat.

'Sick of shit for breakfast, shit for lunch, shit for dinner, shit for tea – shit all day long. I'm just sick of it,' says the first rat.

'Don't worry,' replies the second. 'I know what will cheer you up – tonight we'll go on the piss... '

▶ What's brown and sits on a piano stool? Beethoven's first movement.

▶ What's in the toilet of the Starship Enterprise? The captain's log.

▶ *Types of poo:*

● Ghost poo: You know you've pooed. There's poo on the toilet paper, but not in the toilet. Where is it?

● Teflon poo: So slick and easy you don't even feel it. No trace of poo on the toilet paper. You have to look in the toilet to be sure you did it.

● Goo poo: This has the consistency of hot tar. You wipe 12 times and you still don't come clean. You end up putting toilet paper in your underwear so you don't soil it. Permanent skid marks are left in the toilet.

- Second thoughts poo: You're all done wiping and about to stand up when you realise... there's more to come.

- Pop a vein in your forehead poo: This is the kind of poo that killed Elvis. It doesn't want to come out until you're all sweaty, trembling and purple from straining so hard.

- Weight Watchers poo: You poo so much, you lose several pounds.

- Right now poo: You'd better be within 30 seconds of a toilet. You burn rubber to get there and it usually gets its head out before you can get your pants down.

- King Kong poo: This one is so big, you think it won't go down the toilet unless you break it into smaller chunks. A wire coat hanger usually works well. This kind of poo usually happens when you're at someone else's house.

- Cork poo: Also known as 'floaters'. Even after the third flush, it's still there, floating in the bowl. My God! How do I get rid of it?

- Wet cheeks poo: This poo hits the water sideways and makes a bigger splash than the launching of the QE2, soaking your starfish.

- Wish poo: You sit there all cramped up and fart a few times, but no poo.

- Cement block poo: You wish you'd got a spinal block before you pooed.

- Snake poo: This poo is fairly soft, about as thick as your thumb and at least three feet long.

- Morning after poo: Happens the day after the night before. Normally your poo doesn't smell that bad, but THIS one... Usually you're at someone else's house (normally a girl you're trying to impress) and they're waiting outside to use the bathroom.

- Indian food poo: Also called 'screamers'. You know it's safe to eat again when your bum stops burning.

- Boo hoo poo: Makes you cry with pain and wonder whether your should risk the stitches or go for the fuller figure.

▶ An Indian walks into a trading post and asks for toilet paper. The clerk asks if he would like no name, Charmin or White Cloud.

'White Cloud sounds like good Indian toilet paper,' says the Indian. 'How much is it?'

'$1 a roll,' the clerk replies.

'That seems pretty expensive,' responds the Indian. 'What about the others?'

'Charmin is $2 a roll and no name is 50 cents a roll.'

The Indian doesn't have much money so he opts for the no name.

Within a few hours, he is back at the trading post. 'I have a name for the no name toilet paper,' he announces to the clerk. 'We shall call it John Wayne.'

'Why?' asks the confused clerk.

'Cos it's rough and it's tough and it don't take no crap off an Indian.'

▶ A guy says to a salesgirl, 'I want to buy some toilet paper.'

She says, 'What colour?'

He says, 'Just give me white. I'll colour it myself.'

▶ Jones is checking out of a hotel, when suddenly he has to take a shit real bad. The toilet in his room isn't working, so he bolts down to use the lobby toilets, but all of the stalls are occupied, so he runs back up to his room, and in desperation, drops his pants, uproots a plant and shits in the pot. Then he puts the plant back in the pot and leaves.

Two weeks later, he gets a postcard from the hotel that says, 'Dear Mr Jones, All is forgiven. Just tell us... where is it?'

DATING

▶ The blind daters had really hit it off and, at the end of the evening as they were beginning to undress each other in his apartment, the fellow said, 'Before we go any further, Charlene, tell me, do you have any special fetishes that I should take into account in bed?'

'As a matter of fact,' smiled the girl, 'I do happen to have a foot fetish, but I suppose I'd settle for maybe seven or eight inches.'

▶ How is being at a singles' bar different than being at the circus? At the circus, the clowns don't talk.

▶ What's the difference between a 40-year-old man and a 40-year-old woman? A 40-year-old woman dreams of having children, a 40-year-old man dreams of dating them.

▶ Every time I find Mr Right, my husband scares him away.

▶ Marketing and advertising: the difference explained:

You see a gorgeous woman at a party. You could go over to her and say, 'Hi, I'm great in bed, so what about it?'

That's DIRECT MARKETING.

You could give your best friend £10 so he goes over to her and says, 'Hello, see my friend over there? He's great in bed, so what about it?'

That's ADVERTISING.

She could come over to you and say, 'Hello, I've heard you're great in bed, so what about it?'

That's BRAND RECOGNITION.

You could go over to her and get her telephone number. Then the next day you could call her and say, 'Hello, I'm great in bed, so what about it?'

That's TELEMARKETING.

You could walk over to her, pour her a drink and say, 'May I?' You could then reach up to straighten her hair, at the same time brushing your groin against her leg, and say, 'Hello, I'm great in bed, so what about it?'

That's PUBLIC RELATIONS.

You could talk her into going home with your friend.

That's a SALES REP.

Your friend might not be able to satisfy her and so she could then text you.

That's TECH SUPPORT.

You could leave the party and on your way home realise that there are probably many beautiful women in the houses you're passing. So you could shout out at the top of your voice, 'I'm great in bed.'

That's JUNK MAIL.

▶ A young woman brings her boyfriend, a theology student, home to meet her parents.

'Do you own a house?' asks her father.

'Not yet, but God will provide,' says the student.

'And how do you intend to earn a living?' asks her father.

'I don't know, but God will provide,' replies the student.

'Have you made any long-term plans?' asks her father.

'No,' says the student. 'But I trust God will provide.'

Later the mother asks the father what he thought of their prospective son-in-law.

'Well, he's broke and seems fairly stupid,' replies the father. 'But on the other hand, he thinks I'm God.'

▶ What is the difference between garbage and an ugly girl? Garbage gets picked up at least once a week.

▶ Dear Mr Jones,

Your application to join our online dating agency has been officially rejected.

One of the questions we asked on the application was: 'What do you like most in a woman?'

'My dick' is not an appropriate answer. Thank you for your interest.

▶ The inherent downside in a life of pursuing women is the possibility of inadvertently catching one.

▶ What do you call a man who expects to have sex on the second date? Patient.

▶ I met a girl in a pub last night and we ended up going back to her house. After a few more drinks, we started kissing and having a bit of foreplay on the sofa. She looked at me and said, 'Let's take this upstairs.'

I said, 'OK, you grab one end and I'll grab the other.'

▶ A guy is dropping off a girl at the end of their first date. As he's kissing her goodnight, he pulls down his zip, takes out his cock and puts it in her hand.

She says, 'I've got two words for you! Drop dead!' She jumps out, slams the car door, runs up the drive, storms into the house and slams the front door. Then, there's a knock on the door. She answers it, and the guy is standing there with tears in his eyes.

He says, 'And I've got two words for you... let go!'

▶ I don't have a girlfriend. But I do know a woman who'd be mad at me for saying that.

▶ *Blokes, you know you're on a bad date when...*

● She whispers to the waiter, 'Please kill me.'

● You catch her giving her phone number to the guy cleaning your windscreen.

● She lunges at you several times with a steak knife.

● She keeps calling you 'Bachelor Number Two'.

● 'Whoa! Is it 8.15 already?'

● She changes the conversation by saying, 'I've said enough about me. What do *you* think about me?'

▶ *Girls, you know you're on a bad date when...*

● You order a Double Whopper and he says, 'Hey, I'm not made of money, darling.'

- You've never heard someone speak with such passion about an ant farm.

- He seems to know an awful lot about your shower routine.

- Your dinner reservation is under 'Loser, party of two'.

- He's especially proud of how long he can sustain a burp.

- He calls to tell you he'll pick you up just as soon as the stand-off with the police is over.

- He's been on *Jeremy Kyle* once and *Trisha* twice.

▶ When I got home last night, my girlfriend demanded that I take her out to some place expensive. So I took her to the petrol station.

▶ *Chat-up lines:*

- 'The only thing I want between our relationship is latex!'

- 'If you've lost your virginity, can I have the box it came in?'

- 'I've just received government funding for a four-hour expedition to find your G-spot.'

- 'If you are what you eat, I could be you by morning.'

- 'I'm a great swimmer – can I demonstrate the breaststroke?'

- 'There are 256 bones in your body! Would you like another?'

- 'Nice dress! Can I talk you out of it?'

- 'Hey babe, do you realise that my mouth can generate over 750 psi?'

- 'I wish you were a door so I could bang you all day long.'

- 'Do you want to play army? I will lay down and you can blow the hell outta me.'

- 'I'd walk a million miles for one of your smiles, and even farther for that thing you do with your tongue.'

- 'Do you know what a man with a 12-inch dick has for breakfast? No? Well, I have bacon and eggs!'

- 'If you were a lolly, I would be licking you all night!'

- 'You may not be the best-looking girl here, but beauty is only a light switch away.'

DEAFNESS

▶ My ex-wife was deaf. She left me for a deaf friend of hers. To be honest, I should have seen the signs.

DEATH

▶ How can you tell when your husband is dead? The sex is the same but you get the remote control.

▶ My brother-in-law died. He was a karate expert who joined the army. The first time he saluted, he killed himself.

▶ An elderly man lies dying in his bed. In death's agony, he suddenly smells the aroma of his favourite chocolate-chip cookies wafting up the stairs. He gathers his remaining strength, lifts himself from the bed and slowly makes his way out of the bedroom. With laboured breaths, he staggers down the stairs into the hall and gazes into the kitchen. There, spread out upon racks on the kitchen table and counters are literally hundreds of his favourite chocolate-chip cookies – a final act of love from his devoted wife, seeing to it that he leaves this world a happy man. Mustering one great final effort, the old man throws himself towards the table and lands on his knees. He reaches out a withered hand towards a tray of cookies when – whack! – it's suddenly struck with a spatula.

'You stay out of those,' says his wife. 'Them's for the funeral.'

▶ A man woke up after an operation and, still half-asleep, noticed a figure beside his bed. 'Was my operation a success, Doctor?' he asked.

'I don't know, old chap, I'm St Peter.'

▶ My old grandad's motto in life was 'What you can't see won't hurt you.' He died of radiation poisoning.

▶ The victim of an awful car accident was pronounced dead on arrival at the hospital, and the emergency nurse was ordered to prepare the body for the undertaker.

Removing his clothes, she discovered that the young man had died with the most massive erection she had ever seen. Unable to take her eyes off it, she finally yielded to temptation, took off her panties, straddled the stiff and proceeded to enjoy herself.

She was just getting down from the table, when a second nurse came in and promptly reprimanded her for her obscene behaviour.

'What's the harm?' shot back the first nurse. 'I enjoyed it, and HE surely didn't mind it. Besides, he can't complain and I can't get pregnant. Why don't YOU give it a try, too?'

'Oh, I can't possibly,' said the second nurse, blushing. 'First, he's dead and second, I've got my period. Anyway, listen, the doctor wants you.'

And so the first nurse left. The second nurse got to work but soon found herself terribly excited by this massive hard-on and finally climbed on top of it. Just as she was starting to come, she was astonished to feel the man climax, too! Looking down and seeing his eyelids starting to flutter, she exclaimed in shock, 'I thought you were dead!'

'Lady, I thought I was, too,' said the man, 'until you gave me that blood transfusion.'

▶ A man went into a card shop and said to the woman behind the counter, 'Do you sell bereavement cards?'

She said, 'Yes, sir.'

'Could I exchange one for this get well soon card I bought yesterday?' he replied.

▶ My mate drowned in a half-empty bath tub yesterday. He was normally so optimistic.

▶ My wife has asked me to get her some gloves to wear at her mother's funeral. Does anyone know where I can buy those giant foam fingers?

▶ My grandad gave me some sound advice on his deathbed. 'It's worth spending money on good speakers,' he told me.

▶ An old bloke hires a hitman to kill his wife of 40 years. The hitman says, 'I'll shoot her just below her left tit.'

The husband replies, 'I want her dead, not bloody kneecapped!'

▶ Little Johnny goes into school after being absent the previous day. His teacher demands, 'Where were you yesterday?'

'I'm sorry, Miss, my dad got burned,' replies Johnny.

'Oh, I'm sorry, I hope it wasn't serious,' says the teacher.

To which Johnny replies, 'Well, they don't mess about at the crematorium, Miss.'

▶ A man and his wife were sitting in the living room and he said to her, 'Just so you know, I never want to live in a vegetative state, dependent on some machine and fluids from a bottle. If that ever happens, just pull the plug.' His wife got up, unplugged the TV and threw out all of his beer.

▶ When someone close to you dies, move seats.

▶ News: 'British man plunges to death in Ibiza.' That toilet must have been seriously blocked.

▶ News: 'Local girl Joanna Mow leaps to her death on her birthday.' Her middle name was Ronny.

▶ My mother-in-law came into work at lunch today and I must admit, I was genuinely pleased to see her. I'm an undertaker.

▶ After dying in a car crash, three friends go to heaven. They are all asked the same question: 'When you're lying in your casket, and friends and family are mourning over you, what would you like to hear them say about you?'

The first guy immediately responds, 'I would like to hear them say that I was one of the great doctors of my time, and a great family man.'

The second guy says, 'I would like to hear that I was a wonderful husband and schoolteacher who made a huge difference in the children of tomorrow.'

The last guy thinks for a moment, and then replies, 'I guess I'd like to hear them say, "Oh fuck, he's moving!"'

▶ A bloke working on the buses taking fares pushes one of his passengers off the bus and kills him. At the trial he is found guilty of murder and is sentenced to the electric chair.

As a last meal he asks for a bunch of green bananas, which he duly eats. They sit him down, plug him in and send a million volts through him. When the smoke clears, he is sitting there, right as rain. Checking through the statutes, the governor finds he has no choice but to release him.

The chap goes back to his job on the buses and lo and behold allows another passenger to fall to his death. Once again he is found guilty and sentenced to death.

At the prison he again asks for a bunch of green bananas, which he duly receives and scoffs down. In the chair again and this time he is zapped with two million volts. Smoke clears and there he sits, right as rain.

As before, he goes back to his old job. Through a combination of stupidity and sheer malice he yet again allows another passenger to fall to their death. The judge has no choice but to find him guilty and off he goes to the chair.

As you may have guessed, he asks for his bunch of green bananas, eats them, gets strapped in, three million volts and he's right as rain.

The executioner, who is really pissed off by now, approaches him and asks what the secret is. Is it the green bananas that save his life?

'No,' replies the prisoner. 'I'm just a bad conductor!'

▶ An undertaker was working late one night. He examined the body of Mr Schwartz, about to be cremated, and made a startling discovery. Schwartz had the largest penis he had ever seen! The undertaker decided that he couldn't let such a magnificent specimen be burned and it should instead be preserved for posterity, so he removed it, stuffed it into his briefcase and took it home. 'I have something to show you that you won't believe,' he said to his wife, opening his briefcase.

'My God!' the wife exclaimed. 'Schwartz is dead!'

▶ A meteor falls to earth and destroys New York. Hundreds of thousands die instantly, and a huge queue builds up at the Pearly Gates as the newly dead souls try to get into heaven. Suddenly a huge roar surges from the front of the queue.

'What's going on?' asks a man at the back.

A man further up shouts back, 'Great news! They're not counting adultery!'

DENTISTS

▶ A woman goes to her dentist and after he's given her a thorough examination, he says, 'I am sorry to have to tell you that I am going to have to drill a tooth.'

The woman says, 'No! Oh God, I'd rather have a baby!'

The dentist replies, 'Make your mind up, love, I'll have to adjust the chair.'

▶ Did you hear about the dentist who was voted 'Dentist of the Year'? All he got was a little plaque.

DIARRHOEA

It has recently been discovered that diarrhoea is hereditary. Apparently, it all runs in the jeans.

Government-approved information indicates that you have to eat five portions of fruit and veg a day to stay healthy. Yesterday I ate five mouldy plums and I shat the bed. How is that healthy?

DINOSAURS

Why did dinosaurs have sex underwater? You try to keep 500 pounds of pussy wet!

DIVORCE

My husband and I divorced over religious differences. He thought he was God and I didn't.

There are two sides to every divorce: yours and shithead's.

The happiest time in a man's life is that period of time between his first and second marriage. The problem is he doesn't realise it until the second marriage!

Ever since we got married, my wife has tried to change me. She got me to exercise daily, have a much better diet and stop drinking and smoking.

She taught me how to dress well, enjoy the fine arts, gourmet cooking, classical music and how to invest in the stock market. Now I want a divorce – because I'm so improved, she just isn't good enough for me.

▶ A couple were being interviewed on their golden wedding anniversary.
'In all that time did you ever consider divorce?' they were asked.
'Oh, no, not divorce,' one said. 'Murder sometimes, but never divorce.'

▶ A man was driving home one evening and realised that it was his daughter's birthday and he hadn't bought her a present. He drove to a toy shop and asked the shop manager, 'How much is that new Barbie in the window?'
The manager replied, 'Which one? We have "Barbie goes to the gym" for £19.99... "Barbie goes to the ball" for £19.99... "Barbie goes shopping" for £19.99... "Barbie goes to the beach" for £19.99... "Barbie goes to the nightclub" for £19.99... and "Divorced Barbie" for £375.'
'Why is the Divorced Barbie £375 when all the others are £19.99?' the man asked, surprised.
'Divorced Barbie comes with Ken's car, Ken's house, Ken's boat, Ken's dog, Ken's cat and Ken's furniture.'

▶ Why is divorce so expensive? Because it's worth it.

▶ An ex-spouse is like an inflamed appendix: they cause a lot of pain and suffering but after it's removed, you find you didn't need it anyway!

▶ 'For a while we pondered whether to take a vacation or get a divorce. We decided that a trip to Bermuda is over in two weeks, but a divorce is something you always have.' – *Woody Allen*

▶ A 98-year-old man and a 95-year-old woman went to a lawyer to get a divorce. 'How long have you been married?' he asked.

'Seventy-five rough and rocky years,' they said.

'Then why have you waited so long to file for divorce?'

'Well,' they replied, 'we had to wait for the kids to die!'

DOCTORS

▶ A man walks into the doctors and says, 'Hi Doc, I've got a p-p-p-p-p-p-problem. My w-wife's going t-t-to d-d-d-divorce me because of m-m-my s-s-s-stutter. C-c-c-can you h-h-help?'

The doc says, 'In my experience, most speech impediments are caused by a physical problem, so get behind the screen and remove your clothing for an examination.'

The guy whips his gear off and the doc walks in and exclaims, 'My God, I can see your problem immediately! Your dick is so big, it's pulling the skin tight all the way up your torso to your neck! It's affecting your vocal cords!'

The guy says, 'W-w-what can you d-d-do to s-s-save m-m-my m-marriage then, D-d-doc?'

The doctor then outlines a plan to use a local anaesthetic, chop a few inches out of the centre of the huge member and stitch the pieces together. The guy agrees to come in the following day for the operation.

A few weeks later the man returns to the doctor and says, 'Doctor, this is fantastic! I can talk properly for the first time and it's wonderful. I owe it all to you, but I still have a problem. My wife still wants a divorce as now I can't satisfy her. Can't you sew the old piece back on?'

The doctor turns in his chair, looks the man straight in the eye and says, 'You can f-f-f-f-f-fuck o-o-o-off!!!'

▶ A doctor visits a patient lying in a hospital ward. 'I'm sorry,' says the doctor, 'but I have good news and bad news.'

'Don't hold back,' says the man. 'Tell me the bad news.'

The doctor replies, 'Your illness was worse than we thought. We had to amputate both your legs.'

The man asks, 'So what's the good news?'

The doctor replies, 'The man in the next bed wants to buy your slippers.'

▶ A man is on an operating table having his legs sawn off at the knee by a surgeon. 'Of course,' says the surgeon to the man, 'this doesn't necessarily mean you'll be able to paint like Toulouse-Lautrec.'

▶ What is the difference between a haematologist and a urologist?
A haematologist pricks your finger.

▶ 'Doctor, that rectal exam hurt like hell. What did you do?'
'I used two fingers.'
'What for?'
'I needed a second opinion.'

▶ I just saw this on BBC news: 'WHO DECLARES SWINE FLU PANDEMIC'. Somebody needs to let them know he's not a real doctor.

▶ One night a man and a woman are both at a bar knocking back a few beers. They start talking and come to realise that they're both doctors. After about an hour, the man says to the woman, 'Hey, how about if we sleep together tonight, no strings attached? It'll just be one night of fun.'

The woman doctor agrees to it, so they go back to her place and he goes in the bedroom. She goes into the bathroom and starts scrubbing up like she's about to go into the operating room. She scrubs for a good ten minutes. Finally she goes into the bedroom and they have sex for an hour or so.

Afterwards, the man says to the woman, 'You're a surgeon, aren't you?'

'Yeah, how did you know?' the woman replies.

'I could tell by the way you scrubbed up before we started.'

'Oh, that makes sense,' says the woman. 'You're an anaesthetist, aren't you?'

'Yeah,' replies the man, a bit surprised. 'How did you know?'

The woman answers, 'Because I didn't feel a thing.'

▶ 'Doctor, doctor I keep hearing funny voices from my trousers!'

'Don't worry, they're just talking bollocks.'

▶ I went to see the doctor today and before I could say a word he said, 'Oh, this takes me back to my youth.'

'What does?' I asked.

'The Tardis over there in the corner.'

▶ I went to see the doctor for help with my neuroses. He told me to cut the stems about half an inch from the bottom and put them in a vase.

▶ There's a doctor in my village who hands out body parts. He gives me the willies.

▶ *The British Medical Association has weighed in on prime minister David Cameron's health care proposals:*

• The allergists voted to scratch it, but the dermatologists advised not to make any rash moves.

- The gastroenterologists had a sort of gut feeling about it, but the neurologists thought the administration had a lot of nerve.

- The obstetricians felt they were all labouring under a misconception.

- Ophthalmologists considered the idea shortsighted.

- Pathologists yelled, 'Over my dead body!', while the paediatricians said, 'Oh, grow up!'

- The psychiatrists thought the whole idea was madness, while the radiologists could see right through it.

- The surgeons were fed up with the cuts and decided to wash their hands of the whole thing.

- The ENT specialists didn't swallow it, and just wouldn't hear of it.

- The pharmacologists thought it was a bitter pill to swallow, and the plastic surgeons said, 'This puts a whole new face on the matter... '

- The podiatrists thought it was a step forwards, but the urologists were pissed off at the whole idea.

- The anaesthetists thought the whole idea was a gas, but the cardiologists didn't have the heart to say no.

- In the end, the proctologists won out, leaving the entire decision up to the arseholes in London.

▶ I think my doctor might be gay. When I cough, he tells me to hold his balls.

▶ I explained to the doctor, 'Whenever I harvest our cornfields, I get a really bad headache.'

'It's a migraine,' he explained.

'No, it's not, it's mine – and why the hell have you started speaking Italian?'

▶ According to a new study, 63 per cent of men surveyed said they like to settle an argument by having sex. The other 37 per cent of the men said they would never want to get into an argument with those men.

▶ I went to the doctor the other day and found out my new doctor's a young, drop-dead gorgeous female! I was embarrassed but she said, 'Don't worry, I'm a professional, I've seen it all before – just tell me what's wrong and I'll help you in any way I can.'

I said, 'I think my cock tastes funny... '

▶ My doctor suggested that, for my back problems, I should visit a homeopath. Quite what a gay serial killer can do for my back, I have no idea!

▶ A mute was walking down the street one day and chanced upon a friend of his (also a mute). In sign language, he enquired how his friend had been doing. The friend replied (vocally!), 'Oh, you can forget that hand-waving shit. I can talk now!'

Intrigued, the mute pressed him for details. It seems that he had gone to a specialist, who, seeing no physical damage, had put him on a treatment programme that had restored the use of his vocal cords. Gesturing wildly, the mute asked if he might meet this specialist. They got an appointment that very afternoon.

After an exam, the specialist proclaimed that there was no permanent damage, that the mute was essentially in the same condition as his friend and that there was no reason why he couldn't be helped as well.

'Yes, yes,' signed the mute. 'Let's have the first treatment right now!'

'Very well,' replied the specialist. 'Kindly go into the next room, drop your pants and lean over the examining table. I'll be right in.'

The mute did as instructed and the doctor sneaks in with a broomstick, mallet and jar of Vaseline. Greasing the broom handle, he 'sent it home' with a few deft swipes of the mallet.

The mute jumped from the table, screaming, 'AAAAAAAAaaaaaaaaaa!'

'VERY good,' smiled the doctor. 'Tuesday, we continue with "B".'

▶ 'Doctor, I keep thinking I'm a cowboy.'

'How long have you had these feelings?'

'Oh, about a yeehaa.'

▶ A woman went to the doctor with a bad cough.

The doctor said, 'Do you ever get a tickle in the morning?'

'Well, I used to, but now they've changed the milkman.'

▶ My doctor knows nothing about astrology. Cancer? I'm Capricorn.

▶ A woman went to see her doctor. She complained that her husband said she'd developed a bum like a horse. The doctor asked her to take off her clothes and lie on the examination bad.

After examining her, he told her to get dressed, went back to his desk and began writing.

'What are you writing, Doctor?' she asked.

'Ah,' said the doctor, 'it's a permit letter, allowing you to shit in the street.'

▶ Mrs Jones went to see her doctor. When he enquired about her complaint, she replied that she suffered from a discharge.

He instructed her to get undressed and lie down on the examining table. She did so. The doctor put on rubber gloves and began to massage her private parts. After a couple of minutes, he asked, 'How does that feel?'

'Wonderful,' she replied, 'but the discharge is from my ear... '

▶ A doctor knocked at the hospital door before entering a female patient's room. She called out to come in. The doctor then proceeded to tell her to remove all of her clothing, after which he gave her a thorough examination, from top to bottom, front to back, leaving no part of her body untouched. When he had finished, she looked the doctor straight in the eye and asked, 'Doctor, can I ask you a question?'

'Of course,' he replied.

'Why did you bother to knock?'

▶ A man goes to his doctor and tells him that his wife hasn't wanted to have sex with him for the last six months. The doctor tells the man to send his wife in so he can talk to her. So the wife comes into the doctor's office and the doctor asks her what's wrong, and why doesn't she want to have sex with her husband anymore.

The wife tells him, 'For the last six months, every morning I take a cab to work. I don't have any money so the cab driver asks me, "So are you going to pay today or what?" so I take a "or what". When I get to work I'm late, so the boss asks me, "So are we going to write this down in the book or what?" so I take a "or what". Back home again I take the cab and again I don't have any money so the cab driver asks me again, "So are you going to pay this time or what?" so again I take a "or what". So you see, Doctor, when I get home I'm all tired out, and I don't want it anymore.'

The doctor thinks for a second and then turns to the wife and says, 'So are we going to tell your husband or what?'

▶ Two male medical students were discussing their answers after a tough examination. 'What did you put for question six?' asked one.

'Oh, that was easy', replied the other. 'Fill in the missing letters to find out what you feel when a lady has fainted: pu_s_. The answer was pulse.'

'Damn,' said his friend. 'I got that one wrong.'

DOGS

▶ Why do dogs like to lick their penis? Because they can't make a fist.

▶ If there is H_2O on the inside of a fire hydrant, what's on the outside? K9P.

▶ What's the most popular name for a dog in China? Starters.

▶ A dog goes into a job centre and asks for employment. 'Wow, a talking dog,' says the clerk. 'With your talent, I'm sure we can find you a job at the circus.'

'The circus?' says the dog. 'What does a circus want with a plumber?'

▶ I was eating some food in the park the other day and this old lady came by with her dog, which began barking and jumping up at me.

I said, 'Do you mind if I throw your dog a bit?'

'No,' the old lady said.

So I picked it up and threw it into the lake.

▶ Two men walking through a graveyard with their dogs meet and one man says to the other, 'Morning.'

The other man replies, 'No, just walking the dog.'

▶ Three guys sitting in a bar around a log fire with their dogs get to discussing the merits of their own hounds.

The first one says, 'My dog is called Woodworker... Go, Woodworker.'

The dog grabs a log from fire and with his teeth and paws fashions a beautiful figurine.

The next one says, 'My dog is called Stoneworker... Go, Stoneworker.'

The dog drags a rock from the fire front and a beautiful carving emerges.

The third one says, 'My dog is called Ironworker.' He puts the fire tongs into the fire and gets them red hot. 'Now,' he says, 'I'll just touch him on the balls and you watch him make a bolt for the door.'

▶ Two dogs walk over to a parking meter. One says to the other, 'How do you like that? Pay toilets!'

▶ What type of dog will bring you wine? A Bordeaux collie.

▶ Women just don't understand me – that's why I bought a dog. And this dog is like my dream date. As soon as I get her in the house, she's all over me, rubbing against my leg, licking my nuts. I can't even get a girl to do that. I can't even get a girl to shit on my carpet!

▶ How do you know your dog fancies someone else? He closes his eyes when he humps your leg.

▶ How do you stop a dog humping your leg? Pick him up and suck his cock.

▶ I went to the park this morning to play frisbee with my dog. He was useless. I think I need a flatter dog.

▶ Outside of a dog, a book is man's best friend. Inside of a dog, it's too dark to read.

▶ My Labrador is completely blind. For a laugh I like to wear a fluorescent jacket and take him for a walk.

▶ My kids want a dog but I've refused to get them a Labrador. It's frightening how many Labrador owners you see that have gone blind.

▶ A man takes his puppy to a bar and is told in no uncertain terms to leave immediately.

'But this isn't just any dog,' the man says. 'This dog can play the piano.'

'Well, if he can play that piano, you both can stay, and I'll give you a drink on the house.'

The man sits the dog on the piano stool, and the dog starts playing – ragtime, Mozart, Gershwin – and the bartender and patrons love it. Suddenly a bigger dog runs in, grabs the small dog by the scruff of the neck and drags him out.

'What the hell was that all about?' the bartender asks.

'Oh, that's his mother,' the man says. 'She wants him to be a doctor.'

▶ Did you hear about the man who bought his dog an anti-ageing lead? It's got a new leash of life.

▶ A shepherd sent his sheepdog out to gather and count the flock to make sure none were missing. The dog returns and says that there are 40 sheep.

The shepherd says, 'Forty? I only started with 38!'

The dog replies, 'Yeah, but you told me to round them up.'

▶ Have you heard about the dog who can find anything? He's a Labragoogle.

▶ Two dogs were walking along the road. One dog stopped and said, 'My name is Fido. What's yours?'

The other dog thought for a minute, and then replied, 'I think it's Down Boy.'

▶ I'm having some problems with my new Staffordshire bull terrier so I rang the vet for some advice.

I explained he was brown, stupid, aggressive and liable to attack anyone for no good reason.

The vet replied, 'Muzzle 'im?'

'No,' I said, 'I think he's an atheist.'

▶ Why did the dog hump the cabbage? It thought it was a collie!

▶ Did you hear about the dog who jumped into a washing machine and was killed? At least he died in comfort.

▶ A guest at dinner noticed the small family dog looking hungrily at every bite she took. Finally, she took a small piece of meat from her plate and held it up for him.

'Speak!' she said to the dog.

The dog answered, 'Under the circumstances, I hardly know what to say!'

▶ A redneck walked down to his favourite bar, tied his dog to a tree outside and went in to have a beer.

Twenty minutes later, a policeman entered the bar and asked, 'Who owns the dog tied under that tree outside?'

The redneck said it was his.

'Your dog seems to be in heat,' the officer said.

The redneck replied, 'No way. She's cool cos she's tied up under that shady tree.'

The policeman said, 'No! You don't understand. Your dog needs to be bred.'

'No way,' said the redneck. 'That dog don't need bread. She ain't hungry cos I fed her this mornin'.'

The exasperated policeman said, 'NO! You don't understand! Your dog wants to have sex!'

The redneck looked at the cop and said, 'Well, go ahead. I always wanted a police dog.'

▶ A man is sitting in a plane which is about to take off, when another man with a Labrador retriever occupies the two empty seats beside him. The Lab is situated in the middle, and the first man is looking quizzically at the dog, when the second man explains that they work for the airline.

The airline rep says, 'Don't mind Sniffer; he's a sniffing dog, the best there is. I'll show you once we get airborne when I put him to work.'

The plane takes off and levels out when the handler says to the first man, 'Watch this.' He tells the dog, 'Sniffer, search.'

Sniffer jumps down, walks along the aisle and sits next to a woman for a few seconds. He then returns to his seat and puts one paw on the handler's arm. He says, 'Good boy.'

The airline rep turns to the first man and says, 'That woman is in possession of marijuana, so I'm making a note of this and her seat number for the police, who will apprehend her on arrival.'

'Fantastic!' replies the first man.

Once again the airline rep sends Sniffer to search the aisles. The Lab sniffs about, sits down beside a man for a few seconds, returns to his seat and places two paws on the handler's arm.

The airline rep says, 'That man is carrying cocaine, so again I'm making a note of this and the seat number.'

'I like it!' says the first man.

A third time the rep sends Sniffer to search the aisles. Sniffer goes up and down the plane and after a while sits down next to someone. He then comes racing back, jumps up onto his seat and poops all over the aisle and the seat.

The first man is really grossed out by this behaviour from a supposedly well-trained sniffing dog and asks, 'What the hell is going on with this stupid dog?'

The handler nervously replies, 'He just found a bomb.'

▶ It's two in the morning and the travelling salesman calls the front desk at his motel and asks for some female company but with certain physical characteristics.

'She's got to be taller than six foot and weigh no more than 100 pounds,' he tells the desk clerk.

Thirty minutes later, there's a knock on his door and he opens it to see a tall, lithe young lady.

'I'm here for your pleasure, sir,' she says.

'What do you weigh and how tall are you?'

She replies, 'Six foot two and 97 pounds.'

'Perfect,' he says. 'Now take off all your clothes and get down on all fours on the floor.'

As she does this, he walks to the bathroom door, opens it and ushers in a big St Bernard dog.

The dog looks at the girl and the girl looks at the dog and the salesman says, 'Now, Fritz, do you see what you're going to look like if you don't finish your dinner?'

▶ A salesman dropped in to see a business customer. Not a soul was in the office, except a big dog emptying wastebaskets.

The salesman stared at the animal, wondering if his imagination could be playing tricks on him.

The dog looked up and said, 'Don't be surprised. This is just part of my job.'

'Incredible!' exclaimed the man. 'I can't believe it! Does your boss know what a prize he has in you? An animal that can talk!'

'No, no,' pleaded the dog. 'Please don't tell him! If that man finds out I can talk, he'll make me answer the phone as well!'

▶ A wealthy man decides to go on a safari in Africa. He takes his faithful pet dog along for company. One day the dog starts chasing butterflies and before long he discovers that he is lost. So wandering about, he notices a leopard heading rapidly in his direction with the obvious intention of having lunch.

The dog thinks, 'I'm for it now.' Then he notices some bones on the ground close by, and immediately settles down to chew on them with his back to the approaching cat.

Just as the leopard is about to leap, the dog exclaims loudly, 'Man, that was one delicious leopard. I wonder if there are anymore around here?'

Hearing this, the leopard halts his attack in mid-stride, a look of terror comes over him and he slinks away into the trees. 'Whew,' says the leopard. 'That was close. That dog nearly had me.'

Meanwhile, a monkey who has been watching the whole scene from a nearby tree figures he can put this knowledge to good use and trade it for protection from the leopard. So off he goes. But the dog sees him heading after the leopard with great speed and figures that something must be up.

The monkey soon catches up with the leopard, spills the beans and strikes a deal for himself with the leopard. The cat is furious at being made a fool of and says, 'Here, monkey, hop on my back and see what's going to happen to that conniving canine.'

Now the dog sees the leopard coming with the monkey on his back and thinks, 'What am I going to do now?' But instead of running, the dog sits down with his back to his attackers, pretending he hasn't seen them yet.

And just when they get close enough to hear, the dog says, 'Where's that monkey? I just can never trust him. I sent him off half an hour ago to bring me another leopard, and he's still not back!'

▶ A couple has a dog that snores. Annoyed because she can't sleep, the wife goes to the vet to see if he can help. The vet tells the woman to tie a ribbon around the dog's testicles and he will stop snoring. 'Yeah, right!' she says.

A few minutes after going to bed, the dog begins snoring as usual. The wife tosses and turns, unable to sleep. Muttering to herself, she goes to the closet and grabs a piece of ribbon and ties it carefully around the dog's testicles. Sure enough, the dog stops snoring. The woman is amazed!

Later that night, her husband returns home drunk from being out with his buddies. He climbs into bed, falls asleep and begins snoring loudly. The woman thinks maybe the ribbon will work on him. So, going to the closet again, she grabs another piece of ribbon and ties it around her husband's testicles. Amazingly, it also works on him! The woman sleeps soundly.

The husband awakes from a drunken stupor and stumbles into the bathroom. As he stands in front of the toilet, he glances in the mirror and sees a blue ribbon attached to his privates. He is very confused, and as he walks back into the bedroom, he sees a red ribbon attached to his dog's testicles. He shakes his head and looks at the dog and says, 'I don't know where we were or what we did, but we got first and second place!'

▶ Whenever two shepherds get together, there is the inevitable argument about who has the best sheepdog. So the merits of their respective dogs was the subject of the debate at the bar at a shepherds' convention.

'My dog's so smart,' said one, 'I can give him five instructions at the same time and he will carry them out to perfection.'

'That's nothing,' said his mate. 'I only whistle and point and Rover anticipates the whole exercise.'

Finally they decided to put their dogs to the test. The first shepherd whistled for his dog and told him to dash to the sale yards, select the oldest ram, bring him back into town and load it into the truck which was parked outside the pub.

The dog sped off in a cloud of dust and ten minutes later was seen bringing a large ram down the main street. He jumped into the truck, dropped the tailgate and ushered the ram in.

'Well, that's not bad,' conceded the second drover. 'But watch this.' 'Rover, what about some tucker?'

In a cloud of dust Rover streaked down the main street to a farm five miles out of town. Rover raced into the henhouse, nudged a hen off the nest and gently picked up an egg.

The dog then sped back to town and gently placed the egg at his master's feet. But without waiting for a pat on the head, the dog gathered a few sticks and lit a fire, grabbed a pan in his teeth and dashed to the creek, put the pan on the fire and dropped the egg into the simmering water.

After exactly three minutes, Rover rolled the pan off the fire, laid the boiled egg at his master's feet and stood on his head.

'Well, that beats all,' conceded the first shepherd, 'but why is he standing on his head?'

'Well, he knows I haven't got an egg cup,' said the proud owner.

▶ A German Shepherd went to a telegram office, took out a blank form and wrote: 'Woof. Woof. Woof. Woof. Woof. Woof. Woof. Woof. Woof.'

The clerk examined the paper and politely told the dog, 'There are only nine words here. You could send another "Woof" for the same price.'

'But,' the dog replied, 'that would make no sense at all.'

▶ A farmer was down on his luck having suffered a bad growing season, lack of crops and poor prices. To make ends meet, he decided he'd have to sell his dog – a most intelligent animal.

A few days after placing the ad, a man came to see this 'intelligent' dog. When asked what the dog could do, the farmer pointed to a stand of trees nearby and informed the man there was a pond on the other side. He turned to the dog and commanded, 'Hunt.'

Immediately the dog took off for the trees, came back a few moments later and barked twice. The farmer said, 'He just told me there are two ducks down at the pond.'

'That's absurd,' said the potential buyer. 'Dogs can't count. He was probably just barking for the heck of it.' Just then a duck flew overhead, descended just past the trees and apparently landed on the pond.

'Now send him back and have him count!' said the man. The farmer again commanded, 'Hunt!' and off went the dog. He came back shortly and barked three times. The buyer finally believed the dog was smart and bought him on the spot.

A few days later the man took his new dog out into the woods, where he knew there was a pond nearby. He commanded the dog, 'Hunt!' and the dog took off towards the pond and came back a few minutes later with a stick in its mouth. He came up to the man swinging the stick wildly around and began humping his leg.

'Smart, my ass!' said the new owner and promptly shot the dog. When he got home, he immediately called the farmer to complain. 'Some dog you sold me! When I told him to hunt, he came back waving a stick and started humping my leg so I shot the critter.'

And the farmer replied, 'You idiot! He was trying to tell you there were more ducks than you could shake a stick at!'

▶ If your dog is barking at the back door and your wife is yelling at the front door, who do you let in first? The dog – you know he'll shut up when he comes in.

▶ A young girl is wandering through a park in the pouring rain, when she comes across three dogs. Being a bit of an animal lover, she approaches them, bends down and starts to stroke one of them.

'Ah, you're lovely, aren't you,' she says to the first dog. 'What's your name, then?'

To her surprise, the dog actually answers her. 'My name's Huey, and I've had a great day going in and out of puddles.'

Delighted with this discovery, she moves on to the next dog. 'And what's your name, then?'

Again, unbelievably, the second dog answers her. 'My name's Lewy, and I've had a great day going in and out of puddles.'

And so she moves on to the last dog. 'Let me guess,' she says. Your name's Dewy, and you've had a great day going in and out of puddles.'

'No,' replies the last dog. 'My name's Puddles, and I've had a terrible day.'

▶ A man has a dog which he is attempting to train, but alas has very little success. He is on the verge of despair, when he happens across a very charismatic American evangelist. He unburdens his soul to the American, who promptly informs him to leave the dog with him, and he will have it trained in a jiffy.

The next day the man returns and asks how the evangelist got on. The reply is positive and the evangelist called the dog to give a demonstration.

Picking up a stick, he throws it and says, 'Fetch.' Instantly the dog takes off, grabs the stick and returns. The evangelist says, 'Drop,' and the dog drops the stick at his feet. 'Roll over,' and the dog rolls over. By this time the dog's owner is very excited and asks if he can have a go.

'Sure,' replies the evangelist.

'Heel,' says the owner.

And the dog lifts one paw, places it on the man and says, 'I command this sickness to leave you... '

▶ *How dogs and men are the same...*

• Both take up too much space on the bed.

• Both have irrational fears about vacuum cleaning.

• Both mark their territory.

• Neither tells you what's bothering them.

• The smaller ones tend to be more nervous.

• Both have an inordinate fascination with women's crotches.

• Neither does any dishes.

• Both fart shamelessly.

- Neither of them notice when you get your hair cut.

- Both like dominance games.

- Both are suspicious of the postman.

- Neither understands what you see in cats.

▶ *How dogs are better than men...*

- Dogs do not have problems expressing affection in public.

- Dogs miss you when you're gone.

- Dogs feel guilty when they've done something wrong.

- Dogs admit when they're jealous.

- Dogs are very direct about wanting to go out.

- Dogs do not play games with you, except fetch (and they never laugh at how you throw).

- You can train a dog.

- Dogs are easy to buy for.

- The worst social disease you can get from dogs is fleas.

- Dogs understand what 'no' means.

- Dogs mean it when they kiss you.

▶ *Why dogs are better than women...*

- Dogs understand that instincts are better than asking for directions.

- Dogs like beer.

- Dogs don't hate their bodies.

- Dogs don't criticise.

- Dogs agree that you have to raise your voice to get your point across.

- Dogs never expect gifts.

- Dogs don't want to know about every other dog you've ever had.

- Dogs don't let a magazine article guide their lives.

- You never have to wait for a dog; they're ready to go 24 hours a day.

- Dogs don't cry.

- Dogs love it when your friends come over.

- A dog's time in the bathroom is confined to a quick drink.

- Dogs don't expect you to call when you're running late – the later you are, the more excited they are to see you.

- Anyone can get a good-looking dog.

- Dogs enjoy heavy petting in public.

- Dogs find you amusing when you're drunk.

- Dogs don't mind if you give their offspring away.

- Dogs don't notice if you call them by another dog's name.

- If a dog is gorgeous, other dogs don't hate it.

- A dog's parents never visit.

▶ *Why women are better than dogs...*

• It is socially acceptable to have sexual relations with a woman.

▶ *Dog haiku*

• I love my master;
  Thus I perfume myself with
  This long-rotten squirrel.

• I lie belly-up
  In the sunshine, happier than
  You ever will be.

• Today I sniffed
  Many dog butts – I celebrate
  By kissing your face.

• I sound the alarm!
  Paperboy – come to kill us all –
  Look! Look! Look! Look! Look!

• I sound the alarm!
  Bin man – come to kill us all –
  Look! Look! Look! Look! Look!

• I lift my leg and
  Piss on each bush. Hello, Spot
  Sniff this and weep.

• How do I love thee?
  The ways are numberless as
  My hairs on the rug.

- My human is home!
  I am so ecstatic, I have
  Made a puddle.

- I hate my choke chain.
  Look, world, they strangle me!
  Ack Ack Ack Ack Ack Ack!

- Sleeping here, my chin
  On your foot – no greater bliss – well,
  Maybe catching rats.

- The cat is not all
  Bad – she fills the litter box
  With fig rolls.

- Dig under fence – why?
  Because it's there. Because it's
  There. Because it's there.

- I am your best friend,
  Now, always and especially
  When you are eating.

- You may call them fleas,
  But they are far more – I call
  Them a vocation.

- My owners' mood is
  Romantic – I lie near their
  Feet. I fart a big one.

DONKEYS

▶ Did you hear about the bisexual donkey? He had a hee in the morning and a haw at night.

▶ What do you call a donkey with three legs? Eligible for benefit.

DOWN ON THE FARM

▶ A man rang the doctor in a panic. 'A mouse has just run up my wife's vagina. What should I do?'

The doctor replied, 'Stay right there – I'll come over now, but in the meantime try to lure it out with a piece of cheese.'

When the doctor arrived, he found the man waving a piece of cod under his wife's vagina.

'What's going on?' said the doctor. 'I said use cheese.'

'I know, but I've got to get the cat out first.'

▶ I've just been convicted of bestiality. 'Little harsh on my wife, though,' I thought.

▶ Why do farmers screw goats on the edge of cliffs? So the goats will push back.

▶ A little boy asked his mother: 'Mummy, why are you white and I am black?'

'Don't even ask me that! When I remember that party... you're lucky that you don't bark!'

▶ An officer is posted to a remote desert outpost to look after a unit of malcontents. When he arrives, he realises that there's not much in the way of entertainment, so he asks one of the troops, 'What do you do for sex around here?' The trooper points to a donkey tied to a post nearby. The officer is outraged and orders the donkey to be put out in the field and should any man touch it, he would be shot. After several weeks pass the officer begins to feel a bit edgy and with the lack of women has no lasting way to get relief. There were only so many times he could pleasure himself before it got tiresome. Finally he cracked and demanded that the donkey be brought back to the command tent. When it arrives, he figures that he's going to be the one to go first and so drops his pants and begins to have his way with the donkey. He then realises that all the troops are looking at him aghast.

'What?' he demands. 'Isn't this the way you all did it?'

'No, sir,' one replies. 'We rode the donkey into town to meet girls.'

▶ What's the difference between a farmer and a redneck? Both breed animals, but the redneck gets emotionally involved.

▶ Travelling vacuum salesman knocks on a farmhouse door. 'Excuse me. Before I tell you about my vacuums, I think you should know there's a man fucking a donkey out in your field.'

The kid who answered the door looks past the salesman's shoulder and shrugs. 'That's my dad. He hawwwwlways does that.'

▶ What's the difference between a Rolling Stone and a Scotsman?
A Rolling Stone says, 'Hey, you, get off of my cloud!' and a Scotsman says, 'Hey, McLeod, get off my ewe!'

▶ Forty per cent of people who have worked on farms have had 'inappropriate' contact with animals. The other 60 per cent asked for consent.

▶ A young hillbilly always went out to the barn to beat off and when he was done, he would shoot his load into a coffee can and hide it under the bench. One day his father caught him and told him, 'Son, every time you do that, you are killing a baby.' The next time the boy went to the barn he was about to shoot his load and reached down to grab his can but a little frog had jumped in. The boy looked in the can, saw the frog and said, 'Son, you're ugly but Daddy loves ya.'

▶ My girlfriend wasn't impressed with my new memory-foam mattress. I think it was the imprints of me and a donkey that made her mind up.

▶ A doctor had just finished a marathon sex session with one of his patients. He was resting afterwards and feeling a bit guilty because he thought it wasn't really ethical to screw one of his patients.

However, a little voice in his head said, 'Lots of other doctors have sex with their patients so it's not like you're the first... '

This made the doctor feel a little bit better until still another voice in his head said, 'But they probably weren't veterinarians.'

▶ A man goes to the doctor and says, 'I've got a mole on the end of my penis.'

The doctor says, 'Drop your trousers and show me.'

After a look the doctor says, 'I can get rid of the mole but I'm going to have to report you to the animal welfare people.'

▶ According to the latest issue of *Nature Biotechnology*, scientists have implanted human DNA into female goats. Is that really new? Lonely farmers have been doing that for years.

▶ A group of prisoners were in a rehabilitation meeting, at which they had to admit their crimes to their fellow inmates.

'I'm Vern, and I'm in for armed robbery,' said the first prisoner, while the other prisoners patted him on the back for having the courage to own up.

'I'm Terry, and I'm in for GBH,' said another prisoner, and his comrades all murmured their support.

'I'm Keith', piped up a third prisoner. 'But I'm not telling you what I did.'

The group leader intervened. 'You must. It's the only way you can move forwards in your life,' he said

'OK,' said Keith. 'Here goes. I'm in here for having sex with dogs.'

'Disgusting!' shouted the other prisoners. 'How low can you get!'

'Chihuahuas,' replied Keith.

▶ What do a walrus and Tupperware have in common? They both like a tight seal.

▶ A taxidermist is on vacation down South. He is feeling a little thirsty and decides to have a few drinks at the nearest tavern. Upon entering the tavern, the conversation stops and all eyes turn to him. Feeling a little uneasy, he makes his way to the bar to order a beer. The bartender serves him and says, 'Ya'll ain't from round these parts, is ya?'

'No,' replies the man, 'I am from Connecticut.'

'What is it you do up there in Connecticut?' asks the barman.

'I'm a taxidermist,' says the man.

'A taxidermist!' the barman shouts, 'Hey, George, you ever heard of a taxidermist?'

'No, never heard of it!' says George.

'So, Mr Taxidermist, what is it you do exactly?' asks the barman.

'Well,' explains the man, 'I mount dead animals.'

'Oh,' says the barman. 'It's OK, boys – he's one of us!'

DRINKING

▶ A man is driving happily along, when he is pulled over by the police. The copper approaches him and politely asks, 'Have you been drinking, sir?'

'Why?' snorts the man. 'Is there a fat bird in my car?'

▶ What is £26 a gallon and full of water? Lager.

▶ The great thing about a hotel mini-bar is that it allows you to see what drinks will cost in 2020.

▶ What is the difference between a dog and a fox? About nine pints.

▶ Why did God create alcohol? So ugly people would have a chance to have sex.

▶ 'Hey, pal, what's a breathalyser?' says one drunk to another.

'Well, I'd have to say that it's a bag that tells you when you've drunk way too much,' replies his drunken friend.

'Hey, what do you know? I've been married to one of those for years!'

▶ Mr O'Malley had worked at the local brewery for years, but one day he wasn't paying attention, tripped on the walkway and fell into the beer vat and drowned. The foreman thought it should be his job to inform Mrs O'Malley of her husband's death. He showed up at the front door and rang the bell. When she came to the door, he said, 'I'm sorry to tell you, but your poor husband passed away at work today when he fell into the vat and drowned.'

She wept and covered her face with her apron and after a time, between sobs, she asked, 'Tell me, did he suffer?'

'Knowing Brian O'Malley as well as I did, I don't think so,' said the foreman. 'He got out three times to go to the toilet.'

▶ Gareth Gates got stopped for drink-driving last night. The police say he'll probably be sent to prison, but is unlikely to complete his sentence.

▶ Saw a drunk earlier wandering the streets shouting, 'Vodka!' at random passers-by. I thought to myself, 'That's the spirit...'

▶ My wife told me I had to give up drinking, so I joined the AA. Unfortunately, I joined the Automobile Association by mistake. At least either way I'm on the road to recovery.

▶ A_C_H_L
Sometimes alcohol *is* the answer.

▶ I got home from the pub last night and my wife said, 'I can't believe how intoxicated you are.'

Denying it, I said, 'I'm not drunk.'

She said, 'Yes, you are.'

I said, 'No, I'm bloody not.'

She said, 'Can you tell the time?'

I walked up to the clock and said, 'I'm not bloody drunk.'

▶ It was 40 below zero one winter's night in Alaska. In the town saloon, the bartender told Ed, 'You owe me quite a bit on your tab.'

'Sorry,' said Ed, 'I'm flat broke this week.'

'OK,' said the bartender, 'I'll just write your name and the amount you owe me right here on the wall.'

Ed looked concerned. 'I don't want any of my friends to see that.'

'They won't,' said the bartender. 'I'll just hang your parka over it until it's paid... '

▶ A Scotsman, an American and an Irishman are in a bar. They are having a good time and all agree that the bar is a nice place.

Then the Scotsman says, 'Aye, this is a nice bar, but where I come from, back in Glasgow, there's a better one. At MacDougal's, you buy a drink, you buy another drink and MacDougal himself will buy your third drink!'

The others agree that sounds like a good place.

Then the American says, 'Yeah, that's a nice bar, but where I come from, there's a better one. Over in Brooklyn, there's this place, Vinny's. At Vinny's, you buy a drink, Vinny buys you a drink. You buy another drink, Vinny buys you another drink.'

Everyone agrees that sounds like a great bar.

Then the Irishman says, 'You think that's great? Where I come from in Dublin, there's this place called Murphy's. At Murphy's, they buy you your first drink, they buy you your second drink, they buy you your third drink and then they take you in the back and get you laid!'

'Wow!' say the other two. 'That's fantastic! Did that actually happen to you?'

'No,' replies the Irish guy, 'but it happened to me sister.'

▶ *Things that are difficult to say when you're drunk:*

• Innovative

• Preliminary

• Proliferation

• Cinnamon

▶ *Things that are VERY difficult to say when you're drunk:*

• Specificity

• British Constitution

• Passive-aggressive disorder

• Transubstantiate

▶ *Things that are ABSOLUTELY IMPOSSIBLE to say when you're drunk:*

• 'Thanks, but I don't want to sleep with you.'

• 'Nope, no more booze for me.'

• 'Sorry, but you're not really my type.'

• 'No kebab for me, thank you.'

• 'Good evening, officer, isn't it lovely out tonight?'

• 'I'm not interested in fighting you.'

- 'Oh, I just couldn't – no one wants to hear me sing.'

- 'Thank you, but I won't make any attempt to dance, I have no co-ordination. I'd hate to look like a fool.'

- 'Where is the nearest toilet? I refuse to vomit in the street.'

- 'I must be going home now as I have work in the morning.'

▶ A man feeling very depressed walked into a bar and ordered a triple Scotch. As the bartender poured him the drink, he remarked, 'That's quite a heavy drink. Is something wrong?'

After quickly downing his drink, the man replied, 'I got home and found my wife in bed with my best friend.'

'Wow!' exclaimed the bartender as he poured the man a second triple Scotch. 'No wonder you needed a stiff drink. This one's on the house.'
As the man finished the second Scotch, the bartender asked him, 'So what did you do?'

'I walked over to my wife,' the man replied, 'looked her straight in the eye and told her that we were through. I told her to pack her stuff and to get the hell out.'

'That makes sense,' said the bartender, 'but what about your best friend?'

'I walked over to him, looked him right in the eye and said, "Bad dog!"'

▶ One night in the pub, the owner is lamenting the fact that business is so quiet on Mondays, Tuesdays and Wednesdays. As he moans and groans to some of the regulars at the bar, a stranger dressed in a tweed jacket and wearing glasses wanders over and says, 'I'm sorry, but I couldn't help overhearing your conversation just then. I'm a doctor at the mental hospital up the road, and as part of our outreach programme I'm trying to integrate some of our more sane individuals back into the community. Why don't I bring some of my patients along, say next Tuesday? You'll have some customers, and my patients will have a good night out; it's a win-win situation. What do you think?'

Well, the publican isn't sure but, being a licensed vintner and all that, the thought of more paying customers on a quiet night has a certain appeal, so he agrees.

The following Tuesday the guy in the tweed jacket and glasses shows up with about ten of his mental patients. He explains to the publican, 'They might try to pay for their drinks in unusual ways, so could you just accept whatever they give you, put it all on a tab and I'll settle up the account at the end of the night.'

The barmen have a great time selling a load of pints and encouraging the mental patients to eat crisps and peanuts. The new customers appear to be having a great time, having a sing-song, getting merrily drunk and paying for their drinks with empty Coke cans, banana skins, used teabags and plastic shopping bags.

At closing time the head barman adds up the bill and it comes to just over 300 quid! The bloke with the glasses and the tweed jacket starts to organise the mental patients and get them ready to get on the bus and drive back to the asylum. Finally he comes over and asks for the bill. The publican, feeling that he's charged them rather a lot and that he should do his bit to help these poor unfortunate people, gives him a discount.

'Let's call it £250,' he says.

The guy in the tweed jacket smiles and says, 'That's fine. Have you change for a wheelie bin?'

▶ A beautiful, sexy woman went up to the bar in a quiet rural pub. She gestured alluringly to the bartender, who approached her immediately.

She seductively signalled that he should bring his face closer to hers. As he did, she gently caressed his full beard.

'Are you the manager?' she asked, softly stroking his face with both hands.

'Actually, no,' he replied.

'Can you get him for me? I need to speak to him,' she said, running her hands beyond his beard and into his hair.

'I'm afraid I can't,' breathed the bartender. 'Is there anything I can do?'

'Yes. I need for you to give him a message,' she continued, running her forefinger across the bartender's lips and slyly popping a couple of her fingers into his mouth and allowing him to suck them gently.

'What should I tell him?' the bartender managed to say.

'Tell him,' she whispered, 'there's no toilet paper, hand soap or paper towels in the ladies' room.'

▶ Charles Dickens walks into a bar and orders a Martini. The bartender says, 'Olive or twist?'

▶ A homeless man is travelling down a country lane. Tired and hungry, he comes across a pub called the George and Dragon. Although it's late and the pub is closed, he knocks on the door.

The innkeeper's wife sticks her head out of a window.

'Could I have some food?' he asks.

The woman glances at his shabby clothes and obviously poor condition and sternly says, 'No!'

'Any chance of a pint of ale, then?'

'No!' she says again.

'Could I at least sleep in your barn?'

'No!' By this time, she was fairly shouting.

The down-and-out says, 'OK, then, might I please... ?'

'What now?' the woman interrupts impatiently.

'Might I please have a word with George?'

▶ A guy walks into a bar and says to the woman bartender, 'Hey, babe, Anheuser Busch?'

'Fine,' she says, 'and how's your dick?'

▶ A man sitting in the bar found that the front of his trousers was all wet. Turning to the man on his right, he asked, 'Did you pour beer on my trousers?'

'Nope,' came the reply.

Then, turning to the man on his left, he asked, 'Did you pour beer on my trousers?'

The man also replied, 'Nope.'

'Oops, it must have been an inside job.'

▶ Two guys get off a ship and head for the nearest bar. Each one orders two whiskies and immediately downs them. They then order two more whiskies and once again quickly throw them back. They then order another two whiskies apiece.

One of them picks up one of his drinks and, turning to the other man, says, 'Cheers!'

The other man turns to the first man and asks, 'Hey, did you come here to chat or did you come here to drink?'

▶ A golf club walks into a local bar and asks the barman for a pint of beer. The barman refuses to serve him.

'Why not?' asks the golf club.

'You'll be driving later,' replies the bartender.

▶ Two old drunks were at a bar one night. The first old drunk said, 'Y'know, when I was 30 years old and got a hard-on, I couldn't bend it with both hands. By the time I was 40, I could bend it about ten degrees if I tried really hard. By the time I was 50, I could bend it about 20 degrees, no problem. I'm gonna be 60 next week, and now I can almost bend it in half with just one hand.'

'So,' says the second drunk. 'What's your point?'

'Well,' says the first, 'I'm just wondering how much stronger I'm gonna get!'

▶ Mick and Murphy fancied a pint or two but didn't have a lot of money; between them, they could only raise the sum of 50 pence.

Murphy said, 'Hang on, I have an idea.' He went next door to the butcher's shop and came out with one large sausage.

Mick said, 'Are you crazy? Now we don't have any money left at all.'

Murphy replied, 'Don't worry – just follow me.' He went into the pub, where he immediately ordered two pints of Guinness and two glasses of whisky.

Mick said, 'Now you've lost it. Do you know how much trouble we'll be in? We haven't got any money!'

Murphy replied, with a smile, 'Don't worry, I have a plan. Cheers!' They downed their drinks. Murphy said, 'OK, I'll stick the sausage through my zipper and you go on your knees and put it in your mouth.'

They did it, the barman noticed them, went berserk and threw them out. They continued this, pub after pub, getting more and more drunk all for free. At the tenth pub Mick said, 'Murphy, I don't think I can do any more o'this. I'm pissed and me knees are killin' me!'

Murphy said, 'How do you think I feel? I lost the sausage in the third pub.'

▶ A lady goes to the bar on a cruise ship and orders a Scotch with two drops of water. As the bartender gives her the drink, she says, 'I'm on this cruise to celebrate my 80th birthday and it's today.'

The bartender says, 'Well, since it's your birthday, I'll buy you a drink. In fact, this one is on me.'

As the woman finishes her drink, the woman to her right says, 'I would like to buy you a drink, too.'

The old woman says, 'Thank you. Bartender, I want a Scotch with two drops of water.'

'Coming up,' says the bartender. As she finishes that drink, the man to her left says, 'I would like to buy you one, too.'

The old woman says, 'Thank you. Bartender, I want another Scotch with two drops of water.'

'Coming right up,' the bartender says. As he gives her the drink, he says, 'Ma'am, I'm dying of curiosity. Why the Scotch with only two drops of water?'

The old woman replies, 'Sonny, when you're my age, you've learned how to hold your liquor. Holding your water, however, is a whole other issue.'

▶ A cowboy walks into a bar and orders a whisky. When the bartender delivers the drink, the cowboy asks, 'Where is everybody?'

The bartender replies, 'They've gone to the hanging.'

'Hanging? Who are they hanging?'

'Brown Paper Pete,' the bartender replies.

'What kind of a name is that?' the cowboy asks.

'Well,' says the bartender. 'He wears a brown paper hat, brown paper shirt, brown paper trousers and brown paper shoes.'

'How bizarre,' says the cowboy. 'What are they hanging him for?'

'Rustling,' says the bartender.

▶ Did you hear about the rheumatoid alcoholic? Every night he gets stiff in a different joint.

▶ When are beer and your mother-in-law at their best? When they're cold, opened up and on the table.

▶ *Beer vs pussy:*

• A beer is always wet. A pussy needs encouragement.
Advantage: beer.

• A beer tastes horrible served hot. A pussy tastes better served hot.
Advantage: pussy.

• Having an ice-cold beer makes you satisfied. Having an ice-cold pussy makes you Ann Widdecombe.
Advantage: beer.

• Beers have commercials making fun of bad ones. Pussy does not.
Advantage: draw.

• If you get a hair in your teeth consuming pussy, you are not disgusted.
Advantage: pussy.

• Twenty-four beers come in a box. A pussy is a box you can come in.
Advantage: pussy.

• Too much head makes you angry at the person giving you a beer.
Advantage: pussy.

• If a beer is brewed with yeast, it is still edible.
Advantage: beer.

- If you come home smelling like beer, the Woman may get angry.
  If you come home smelling like pussy, she will definitely get angry.
  Advantage: beer.

- Six beers in a night and you better not drive. Six pussies in a night and you have done all the driving you need.
  Advantage: pussy.

- Buy too much beer and you will get fat. Buy too much pussy and you will get poor.
  Advantage: draw.

- It is socially acceptable to have a beer in the stands at a football game.
  You are a legend if you have a pussy in the stands at a football game.
  Advantage: pussy.

- If a cop smells beer on your breath, you are going to get a breathalyser.
  If a cop smells pussy on your breath, you are going to get a high five.
  Advantage: pussy.

- With beer, bigger is better.
  Advantage: beer.

- Wearing a condom does not make a beer any less enjoyable.
  Advantage: beer.

- Pussy can make you see God. Beer can make you see the porcelain God.
  Advantage: pussy.

- If you think all day about the next pussy you will have, you are normal.
  If you think all day about your next beer, you are an alcoholic.
  Advantage: pussy.

- Peeling labels off of beers is fun. Peeling panties off pussy is more fun.
  Advantage: pussy.

- If you try to grab a beer at work, you get fired. If you try to grab a pussy at work, you get hit with sexual harassment.
  Advantage: draw.

- If you suddenly drop a beer, it may break. If you suddenly drop a pussy, it may hunt you down like the dog you are.
  Advantage: beer.

- If you change to another beer, your old brand will gladly have you back.
  Advantage: beer.

- The best pussy you have ever had is not gone once you have enjoyed it.
  Advantage: pussy.

- The worst pussy you have ever had is not gone once you have enjoyed it.
  Advantage: beer.

- The government taxes beer.
  Advantage: pussy.

▶ A man walks into a bar after a long ride on his horse. He walks up to the bar and asks the bartender for a beer. When he gets his beer, he starts eyeing this beautiful lady in the corner. Just as he turns back, a monkey runs up to the beer, dunks his balls in the beer and runs off.

Agitated, the man says to the bartender, 'I can't drink this now! Give me another beer!' So, the bartender brings him another beer. Before the man can do anything about it, the monkey runs back over, dunks his balls in the beer and runs off before the man can grab him. Even more angry, the man says, 'I can't drink this now. Bring me another beer!' He gets another beer and guards it with his life. The monkey sneaks up behind him, knocks the stool out from underneath the man, hops up onto the bar and dunks his balls in the beer. Now the man is thoroughly pissed off. He grabs the bartender and says, 'Man, I've had it. Whose stupid monkey is this anyway?'

The bartender replies, 'It belongs to the piano player.'

The man walks over to the piano player and says, 'Excuse me, do you know your monkey is dunking his balls in my beer?'

To which the piano player replies, 'No, I sure don't, but if you hum a few notes, I'll play it.'

▶ A fellow in a bar notices a woman, always alone, who comes in on a fairly regular basis. After the second week, he makes his move.

'No thank you,' she says politely. 'This may sound rather odd in this day and age, but I'm keeping myself pure until I meet the man I love.'

'That must be rather difficult,' the man replies.

'Oh, I don't mind too much,' she says. 'But it has my husband really pissed off.'

▶ The boss at a restaurant went up to the bartender and asked, 'Have you been fooling around with the waitress?'

'Oh no, sir, I haven't,' replied the bartender.

The boss replied, 'Good, then YOU fire her!'

▶ What's the difference between a bartender and a proctologist?
A proctologist waits on one arsehole at a time.

▶ My dad was the town drunk. Most of the time that's not so bad; but in New York City?

▶ After the tourist had been served in a Las Vegas cocktail lounge, he beckoned the waitress back and said quietly, 'Miss, y'all sure are a luvly, luvly lady; can ah persuade y'all to give me a piece of ass?'

'Lord, that's the most direct proposition I've ever had!' gasped the girl. Then she looked around the room, smiled and added, 'Sure, why not? You're nice-lookin', too, and it's pretty slow here right now, so why don't we just slip away up to your room?'

When the pair returned half an hour later, the man sat down at the same table and the waitress asked, 'Will there be anything else, sir?'

'Why, yes,' replied the southern gentleman. 'Ah sure 'preciate what y'all just did for me; it was real sweet and right neighbourly, but where ah come from in Arkansas, we lack our bourbon real cold, so ah still need to trouble y'all for a piece uh ass for mah drink.'

▶ A guy walks into a bar and orders three whisky sours, drinks them down, BAM! BAM! BAM! Then he orders three more. The bartender's having a slow night and appreciates the business, but is also concerned.

'Hey buddy, slow down. What seems to be the problem?'

The guy answers, 'I went on a week-long business trip and had to leave my wife alone. I've had my suspicions about our next-door neighbour, so I hung a weight from the bottom of the bedspring just above a bowl of cream.'

The bartender nods sympathetically and pours the guy another. 'So you came home and found cream on the weight?'

The guy downs his fourth whisky sour and says, 'It's worse than that. The cream had been churned into butter.'

▶ The two buddies had been out drinking for hours, when their money finally ran out. 'I have an idea,' mumbled Al. 'Lesh go over to my housh and borrow shum money from my wife.' The two of them reeled into Al's living room, snapped on the light and, lo and behold, there was Al's wife making love on the sofa to another man. This state of affairs considerably unnerved Al's friend but didn't seem to affect Al.

'Shay, dear, you have any money for your ever-lovin' hushban?' he asked.

'Yes, yes,' she snapped. 'Take my purse from the mantel and, for Pete's sake, turn off those lights.'

Outside, they examined the purse, and Al proudly announced, 'There's enough here for a pint for you and a pint for me. Pretty good, eh, old buddy?'

'But, Al,' protested his friend, somewhat sobered by the spectacle he'd just witnessed, 'what about that fellow back there with your wife?'

'The hell with him,' replied Al, 'let him buy his own pint.'

▶ A man walked into the bar. As he waited for his drink, he noticed a gorgeous young Indian girl sipping a soft drink at the other end of the bar. He told the bartender to give her a real drink. The bartender replied, 'I can't. The C.P. would be on my ass.'

'What's the C.P.?'

'City Police.'

The man finished his drink and ordered another. Again, he asked the bartender to give the Indian girl a real drink, but this time the bartender said, 'I can't. The S.P. would shut me down.'

'What's the S.P.?'

'State Police.'

Just then the Indian girl got up and walked out of the bar. The man hurried out after her. An hour later, he staggered back into the bar, his clothes covered with blood, his nose broken.

'The F.B.I. got me!' the man moaned.

'What do you mean the F.B.I?' the bartender asked.

'A Fucking Big Indian!'

▶ In a nearly empty London bar on a filthy winter's day, there were several patrons quietly drinking when in comes your stereotypical American visitor, obviously unimpressed by the country, its weather and everything else about it.

He says loudly, 'What a lousy country. The bars are shut half the time, it's cold, wet and windy, the beer tastes like piss and is served at the same temperature, the streets are packed and you can't even get a cab.'

Several people quietly leave.

He looks at a gentleman quietly sipping a pink gin and says, 'Hey, limey. How can you bear to live in such a miserable place?'

He is ignored; more people leave. After much more of this, only the gentleman with the pink gin, the barman and the American are left.

He says, 'Hey, limey, I'm talking to you. I've been to damn near every country in the world and this is the lousiest. I dunno how you can bear to live here. This country is just the arsehole of the world.'

The gentleman with the pink gin pauses, takes another sip and, turning, delicately, enquires of the American. 'Oh, yes. Just passing through, are you?'

▶ A man dressed in painter's overalls walks into a hardware store and asks for a bottle of white spirit. The proprietor looks at him. 'No. You're that alcoholic bum who used to always hang around the village green – you'll just drink this.'

The man is shocked: 'Oh no, you are mistaken – I used to be that man, but I have a home now, have started up my own painting and decorating business, have given up drinking and cleaned up my life entirely. I need the white spirit to clean my brushes, or they'll be ruined. Why is it that nobody can recognise me for the person I want to be, rather than the person I used to be?'

The hardware proprietor pauses to think. 'You're right. I'm sorry for judging you based on your past. Would you like a litre?'

'Thank you! Yes, a litre bottle. Do you have a cold one?'

▶ Quasimodo walks into a bar, strolls straight up to the barman and says, 'I'll have a whisky, please.'

The barman says, 'Bells all right?'

'Mind your own business.'

▶ A man walked into a bar and ordered a Scotch. 'And,' he added ominously, 'I want a ten-year-old Scotch. And don't try to fob me off with something younger because I can tell the difference.'

The bartender thought the customer was all talk and decided to trick him by giving him a five-year-old Scotch. But the man took one sip, grimaced and snapped, 'Bartender, this is five-year-old Scotch. I told you I wanted ten-year-old Scotch. The bartender was still not convinced and tried to fool the customer with a seven-year-old Scotch, but once again the man said, 'I told you I wanted ten-year-old Scotch. This is only seven years old.'

Admitting defeat, the bartender served him the ten-year-old Scotch, and the customer purred. 'Perfect. At last, the real thing.'

Observing all this was a drunk, who then staggered over, slammed a glass down in front of the Scotch connoisseur and said, 'Here, try this.'

The man took a sip and immediately spat it out. 'Ugh! It tastes like piss!'

'Yeah,' said the drunk. 'Now tell me how old I am.'

▶ Harry, Bill and Steve are sitting at the corner bar enjoying themselves, when Ted walks in looking distressed.

'Ted, you look awful. What's wrong?' Harry asks.

Ted says, 'Last night I got really drunk, and then somewhere between here and my house, I was abducted by an alien.'

Everyone is shocked. 'I heard about this kind of thing happening!' Bill says, 'What did the alien do to you?'

'I don't remember all the details,' Ted says. 'All I remember is being anally probed by the alien.'

Everyone is horrified. 'I heard that they'll do that!' Steve says. 'What did the alien look like?'

Ted responds, 'Carl.'

▶ I went to the pub last night and the barman asked me what I wanted, so I said, 'Surprise me!'

He showed me a naked picture of my daughter.

▶ A guy walks into a pub and approaches the barman. 'Can I have a pint of Less, please?'

'I'm sorry, sir,' the barman replies, looking slightly puzzled. 'I've not come across that one before. Is it one of those European beers?'

'I've no idea,' replies the guy. 'The thing is, I went to see my doctor last week and he told me that I should drink less.'

▶ A Roman centurion walks into a bar.

'What can I get you?' says the barman.

'I'd like a Martinum, please.'

'Do you mean a Martini?'

'If I want a double, I'll ask.'

▶ A squaddie comes back from Afghanistan on leave and goes into his local for a few pints. The local university has organised an anti-war demo of 100 students that walks past the pub chanting, 'Troops out', 'Murderers', etc.

He walks out, whips out his sheath knife and, in a blur, kicks the hell out of all 100 of them in about ten seconds. He finishes up by lopping off the head student's ear before strolling back into the pub and ordering another pint and a pork pie.

He opens the pork pie, flips the ear into it and eats it with one bite.

The barman, obviously impressed, says, 'Special forces, right?'

'Nah,' he replies. 'Pioneer corp.'

▶ My mate told me he could make vodka out of cow faeces. I think that's Absolut Bullshit.

▶ Two fellows stopped in a pub for a drink. They called the proprietor over and asked him to settle an argument. 'Are there two pints in a quart or four?' asked one.

'There are two pints in a quart,' confirmed the proprietor.

They moved back along the bar and soon the barmaid asked for their order.

'Two pints please, miss, and the bartender offered to buy them for us.'

The barmaid doubted that her boss would be so generous, so one of the fellows called out to the proprietor at the other end of the bar, 'You did say two pints, didn't you?'

'That's right,' he called back, 'two pints.'

▶ A drunk gets on a bus. The driver, impatient while the drunk fumbles in his pocket for change, drives off. As the bus starts rolling, the drunk reacts to the sudden movement by stumbling all the way to the back of the bus.

The bus stops at the next stop. He reacts by stumbling to the front of the bus. Still the drunk man is fumbling in his pocket for change. The bus jerks forwards once again, and the drunk stumbles uncontrollably to the back of the bus once again. Next stop, the same thing happens. In fact, every time the bus stops, the man staggers to the front. Every time the bus starts, he staggers uncontrollably to the back. A few stops later, the drunk starts to exit the bus from the front.

'Hey,' shouts the bus driver. 'You didn't pay your fare yet!'

The drunk, still reeling, shouts back, 'Why should I?! I walked all the way!'

▶ I was waiting at the counter in a cocktail bar the other day.

'Sex on the beach?' asked the barman

'No, thanks,' I replied. 'I just had a wank on the train.'

▶ An old soldier hopped in, crutch under one arm, and called to the barman, 'A pint of the dark stuff.'

'Too late,' said the barman, 'we've just closed up.'

'Ah come on,' said the soldier. 'I lost my leg at Dunkirk.'

'Well, you won't find it in this pub,' said the barman.

▶ A blonde was hunched over the bar, toothpick in hand, spearing futilely at the olive in her drink. A dozen times the olive eluded her. Finally, another patron, who had been watching intently from the next stool, became exasperated and grabbed the toothpick.

'Here, this is how you do it,' he said, as he easily skewered the olive.

'Big deal,' muttered the blonde. 'I already had him so tired out, he couldn't get away.'

▶ An ugly girl in a pub says, 'If you can guess my weight, you can shag me all night long.'

A bloke says, 'Oh, about 93 stone, you ugly fat cow.'

She replies, 'That's close enough, you lucky bastard.'

▶ As I pulled back the ringpull on my can of Stella, I heard 'Hello'. I thought to myself, 'It must be the drink talking.'

▶ Two drunks are standing at a whorehouse door. The first drunk says, 'I heard half these girls have the clap and that none of them would think twice about stealing every penny we've got.'

The second drunk says, 'Not so loud, or they won't let us in.'

▶ Did you hear about the half-Irish, half-Scottish man? He was desperate for a drink but couldn't bring himself to buy one.

▶ Female wanted, must have your own pub. Apply with inn.

▶ Three drunk men stopped a taxi after a heavy night of bingeing. The taxi driver had figured they were wasted, so when the men got in the taxi, he switched on the engine, then switched it off again and told them they'd arrived.

The first guy gave him the money, the second guy said thanks, but the third guy gave him a slap.

The taxi driver was stunned as he didn't think they would realise the taxi hadn't moved an inch, so he asked, 'What was that for?'

The man replied, 'Control your speed next time – you could have killed us.'

▶ Every time I get something stuck in my throat, I just dislodge it by drinking a pint of lager. It's called the Heineken Manoeuvre.

▶ An Englishman, a Scotsman, an Irishman, a Latvian, a Turk, an Aussie, a Yank, an Egyptian, a Mexican, a Spaniard, a Greek, a Russian, an Estonian, a German, an Italian, a Pole, a Lithuanian, a Swede, a Finn, an Israeli, a Romanian, a Bulgarian, a Serb, a Czech and a Swiss man walk into a pub.

The landlord says, 'I can't let you in without a Thai.'

▶ Have you heard about the awful pub called The Fiddle? It really was a vile inn.

▶ What's the best thing for a hangover? Drink loads the night before.

▶ Did you hear about the man who was worried by his solitary drinking? He got a cat.

▶ When should you never drive home from the pub? When you walked there in the first place.

▶ A suave playboy picked up an elegant young lady in a bar and took her back to his apartment. Eager to impress her, he showed her his collected works of art and some rare first editions. He then offered her a drink, asking her whether she would prefer a glass of sherry or port.

'Oh, definitely sherry,' she said. 'Sherry is like the nectar of the gods. Just looking at it in this crystal decanter fills me with anticipation. When the stopper is removed and the beautiful liquid is poured into the glass and I inhale the delicious tangy aroma, I am lifted on the wings of ecstasy. As I taste the magical potion, my whole being glows, it seems like a thousand violins are playing in my ears, and I'm transported into another world. Port, on the other hand, makes me fart.'

▶ Why did God invent alcohol? So that fat women can get laid, too.

▶ Alcohol doesn't make you fat, it makes you lean... against tables, chairs, floors, walls and ugly people.

▶ A drunk staggers into the back of a taxi. He leans towards the driver and says, 'Excuse me, have you got room for a lobster and three bottles of wine on your front seat?'
  'I think so,' says the driver.
  'Good,' replies the drunk and throws up.

▶ A man walked into a bar and said to the barman, 'Beer for me, beer for you and beer for everyone who is in the bar now.' After finishing his beer, the man began to walk out of the bar.
  'Hey,' shouted the barman. 'You haven't paid for the drinks!'
  'Sorry,' said the man, 'I haven't got any money.'
  Furious at being duped, the barman whacked him around the head and threw him out onto the street.
  The same man returned to the same bar the following evening and said to the barman, 'Beer for me, beer for you and beer for everyone who is in the bar now.'
  Thinking that nobody would be crazy enough to pull the same stunt twice, the barman figured that the customer must have the money this time, so he handed out the beers. But as the man finished his drink, he headed for the door.
  'Hey!' yelled the barman. 'You haven't paid again!'
  'Sorry,' said the customer, 'I've got no money.'
  Red with rage, the barman hit the man to the ground and hurled him out onto the street.

The next night, the same man was back in the same bar. He said to the barman, 'Beer for me and beer for everyone who is in the bar now.'

Disgusted, the barman asked, 'What, no beer for me this time?'

'No,' said the man. 'You get violent when you drink.'

▶ My doctor asked me if I drank to excess. I told him I would drink to anything.

▶ You know you're drunk when you've got to swerve a pine tree in the middle of the road, only to realise it was the air freshener hanging from your rear-view mirror.

▶ My wife said that I'll find any excuse to drink. I said, 'Speaking of beer... '

▶ Woke up this morning after a heavy night of drinking to find out that I'd gone bald. Which is strange, because normally I go for brunettes.

▶ It's my mate's birthday today. He doesn't drink, smoke, gamble or cheat on his missus. We've got no idea how to celebrate it.

▶ I knew that I had a drink problem when my piss began to smell of alcohol. I knew that I was an alcoholic when I discovered that it tasted like it, too.

▶ What's made of paper and takes an hour to drink? The family allowance cheque!

▶ You've never been truly drunk until you've had to use a bar stool as a walker to get home.

▶ I went to the doctor today and he said he was worried about how much alcohol I was consuming. He asked me how many units of booze I had consumed this week and, after I told him 21, he told me 28 was the maximum, and that I'm fine after all.
It was a good idea to go and see him on a Monday.

▶ Got on the bus, pissed and stoned out of my mind. An old lady said to me, 'You're going to hell, young man.' So I got off the bus.

▶ A woman walked into a bar and asked for a double entendre. So the bartender gave her one.

▶ I found my girlfriend slumped over Hadrian's Wall with an empty vodka bottle in her hand. I think she might be a borderline alcoholic.

▶ A woman walked into a bar and ordered two shots. She downed the first one, saying, 'This is for the shame.' Then she downed the second one, saying, 'This is for the glory.' Then she ordered two more shots and repeated the shame/glory routine.

She was about to order another two shots when the barman asked her, 'What's all this about shame and glory?'

'You see,' she explained, 'I like to do my housework naked. But last week when I bent over to pick something up, my Great Dane dog mounted me from behind.'

'Ah, right,' said the barman. 'That must be the shame.'

'No,' she said, 'that was the glory. The shame was when we got locked out and he dragged me around the front yard for half an hour.'

▶ My teenage daughter came home after hanging around the park, drinking Diamond White with her friends.

'Dad, I feel sick and the room's spinning,' she slurred.

'Well,' I replied, 'those are just some of the ciderfects.'

▶ A man goes into a bar with an ostrich and a cat. The bartender says, 'What would you like, sir?'

The man says, 'I'll have a pint of beer.' He looks at the ostrich and says, 'What will you have?'

'I'll have a pint of beer,' says the ostrich.

He looks at the cat. 'What will you have?'

'Half a pint of beer but I'm not paying!'

'That will be £12.65,' says the bartender.

So the man reaches into his pocket and pulls out exactly £12.65.

The next day after work the man goes into the same bar. The bartender says, 'What would you like, sir?'

The man says, 'I'll have a pint of beer.' He looks at the ostrich and says, 'What will you have?'

'I'll have a pint of beer,' says the ostrich.

He looks at the cat. 'What will you have?'

'Half a pint of beer but I'm not paying!'

'That will be £12.65,' says the bartender.

So the man reaches into his pocket and pulls out exactly £12.65.

The next day after work the man goes into the same bar. 'What'll it be today?' says the bartender.

'Double whisky on the rocks,' says the man. He looks at the ostrich and says, 'What will you have?'

'I'll join you in a double whisky,' says the ostrich.

He looks at the cat. 'What will you have?'

'Half a pint of beer but I'm not paying!'

'That will be £21.95,' says the bartender.

So the man reaches into his pocket and pulls out exactly £21.95.

The next day after work the man goes into the same bar. 'Excuse me,' the bartender says, 'I was just wondering why, no matter what the price, you always have the exact change in your pocket?'

'Well,' says the man, 'when my grandmother died she left me everything in her house and inside there was a lamp so I rubbed it and out popped a genie. It granted me three wishes so I asked that every time I wanted to buy something I would have the exact change in my pocket.'

'That's brilliant,' says the bartender 'You'll never ever run out of money. What else did you ask for?'

'A bird with long legs and a tight pussy.'

▶ My grandmother is over 80 and still doesn't need glasses. She drinks straight from the bottle.

▶ A popular bar installed a new robotic barman that was programmed to strike up a conversation according to the customer's IQ. So when a man came in for a drink, the robot asked him, 'What's your IQ?' The man replied, '130.' The robot then proceeded to make conversation about nuclear physics, astronomy and advanced maths. The customer was impressed.

Then another man came in for a drink and the robot asked him, 'What's your IQ?' The man responded, '120.' So the robot started talking about football, cycling and cricket. The customer thought it was really cool.

Then a third man came into the bar and, as before, the robot asked him, 'What's your IQ?' The man replied, '80.' The robot said, 'So, how are things in Essex these days?'

▶ Fred started chatting up a good-looking girl in a bar. Seeing that she didn't back off, he asked her name. 'Carmen,' she replied.

'That's a nice name,' he said. 'Who named you, your mother?'

'No, as a matter of fact, I named myself,' she replied.

'That's interesting. Why Carmen?'

'Because I like cars, and I like men.' Looking him directly in the eyes, she asked, 'What's your name?'

'Beerfuck,' he quickly replied.

DRUGS

▶ What's the difference between a hooker and a drug dealer? A hooker can wash her crack and sell it again.

▶ A Rastafarian walks into a bank and hands the cashier a bag full of marijuana.

'Sir, what's this for?' says the surprised lady.

The Rasta replies, 'Me come to open a joint account.'

▶ The long-term implications of modern drugs must be fully considered. Because over the past few years, more money has been spent on breast implants and Viagra than is spent on Alzheimer's disease research, it is believed that by the year 2030 there will be a large number of people wandering around with huge breasts and erections who can't remember what to do with them.

▶ I was talking to my dad yesterday. He's getting a little older and complaining about joint pain.

I said. 'Is it your hip?'

He said, 'No, I burned my lip smoking pot.'

▶ Why are roach clips called roach clips? Because 'pot holder' was already taken.

▶ A teenager comes in and asks, 'Gran, have you seen my pills – they were labelled LSD?'

His granny replies, 'Forget that. Have you seen the dragon in the kitchen?'

▶ What do you do if your drug test comes back negative? Change your dealer.

▶ What do you get if you add one eighth to one quarter? Stoned.

▶ My younger brother's an example of what can happen to people who get involved with drugs. A Porsche and his own house by the age of 20.

▶ Why do junkies steal? Just for the crack.

▶ What do you get if you cross an LSD tablet with a contraceptive pill? A trip without the kids.

▶ I was shocked and disappointed to learn that my son has been experimenting with drugs. I honestly don't care what pH it is, cocaine is too expensive to waste on litmus paper.

▶ Ketamine – just say neigh.

▶ Ketamine – only fools and horses.

▶ What should you do for stiff joints? Roll them thinner.

▶ Did you hear about the junkie Christmas tree? It comes with its own pot but it leaves needles everywhere.

DWARVES

▶ What does a dwarf get if he runs through a woman's legs? A clit around the ear and a flap across the face.

▶ Every day at work a man sidled up to a woman and, taking a deep breath in, told her her hair smelled nice. After a week of this, the woman could take no more and reported him for sexual harassment.

The boss was mystified. 'What's wrong with someone telling you your hair smells nice?' he said.

The woman replied, 'He's a midget.'

▶ Why do dwarves laugh when they run? Because the grass tickles their balls!

▶ Make little things count: teach arithmetic to dwarves.

▶ A dwarf sidles up to a tall blonde and says, 'Hey, what do you say to a little fuck?'

She says, 'Hello, you Little Fuck.'

▶ A chap was in the toilet having a piss when he noticed a dwarf to his left. This dwarf's head was shaking quite badly, so the fellow asked him what the problem was. The dwarf replied that he was with the circus and for years he had been a human cannonball, and this head shaking was the result of years being fired out of a cannon.

As the dwarf left the toilet, the chap noticed another dwarf standing to his right. He, too, had a shaking head, so naturally the chap asked him if he was with the circus as well.

'No!' shouted the dwarf. 'When you were busy talking to that other bloke, you were pissing in my ear!'

DYSLEXIA

▶ Did you hear about the dyslexic pimp? He bought a warehouse!

▶ Dyslexics of the world – untie!

▶ Two dyslexics were chatting on the Tube.
   'Can you smell gas?' the first chap asked
   'I can't even smell my own name,' was the reply.

▶ Dyslexia means never having to say that you're yrros.

▶ Old MacDonald was dyslexic... K,Y, J, E, O.

▶ What is the motto of the dyslexic bestiality society? In dog we thrust.

▶ Two dyslexic bank robbers walk into a bank, shouting, 'Air in the hands, motherstickers, this is a fuckup!'

▶ Spoke to a mate today, said he had some bad news from the doctor – the big C!

'Bloody hell, mate, cancer?' I asked.

'No,' he said. 'Dyslexia.'

▶ I'm sick of these people who keep making jokes about dyslexia. It's not big and it's not furry.

▶ A G N B: That's bang out of order.

EGO

▶ Three words to ruin a man's ego: 'Is it in?'

EINSTEIN

▶ What's the most intelligent thing that has ever slipped out of a woman's mouth? Albert Einstein's cock!

ELEPHANTS

▶ A bloke walks into a bar with an elephant. 'This elephant will do anything,' he announces proudly.

'All right,' says the barman. 'Make it stand on one leg.'

So the bloke lifts the elephant's ear up and whispers something to the elephant. Moments later the great grey beast lifts itself up onto its hind legs, then carefully balances itself up on one leg. The crowd in the bar go wild with enthusiastic cheering.

'Very clever,' says the barman. 'Now let's see it fuck my cat.' And so saying, he plonks the genial bar cat onto the bar.

The bloke with the elephant thinks a moment, then takes the cat and places it on the floor in front of the elephant (who is still poised Bolshoi-like on one leg). He gets up on tiptoe and whispers something in the elephant's ear. As silence descends on the drinkers in the bar, the man steps back and the elephant teeters over and comes crashing down, splattering Tiddles across the floor.

'There you go,' says the bloke. 'That's fucked it.'

▶ Two old ladies go to the zoo and see an angry male elephant with a huge erection. The elephant is rampaging round the enclosure.

One of the old ladies says, 'Gracious, d'you think he'll charge?'

The other old lady looks at the erection and says, 'Well, yes – I think he'd be entitled to!'

▶ What do you get when you cross an elephant with a poodle? A dead poodle with an 18-inch arsehole.

▶ What's big, grey and doesn't matter? An irr-elephant.

▶ An elephant asked a camel, 'Why are your breasts on your back?'

'Well,' said the camel, 'I think that's quite an inappropriate question from someone whose dick is on his face.'

▶ An elephant and a monkey are sitting by a river chatting, when a turtle crawls out and quick as a flash the elephant stamps on it, squashing it flat.

'What the hell was that about?' shouts the monkey.

'That turtle,' replies the elephant 'bit my trunk 20 years ago. I'd know him anywhere.'

The monkey looks amazed and says, 'Whoa, turtle recall.'

▶ A young woman goes out drinking one night, something that she normally doesn't do, and she gets really plastered. The next morning she rolls over and discovers there is an elephant in bed with her.

She looks at the elephant and says, 'Oh no, I must have been really tight last night!'

The elephant looks at her and waves his trunk a little and says, 'Only the first time.'

▶ What should you do if an elephant comes in your window? Learn to swim.

▶ A female elephant was walking through the jungle one day, when she got a thorn in her foot. The further she walked, the more it hurt, until eventually she began to limp. After a while, an ant came over to her and asked, 'What's the matter?'

The elephant replied, 'I've got this thorn in my foot, and I would do anything to get it out.'

The ant said, 'Anything? Would you let me butt-fuck you?'

The elephant thought about it for a minute and decided, 'What the hell. How bad could an ant be?' So she agreed. The ant started pulling on the thorn and soon got it out. True to her word, the elephant lay down on her side and moved her tail out of the way. The ant crawled up on her and started getting to work. This unlikely scene was watched from the top of a tree by a monkey who laughed so much that he accidentally knocked a coconut out of the tree. The coconut crashed down on the elephant's head, right between her ears. 'Aaaaargh!' moaned the elephant in pain.

The ant yelled, 'Take it all, bitch, take it all!'

▶ A man went to the doctor and said, 'I've got a huge hole in my arse.'

The doctor said, 'Drop your pants, bend over and I'll take a look.' The man did as requested and the doctor examined him. 'My God!' exclaimed the doctor. 'What on earth could have made a hole as big as that?'

The patient replied, 'I've been fucked by an elephant!'

The doctor said, 'But an elephant's penis is long and thin, this hole is enormous.'

'Yes,' said the patient, 'but he fingered me first.'

▶ A man in a bar started playing the piano and an elephant drinking in the corner burst into tears. The man asked, 'Do you recognise the tune?'

'I recognise the ivory,' replied the elephant.

▶ A jeweller called the police station to report a robbery.

'You'll never believe what happened, Sergeant. A truck backed up to my store, the doors opened and an elephant came out. He broke my plate-glass window, stuck his trunk in, sucked up all the jewellery and climbed back into the truck. The doors closed and the truck pulled away.'

The desk sergeant said, 'Can you tell me, for identification purposes, whether it was an Indian elephant or an African elephant?'

'What's the difference?' asked the jeweller.

'Well,' said the sergeant, 'an African elephant has great big ears and an Indian elephant has little ears.'

'Come to think of it, I couldn't see his ears,' said the jeweller. 'He had a stocking over his head.'

ERECTIONS

▶ Bone of contention: a hard-on that causes an argument. E.g., one that arises when a man is watching Olympic beach volleyball on TV with his girlfriend.

▶ An army colonel was reviewing the troops. One man he passed sported an enormous erection.

'Sergeant!' the colonel shouted. 'Give this man 30 days' compassionate home leave.'

'Yes, sir,' the sergeant replied.

A few months later the same thing occurred with the same man. 'Sergeant! Give this man another 30 days' compassionate home leave,' the colonel barked.

A few months later, same guy, same problem. The colonel was angry.

'Sergeant! Haven't we given this man two compassionate home leaves?'

'Yes, sir,' the sergeant replied.

'Then what's his problem?' the colonel asked.

The sergeant saluted and said, 'Sir, it's you he's fond of.'

▶ This bloke goes into see his doctor and says, 'Every time I see a lorry, I get an erection.'

The doc laughs and says, 'Impossible.'

So the bloke stands up and walks over to the window and, after a lorry passes by, he pulls his trousers down to reveal a huge hard-on.

The doctor says, 'This defies medical science, but give me a sample of blood, then come back in three weeks and I'll have a result.'

Three weeks pass by and the bloke returns to the doctor. On entering his office, the doctor says, 'Sit down, I have some bad news for you.'

The bloke slumps into a chair and says, 'What is it, Doc?'

The doctor explains, 'You're HGV positive.'

▶ What's stiff and excites women? Elvis Presley.

▶ The young Swedish au pair had been working for the Schmitts for more than a year. While hard-working and efficient, she still struggled with English.

One day she told Mrs Schmitt that she had received good news from her boyfriend Sven. 'He is coming visit me from army next week!'

'That's wonderful,' Mrs Schmitt replied. 'How long is his furlough?'

'Oh,' the young woman said, 'about long as Mr Schmitt's. Maybe little thicker.'

▶ A man had to go to the doctor to get a lump on one of his testicles checked out.

As the doctor was fondling his balls, he suddenly stopped and said, 'Don't worry, it's perfectly normal to get an erection.'

'WHAT?! I don't have an erection,' said the man.

He replied, 'No, I know you don't, I was talking about me!'

ESKIMOS

▶ How do Eskimos stop their mouths from freezing up? They grit their teeth.

▶ Two Eskimos sitting in a kayak were getting chilly. They lit a fire in the craft and it sank, proving that you can't have your kayak and heat it, too.

▶ What do Eskimos get from sitting on the ice too long? Polaroids.

▶ Why did it take Bill six months to sing *Night and Day*? Bill is an Eskimo.

ESSEX GIRLS

▶ How do you make an Essex girl's eyes sparkle? Shine a torch into her ear.

▶ Did you hear about the big power cut at the Bluewater Centre? Forty Essex girls were stuck on the escalator for three hours.

▶ What is the difference between an Essex girl and a Creme Egg? It costs 40 pence to lick out a Creme Egg!

▶ How do you know when an Essex girl has an orgasm? She drops her chips.

▶ What's the difference between an Essex girl and an ironing board? Occasionally you have trouble getting the legs apart on an ironing board.

▶ What does an Essex girl say after her doctor tells her that she's pregnant. 'Is it mine?'

▶ What does it mean if you see an Essex girl with square boobs? She forgot to take the Kleenex out of the box.

How do you plant dope? Bury an Essex girl.

How do you make an Essex girl laugh on a Saturday? Tell her a joke on a Wednesday.

What is the difference between a supermarket trolley and an Essex girl? A supermarket trolley has a mind of its own.

What does an Essex girl do with her arse after sex? She takes him down the pub.

What's the similarity between an Essex girl and a dog turd? The older they get, the easier they are to pick up.

What's the difference between an Essex girl and the Panama Canal? One's a busy ditch.

Why do Essex girls write 'TGIF' on their shoes? Toes Go in First.

What's the mating call of an Essex girl? 'I'm so drunk!'

What do you call an Essex girl with half a brain? Gifted.

How is an Essex girl like a beer bottle? They are both empty from the neck up.

What's an Essex girl's favourite wine? 'Awwww, why can't I go Bluewater?'

▶ What's the difference between an Essex girl and a Porsche? You don't lend the Porsche out to your friends.

▶ Why do Essex girls wash their hair in the sink? Because that's where you wash vegetables.

▶ How do you pull an Essex girl? By her earrings!

▶ What do you see when you peer into an Essex girl's eyes? The back of her head.

▶ How do you confuse an Essex girl? You don't; they're born that way.

▶ Did you hear about the Essex lesbian? She kept having affairs with men.

▶ What did the Essex girl say when asked, 'Ever been picked up by the fuzz?' 'No, but I've been swung around by the tits.'

▶ What do you call 15 Essex girls in a circle? A dope ring.

▶ Why did the Essex girl drown in the pool? Someone stuck a 'scratch & sniff' sample at the bottom.

▶ Why do Essex 18-year-olds take sex education courses? So they can learn what they've been doing wrong for the past five years.

▶ What do you call a fly buzzing inside an Essex girl's head? A Space Invader.

▶ Why did God create Essex girls? Because sheep can't bring beer from the fridge.

▶ How can you tell if an Essex girl has been using a computer? There's a note in the disk drive and a condom on the joystick.

▶ What goes blonde, brunette, blonde, brunette? An Essex girl doing naked cartwheels.

▶ How do you stop an Essex girl getting pregnant? Cut her brother's bollocks off.

▶ What designer label does an Essex girl have in her knickers? Next.

▶ What does an Essex girl use for protection during sex? A bus shelter.

▶ What does an Essex girl say after sex? 'Do you all play for the same team?'

▶ An Essex girl goes to the council to register for child benefit.
   'How many children?' asks the council worker.
   'Ten,' replies the Essex girl.
   'Ten?' says the council worker. 'What are their names?'
   'Wayne, Wayne, Wayne, Wayne, Wayne, Wayne, Wayne, Wayne, Wayne and Wayne'.
   'Doesn't that get confusing?'
   'Naah... ' says the Essex girl. 'It's great because if they are out playing in the street I just have to shout, "Waayne, yer dinner's ready!" or "Waayne, go to bed now!" and they all do it.'

'What if you want to speak to one individually?' says the perturbed council worker.

'That's easy,' says the Essex girl. 'I just use their surnames.'

ETHICAL GUIDE FOR MEN

▶ Under no circumstances may two men share an umbrella.

▶ If you've known a guy for more than 24 hours, his sister is off limits forever. Unless you actually marry her.

▶ When questioned by a friend's girlfriend, you need not and should not provide any information as to his whereabouts. You may even deny his very existence.

▶ Unless he murdered someone in your immediate family, you must bail a friend out of jail within 24 hours.

▶ You may exaggerate any anecdote told to your friends by 50 per cent without recrimination. Beyond that, anyone within earshot is allowed to yell out, 'Bullshit!' (Exception: when trying to pick up a girl, the allowable exaggeration is 400 per cent.)

▶ The minimum amount of time you have to wait for another man is five minutes. The maximum is six minutes. For a girl, you are required to wait ten minutes for every point of hotness she scores on the internationally accepted 1–10 scale.

▶ Bitching about the brand of free beer in your friend's refrigerator is forbidden. But gripe at will if the temperature is not correct.

▶ A friend must be permitted to borrow anything you own – grill, car, first-born child – within a 12-hour notice. Women or anything considered 'lucky' are not applicable in this case.

▶ Falling on a grenade for a buddy (agreeing to distract the skanky friend of the hot babe he's trying to score) is your legal duty. But should you get carried away with your good deed and end up getting on the beast, your pal is forbidden to ever speak of it.

▶ On a road trip, the strongest bladder determines pit stops, not the weakest.

▶ Before dating a buddy's ex, you are required to ask his permission. He must grant it. He is, however, obliged to say, 'Man, you're gonna love the way she licks your balls.'

▶ Women who claim they 'love to watch sports' must be treated as spies until they demonstrate knowledge of the game and the ability to eat a large doner.

▶ If a man's zip is down, that's his problem – you didn't see anything!

▶ No man shall ever be required to buy a birthday present for another man.

▶ You must offer heartfelt condolences over the death of a girlfriend's cat, even if it was you who secretly set it on fire and threw it into a ceiling fan.

▶ While your girlfriend must bond with your buddies' girlfriends within 30 minutes of meeting them, you are not required to make friends with her gal pals' boyfriends – low-level sports bonding is all the law requires.

▶ Unless you have a lucrative endorsement contract, do not appear in public wearing more than one Nike swoosh.

▶ When stumbling upon other guys watching a sporting event, you may always ask the score of the game in progress, but you may never ask who's playing.

▶ If your girlfriend asks to set your friend up with her ugly, whiny, loser friend, you must grant permission, but only if you have ample time to warn your friend to prepare his excuse about joining the priesthood.

▶ Unless you're in prison, never fight naked. This includes men who aren't wearing shirts.

▶ Friends don't let friends wear Speedos. Ever. Case closed.

▶ When picking players for sports teams, it is permissible to skip over your buddy in favour of better athletes – as long as you don't let him be the last sorry son of a bitch standing on the sideline.

▶ If you ever compliment a guy's six pack, you better be talking about his choice of beverage.

▶ Never join your girlfriend in ragging on a buddy of yours, unless she is withholding sex, pending your response.

▶ Never hesitate to reach for the last beverage or pizza, but not both. That's just mean.

▶ Never talk to another man in the bathroom unless you are on equal footing: both urinating. Both waiting in line for all other situations, an 'I recognise you' nod will do just fine.

▶ Never allow a telephone conversation with a woman to go on longer than you are able to have sex with her. Keep a stopwatch nearby, hang up if necessary.

▶ You cannot rat out a friend who shows up to work with a massive hangover; however, you may hide the aspirin, smear his chair with cheese, turn the brightness on his computer way up so he thinks it's broken or have him paged every seven minutes.

▶ If you catch your girl messing around with your best friend, let your national 'crime of passion' laws be your guide.

▶ If your buddy is trying to hook up with a girl, you may sabotage him only in a manner that gives you no chance of getting any, either.

▶ Before allowing a drunken friend to cheat on his girl, you must attempt one intervention. If he can get up on his feet, look you in the eye and deliver a 'fuck off', then you are absolved from all responsibility. Later on it is OK that you have no idea what his girlfriend is talking about.

▶ The morning after you and a babe, who was formerly 'just a friend', go at it, the fact that you're feeling weird and guilty is no reason not to jump on her again before there is a discussion about what a big mistake it was.

▶ If a buddy has an eyelash or any other foreign object on his hair or face, under no circumstances are you permitted to remove it. However, an appropriate hand gesture may be made to make him aware of it.

▶ An anniversary is recognised on a yearly basis. Under no circumstances will anything be celebrated in an interval other than a year.

▶ When using a urinal in a public restroom, a buffer zone of at least one urinal will exist at all times. If the only empty urinal is directly next to an occupied one, then you are still required to wait. (Exception: at a sporting event where a line has formed to use even the handbasins.)

▶ When coming to a room which you know is occupied by your friend and possibly a girl, you must knock and wait for an adequate response. If no response occurs, and the door is locked, a ten-minute period is required before knocking again.

▶ No man shall ever watch any of the following programmes on TV:

• Figure skating

• Men's gymnastics

• Any sport involving women (unless viewed for sexual purposes)

▶ If you accidentally touch or brush against any part of another man below the waist, it is an understood accident, and NO apologies or any reference to the occurrence is necessary.

▶ No man shall spend more than two minutes in front of a mirror. If more time is required, a three-minute waiting period must be allowed before returning to the mirror.

▶ Any dispute lasting longer than three minutes will and must be settled by rock, paper, scissors. There is no argument too important for this determining method.

▶ No man will ever willingly watch a movie in which the main theme is dancing, and if a man shall happen to view such a movie, it is only acceptable if it's with a girlfriend.

▶ Only acceptable time when a man is allowed to cry:

• When a heroic dog dies to save his master.

• After being struck in the testicles with anything moving faster than 7 miles per hour.

• When your date is using her teeth.

• The day Keira Knightley chooses a husband.

▶ If a bet is made, and the challenge is completed, then the bettor may recoup his money by immediately completing a more daring challenge. If he refuses the challenge or chooses not to propose one, then and only then must the money be paid.

▶ If a hot girl shall happen to pass by while you are in an arm's reach of your buddy, you will, and must, tap him on the shoulder to make him aware of the babe.

▶ A man's shoes may not intentionally match any other article of clothing on his body.

▶ No comment shall ever be made to a man about how much he is sweating. In fact, there is no need to bring notice to any body part which he may be sweating from.

▶ No man shall ever allow anyone to speak ill of *The Simpsons* or any *Rocky* movie. (Exception: *Rocky V.*)

▶ You have not made any mistake if you find that there are extra pieces after reassembling or assembling an object. In fact, you have just found a way to make that object more efficient.

▶ There is never an occasion in which any shirt without buttons may be tucked in. (Exception: when you are participating in an organised sporting event.)

▶ Any object thrown with reasonable speed and accuracy MUST be caught.

▶ No man shall ever keep track of, or count, the amount of beers he has had in a night. Estimated measures are acceptable the next day, e.g., 'I had at least a gallon.'

▶ Under no circumstances may two non-related men share a bed or anything which can be perceived as a mattress.

▶ In an empty room, car, etc., a man cannot ask another man if he is mad because he isn't talking.

▶ If you jiggle more than twice, you're playing with it.

▶ A man shall never help another man apply suntan oil.

▶ The guy who wants something the most is responsible for getting it.

▶ If your friend says, 'Lick my nuts,' as a way to put you down, don't try to be funny by saying, 'OK,' and moving your head towards his crotch. Two homosexual references in a row are just plain scary...

▶ If you say ouch, you are a pussy.

▶ It is the God-given duty of every man to assist any other man that may be in need of assistance in obtaining every guy's dream (a threesome with two girls).

EXERCISE

▶ How do you get a man to do sit-ups? Put the remote control between his toes.

▶ I've started a new exercise programme. I do 20 sit-ups every morning. That may not sound like a lot, but I can only hit that snooze button so many times!

▶ What's better than seeing a woman wrestle? Seeing her box.

▶ The missus just found out I replaced our bed with a trampoline. She hit the roof.

▶ Two old women are sitting on a bench talking.

One says to the other, 'How's your husband holding up in bed these days?'

The second replies, 'He makes me feel like an exercise bike. Each day he climbs on and starts pumping away, but we never seem to get anywhere.'

EX-WIVES

▶ 'I bought my ex a gift for her birthday but she didn't use it so I'm not going to get her another.'

'What did you get her?'

'A cemetery plot!'

▶ I still miss my ex-wife... but my aim is getting better.

FACTS OF LIFE

▶ A farmer was helping one of his cows to give birth, when he noticed his son watching wide-eyed. 'Oh dear,' thought the farmer, 'I can see I'm going to have to explain the facts of life.' So when he finished, he asked the boy, 'Well, do you have any questions?'

'Just one,' gasped the boy. 'How fast was that calf going when it hit that cow?'

▶ A teenager came home from school and asked her mother, 'Is it true what Olivia just told me, that babies come out of the same place where boys put their thingies?'

'Yes, dear,' replied her mother, pleased that the subject had finally come up and that she wouldn't have to explain it.

The girl looked mystified. 'But then when I have a baby, won't it knock my teeth out?'

FAIRY TALES

What's the difference between a Northern fairy tale and a Southern fairy tale? A Northern fairy tale starts, 'Once upon a time... ' A Southern fairy tale starts, 'Y'all ain't gonna believe this shit.'

What did Cinderella say when she got to the ball? Cough, gag, choke, etc.

What fruit has seven dents? Snow White's cherry.

How do you piss off Winnie the Pooh? By sticking your finger in his honey.

Define 'Egghead': What Mrs Dumpty gives to Humpty.

What's brown and lives in a bell tower? The lunch bag of Notre Dame.

A man walking along comes across a genie shaking a rug. 'What's wrong?' he asks. 'Won't it start?'

A flat-chested woman was delighted when her fairy godmother said her breasts would increase in size each time a man said, 'Pardon' to her.

Walking down the street, the woman accidentally bumped into a man who said, 'Pardon me.' To her delight, her breasts immediately grew an inch. The next day, she bumped into a man in the corner shop, and when he begged her pardon, another inch was added to her breasts. She was in seventh heaven. That evening, she walked into an Indian restaurant, and collided with a waiter, who bowed and said, 'A thousand pardons for my clumsy behaviour.'

The headline in the following morning's paper read: 'Indian waiter crushed to death.'

▶ The seven dwarfs are all excited as the new pope is visiting fairy-story land. All week they nudge Dopey, sniggering, 'Well, you can finally ask your question!', to which Dopey replies every time, 'Shut up!' Finally the day arrives and all the dwarfs are lined up with the other characters from the Snow White story. He shakes hands with the evil queen, then Snow White, then slowly makes his way down the line of dwarfs. As he approaches Dopey, there's a small murmur which gets louder and louder: 'Ask him, ask him... ask him, ASK HIM!'

Ask me what?' questions the pope.

The dwarfs shove Dopey forwards. 'ASK HIM!'

'What would you like to know?' says his holiness.

'Well,' begins Dopey, 'are any of your nuns black?'

'Hmm,' ponders the pope. 'As a religion we Catholics don't differentiate between races so it's more than probable that quite a few of our nuns are black. Does that answer your question?'

'ASK HIM!!' shout the dwarfs.

'Is there more to your question, young man?'

'Erm... do any of your nuns work in Antarctica?'

'Well, young man, we have nuns all around the globe so it's more than likely that we have a couple in Antarctica. Does that answer your question?'

'ASK HIM!!!!!!!!!!!!!!' yell the dwarfs.

'Is there more to this question?' asks the pope, now getting more than annoyed.

'Erm... are any of these black nuns in Antarctica dwarfs?'

'WHAT?!' splutters the pope. 'I'm sure if we had a black dwarf nun in Antarctica, I would have heard of it. So in answer to your question, NO!'

All the dwarfs collapse on the floor pissing themselves laughing. 'DOPEY SHAGGED A PENGUIN! DOPEY SHAGGED A PENGUIN!'

▶ What looks like Blu-tak, feels like Blu-tak, tastes like Blu-tak, but isn't? Blue Smurf poo.

FARTING

▶ Why do men fart more than women? Cos women never shut their mouth for long enough to let the gas build up.

▶ A lady walks into a shop that sells very expensive Persian rugs. She browses around, then spots the perfect rug and walks over to inspect it. As she bends to feel the texture of the rug, she farts loudly. Very embarrassed, she looks around nervously to see if anyone has noticed her little accident and hopes a salesperson does not pop up right now.

As she turns back, there, standing next to her, is a salesman. 'Good day, madam. How may we help you today?'

Very uncomfortably, she asks, 'Sir, what is the price of this lovely rug?'

He answers, 'Madam, if you farted just touching it, you are very likely to shit when you hear the price!'

▶ A woman leaning at the bar said to me, 'I love the strong silent type.'

'You mean a man like me?'

'No, farts. Like the one I've just done!'

FAT BLOKES

▶ The wife's been moaning at me for a while as I've piled on the pounds and developed a spare tyre, so I went along to the doctor and asked if there was anything I can do.

He said, 'It's simple. Don't panic. Just do something a couple of times a week that gets you slightly out of breath.'

So I started smoking again.

▶ As a woman steps out of the shower, her husband grabs one of her breasts and says, 'If you firmed these up a bit, you wouldn't have to keep using your bra.' He laughs and laughs.

The next morning, he again catches her as she finishes her shower and grabs her ass and says, 'If you firmed this up a bit, you wouldn't have to keep using your girdle.' Again he laughs and laughs, while his wife plots her revenge.

The next morning as he steps out of the shower, his wife grabs his penis and says, 'If you firmed THIS up a bit, I wouldn't have to keep using your brother.'

▶ You know you're getting fat when you sit in your bath tub and the water in the toilet rises.

▶ Life is like a box of chocolates. Finished too quickly by the clinically obese.

Doctors tell us there are 7,000,000 overweight people. These, of course, are just round figures.

Britain has some of the most violent teenagers in the world but also the most obese. Which is why when I'm getting chased by a gang of youths, I always like to make sure I run past a Greggs.

I watched *Mission Impossible* tonight. It was the local Weight Watchers club trying to touch their toes.

Before he died, Giant Haystacks went on a course of acupuncture. They never found any of the needles.

FAT GIRLS

What do fat women and mopeds have in common? Both are fun to ride but you don't want your friends to see you on them.

▶ How do you get a fat girl into your bed? Piece of cake.

I shagged a fat chick in an elevator last night. It was wrong on so many levels.

A young woman was having a physical examination and was very embarrassed because of a weight problem. As she removed her last bit of clothing, she blushed. 'I'm so ashamed, Doctor,' she said, 'I guess I let myself go.'

The physician was checking her eyes and ears. 'Don't feel ashamed, miss. You don't look that bad.'

'Do you really think so, Doctor?' she asked.

The doctor held a tongue depressor in front of her face and said, 'Of course. Now just open your mouth and say, "Moo!"'

▶ Queen guitarist Brian May has finally had his doctoral thesis in astrophysics published. Does this mean he can now prove categorically that fat-bottomed girls make the rocking world go round?

▶ A balanced American diet is when every McNugget weighs the same.

▶ Ben & Jerry: the men who complete a fat girl's threesome.

▶ My wife is the double of Kate Moss. Kate is eight stone and my wife is 16 stone.

▶ What's the best way to pick up American girls? Use a crane.

▶ A waiter approached our table and asked us if we enjoyed our meal.
'It was absolutely delicious, I ate every last bit!' said my wife.
'And, sir?' said the waiter. 'How did you find the pork belly?'
'Oh, about six years ago, we met on holiday.'

▶ A guy is shagging his overweight missus, when his phone rings.
'You'll have to phone back, mate,' he says. 'I'm in the tub.'

▶ A woman goes in to see the psychiatrist about her low self-esteem. She is unhealthy, pale and obese. After tearfully explaining her predicament, the doc says, 'Hmm, yes, could you please lie on the floor under the window? Now over next to the door. Now under the bookshelves. Thank you.'

He then occupies himself with writing. The patient, exasperated, interrupts him and asks if he has anything he can offer her. 'No,' he says, 'you need to see your internist about your poor health.'

'Then what was all that stuff you had me do, lying on the floor?'

'Oh, I'm having a new white sofa delivered next week and was wondering where to put it.'

▶ I am a single man (30) seeking a life partner to share my soul with. I am sensitive, caring and have a deeply loving nature. If you wish to give me your heart, I will give you mine and know that, held within your gentle hands, it will be safe forever. No fat chicks.

▶ My wife's been told she'll have to lose weight if she wants to become pregnant. I told her.

▶ I was staring at my girl this morning and I said, 'You know, there are three things I really don't like about you.'

'Oh, what are they?' she asked.

'Your chin.'

▶ My wife applied to go on *How to Look Good Naked*. She got a letter back from Channel 4 saying she wasn't a suitable candidate, but had she considered *Scrapheap Challenge*?

▶ A man is about to have sex with a really fat woman, so he climbs on top of her.

'Can I turn the light off?' he asks.

'Why?' she replies. 'Are you feeling a bit shy?'
'No,' he says, 'it's burning my arse!'

▶ I wouldn't say my wife is fat, but when she walks past the TV, I miss three adverts.

▶ I got my heavy goods licence today. My wife prefers to call it a marriage certificate.

▶ How do you know if a girl is too fat to shag? When you pull her knickers down, her arse is still in them.

▶ My girlfriend asked, 'What can I do to make my bum look smaller?'
So I told her to emigrate to America!

▶ I'm not saying my wife is fat, but she has to put her belt on with a boomerang.

▶ My wife's got a brilliant Halloween costume. She's wearing a leotard and no make-up.

▶ Have you heard about the new lingerie shop for obese women? It's called Thong in Cheek.

▶ Did you hear about the man who shagged five fat girls in one weekend? He was on a massive roll.

▶ My girlfriend is so fat, her arse looks like two pigs fighting over a Malteser.

FATHERHOOD

▶ A girl brings her new boyfriend home and decides to introduce him to her parents. She walks into the living room, only to be confronted by her father leaning over the sofa and banging the side of his head with his fist. In some pain, he tells her that he was throwing peanuts up in the air and catching them in his mouth, but had somehow managed to get one stuck in his ear. Sensing the opportunity to impress his girlfriend's family, the boyfriend sticks two fingers up her father's nose and tells him to blow. He does, and the peanut comes shooting out of his ear, just missing his wife, who is coming into the room.

The girl takes her boyfriend into the kitchen to get a drink, and the man's wife leans over and whispers to him, 'Who is that young man?'

'By the smell of his fingers, I'd say he was our son-in-law-to-be,' he replies.

▶ *Ten things you'll never hear a dad say:*

- 'Well, how about that? I'm lost! Looks like we'll have to stop and ask for directions.'

- 'You know, Pumpkin, now that you're 13, you'll be ready for dates. Won't that be fun?'

- 'I noticed that all your friends have a certain hostile attitude. I like that.'

- 'Here's a credit card and the keys to my car. Have some fun!'

- 'What do you mean you want to play football? Ballet's not good enough for you, son?'

- 'Your mother and I are going away for the weekend. You might want to consider throwing a party.'

- 'Well, I don't know what's wrong with your car. Probably one of those thingy-me-bobs, you know, that makes it run or something. Just have it towed to a mechanic and pay whatever he asks.'

- 'No son of mine is going to live under this roof without an earring. Now quit moaning, and let's go to the jewellers.'

- 'What did you get a job for? I make plenty of money for you to spend. Here's £100.'

- 'What do I want for Father's Day? Aahh – don't worry about that. It's no big deal.'

▶ An old man is sitting on a bus, when a punk rocker gets on. The punk rocker's hair is red, green, yellow and orange. He has feather earrings.

When he sees the old man staring at him, the punk rocker says, 'What's the matter, old man? Didn't you ever do anything wild when you were a young man?'

The old man replies, 'Yeah. Years ago I shagged a parrot. I thought maybe you were my son.'

▶ *The difference between fathers of today and yesterday:*

- In 1900, a father waited for the doctor to tell him when the baby arrived. Today, a father must wear a smock, know how to breathe and make sure film is in the video camera.

- In 1900, fathers passed on clothing to their sons. Today, kids wouldn't touch Dad's clothes if they were sliding naked down an icicle.

- In 1900, fathers could count on children to join the family business. Today, fathers pray their kids will soon come home from university long enough to teach them how to work the computer and set up the DVD recorder.

- In 1900, a father smoked a pipe. If he tries that today, he gets sent outside after a lecture on lip cancer.

- In 1900, a father came home from work to find his wife and children at the supper table. Today, a father comes home to a note, 'Oscar's at football, Olivia's at gymnastics, I'm at aerobics, pizza in fridge.'

- In 1900, fathers and sons would have heart-to-heart conversations while fishing in a stream. Today, fathers pluck the headphones off their sons' ears and shout, 'WHEN YOU HAVE A MINUTE... '

- In 1900, a father gave a pencil box for Christmas, and the kid was all smiles. Today, a father spends £500 at Toys 'R' Us, and the kid screams, 'I wanted an Xbox!'

- In 1900, a happy meal was when Father shared funny stories around the table. Today, a Happy Meal is what Dad buys at McDonald's.

- In 1900, when fathers entered the room, children stood to attention. Today, kids glance up and grunt, 'Dad, you're in the way of the TV.'

- In 1900, fathers threatened their daughters' boyfriends with shotguns if the girl came home late.

Today, fathers break the ice by saying, 'So... how long have you had that earring?'

FEMINISM

▶ What do you say to a feminist with no arms and no legs?
Option A: 'NICE TITS!'
Option B: 'How are you going to do the dishes?'

▶ Two men were talking. 'My son asked me what I did during the Sexual Revolution,' said one. 'I told him I was captured early and spent the duration doing the dishes.'

▶ Why did God invent lesbians? So feminists wouldn't breed.

▶ How many feminists does it take to change a lightbulb? Trick question – feminists can't change anything!

▶ I don't know what feminists are going on about when they say television never shows any positive, dynamic female role models. I mean, what was Lassie all about?

FIANCÉES

▶ A man was extolling the virtues of his glamorous fiancée. One of his friends said, 'You can't be serious about marrying her. She's been with every man in Leeds.'
The man thought before replying, 'Leeds isn't such a big city... '

FIRE

▶ A hillbilly farmer from back in the hills walked 12 miles, one way, to the general store.

'Heya, Wilbur,' said Ron, the store owner. 'Tell me, are you and Myrtle still making fires up there by rubbing stones and flint together?'

'You betcha, Ron. Ain't no other way. Why?'

'Got something to show you. Something to make fire. It's called a match.'

'Match? Never heard of it.'

'Watch this. If you want a fire, you just do this,' Ron said, taking a match and striking it on his trousers.

'Huh. Well, that's something, but that ain't for me, Ron.'

'Well, why not?'

'I can't be walking 12 miles every time I want a fire to borrow your trousers.'

▶ A woman phones the fire brigade. 'Help me! My house in on fire!'

'Tell me your address and we'll be there as soon as possible,' replies the operator.

'I can't tell you that, I'm too confused to think straight,' complains the woman.

'Then how do you expect us to get there?' replies the operator.

'What do you mean?' says the woman. 'Don't you have those big red trucks?'

▶ Did you hear about the two Mexican firefighting brothers? They were called Hose A and Hose B.

▶ My dad used to say, 'Always fight fire with fire.' Which is probably why he got thrown out of the fire brigade.

▶ Ted bought himself a new smoke alarm. He stuck it on the ceiling, then read the instructions: 'Now test your alarm is working properly.' So he set fire to his sofa.

FIRST AID

▶ Michael Jackson was found lying unconscious by two ambulance men.
Paramedic 1: 'His heart has stopped.'
Paramedic 2: 'Just beat it, beat it!'

▶ *First aid for non-medically minded people:*

- ELECTROCUTION
Is he/she still connected to the power supply? If so, SWITCH OFF THE POWER IMMEDIATELY. Electricity costs an absolute fortune, and it would be going to waste. Check the victim's pulse (if you can find their wrist amongst the stack of charred bones and greasy, bubbling flesh that was once a human being). And do try not to be squeamish about it. Drive the victim to the nearest accident and emergency. You can use him/her to jump start the engine as well, if need be.

- TREATING BURNS AND SCALDS
Run the affected area under cold tap water as soon as possible (if the victim's entire body is a swirling mass of flames, it may a little too late for this). If the victim has spilled hot liquid over his/her clothes, then REMOVE CLOTHING IMMEDIATELY. You can never tell, the sight of you

parading around naked may cheer them up and take their mind off their injury. Remind the victim that worse things happen at sea. Cite drowning as an example.

- FRACTURES AND BROKEN LIMBS
  Check the injured area to see if the break or fracture has resulted in a tubular shard of shearing white bone jutting outwards through the bloody mass of flesh. If it has, then tell the victim that they are going to die. That always perks them up. Tie a splint to the victim's leg and ask them to walk back and forth for a few minutes. They will probably fall down nconscious, making the rest of your job easier. Do not move the broken or fractured limb, as this may result in an abnormal position. However, if you're feeling daring, try pointing legs in the wrong direction, bending wrists through 180 degrees, etc. It really is amazing the number of fascinating contortions that can be achieved. Far better than Play-Doh.

- CHOKING ON FOOD
  Try to dislodge the article blocking the victim's windpipe by punching them hard in the stomach. Do remember to duck before the particles of food hit you in the eye, however. Call the waiter and ask for a 20 per cent reduction on the bill. Make a mental note to order soup next time.

- OBJECTS STUCK IN VICTIM'S EYE
  Rinse the victim's eye in lukewarm water. DO NOT USE SOAP AS WELL. Offer to pick the object out of the victim's eye with your teeth. This usually results in the object mysteriously 'going away' and not bothering the victim anymore before you can get to it.

- CONCUSSION
  When the victim comes around, ask them what day it is, who the president of the USA is, how many fingers you are holding up. To make

it more difficult, hold the fingers up behind your back. Talk in Swahili to disorient the victim a bit more. Switch off all the lights. When he/she regains consciousness, shout, 'Thank God! We thought you might be dead, or blinded or something.'

FISHING

▶ Three guys are fishing, when Fred gets up to get a beer, loses his balance and falls out of the boat.

Ed says, 'What should we do?'

Bill says, 'You better jump in after him, he's been underwater for a while, he might need some help.'

So Ed jumps in, and after some time, he surfaces. He says, 'Help me get him in the boat.'

They wrestle Fred back into the boat. Ed says, 'What do we do now? It doesn't look like he's breathing.'

Bill says, 'Give him mouth to mouth.'

Ed starts to blow air into Fred's mouth and says, 'Whoa, I don't remember Fred having such bad breath.'

Bill says, 'Come to think of it, I don't think Fred was wearing a rotting snowmobile suit, either.'

▶ Did you hear about the girl who went on a fishing trip with six guys? She came back with a red snapper.

▶ Mike and Bill are old fishing buddies who haven't seen each other in years. They grew up together in the old neighbourhood and went fishing every chance they could.

Deciding it was finally time to catch up with each other, the two friends embarked on a fishing trip and began talking about what was going on in their lives.

'Hey, Bill,' Mike says. 'Remember Ellen Banks?'

Bill smiles. 'You mean Easy Ellen? You mean Every Input Ellen? Yeah. I remember her all right! Didn't she have sex with the entire football team?'

'Yep. That's her,' Mike replies.

'Well, what about her?'

Mike smiles as he unpacks his fishing gear. 'I married her,' he says proudly.

Feeling embarrassed, Bill tries to make up for insulting his friend's wife.

'Boy... I guess you must have a pretty great sex life with that Ellen!' he says uneasily.

Mike sighs and says, 'Well, not really. Her pussy is covered with sores and lesions and it's really dirty. I actually can't have sex with her at all.'

'Well, Ellen had some great tits! I bet at least those keep you happy!'

Mike shakes his head no. 'Her breasts are covered with scabs and they really can't be touched.'

'But Ellen was known for giving great blowjobs! Those must get you through the night.'

Mike shrugs his shoulders. 'Nope. She can't do that, either, anymore. Her mouth is riddled with herpes and mucus. I'm not even supposed to kiss her.'

Bill looks over at his friend, perplexed. 'So if you can't fuck her, suck her tits, get a blowjob or even kiss her... why did you marry her?'

Casting his fishing line out into the water, Mike grins at his friend and says, 'She shits the best worms!'

▶ A man is ice-fishing on a frozen lake and not having much luck. A small boy comes along, bores a hole in the ice a short distance away and starts fishing himself. After a few minutes the boy catches a huge fish. A few minutes later another large fish is caught, then another, then another. The man is mystified and, after the boy has caught his fifth fish, he goes over to investigate.

'Hey, son,' says the man. 'What's your secret?'

The boy replies, 'Yu haf tu kip yr wrms wrm.'

'What was that?' says the man.

The boy spits into a bucket. 'I said, "You have to keep your worms warm."'

▶ What can you do in radiation-contaminated rivers? Nuclear fission.

▶ A man walks into a fishmongers carrying a salmon under his arm.

'Do you make fishcakes?' he asks.

'Of course,' says the fishmonger.

'Oh good,' says the man. 'It's his birthday.'

FOOD

▶ What do horny women order at Subway? Footlongs.

▶ There once was a man who was half-French and half-pygmy. He was very sad. He was a fantastic cook, but he couldn't reach the grill.

▶ What's the biggest fish in the world? A hore. If you catch one, you can eat her for months.

▶ Two bachelors are talking about cooking. 'I got a cookbook once,' says one. 'But I could never do anything with it.'

'Were the recipes too hard?' asks the other.

'No,' he replies. 'But each of the recipes began the same way – take a clean dish... '

▶ Two little potatoes are standing on the street corner. One is a prostitute. How can you tell which one is the prostitute? It's the one with the little sticker that says, 'I-DA-HO'.

▶ How does an Englishman get his apples down? He uses a Pole.

▶ What do you call two rows of cabbages? A dual-cabbage way.

▶ I got a herb belt for Christmas. Complete waist of thyme.

▶ I had a stroke of luck on the stock exchange yesterday. I managed to swap three Oxo cubes for a jar of Bovril.

▶ Koreans have recently brought out their own vegetarian version of an instant noodle snack. It's called Not Poodle.

▶ I went for some fish and chips the other day. I took them back and said, 'Are you sure this fish is cooked?'

The bloke said, 'Yes, why?'

I said, 'Because it's eaten all the bloody chips!'

▶ All this talk of dangerous, genetically modified food tasting horrible is nonsense. I mean, just today I had a delicious leg of salmon.

▶ Whenever I eat out at McDonald's, I like to have a Happy Meal. So I leave the wife and kids at home.

▶ What's the Hiroshima breakfast? A giant mushroom with burned soldiers.

▶ Tea is for mugs.

▶ *20 reasons why chocolate is better than sex:*

• You can always get chocolate.

• With chocolate, size doesn't matter; it's always good.

• Chocolate satisfies, even when it has gone soft.

• You can safely have chocolate while you are driving.

• You can make chocolate last as long as you want it to.

• You can have chocolate, even in front of your mother.

• If you bite the nuts too hard, the chocolate won't mind.

• Two people of the same sex can have chocolate without being called nasty names.

• The word 'commitment' doesn't scare off chocolate.

• You can have chocolate on top of your desk without upsetting your workmates.

• You can ask a stranger for chocolate without fear of getting into trouble.

• You don't get hairs in your mouth with chocolate.

- With chocolate, there's no need to fake it.

- Chocolate doesn't make you pregnant.

- You can have chocolate at any time of the month.

- Good chocolate is easy to find.

- You can have as many kinds of chocolate as you can handle.

- You are never too young or too old for chocolate.

- When you have chocolate, it does not keep your neighbours awake.

- 'If you love me, you'll swallow that' has real meaning with chocolate.

▶ My mate asked if I wanted to join his religious sect where they worship a probiotic drink. I said, 'I'm not interested in Yakult.'

▶ I ate horse meat last night. It tasted all right, but it gave me the trots.

▶ I have just had a bitter row with the missus. She thinks Tetley's is better than Boddingtons.

▶ I went for an Indian last night. The waiter came over and said, 'Curry OK?'
  I said, 'Go on, then – one song, then you can bugger off.'

▶ I accidentally left the fridge door open and all the food went off. My wife was furious. 'What am I supposed to do with all this food?'
  I said, 'Look, love, don't make a meal out of it.'

▶ What do you do if a cat spits at you? Turn the grill down.

▶ I ate 20 yoghurts in a row last night. I was Mullered.

▶ On a traffic light green means go and yellow means yield, but on a banana it's just the opposite. Green means hold on, yellow means go ahead and red means where the fuck did you get that banana?

▶ A man goes to a local business adviser to seek advice on starting up a business in a different country. 'I'd like to open up a cheese shop in Holland.'

The adviser replies, 'That's not such a good idea. There are too many cheese shops in Holland.'

The man goes back six months later. 'You were quite right about Holland.'

'What have you decided to do, then?' asks the adviser.

'I'm going to open a cheese shop in Israel.'

'Good choice. What are you going to call it?'

'Cheeses of Nazareth!'

▶ We are so poor, my wife's having Ordinary K for breakfast.

▶ Did you hear about the Chinese magician who did magic with chocolate? He had loads of Twix up his sleeve.

▶ A man goes into a greasy spoon restaurant and orders a bowl of chicken noodle soup. 'What's this?!' he screams. 'There's a pussy hair in my soup! I'm not payin' for it!' and he storms out.

The waitress gets very upset at this and follows him out and sees him go to the whorehouse across the street. He pays the madam and retires to a room with a lovely blonde and goes down on her with gusto. The waitress bursts in and yells, 'You complain about a hair in your soup and then come over here and do THIS?!'

He lifts his head, turns to her and says, 'Yeah! And if I find a noodle in here, I ain't payin' for it, EITHER!'

FOOTBALL

▶ Latest football scores from Spain. Real Madrid, one, Surreal Madrid, fish.

▶ 'BBC study finds ADHD genetic link.' I was talking to my dad about this, and we both came to the conclusion that Chelsea will win the league.

▶ What's the difference between Gary Glitter and football? Your wife will probably let you take her up the football.

▶ The president of Fifa, Sepp Blatter, has come under more criticism about goal-line technology, this time from his wife.

She said, 'It doesn't surprise me – I've been asking him for years whether it was in or not.'

▶ Fabio Capello was wheeling his shopping trolley across the supermarket car park, when he noticed an old lady struggling with her bags of shopping. He stopped and asked, 'Can you manage, dear?'

To which the old lady replied, 'No way. You got yourself into this mess – don't ask me to sort it out!'

▶ What do you call an Englishman in the knockout stages of the World Cup? A referee.

▶ Why doesn't Pakistan have an international football team? Because each time they get a corner, they open a shop.

▶ A tourist is in North London one Saturday and he decides he would very much like to go to a football match, so he asks a man in the street if there are any local matches being played that afternoon.

'Well,' replies the man, 'the Arsenal ground is very close but they're playing away today. If you feel you really must see a match, the Tottenham ground is not that far away. You go straight down this road and you'll see two queues, a big queue and a small queue. You should go to the small queue because the big one is for the fish and chip shop.'

FOREPLAY

▶ What is the Australian for foreplay? 'Brace yourself, Sheila.'

▶ A man was on a date with the easiest girl in town. After they parked the car, she wasted no time in climbing into the back and encouraging him to put his hand inside her knickers. The petting grew heavier and she began moaning in pleasure until she suddenly cried, 'Ow, that ring is hurting me!'

He replied, 'That's no ring – that's my watch!'

▶ A married couple were lying in bed at night. The wife had settled down ready to go to sleep, but the husband was reading a book by the light of his bedside lamp. As he was reading, he paused momentarily, reached over to his wife and started fondling her pussy before resuming reading his book. Aroused by his touch, she got out of bed and slipped off her nightdress. The husband was mystified.

'What are you doing?' he asked.

'You were playing with my pussy,' replied the wife. 'I thought it was foreplay for something heavier.'

The husband exclaimed, 'No! I was just wetting my fingers so I could turn the pages.'

▶ Why don't women blink during foreplay? They don't have time.

▶ What is a man's idea of foreplay? A half hour of begging.

▶ Why do so many women fake orgasm? Because so many men fake foreplay.

▶ What's a redneck's idea of foreplay? 'Are you awake yet, sis?'

▶ As things start hotting up, a girl said to her boyfriend, 'Hey honey, slow down – foreplay is an art.'

'Well, you'd better get my canvas ready soon,' he panted, 'because I'm about to spill my paint!'

▶ MAKING COFFEE
Making a cup of coffee is like making love to a beautiful woman.

It's got to be hot, you've got to take your time, you've got to stir... gently, and firmly, you've got to grind your beans until they squeak and then you deposit your milk.

▶ LAYING A CARPET
Laying a carpet is very much like making love to a beautiful woman.

You check the dimensions, lay her out on the floor, pin her down and walk all over her. If you're adventurous – like me – you might like to try an underlay.

▶ HANGING WALLPAPER

Well, hanging wallpaper is also very much like making love to a beautiful woman.

Clean all the relevant surfaces, spread her out on the table, cover her with paste and stick her up. Then you clean your brush, light your pipe, stand back and admire your handiwork.

▶ PUTTING UP A TENT

Putting up a tent is very much like making love to a beautiful woman.

You rent her, unzip the door, put up your pole and slip into the old bag.

▶ WASHING A CAR

Washing a car is very much like making love to a beautiful woman.

You've got to caress the bodywork, breathe softly and gently, give every inch of it your loving attention and make sure you've got a nice wet sponge.

▶ BEING IN THERAPY

And yet having therapy is very much like making love to a beautiful woman.

You get on the couch, string them along with some half-lie and evasions, probe some deep dark holes and then hand over all your money.

▶ BEING IN A CRASH

Going to the brink of death and back, in a nine-car pile-up on a dual-carriage way, is very much like making love to a beautiful woman.

First of all brace yourself. Hold on tight – particularly if it's a rear-ender – and pray you make contact with her twin airbags as soon as possible.

▶ GOING FISHING
Fishing is very much like making love to a beautiful woman.

First of all, clean and inspect your tackle. Carefully pull back your rod cover and remove any dirt or gunge that may have built up while not in use. Then, extend your rod to its full length and check that there are no kinks or any wear, particularly at the base where the grip is usually applied. Make sure you've got a decent float, the appropriate bait and that there's plenty of shot in your bag.

FRENCH

▶ What do you get when you toss a hand grenade into a kitchen in France? Linoleum Blownapart.

▶ How do you hint to someone they have a hygiene problem? Start talking to them in French.

▶ Once upon a time in the Kingdom of Heaven, God went missing for six days. Eventually, Archangel Michael found him on the seventh day resting. He enquired of God, 'Where have you been?'

God pointed downwards through the clouds. 'Look, Michael, look what I've made... ' said God.

Archangel Michael looked puzzled and said, 'What is it?'

'It's a planet,' replied God, 'and I've put LIFE on it. I'm going to call it earth and it's going to be a great place of balance.'

'Balance?' enquired Michael, still confused.

God explained, pointing down to different parts of the earth. 'For example, North America will be a place of great opportunity and wealth while South America is going to be poor. The Middle East over there will be a hot spot and Russia will be a cold spot. Over there I've placed a continent of white people and over there is a continent of black people.' God continued, pointing to the different countries, 'This one will be extremely hot and arid while this one will be very cold and covered in ice.'

The archangel, impressed by God's work, then pointed to another area of land and asked, 'What's that?'

'Ah,' said God. 'That's England, the most glorious place on earth. There will be beautiful people, dozens of Premiership football teams and very many impressive cities; it will the home of the world's finest artists, musicians, writers, thinkers, inventors, explorers and politicians. The people of England are going to be modest, intelligent and humorous and they're going to be found travelling the world. They'll be extremely sociable, hard-working and high-achieving and they will be known throughout the world as speakers of truth.'

Michael gasped in wonder and admiration but then proclaimed, 'What about balance, God? You said there will be BALANCE!'

God replied very wisely, 'Wait till you see the bunch of tossers I'm putting down next to them in France!'

▶ Did you hear about the Frenchman who could only count to seven?
He had a *huit* allergy.

▶ A Frenchman walks into a library and asks for a book on war.
The librarian replies, 'No, mate, you'll lose it.'

▶ What's black and crispy and comes on a stick? Joan of Arc.

▶ An Englishman, a Frenchman, a Spaniard and a German are all standing watching a street performer do some excellent juggling. The juggler notices that the four gentlemen have a very poor view, so he stands up on a large wooden box and calls out, 'Can you all see me now?'

'Yes.'

'Oui.'

'Si.'

'Ja.'

▶ A woman walking past a shop sees an advert in the window: 'Good home wanted for clitoris-licking frog.'

She goes inside and says to the guy behind the counter, 'I've come about the clitoris-licking frog.'

'Oui, madame,' the assistant says.

▶ A plane carrying an Englishman, a Frenchman, a Mexican and a Texan is about to crash. The pilot shouts back at them, 'We have to lose weight! If three of you jump, the fourth might be saved!'

The Englishman stands up, shouts, 'God save the Queen!', and jumps.

The Frenchman stands up, shouts, *'Vive la France!'*, and jumps.

The Texan stands up and shouts, 'Remember the Alamo!' – and throws out the Mexican.

▶ Did you know the toothbrush was invented by the French? If it had been invented by anyone else, it would have been called the teethbrush.

▶ Why don't the French barbecue? The snails keep slipping between the grills.

▶ How do you get a French waiter's attention? Start ordering in German.

▶ Computer tip: if you install the French versions of your favourite programs, they run a lot faster.

▶ The makers of French's mustard made the following recent statement: 'We at the French's company wish to put an end to statements that our product is manufactured in France. There is no relationship, nor has there ever been a relationship, between our mustard and the country of France. Indeed, our mustard is manufactured in Norwich, England. The only thing we have in common is that we are both yellow.'

▶ Why wouldn't the Statue of Liberty work in France? Because she has only one arm raised.

▶ How do you stop a French tank? Say, 'Boo'.

▶ Why do the French get more votes in the UN? They vote with both hands.

▶ What is the difference between a Frenchwoman and a basketball team? The basketball team showers after four periods.

▶ What is French people's favourite film? *The Running Man*.

▶ How did the French react to German reunification? They put up speed bumps at the borders to slow down the panzers.

▶ Why does the French flag have Velcro? So the blue and red sections are easily removed during a time of war.

FRIENDS

▶ My wife ran off with my best friend. I really miss him.

▶ I had a strange friend who said he had dug a hole and filled it with water. I thought to myself, 'He means well.'

▶ Steve comes home from work and hears strange noises coming from the bedroom. He runs upstairs, only to burst in and find his best mate pumping away with Steve's rather ugly wife. He looks at the pair in utter disgust before turning to his friend. 'Honestly, Dave,' he says. 'I have to, but you?'

FROGS AND TOADS

▶ What's green and hard? A frog with a flick knife.

▶ Do you know how to eat a frog? You put one leg over each ear.

▶ Once upon a time there was a little yellow toad crying in the forest.
   The good witch came along and asked the little yellow toad, 'Why are you crying, my friend?'
   The little yellow toad said, 'All my friends are green and I'm yellow. I want to be green like all my friends... sniff, sniff.'
   The good witch replied, 'No problem!'
   And she tapped the little yellow toad with her magic wand and the little yellow toad turned green... all except his private parts, which remained yellow.

'Oh no!' exclaimed the little toad, 'I can't go through life all green except for my private parts! You have to make me green all over!'

The good witch said, 'Sorry, I don't do private parts. You will have to go see the wizard!'

So, off the little toad went to see the wizard.

The good witch continued on into the forest, where she came upon a little brown squirrel crying very hard.

'Why are you crying, little brown squirrel?' the good witch asked.

'Because,' said the little brown squirrel, 'all my friends are red and I want to be red, too... sniff, sniff.'

'No problem!' said the good witch.

And she tapped the little brown squirrel and turned him red... all except his private parts, which remained brown.

'Oh, no!' exclaimed the little squirrel, 'I can't go through life all red except my private parts! You have to make me red all over!'

But the good witch said, 'Sorry, I don't do private parts. You will have to go see the wizard!'

But the little squirrel started crying harder and said, 'But I'm new around here! I don't know the wizard! How will I find him?'

And the good witch said, 'Oh, that's easy! Just follow the yellow dick toad... '

▶ Why can't Miss Piggy count to 70? Because she gets a frog in her throat at 69.

▶ A princess is walking along a pond in the royal gardens, when she looks down and sees a really ugly frog. Picking the frog up, she comments on the creature's rather hideous appearance.

Princess: 'My, but you are really an ugly frog!'

Frog: 'I know, I know, I got a really bad spell on me.'

Princess: 'Well I've seen frogs with spells, but none as ugly as you.'

Frog: 'Look, leave me alone, my dear. I told you, it's a really bad spell.'

Princess: 'Well, even so, if I kiss you, will you turn into a prince?'

Frog: 'I don't know, dear. A spell this bad will probably take a blowjob.'

▶ A woman went into a store to buy her husband a pet for his birthday. After looking around, she found that all the pets were very expensive. She told the clerk she wanted to buy a pet, but she didn't want to spend a fortune.

'Well,' said the clerk, 'I have a very large bullfrog – they say it's been trained to do blowjobs.'

'Blowjobs?' the woman asked.

'It hasn't been proven, but we've sold 30 of them this month,' he said.

The woman thought it would be a great gag gift and what if it's true… no more blowjobs for her! She bought the frog.

When she explained the animal's ability to her husband, he was extremely sceptical and laughed it off. The woman went to bed happy, thinking she may never need to perform this tiresome act again.

In the middle of the night, she was awakened by the noise of pots and pans flying everywhere, making loud banging and crashing sounds.

She ran downstairs to the kitchen, only to find her husband and the frog reading cookbooks.

'What are you two doing at this hour?' she asked.

The husband replied, 'If I can teach this frog to cook, your arse is out of here.'

GEEKS

▶ Two IT guys are chatting in a pub after work. 'Guess what, mate?' says the first IT guy. 'Yesterday, I met this gorgeous blonde girl in a bar.'

'What did you do?' says the other IT guy.

'Well, I invited her over to my place, we had a couple of drinks, we got into the mood and then she suddenly asked me to take all her clothes off.'

'You're kidding me!' says the second IT guy.

'I took her miniskirt off, and then I lifted her and put her on my desk next to my new laptop.'

'Really? You got a new laptop?'

▶ It has been reported in the press that Stephen Hawking suffered a terrible crash today. Luckily, though, he was able to reboot.

▶ Stephen Hawking masturbating. Now there's a stroke of genius.

▶ How do you know if a Korean has been in your house? Your PC is warm, your homework is done and your dog is missing.

▶ Particle physics gives me a hadron.

GENIE

▶ A man goes into a bar with a lamp. After he's had a few drinks, the man says to the barman, 'This lamp is magic, y'know. If you rub it, a genie comes out and grants you a wish.'

'Oh, yes?' replies the barman. 'Let's have a go then.' He rubs the lamp with a bar cloth and out pops a genie. 'Fantastic,' says the barman. 'It works. Er, let's see. Can I have a million bucks, please.'

'As you wish,' replies the genie and the bar is suddenly full of ducks.

'I forgot to mention,' says the man. 'He's a little deaf.'

▶ Harry and Tom are adrift in a lifeboat. Harry finds a lamp and, giving it the customary rub, is not surprised when a genie appears. The genie apologises to Harry and Tom and says that, due to cut-backs, it can only grant them one wish.

Harry doesn't think, he just knows he is thirsty so he blurts out, 'Turn the entire ocean into beer!' The genie claps its hands, the salt water changes to beer and the genie vanishes. There's a pregnant pause as Harry and Tom consider their new circumstances.

Tom looks at Harry with disgust, 'Well, isn't that great,' he says. 'Now we're going to have to pee in the boat.'

GINGER

▶ What do you call a good-looking woman with a ginger man? A hostage.

▶ Just watched that *Harry Potter* film, but it's pretty unrealistic. I mean... a ginger kid with two friends.

▶ Have you heard the one about the ginger at the party? Neither have I.

▶ Ginger kids are lucky in one respect. When they went for a sleepover at Michael Jackson's, they got their own room.

▶ How can two redheads become invisible in a crowd of three? When they're with a blonde.

▶ Why do redheads take the pill? Wishful thinking.

▶ What do you call a redhead with large breasts? A mutant.

▶ Why was the first football pitch sketched out on a redhead's chest? They needed a level playing field.

▶ Why are redheads flat-chested? It makes it easier to read their T-shirts.

▶ Apparently, in about 70 years there will be no more newborn kids that are naturally ginger. See, even Mother Nature hates them.

GIRLFRIENDS

▶ A man split up with his girlfriend. His friend told him, 'There's plenty more fish in the sea.'
  He replied, 'But it's not the smell I miss.'

▶ My friend has got a new epileptic girlfriend. She's well fit.

▶ Girlfriends are like applying to university. You rarely get an unconditional offer.

▶ What's the best part of having a homeless girlfriend? You can drop her off wherever you want!

GOD

▶ Why did God create Adam before he created Eve? Because he didn't want anyone telling him how to make Adam.

▶ What does an atheist shout when she's having an orgasm? 'Darwin! Oh, Darwin!'

▶ Why did God create Eve? To iron Adam's leaf.

▶ Who was the greatest inventor of all time? God was! He took a rib from Adam and made a loudspeaker.

▶ God creates Adam, and soon Adam is complaining that he's all alone in the Garden of Eden.

So God says, 'OK, I'll make you a companion, a beautiful creature who'll cook and clean for you. It will be able to converse intelligently on any subject and never ever complain or argue.'

Adam says, 'That sounds great.'

God says, 'The only thing is, it will cost you an arm and a leg.'

Adam says, 'Damn, that's expensive. What can I get for a rib?'

▶ God is talking to one of his angels. He says, 'Do you know what I have just done? I have just created a 24-hour period of alternating light and darkness on earth. Isn't that good?'

The angel says, 'Yes, but what will you do now?'

God says, 'I think I'll call it a day.'

▶ After a few days, the Lord called to Adam and said, 'It is time for you and Eve to begin populating the earth, so I want you to kiss her.'

Adam answered, 'Yes, Lord, but what is a kiss?'

So the Lord gave a brief description to Adam, who took Eve by the hand and took her to a nearby bush.

A few minutes later, Adam emerged and said, 'Thank you, Lord, that was enjoyable.'

And the Lord replied, 'Yes, Adam, I thought you might enjoy that and now I'd like you to caress Eve.'

And Adam said, 'What is a caress?'

So the Lord again gave Adam a brief description and Adam went behind the bush with Eve.

Quite a few minutes later, Adam returned, smiling, and said, 'Lord, that was even better than the kiss.'

And the Lord said, 'You've done well, Adam. And now I want you to make love to Eve.'

And Adam asked, 'What is make love, Lord?'

So the Lord gave Adam directions and Adam went again with Eve behind the bush, but this time he reappeared in two seconds.

And Adam said, 'Lord, what is a headache?'

▶ Little boy: 'Mummy, is God a girl or a boy?'

Mummy: 'God is both girl and boy.'

Little boy: 'Mummy, is God black or white?'

Mummy: 'God is both black and white.'

Little boy: 'Mummy, is God gay or straight?'

Mummy: 'God is both gay and straight'.

Little boy: 'Mummy, is God Michael Jackson?'

▶ Three blond men are stranded on one side of a wide river and don't know how to get across. The first blond man prays to God to make him smart enough to think of a way to cross the river. God turns him into a brown-haired man, and he swims across.

The second blond man prays to God to make him even smarter, so he can think of a better way to cross the river. God turns him into a red-haired man and he builds a boat and rows across.

The third blond man prays to God to make him the smartest of all, so God turns him into a woman and he walks across the bridge.

GOLF

▶ A couple of women were playing golf one sunny Saturday morning. The first of the twosome teed off and watched in horror as her ball headed directly towards a group of men playing the next hole.

The ball hit one of the men, and he immediately clasped his hands together at his crotch, fell to the ground and proceeded to roll around in evident agony.

The woman rushed down to the man and immediately began to apologise. 'Please allow me to help. I'm a nurse and I know I could relieve your pain if you'd allow.'

'I'll be all right... I'll be fine in a few minutes,' he replied breathlessly as he remained in the foetal position, still clasping his hands together at his crotch.

But she persisted, and he finally allowed her to help him. She gently took his hands away and laid them to the side, then she loosened his trousers and put her hands inside. She began to massage him. 'How does that feel?'

'It feels great, but my thumb still hurts like hell.'

▶ Two golfers are just about to tee off, when suddenly a naked blonde runs across the fairway, followed by two men in white coats, a man carrying two buckets of sand and an old man hobbling at the rear. One of the golfers asks the old man what is going on.

'That's a nymphomaniac from the asylum. Us attendants are trying to catch her,' he tells them.

'And what about the man with the buckets of sand?' they ask.

'That's his handicap. He caught her last time.'

▶ What's the difference between a downhill putt and a blowjob? You'll never hear a guy getting a blowjob say, 'Slow down! Stop! BITE, YOU COCKSUCKER!'

▶ A golfer was involved in a terrible car crash and was rushed to the hospital. Just before he was put under, the surgeon popped in to see him.

'I have some good news and some bad news,' said the surgeon. 'The bad news is that I have to remove your right arm.'

'Oh no!' cried the man. 'My golfing is over! Please, Doc, what's the good news?'

'The good news is, I have another one to replace it with but it's a woman's arm. I'll need your permission before I go ahead with the transplant.'

'Go for it, Doc,' said the man. 'As long as I can play golf again.'

The operation went well and a year later the man was out on the golf course, when he bumped into the surgeon.

'Hi, how's the new arm?' asked the surgeon.

'Just great,' said the man. 'I'm playing the best golf of my life. My new arm has a much finer touch and my putting has really improved.'

'That's great,' said the surgeon.

'Not only that,' continued the golfer, 'my handwriting has improved, I've learned how to sew my own clothes and I've even taken up painting landscapes in watercolours.'

'Unbelievable!' said the surgeon. 'I'm so glad to hear the transplant was such a great success. Are you having any side effects?'

'Well, just one problem,' said the golfer. 'Every time I get an erection, I also get a headache.'

GOOD DAYS

▶ *The perfect day – Her*

8.45 Wake up to hugs and kisses

9.00 Five pounds lighter on the scales

9.30 Light breakfast

11.00 Sunbathe

12.30 Lunch with best friend at outdoor café

1.45 Shopping

2.30 Run into boyfriend's/husband's ex and notice she's gained 30 pounds

3.00 Facial, massage, nap

7.30 Candlelit dinner for two and dancing

10.00 Make love

11.30 Pillow talk in his big strong arms

▶ *The perfect day – Him*

6.45 Alarm

7.00 Shower and massage

7.30 Blowjob

7.45   Massive dump while reading sports section

8.15   Limo arrives, Bloody Marys

8.30   Private jet to St Andrew's

9.30   Front nine holes

11.30 Lunch – two dozen oysters, steak, three beers

12.30 Blowjob

12.45 Back nine holes, St Andrew's

2.30   Limo to airport, Martini in limo

3.30   Nice, South of France. Afternoon fishing with all-female crew (topless). Sex for each fish caught. Catch 1,249-pound Blue Marlin. Grilled tuna and steamed lobster snack, six beers, nap

6.15   Blowjob

6.30   Learjet return flight, total body massage in transit

7.30   Shit, shower, shave

8.00   Watch live coverage of all-female wrestling

9.00   Dinner at Ritz, Oysters, 20-ounce steak (rare), Chateau Lafite Rothschild 1963 (magnum), Louis XII Cognac, Cuban cigar

10.30 Sex with three women, all from different countries

11.30 Whirlpool, steam, massage. Women quietly get dressed, hail cab, leave

Midnight   Blowjob. Sleep

GORILLAS AND MONKEYS

▶ A gorilla and a rhino were best friends until one day, as the rhino bent over to drink from a watering hole, the gorilla took advantage of the situation and buggered him. The rhino reacted angrily and chased the gorilla all over the game reserve. Half an hour later and still hotly pursued by the charging rhino, the gorilla spotted an explorer sitting in a chair reading a newspaper. Creeping up behind the explorer, the gorilla killed him, put on his clothes, threw his body in a bush and sat down in the chair to read the paper.

Moments later the rhino arrived. 'Excuse me,' he said, 'have you seen a gorilla round here?'

Holding up the paper to hide his face, the gorilla replied, 'What, the one that buggered a rhino by the watering hole?'

'Oh Lord,' said the rhino, 'don't tell me it's made its way into the papers already!'

▶ A monkey is having a pint in his local. When he's down to the last sip, he spits the beer at the barman.

The monkey apologises to the barman, 'Please forgive me, you probably think we do this in the jungle all the time. Actually, it's a nervous habit I just can't seem to break. It is so embarrassing.'

'You'd better see a psychiatrist,' says the barman.

A few weeks later, the monkey comes in the bar again. He sits down and orders a beer. Just as he's about to take the last sip, he spits at the barman.

'Hey, I thought you were going to see a psychiatrist!'

'I have been,' says the monkey.

'Well, it's not doing any good.'

'Yes, it is,' says the monkey. 'Now I'm not embarrassed about it.'

▶ Did you hear about the man who fed gorillas with a golf club? He drove them bananas.

▶ A student attends a lecture on the subject of 'Hunger or sex, which instinct is the stronger?'

The lecturer describes to the audience a series of tests he has conducted to find a scientific answer. 'For my tests,' he says, 'I used one healthy male and one healthy female chimpanzee. Before each test, I kept them apart so they could not see or hear each other. I also starved the male of both food and sex for a week.

'For my first test, I put a bowl of food in the middle of my lab and then placed the male in one corner and the female in the opposite corner. The male looked at the female, then looked at the food, then rushed to the bowl of food and devoured it. So, ladies and gentlemen, it looked like hunger prevailed over the sexual instincts of the male.

'But as a true scientist, I did a second test to see whether the earth's magnetic field had influenced the outcome. Again I kept the apes separate, starved the male and put the bowl of food in the middle of the lab. Then I put the male in the south-west corner and the female facing him in the north-east corner. The male immediately looked at the female, then at the food, then rushed to the bowl of food and devoured it. So once again the male preferred food to sex.

'But I wanted to be absolutely sure of the results so I carried out a third test, this time placing the male much closer to the female than to the food. The result was the same. The male looked at the female, then at the food, then rushed to the bowl of food and devoured it.

'So, ladies and gentlemen, I can say with some confidence that hunger is a much stronger drive than sexual instincts in the male animal. Thank you.'

After the applause has died down, the student stands up and asks, 'I have a question for you, Mr Lecturer. Have you tried doing the experiments with a different female ape?'

▶ A man wakes up one morning to find a gorilla on his roof. So he looks in the Yellow Pages and, sure enough, there's an ad for 'gorilla removers'.

He calls the number, and the gorilla remover says he'll be over in 30 minutes.

The gorilla remover arrives and gets out of his van. He's got a ladder, a baseball bat, a shotgun and a mean old pit bull.

'What are you going to do?' the homeowner asks.

'I'm going to put this ladder up against the roof, then I'm going to go up there and knock the gorilla off the roof with this baseball bat. When the gorilla falls off, the pit bull is trained to grab his testicles and not let go. The gorilla will then be subdued enough for me to put him in the cage in the back of the van.'

He hands the shotgun to the homeowner.

'What's the shotgun for?' asks the homeowner.

'If the gorilla knocks me off the roof, shoot the dog.'

▶ There was a man who owned a giant gorilla and he'd never left it on its own. But eventually he had to take a trip, so he left his gorilla in the care of his next-door neighbour. He explained to his neighbour that all he had to do was feed his gorilla three bananas a day at three, six and nine o'clock. But he was never ever to touch its fur.

So the next day the man came and gave the gorilla a banana and looked at it for a while, thinking, 'Why can't I touch its fur? Nothing seems to be wrong with it.'

Every day he came in and sized up the gorilla for a little while longer as he still couldn't understand. About a week later, he'd worked himself into a frenzy and decided that he was going to touch the gorilla. He passed it the banana and very gently brushed the back of his hand against its fur.

Suddenly the gorilla went 'ape' and started to violently jump around. Then it turned and began to run towards the man who, in turn, ran through the front door, over the lawn, across the street, into a sports car and drove off.

In the rear-view mirror, he could see the gorilla in another sports car, driving right behind him and motioning for him to pull over. He drove for two hours until the engine began to splutter and the car just stopped.

He jumped out and began to run down the street, over a brick wall, into someone's front garden and turned around to find the gorilla right behind him, beating its chest.

The man jumped down and ran back into the street screaming, until it got dark and he thought he'd lost the gorilla. The man ran into an alleyway, then suddenly he saw a giant shadow coming down the street ahead. It was the gorilla!

This time there was no escape. As the gorilla neared him, the man began to feel faint. The giant beast came face to face with him, slowly raised its mighty hand and said, 'Tag! You're it!'

▶ A guy was standing in front of the gorilla cage at the zoo one day, when a gust of wind swept some dust into his eye.

As he rubbed his eyelid, the gorilla went crazy, bent open the bars and beat the guy senseless.

When the guy came to his senses, he reported the incident to the zookeeper.

Nodding, the zookeeper explained that pulling down your eyelid means 'screw you' in gorilla language.

The explanation didn't make the victim feel any better and he vowed revenge.

The next day, he purchased two large knives, two party hats, two party horns and a large sausage.

Putting the sausage in his pants, he hurried to the zoo and went right up to the gorilla's cage, where he opened up his bag of goodies. Knowing that gorillas are natural mimics, he put on a party hat.

The gorilla looked at him, reached through the bars, grabbed a hat from the bag and put it on.

Next, the guy picked up his horn and blew on it. The gorilla reached out, picked up his horn and did the same.

Then the man picked up his knife, whipped the sausage out of his pants and sliced it in half.

The gorilla looked at the knife, looked at his own crotch, looked at the man and pulled down his eyelid.

GRAFFITI

▶ Why is there so little Puerto Rican literature? The spray can wasn't invented until 1949.

GREEKS

▶ How do Greeks separate the men from the boys? With a crowbar.

▶ Why do Greek men wear gold neck chains? So they know where to stop shaving.

▶ What's the Greek army motto? 'Never leave your buddy's behind.'

GUNS

▶ Guns don't kill people. Husbands who come home early kill people.

▶ My uncle had his tongue shot off during World War II. He doesn't talk about it, though.

▶ A pregnant woman was living in a violent neighbourhood, where gunfire could often be heard at night. One evening, while popping to the shops, she was caught in the crossfire and took three bullets in her stomach. Worried doctors were concerned that the bullets may have harmed the unborn baby, but when they gave her a scan, they found that there were in fact triplets inside her. The good news was that the bullets had done no harm, and doctors assured the woman that the bullets would be harmlessly passed by the children when they were born. A number of years passed and the children all grew up fine, with no problems.

One day their mother was cooking dinner, when her first 15-year-old daughter rushed in and said, 'Mummy, I was going to the toilet and a bullet fell out!'

'Don't worry,' replied the mother. 'It's what we expected to happen. Everything is fine.'

Relieved, the girl went away.

Five minutes later her sister rushed down the stairs, shouting for her mum. 'Mum, I went to the toilet and a bullet fell out.'

The mother reassured her daughter that everything was fine and went back to cooking the dinner.

Suddenly her son burst in. 'Mum, Mum, you'll never guess what's just happened!'

'Don't tell me, you were going to the toilet and a bullet fell out?'

'I was having a wank and I've shot the cat!'

▶ A blonde suspects her boyfriend of cheating on her. She goes out and buys a gun and turns up at his flat unexpectedly. Sure enough, she opens the door and finds him in the arms of a redhead. Well, the blonde is angry. She opens her bag to take out the gun, but as she does so she is overcome with grief. She takes the gun and points it to her own head.

The boyfriend yells, 'No, darling, don't do it!'

The blonde replies, 'Shut up, you're next.'

▶ An ex-US Marine Virginian hillbilly came to town carrying a jug of moonshine in one hand and a shotgun in the other. He stopped a man on the street and said, 'Here, friend, take a drink outta my jug.' The guy protested, saying he never drank, but the hillbilly pointed the shotgun at him and commanded, 'Drink!'

The stranger drank, shuddered, shook, shivered and coughed. 'My God!' he said. 'That's awful stuff you've got there!'

'Ain't it, though!' replied the hillbilly. 'Now, you hold the gun on me while I take a swig.'

GYMNASTICS

▶ Did you hear about the naked men's gymnastics team? Their favourite display was to stand on each other's shoulders, starkers. They call it the scrotum pole.

GYNAECOLOGY

▶ What do a gynaecologist and a pizza delivery man have in common? They can smell it but they can't eat it!

▶ What is the difference between a genealogist and a gynaecologist? A genealogist looks up your family tree, while a gynaecologist looks up your bush.

▶ Did you hear about the blind gynaecologist? He could lip-read.

▶ Did you hear about the dyslexic gynaecologist? He wants to look at your vinegar.

▶ It's a young girl's first time at the gynaecologist. She's up in the stirrups, and she's scared to death.
   The gynaecologist says, 'You're nervous, aren't you?'
   She says, 'Yes. It's my first time at the gynaecologist.'
   He says, 'Would you like me to numb you down there?'
   She says, 'Please.'
   He sticks his head between her legs and goes, 'Num, num, num... '

▶ A lady goes to the gynaecologist but won't tell the receptionist what's wrong with her, just that she must see a doctor. After hours of waiting, the doctor sees her and asks what the problem is. She explains that her husband is a compulsive gambler and every penny he can get his hands on he gambles. So when she had £500, she stuffed it in her vagina but now can't get it out.

The doctor says, 'Don't be nervous, I see this happen all the time.' He asks her to pull down her underwear, sits her down with her legs wide open, puts his gloves on and says, 'I only have one question. What am I looking for? Bills or loose change?'

▶ Medical ethics experts are still struggling with the question as to whether or not it's fitting for young male gynaecologists to keep looking up old girlfriends.

▶ A woman goes to her gynaecologist and complains of a pain in her aviaries.

'Don't you mean ovaries?' the doc says.

'No,' she says.

'We had better have a look,' says the doc. After a minute of peering, he says, 'You're right. It looks like there's been a cockatoo up there.'

▶ A young blonde went to a gynecologist and said that she and her husband were desperate to start a family.

'We've been trying for months and I just don't seem able to get pregnant,' she said.

'I'm sure we can solve your problem,' said the gynecologist. 'Just take off your underwear and get on the examination table.'

'Well, OK,' said the blonde. 'But I'd rather have my husband's baby.'

▶ What did the gynaecologist say to his wife when he came home after a tiring day?

'Whew, I'm bushed.'

▶ Knock knock!
Who's there?
Jenny Tull.
Jenny Tull who?
Jenny Tull Warts.

HAIR

▶ Boycott shampoo! Demand the REAL poo!

▶ A man was looking all over town to find a friend of his. He walked down the street and came to a barber shop. He stuck his head inside and asked, 'Bob Peters here?'
   The barber replied, 'Nah, we just do shaves and haircuts.'

▶ A blonde and a brunette were talking one day. The brunette said that her boyfriend had a slight dandruff problem but she gave him Head and Shoulders and it cleared it up.
   The blonde asked inquisitively, 'How do you give shoulders?'

▶ Did you know the longest hair on the human body is the eyelash? It stretches from the lids over the top of the skull, down the spine and comes out of your backside. Don't believe me? Try pulling a hair out your arse and feel your eyes water.

▶ I haven't slept for ten days, because that would be too long.

▶ A barber runs out of his shop and down to the nearest corner, where a policeman is standing.

'Officer,' he asks, 'have you seen a man run by here in the last few minutes?'

'No, I haven't. What's the problem?'

'The lousy cheat ran out of my shop without paying me!'

'Does this fellow have any distinguishing features?' the officer asks.

'Well, yes,' the barber replies. 'He's carrying one of his ears in his left hand.'

HALLOWEEN

▶ *The top five reasons why trick or treating is better than sex:*

- You're guaranteed to get at least a little something in the sack.

- If you get tired, wait ten minutes and go at it again.

- The uglier you look, the easier it is to get some and if you wear your Batman mask, no one thinks you're kinky.

- It doesn't matter if kids hear you moaning and groaning.

- If you don't get what you want, you can always go next door.

HAREMS

▶ Three guys were on a trip to Saudi Arabia. One day, they stumbled into a harem tent filled with over 100 beautiful women. They started getting freaky with all the women, when suddenly the sheik came in.

'I am the master of all these women. No one else can touch them except me. You three men must pay for what you have done today. You will be punished in a way corresponding to your profession.'

The sheik turned to the first man and asked him what he did for a living.
'I'm a cop,' said the first man.
'Then we will shoot your dick off!' said the sheik.
He then turned to the second man and asked him what he did for a living.
'I'm a fireman,' said the second man.
'Then we will burn your dick off!' said the sheik.
Finally, he asked the last man, 'And you, what do you do for a living?'
The third man answered, with a sly grin, 'I'm a lollipop man.'

HAROLD SHIPMAN

▶ Why did Harold Shipman hang himself? He'd run out of patients.

▶ There's going to be a film made about Harold Shipman. The director wants to call it *The Silence of the Grans* but the producer prefers to have Robert De Niro starring in it as 'The Old Dear Hunter'.

▶ What's the difference between Dr Harold Shipman and Tony Blair? Dr Shipman actually did something about hospital waiting lists.

▶ Harold Shipman will be sadly missed by the prison boxing team. A spokesman said that he had a lethal left jab.

▶ What's the connection between Gareth Gates and Harold Shipman? Neither can finish a sentence.

▶ Harold had just finished off his chicken madras, when a guard approached him. 'How was your curry, Dr Shipman?'
'Great,' Harold replied, 'but I could have murdered a nan.'

▶ Old people finally got their revenge. Dr Shipman was finally overcome by a granny knot.

▶ Allegedly before Shipman died, he'd written out his own death certificate. Apparently it said he died of natural causes.

HEAVEN

▶ There was a big earthquake centred on the monastery. It was destroyed and all 50 of the monks there were killed.

When they all arrived at the gates of heaven, they were met by St Peter.

'To save time,' he said, 'we'll do the entrance exam en masse. Right, now hands up those of you who have played around with little boys?'

Forty-nine hands were raised.

'OK,' said St Peter, 'you all can all go down to hell – and take that deaf bastard with you.'

▶ Eve walks over to Adam in the Garden of Eden and kisses him passionately. 'Wow,' says Adam, 'how did you learn to kiss like that?'

▶ Boy to father: 'Daddy, why does Grandma spend so much time reading the Bible?'

Father: 'Ssh, son. She's cramming for her finals.'

▶ Osama Bin Laden arrives in heaven. He is surprised that there are not 72 virgins waiting for him and even more surprised to be met by St Peter.

St Peter: 'Welcome, Osama. We've been waiting for you and it is good to see you. Now before anything else, is there anything I can do for you?'

OBL: 'Well, would it be possible to see Mohamed?'

St Peter: 'You want to see Mohamed? Well, I'm sure that would be possible, but first I must register you. There now.'

OBL: 'Will it be possible to see Mohamed now?'

St Peter: 'It shouldn't be a problem, but first, I must just take you to meet God; he's been looking forward to seeing you.'

So St Peter takes OBL off to God.

God: 'My dear boy, how good to see you! I began to think you were never coming. Did you have a good journey? Has St Peter shown you around?'

OBL: 'Yes, everything is fine but there is just one thing. Could I see Mohamed?'

God: 'You want to see Mohamed? Of course, dear boy. Tell me, would you like a coffee?'

OBL: 'That would be very nice.'

God goes to the door, opens it and shouts: 'Yo, Mohamed, two coffees, please.'

▶ When Pope John Paul II got to heaven, St Peter told him he was lucky to be there.

John Paul asked, 'Why? What did I do wrong on earth?'

'God was angry with your refusal to admit female priests,' said St Peter.

'He's mad about that?' the late pope asked.

St Peter replied, 'She's furious.'

▶ *In heaven...*

- The cooks are French.

- The policemen are English.

- The mechanics are German.

- The lovers are Italian.

- The bankers are Swiss.

▶ *In hell...*

- The cooks are English.

- The policemen are German.

- The mechanics are French.

- The lovers are Swiss.

- The bankers are Italian.

HELL

▶ An old lady dies and goes to heaven. She is chatting to St Peter at the Pearly Gates, when all of a sudden she hears the most awful blood-curdling screams.

'Oh my goodness,' says the old lady, 'what is happening?'

'Don't worry about that,' says St Peter. 'It's only someone having the holes bored on their shoulder blades for the wings.'

The old lady looks a little uncomfortable but carries on with the conversation. Ten minutes later, there are more blood-curdling screams.

'Oh my goodness,' says the old lady, 'now what is happening?'

'Not to worry,' says St Peter, 'they are just having their head drilled to fit the halo.'

Shaking her head, the old lady says, 'I can't do this. I'm off down to hell.'

'You can't go there,' says St Peter. 'You'll be raped and sodomised.'

'Sure,' says the old lady, 'but I've already got the holes for that!'

HISTORY

▶ According to archaeologists, for millions of years the Neanderthal man was not fully erect. That's pretty easy to understand considering how ugly the Neanderthal women were.

▶ The Pharaoh was dictating, and his scribe was busily chipping away at the stone tablet. 'I have plans... to form,' the monarch said slowly, 'a personal bodyguard... of stalwart... and virile... young men.'

The chips flew, but then suddenly ceased flying and the perspiring chiseller looked up enquiringly. 'Excuse me, Your Majesty, but is virile spelled with one or two testicles?'

▶ Why did Henry VIII put skittles on his lawn? So he could take Anne Boleyn.

▶ Breaking news: 'Archaeologists digging at the site of Shakespeare's house have uncovered thousands of monkey skeletons.'

▶ Napoleon came home tired and weary, wet and wounded, and went straight round to Josephine's flat. He was shocked to find a pair of large gum boots on her front doorstep.

'Josephine! Josephine!' he called out. 'What are those rubber boots doing out here?'

'They're not rubber boots,' said Josephine. 'They're Wellington's.'

▶ On that fateful day, Davy Crockett woke up and rose from his bunk on the main floor of the Alamo. He then walked up to the observation post along the west wall of the fort.

William B Travis and Jim Bowie were already there, looking out over the top of the wall.

These three great men gazed at the countless hordes of Mexicans moving steadily towards them.

With a puzzled look on his face, Crockett turned to Bowie and said, 'Jim, are we having some landscaping done today?'

▶ Hitler walks into the meeting room and turns to his trusted staff. 'I want you to organise the execution of 10,000 Jews and one kitten.'

Everyone looks around the table and after a long silence, Goering pipes up, 'Mein Führer, why do you want to kill a kitten?'

Hitler smiles and turns to the rest of the table. 'You see, no one cares about the Jews.'

HITCHHIKING

▶ A lawyer was going home in his limo, when he saw two men sitting on the side of the road eating grass. He tapped the glass and told his chauffeur to pull over and investigate.

The chauffeur went across to the two men and asked them why they were eating grass. The men replied that they had no money and must eat grass. The chauffeur went back to the car and told the lawyer. The lawyer, deeply moved, invited the men back to his house, where he would feed them. One of the men very timidly said, 'I have a wife and three children.' Then the second man spoke up and said, 'I have a wife and six children.'

The lawyer, filled with compassion, told them to bring their families along.

Both families squeezed into the car and they set off for the lawyer's house. One of the men was overcome with gratitude and took the lawyer's hand. 'Sir, you are too kind and generous, and we are not able to repay you. Thank you for your kindness.'

'Do not worry about it, it's fine and there's plenty for everyone,' replied the lawyer. 'You'll love my house – the grass is about two feet high.'

▶ There's a man hitchhiking on the motorway, when along comes an 18-wheeler. It pulls up and comes to a grinding halt. The hitcher runs to the truck, reaches up, opens the door and jumps in. There sits the driver and beside him is his pet monkey.

'Great-looking monkey,' said the hitcher.

'Yeah, he's great company and he looks after you, too. Check this shit out.' Without further ado, the trucker punches the monkey in the guts with all his might. The monkey dutifully bends down, unzips the trucker's fly, goes down and gets to work on the trucker's manhood at a vigorous pace. Once the lorry driver has unloaded his cargo all over the cabin, the monkey wipes him off, zips up his fly and sits back down in his little monkey seat in the cabin.

'That's GREAT!' says the by-now quite interested hitcher. 'Can I give it a try?'

The driver looks across and says, 'Yeah sure, why not?'

'OK, but just one thing, though,' says the hitcher.

'What's that?' asks the trucker.

'There's no need to smack me in the guts so hard.'

▶ A hitchhiker was standing by the roadside, making vulgar gestures at passing cars. Another hiker came over to him and said, 'You'll never get a lift like that.'

'I don't care,' said the first. 'It's my lunch break.'

HOLIDAYS

▶ An old married couple were on holiday in Morocco. They were touring around the souk looking at the goods, when they passed a small sandal shop. From inside they heard a gentleman with a Moroccan accent say, 'You, foreigners! Come in. Come into my humble shop.'

So the married couple walked in. The shopkeeper said to them, 'I have some special magical sandals I think you'd be interested in. They make you wild at sex like a great desert stallion camel.'

Well, the wife was really interested in buying the sandals after what the man had claimed, but her husband felt he really didn't need them, being the stallion he was. The husband asked the man, 'How could sandals make you into a sex freak?'

The shopkeeper replied, 'Why don't you try them on and see for yourself?'

After much badgering from his wife, the husband finally conceded to try them on. As soon as he slipped them onto his feet, he got this wild look in his eyes, something his wife hadn't seen in many years. Her husband was full of raw sexual power.

In a blink of an eye, the husband rushed at the Moroccan man, threw him on a table and started tearing at the guy's trousers. All the time the shopkeeper man was screaming, 'YOU HAVE THEM ON THE WRONG FEET! YOU HAVE THEM ON THE WRONG FEET!'

▶ What is the smallest hotel in the world? A pussy, cos you have to leave the bags outside.

▶ Tom and Dick are comparing notes on their summer holiday. 'I was staying in a hotel in Poole,' says Tom.

'In Dorset?' asks Dick.

'Certainly,' says Tom. 'I'd recommend it to anyone.'

▶ A man phones a taxi company because his cab hasn't turned up. 'I'm supposed to be at the airport for nine o'clock,' says the man.

'Don't worry,' says the girl. 'The taxi will get you there before your plane leaves.'

'I know it will,' says the man. 'I'm the pilot.'

▶ A husband and wife are on holiday.

'Oh my God!' exclaims the wife. 'I just remembered I left the oven on.'

'Don't worry about it,' replies her husband. 'The house won't burn down. I just remembered I left the bath running.'

▶ Tom arrives at a hotel in a Scottish village on a cold, grey, drizzly day. The weather remains the same for two weeks. Exasperated, Tom stops a little boy in the street. 'Does the weather here ever change?' he asks.

'I don't know,' replies the boy. 'I'm only six.'

▶ The weather was terrible on my holiday. Mind you, I did come home brown – with rust.

HOME

▶ A friend accused me of being homophobic the other day.

'Nonsense,' I said. 'I love my house.'

▶ A book just fell on my head. I've only got myshelf to blame.

▶ First thing this morning, there was a tap on my door. Funny sense of humour my plumber has.

HORSES

▶ Why did the woman get thrown out of the riding stable? She wanted to mount the horse her way.

▶ A horse walks into a bar and orders a drink. The barman gives the horse a drink. Then horse complains loudly, 'Hey, what sort of a barman are you! You forgot the little umbrella!'

He finishes his drink and gallops out of the bar. Another customer, who had been watching the whole scene with increasing astonishment, turns to the barman and says, 'My God, that is incredible! I have never seen anything like that before, never in my entire life!'

The barman replies, 'For God's sake, what's the big deal? Anyone can forget the little umbrella!'

▶ Keith was a famous race horse. Not only was he fast, but he could talk.

Keith was entered in the Gold Cup. A come-from-behind horse, he started at the back of the field and slowly moved up through the rest of the field until he was just behind the leader. Suddenly, he seemed to slow down and ended up in second place at the end of the race.

Afterwards, the owner came up and asked him what had happened.

Keith replied, 'I'm really sorry, boss, but I got behind that little filly and she had the cutest little butt. I just couldn't pass her up.'

The owner voiced his displeasure and told Keith that he would have to put blinkers on him for the next race.

But again Keith repeated his performance, passing up all the horses until he got to the little filly, when he again slowed down behind her.

The owner asked again what had happened. Keith replied, 'Well, boss, it was going great. I couldn't see to the left or right. All of a sudden, that pretty little filly cut right in front of me and I just couldn't pass her up.'

The owner said, 'Keith, I'm really sorry but I'm going to have to have you neutered before the Grand National.'

Keith said, 'I understand, boss. I deserve it for the way I've behaved the last two races.'

Keith recovered from his surgery in time for Aintree. The gate opened up and Keith took off but fell over right past the starting gate.

The owner rushed onto the track. 'Keith, what's wrong? Did I rush you into this? Are you hurt?'

Keith looked up at the owner and said, 'Boss, it's not your fault. I was really ready for this race. My mind was on the race and I didn't even look at that little filly as we were going into the gate.'

'Well, then, what happened?' asked the owner.

Keith replied, 'The gate opened, I started to run and all of a sudden I heard the announcer say "And they're off!" and I got so embarrassed, I crossed my legs.'

HOSPITALS

▶ Who's the coolest guy in a hospital? The ultra-sound guy.

▶ Who takes over when he's on holiday? The hip-replacement guy.

▶ Where do you go for hot women who scream in bed? The burns unit.

HUNTING

▶ A man went bear hunting and saw a large bear by a clearing. He aimed and fired and the bear dropped down. The hunter ran up to look for the bear but it wasn't there. Next minute the bear came up behind him and tapped him on the shoulder and said, 'You now have two choices, I can kill you and eat you or screw you for a while.' The hunter didn't want to die so he let the bear have his way with him and left.

But he was very angry and went back the next day with a shotgun and sure enough there was the bear in the same place. He took aim and fired and the bear dropped. Once again he ran up to get the bear but the bear wasn't there. Once again the bear came up behind him, tapped him on the shoulder and said, 'Same deal as yesterday.' So the hunter let the bear have his way with him again and he left madder than before.

He went home and got an even bigger gun and went back to the same place and sure enough there was the bear again. This time he took a really careful aim and fired and the bear dropped. For the third time the hunter ran up to get the bear and the bear wasn't there. The bear came up behind him and tapped him on the shoulder and said, 'You ain't really into this for the hunting, are you?'

▶ A hunter is walking through the jungle, when he finds a huge dead rhinoceros with a pygmy standing next to it.

Amazed, he asks, 'Did you kill that?'

'Yes,' says the pygmy.

'How could a little bloke like you kill a huge thing like that?'

'I killed it with my club,' says the pygmy.

The astonished hunter asks, 'How big is your club?'

'Oh,' replies the pygmy, 'there's about 60 of us.'

▶ A fellow was telling a couple of his friends about the tragedy that befell him while scouting the woods the weekend prior to opening of deer season. 'I was going through the woods,' he said, 'when, turning behind a big tree, I came face to face with a huge grizzly.'

'Wow!' said one of the friends. 'That must've been really scary.'

'Yeah,' said the man telling the story, 'the grizzly reared up like this (man stands up, raises both hands in front, with hands clawed) and goes GRRRRRRRRRRRRRR!!! Man, I just shit all over myself!'

'Well, hell,' says one of his friends, 'I'd shit all over myself, too, if a bear did that to me.'

'No, no,' said the storyteller, 'I didn't mean then. I meant just now when I reared up and screamed "GRRRRRRRRRRRRRRRR!"'

▶ A man was out duck hunting, when a policeman drove by and asked him for his driving licence.

'OK,' said the hunter.

The policeman then grabbed one of the ducks, stuck his finger up the duck's arse and asked him if he had a licence to own a California duck. The man showed him the licence. The policeman then took another duck and shoved his finger up its arse. He asked the hunter if he had a licence to hunt Florida duck. The man showed him his licence. The policeman finally took the last duck, shoved his finger up the duck's anus and asked him if he had a licence to hunt Louisiana duck. So the man showed him the licence.

The policeman calmed down and started to relax. 'So, where are you from?' the policeman asked.

The man bent over. 'You tell me,' he said.

▶ A city slicker pulled into a one-street town in the middle of Wyoming. The place seemed deserted, apart from an old timer sitting in a rocking chair at the front of the general store. 'What do you folks do around here?' asked the city slicker.

The old timer replied slowly, 'We don't do nothin' but hunt 'n' fuck.'

'What do you hunt?'

'Something to fuck.'

▶ Two guys are out hunting and get lost. The first guy says to the second guy, 'What do you think we should do?'

The second guy says, 'Let's fire three shots into the air. It's the international distress code.'

So they fire three shots into the air and wait an hour but nobody comes. The first guy says to the second guy, 'What do you think we should do now?'

The second guy says, 'Let's fire three more shots into the air.'

So they fire three more shots into the air, wait an hour and still nobody comes. The first guy says, 'What do you think we should do now?'

The second guy says, 'Let's fire three more shots into the air.'

The first guy says, 'Well, I sure hope someone comes soon, these are my last three arrows!'

▶ One Sunday, a priest decided to skip church and go hunting in the forest. While he was hunting he saw a gigantic grizzly bear, which had stopped to get honey from a beehive. The priest thought the bear was good game so he clumsily shot at it but missed. The bear, startled by the shot, jumped up and charged at the priest. The priest used his only option and dropped to his knees and prayed. 'Dear God,' he said, 'please let this bear be a good Christian, a better one than I was.'

As the bear drew closer, it dropped to its knees and said, 'Dear God, thank you for this meal I am about to receive.'

HYGIENE

▶ What is long, hard and stiff, is used inside a warm, wet place and gets moved back and forth for the best effect? A toothbrush.

▶ To truly love another, you must first love yourself... And it wouldn't hurt to wash your hands in between.

HYPOCHONDRIA

▶ My doctor tells me I suffer from extreme hypochondria. He prescribed a strong placebo, but I don't think it's working.

▶ Doctor to patient: 'I have good news and bad news. The good news is that you're not a hypochondriac.'

▶ Why are hypochondriacs such lousy lovers? They prefer to wait until the swelling goes down.

▶ The doctor has prescribed me anti-hypochondria tablets. I'm worried about the possible side effects.

ILLNESS

▶ Have you heard about the anti-road protestor who died? He refused a bypass.

▶ What do you call a leper in a spa? Porridge.

▶ A wife was in intensive care last night after cutting herself badly while shaving her minge. Doctors this morning say her condition is stubble.

▶ Rick Astley walks into rehab. The receptionist says, 'Get lost – you're never gonna give it up.'

▶ I became friends with my best mate through a shared illness – we both suffer from inferiority complexes. His is better than mine, though.

▶ A young couple had only been married for about two weeks, when the wife complained of a burning sensation in her chest. She told her husband, who suggested that she goes to the doctor to be examined. She arranged an appointment and went the following day. The husband, while at work, received a call from the doctor. 'I am sorry to say your wife has acute angina... ' announced the GP.
   'Yeah, I know,' replied the husband. 'She's got a nice pair of tits, too!'

▶ So I parked my big 4x4 V8 in the disabled parking bay at Tesco. Some do-gooder shouted, 'Oi, what's your disability, then, mate?!'
   I shouted, 'Tourettes, you fucking wanker, now piss off!'

▶ I was told today by my doctor I have an enlarged liver. I said, 'That's lucky because I drink a lot.'

▶ A man has a check-up and the doctor finds something seriously wrong. He decides the news is too bad to tell the man directly so he breaks it to his wife. 'Your husband is seriously ill,' says the doctor. 'The only way you can save his life is to offer him a completely stress-free existence. You must not contradict him in any way. He must give up his job so he can concentrate on restful hobbies. He must have three home-cooked meals every day and live in an environment that is as tranquil, tidy and germ free as possible.'

In the car home the husband says, 'So what's going to happen to me?'

The wife answers, 'You're going to die.'

▶ Newsflash: 'Page-3 girl in skin cancer scare.' That's the downside to exposing yourself in the sun on a regular basis.

▶ 'Doctor, doctor, I've got problems with my hearing.'

'What are the symptoms?'

'They're those yellow people on TV.'

▶ Did you hear about the man who tested positive for OCD? He rung the doctor's 25 times to check the results.

▶ A man is recovering from surgery, when a nurse asks him how he is feeling. 'I'm OK but I didn't like the four-letter-word the doctor used in surgery,' he answered.

'What did he say?' asked the nurse.

'OOPS!'

▶ A charity pantomime in aid of Paranoid Schizophrenics descended into chaos yesterday when someone shouted, 'He's behind you!'

▶ Joe's wife was sick. Very sick. None of the doctors could figure out what was wrong with her. He was about to go into her room and visit her, when her doctor approached him. The doctor said, 'These might be her last few days, so you should do whatever she asks of you, so that she may die happy.'

Well... Joe thought this over and decided that that was a great idea. He went in and they talked for about three hours. After a while he asked her if there was anything that he could do for her. She thought for a little bit and said, 'Make love to me... screw me like you never have before... ' He thought this was a little much in her condition, but since it might be one of the last times, he decided to comply.

The next day he came in, and her doctor said that she was much better, and he should do whatever he did yesterday. Well, he walked in and they talked, and she requested they make passionate love again, and again he complied.

After about five days of this she had fully recovered and was able to go home. She walked into the living room to find that Joe was crying. She said, 'What's the matter? I'm fine now. You have nothing to worry about.'

He replied, 'I know, but all this time I can't stop thinking that I could have saved Mum!'

▶ A woman walks into the doctor's office with a huge boil on her arse.

The doctor squeezes it, pushes it and then looks at the hard white pus core. He says this is too big a job for me so he sends her to Gus the pus sucker.

The woman goes to Gus, who looks at the bulging, red, inflamed boil festering with pus and says, 'This is no problem.' He then proceeds to press his lips to her arse and sucks out the pus and core of the boil.

Halfway through, the woman drops a mammoth fart. Gus stops what he's doing, looks up and says, 'You know, lady, it's people like you that make this job fucking disgusting.'

▶ The Centre for Disease Control has released a list of symptoms of bird flu. If you experience any of the following, please seek medical treatment immediately:

1. High fever
2. Congestion
3. Nausea
4. Fatigue
5. Aching in the joints
6. An irresistible urge to shit on someone's windscreen

▶ What sits at the end of your bed and takes the piss? A dialysis machine.

▶ What's blue and doesn't fit? A dead epileptic.

▶ A guy goes to the doc, who gives him suppositories and tells him to put one in his back passage every night for a fortnight and then come back for a progress report.

Two weeks go by and the man returns. The doc asks what effect the suppositories have had.

'None whatsoever,' the man replies, but then again we don't have a back passage so I've been putting them in the cupboard under the stairs.'

▶ Mr Smith went to the doctor's office to collect his wife's test results. The receptionist said, 'I'm sorry, sir, but there has been a bit of a mix-up and we have a problem. When we sent the blood samples from your wife to the lab, the samples from another Mrs Smith were sent as well and we are now uncertain which one is your wife's. Frankly, that's either bad or terrible.'

Mr Smith asked, 'What do you mean?'

The receptionist replied, 'Well, one Mrs Smith has tested positive for

Alzheimer's, and the other for syphilis. However, we cannot tell which is your wife.'

Mr Smith exclaimed, 'That's terrible! What am I supposed to do now?'

The receptionist answered, 'The doctor recommends that you drop your wife off in the middle of town – if she finds her way home, don't sleep with her.'

IMPOTENCE

▶ A man came home with some ice cream. He asked his wife if she wanted any.

'How hard is it?' she asked.

'As hard as my cock,' he replied.

'Pour me some.'

▶ A woman goes to her doctor, complaining that her husband is 300 per cent impotent.

The doctor says, 'I'm not sure I understand what you mean.'

She says, 'Well, the first 100 per cent you can imagine. In addition, he burned his tongue and broke his finger... '

▶ Two eggs boiling in a pan, one male and one female. The female egg says, 'Look, I've got a crack.'

'No good telling me,' replies the male egg. 'I'm not hard yet.'

▶ Kellogg's is coming out with a new cereal for impotent men. It's to be called 'Nut 'N' Raisin Honey'.

▶ 'Doc, you gotta help me,' said Mr Smith, walking into the physician's office. 'I need a prescription for Sex-Lax.'

'Don't you mean Ex-Lax?' asked the doctor.

'No, no, no,' answered Mr Smith testily. 'I don't have trouble going. I have trouble coming.'

▶ A man complained to the urologist that he had fathered too many children. The doctor asked him to return next week so he could make him impotent.

The following week, the man showed up in a tuxedo. The doctor asked, 'Why the tuxedo?'

He said, 'If you're going to make me impotent, I'm going to look impotent!'

▶ What's the difference between anxiety and panic? Anxiety is when, for the first time, you can't do it the second time. Panic is when, for the second time, you can't do it the first time.

▶ A guy was on a business trip in Houston and bought a really cool pair of snakeskin boots. He couldn't wait to show his new boots to his wife. Returning from his trip late the next evening, his wife was in the bathroom getting ready for bed. He quickly stripped naked, except for his new snakeskin boots, and stood in the bedroom to wait for her. As the wife emerged from the bathroom, he asked, 'Well, honey, do you notice anything special?'

She replied, 'Yeah, it's limp.'

'It's not limp!' exclaimed her husband. 'It's admiring my new snakeskin boots!'

'Well, next time buy a hat.'

▶ *Excuses for impotence:*

- 'I can't help it. You're like an angel, and making love to you would be like defiling a sacred thing.'

- 'I can't help it. I love you too much to give you this disease.'

- 'I don't understand it. This is the first time this has happened to me today.'

- 'Listen, are you sure we are doing the right thing?'

- 'I think I twisted my ankle.'

- 'Have YOU ever had this problem before?'

- 'I'm sorry, I just can't imagine anyone I like right now.'

INCONTINENCE

▶ 'Good afternoon, incontinence hotline, can you hold, please?'

INSECTS

▶ Two bees ran into each other. The first bee asked the other how things were going.

'Really bad,' said the second bee. 'The weather has been really wet and damp and there aren't any flowers or pollen, so I can't make any honey.'

'No problem,' said the first bee. 'Just fly down five blocks and turn left. Keep going until you see all the cars. There's a Bar Mitzvah going on and there are all kinds of fresh flowers and fruit.'

'Thanks for the tip,' said the second bee, and he flew away.

A few hours later, the two bees ran into each other again. The first bee asked, 'How'd it go?'

'Great!' said the second bee. 'It was everything you said it would be.'

'Uh, what's that thing on your head?' asked the first bee.

'That's my yarmulke,' said the second bee. 'I didn't want them to think I was a wasp.'

▶ Did you hear about the man who was stung by a bee? £40 for a jar of honey.

▶ Why was the centipede dropped from the insect football team? He took too long to put his boots on!

▶ The bee. Nature's very own suicide bomber.

▶ Why do bees stay in their hives during winter? Swarm.

▶ Why did the bee cross his legs? Because he couldn't find the BP station.

▶ There are two fleas on a pussy. One is smoking dope; what's the other one doing? Sniffing crack.

▶ Two caterpillars were sitting on a leaf when a butterfly flew past.

One caterpillar turned to the other and said, 'You'll never get me up in one of those things!'

▶ I got an ant farm. Them fellas didn't grow shit.

▶ Two ants are playing a fast game of tennis in a saucer.

After the game they sit on the edge of the saucer towelling themselves off and one ant turns around and says, 'Mate, you'll have to improve your game for tomorrow.'

The other ant asks, 'Why?'

The first ant replies, 'We're playing in the cup tomorrow.'

▶ Two fleas were hanging out one day, and one told the other about its night. 'Hey, man, I had a great time last night. I went to the symphony and I had the best seat in the house, in the conductor's beard. Things were cool until the second movement, when he sneezed, and I was flung into the soprano soloist's cleavage. That wasn't bad, nice and warm and all, but she got all worked up and started to sweat, and I slid down between her legs. I stayed there and fell asleep, but there is one thing I don't get. When I woke up, I was in the conductor's beard again.'

INSULTS

▶ 'Hi there, I'm a human being! What are you?'

▶ 'I've seen more life in a down and out's vest.'

▶ 'Your red shirt goes well with your eyes... '

▶ 'Save your breath... You'll need it to blow up your date.'

▶ 'All day I thought of you... I was at the zoo.'

▶ 'He does the work of three men: Curly, Larry and Moe.'

▶ 'I heard that you went to the haunted house and they offered you a job.'

▶ 'Listen, are you always this stupid or are you just making a special effort today?'

▶ 'Well, they do say opposites attract... so I sincerely hope you meet somebody who is attractive, honest, intelligent and cultured.'

▶ 'I heard that you changed your mind. So, what did you do with the nappy?'

▶ 'I know what sign you were born under – "RED LIGHT DISTRICT".'

INVENTIONS

▶ An inventor went to the Patents Office to register a new folding bottle.
'What's it called?' asked the clerk.
'A fottle,' replied the inventor. 'It's short for "folding bottle".'
'That's a silly name,' said the clerk.
'And I've also invented a folding carton called a farton.'
'I'm sorry, there's no way we can allow that. It's too rude.'
'Oh, dear,' said the inventor. 'Then you're going to hate the name of my folding bucket!'

IRISH JOKES

▶ An Irishman went to London for a visit to the circus. While there, he saw a man with an elephant act. The man claimed the elephant could look at a person and tell that person's age. The Irishman was very sceptical and said so, in no uncertain terms.

The man had the elephant look at a small boy, and the elephant stamped its foot nine times. 'Is that right?' he asked the boy.

'Yes, I'm nine!' the boy said.

The Irishman continued his loud heckling, still not believing that this was true.

The man asked the elephant to tell the ages of several other people, and each time the elephant stamped his foot and the people said he was correct. The Irishman got even louder and more abusive towards the man. Finally the man could take it no longer and wagered the Irishman that the elephant could look at him and tell him his age. The Irishman took him up on the wager. The elephant looked closely at the Irishman, turned around, raised his tail and broke wind like you wouldn't believe. Then he turned back around, knocked the Irishman to the ground with his trunk and stomped on him twice.

The Irishman, crumpled and bleeding, staggered back to his feet and with a sound of disbelief in his voice cried, 'Mother of Mary, he's right! Farty-two!'

▶ The Irish are famous for 'the gift of the gab' – but these days you can clear that up with antibiotics.

▶ Why do the police in Dublin travel in threes? They need one who is able to read, another who can write and one to keep an eye on the two intellectuals.

▶ Where did they find the Irish woodworm? Dead in a brick.

▶ Ireland's worst air disaster occurred early this morning, when a small two-seater Cessna plane crashed into a cemetery. Irish search and rescue workers have recovered 1,826 bodies so far and expect that number to climb as digging continues.

▶ Why did God invent alcohol? To prevent the Irish from ruling the world.

▶ An English guy is screwing an Irish girl. The girl asks, 'You haven't got AIDS, have you?'
   He replies, 'No.'
   She responds, 'Oh, thank fuck for that! I don't want to get that again!'

▶ An Irishman goes up to his doctor and says, 'I want the snip.'
   The doctor says, 'Well, that'll be £2,000.'
   The Irishman thinks for a bit and says, 'Hmm, that's a wee bit expensive.'
   The doctor replies, 'Don't worry, though, there is another option. Take this firework and a tin can. Light it and count to ten.'
   So the Irish man goes away, puts the firework in the tin, holds it in one hand and begins counting. 'One, two, three, four, five... ' He puts the tin can between his legs and continues to count on his other hand. 'Six, seven, eight, nine, ten.'
   BOOM!!!

▶ Newsflash: 'The Irish government have announced that, as of next week, all cars in Ireland will now drive on the right-hand side of the road.
If this is a success, all buses and lorries will follow a week later.'

▶ Why do the Irish have potatoes and the Arabs have oil? The Irish had first choice.

▶ Paddy says to Mick, 'I hear that girl who played Pussy Galore in the Bond films has split her fanny open!'

Mick replies, 'Honor Blackman?'

Paddy says, 'No, on a dildo!

▶ An Irish woman was admitted to hospital today after having phone sex. Doctors removed two Nokias, three Motorolas and one Samsung but no Siemen was found.

▶ Did you hear about the Irishman who stepped into the path of a steam train? He was chuffed to bits!

▶ The roof of the church in County Mayo was leaking and the priest asked for volunteers to raise funds for its repair. Keith offered his services.

About a week later, the priest met Keith, who was straggling from side to side as a result of having imbibed too freely.

Keith was apologetic. 'I'm collecting for the roof, Father,' he said. 'Every one of the neighbours I called on insisted on giving me a wee drop after paying his subscription.'

The priest was shocked. 'Are there no teetotallers in the parish, Keith?'

'Oh, yes, to be sure,' said Keith. 'I've written to them.'

▶ Irish terrorist police have surrounded a Dublin department store. They heard Bed Linen was on the second floor.

ITALIAN JOKES

▶ An Italian family is at the dinner table, when the father says to his oldest son, 'Tony! Why you a such a fat a boy?'

Tony says, 'Poppa, it's a Mama's spaghetti. I can't a stop a eating it.'

Poppa says, 'You should a take a smaller bites.'

Then Poppa says to his middle son, 'Michael! Why you a such a fat a boy?'

Michael says, 'Poppa, it's a Mama's lasagne. I can't a stop a eating it, it's a so good.'

Poppa says, 'You should a take a smaller bites.'

Then Poppa says to his youngest son, 'John! How you a stay so slim a and a trim, a?'

John says, 'It's a so easy, Poppa. I eat a lots and lots of a pussy.'

Poppa says, 'Pussy? Pussy a taste like shit!'

John says, 'Poppa, you should a take a smaller bites.'

▶ Why did the new Italian navy buy glass-bottomed boats? So they could see the old Italian navy.

▶ Two blokes are walking down the street. One of them is notorious for his prejudice against Italians. Yet when he sees an Italian organ grinder with a monkey, he throws £20 into the monkey's hat.

The friend is surprised. 'But people have been telling me for years how much you hated Italians, and here you do that.'

To which the bloke replies, 'Well, they're so cute when they're little.'

▶ A band at an Italian wedding decide to take requests. Nunzio walks up and asks, 'Uh, do youse guys know da song "Strangers in da Night"?'

The band leader says, 'Sure we know that one.'

Nunzio says, 'Hey! dat's great! But I got just one favour – could youse play it in five-four time?'

'Isn't it played in four-four time?' the band leader asks.

'Yeah, but dis here's a special occasion, know whut I mean?'

The band discusses amongst themselves, till the leader turns and says, 'I don't think we'll have any problems.'

Nunzio turns and yells out, 'Hey, Uncle Vinnie! C'mon up here and sing!'

Uncle Vinnie walks up to the mike as the band begins the intro, and then starts to sing, 'Strangers in da fuckin' night... '

JAPANESE JOKES

▶ What do Japanese men do when they have an erection? Vote.

▶ A dustman is going along a street emptying the wheelie bins. He gets to one house where the bin hasn't been left out, so he has a quick look for it, and then knocks on the door. Eventually a Japanese man answers.

'Harro,' he says.

'All right, mate, where's your bin?' asks the dustman.

'I bin on toiret,' replies the Japanese bloke, looking perplexed.

'No, mate, where's ya dustbin?'

'I dust bin on toiret, I told you,' says the Japanese man.

'Mate,' says the dustman, 'you're misunderstanding me... Where's your wheelie bin?'

'OK, OK,' says the Japanese guy. 'I wheelie bin having wank.'

JEHOVAH'S WITNESSES

▶ When a Jehovah's Witness dies and gets to heaven, does God hide behind the gates and pretend he's not in?

▶ What do you get if you cross a Hell's Angel with a Jehovah's Witness? Someone who knocks on your door on a Sunday morning and tells YOU to fuck off!

JEWISH JOKES

▶ What's a Jewish threesome? Two headaches and an erection.

▶ Moshe wants to buy a parrot and goes to his local pet shop to see what they have. The assistant shows him a parrot and explains that this one is really quite special – it can speak most languages. So Moshe decides to test this out.

'Do you speak English?' asks Moshe.

'Yes,' replies the parrot.

'*Hablas español?*' asks Moshe.

'*Si,*' replies the parrot.

'*Parlez vouz français?*' asks Moshe.

'*Oui,*' replies the parrot.

'*Sprechen sie deutsch?*' asks Moshe.

'*Jawohl,*' replies the parrot.

'*Falas portugues?*' asks Moshe.

'*Sim,*' replies the parrot.

Moshe pauses for a while, then asks the parrot, 'Do you speak Yiddish?'

The parrot shrugs its shoulders and says, 'Nu? Vis a nose like dis, vot you tink?'

▶ How do you know Jesus wasn't Jewish? He went to the Last Supper. If he was Jewish, he would've gone for the Early Bird.

▶ No matter what this husband did in bed, his wife never achieved an orgasm. Since by Jewish law a wife is entitled to sexual pleasure, they decide to consult their rabbi. The rabbi listens to their story, strokes his beard and makes the following suggestion: 'Hire a strapping young man. While the two of you are making love, have the young man wave a towel over you. That will help your wife fantasise and should bring on an orgasm.'

They go home and follow the rabbi's advice. They hire a handsome young man and he waves a towel over them as they make love. It does not help and the wife is still unsatisfied. Perplexed, they go back to the rabbi.

'OK,' he says to the husband, 'Try it reversed. Have the young man make love to your wife and you wave the towel over them.'

Once again, they follow the rabbi's advice. They go home and hire the same strapping young man.

The young man gets into bed with the wife and the husband waves the towel. The young man gets to work with great enthusiasm and soon she has an enormous, room-shaking, ear-splitting, screaming orgasm.

The husband smiles, looks at the young man and says to him triumphantly, 'See that, you schmuck? THAT'S how you wave a towel!'

▶ Hear about the Jewish detective? He had a tip off.

▶ Adolf Hitler was very keen on the occult, so he went to a fortune-teller hoping that the woman could tell him how long he would live.

After careful charting, she said, 'I can't predict the exact date of your death, but I do know that you will die on a Jewish holiday.'

'And which holiday will this be?' he asked.

'It does not matter,' she replied. 'Any day that you die will be a Jewish holiday.'

▶ A man is talking to his Irish buddy and says, 'I gotta stop drinking that Irish whisky.'

'How come?' asks his friend.

'Because every Saturday night I go out and drink a bottle of the stuff, come home, make mad passionate love to the wife, wake up Sunday morning and go to church.'

'What's wrong with that?' the Irishman asks. 'A lot of good Irishman go out on Saturday night, drink a bottle of good Irish whisky, come home, do the wife and go to Mass on Sunday.'

'I know,' says his friend, 'but I'm Jewish.'

▶ Keith wonders if having sex on the Sabbath is a sin because he is not sure if sex is work or play. So Keith first of all goes to a Catholic priest and asks for his opinion on this question. After consulting the Bible, the priest says, 'My son, after an exhaustive search, I am positive that sex is work and is therefore not permitted on Sundays.'

Keith thinks, 'What does a priest know about sex?' So he goes to a Protestant minister, who after all is a married man and experienced in this matter. Keith queries the minister and receives the same reply. 'Sex is work and therefore not for the Sabbath.'

Not pleased with the replies, Keith then seeks out the ultimate authority, a man of thousands of years' tradition and knowledge. He goes to a rabbi.

The rabbi ponders the question, then states, 'My son, sex is definitely play.'

Keith replies, 'Thank goodness but rabbi, how can you be so sure when so many others tell me sex is work?'

The rabbi answers, 'If sex were work, my wife would have the maid do it.'

▶ A Jewish grandmother is walking home after a long day at a garment factory. Suddenly a flasher jumps out and opens his coat in front of her.

The lady looks at him and says, 'You call that a lining... ?'

▶ How do you know when a Jewish woman has an orgasm? She drops her nail file.

▶ Why do Jewish women always go for men who are circumcised? Because they find it hard to refuse anything with ten per cent off.

▶ Why does a married princess close her eyes while she's making love? Because she can't stand to see her husband enjoying himself.

▶ What is a Jewish nymphomaniac? A wife who does her hair and sleeps with her husband on the same day.

KNIGHTS

▶ A knight and his men returned to their castle after a hard day of fighting.

'How are we faring?' asked the king.

'Sire!' replied the knight. 'I have been robbing and pillaging on your behalf all day, burning the towns of your enemies to the west.'

'What?' shrieked the king. 'I don't have any enemies to the west!'

'Oh!' said the knight. 'Well, you do now.'

▶ The king was wandering around the palace gardens, when he saw the gardener's wife with seven kids.

'Are these all yours?' he asked.

'Yes, Your Majesty, and we have another seven at home.'

'Good God, your husband deserves a knighthood.'

'He's got one, sir, but he never uses it,' she replied.

KNOBS

▶ A woman put a small ad in the paper seeking some male company. 'Looking for man with these qualifications; won't beat me up or run away from me and is great in bed.'

A couple of days later there's a ring at her door. She opens it to find a man lying on the step.

'Hello, I'm Keith,' he calls up to her. 'I saw your ad. I have no arms so I won't beat you up and no legs so I won't run away. I'm your perfect man.'

'There was one more qualification. What makes you think you're great in bed?'

'I rang the doorbell, didn't I?'

▶ Why does a penis have a hole in the end? So men can be open-minded.

▶ Did you hear about the man who sent away for a penis enlarger? They sent him back a magnifying glass.

▶ A guy is in the pub toilet having a piss, when the door opens. In walks a very large, very muscular guy. This guy proceeds to pull down his pants, revealing a monster prick.

To the man's amazement, the muscular guy growls and slams his dick into the sink attached to the wall. It shatters, spraying pieces and water everywhere. Next, the muscular man growls louder and slams it into one of the stalls, making the entire thing collapse. Then he slams it into the wall of the room, knocking a very large hole into it.

The giant approaches the scared guy having a piss.

'Hey, mate, do you see this very large, very strong cock?' he asks.

'Yes,' replies the guy taking a leak.

'Do you know what I am going to do with this very large, very strong cock?'

'No, I'm afraid I don't.'

'I'm going to shove it up your arse!'

'Jesus, that's a relief. I thought you were going to hit me with it!'

▶ A man went to a doctor to have his dick enlarged. The particular procedure involved grafting a baby elephant's trunk onto the end. Overjoyed, the man went out with his girlfriend to a very fancy restaurant.

After cocktails, the man's prick crept out of his pants, felt around the table, grabbed a hard roll and quickly disappeared under the tablecloth.

The girl was startled and exclaimed, 'What was that?'

Suddenly, the prick came back, took another hard roll and just as quickly disappeared.

The girl was silent for a moment, then finally said, 'I don't believe I saw what I think I just saw... can you do that again?'

With a bit of an uncomfortable smile, the man replied, 'I'd like to, but I don't think my arse can take another crusty roll!'

▶ Two poor kids went to a birthday party at a rich kid's house. The birthday boy was so rich that he had his own swimming pool and all the kids went in. As they were changing afterwards, one of the poor kids said to the other one, 'Did you notice how small the rich kid's penis was?'

'Yeah,' said his mate. 'It's probably because he's got toys to play with.'

▶ Why does an elephant have four feet? Six inches isn't enough.

▶ Why are men so concerned about the size of their penises? Because they should be.

▶ *Letter of complaint to the management:*
I, the Penis, hereby request a raise in salary for the following reasons:

● I do physical labour.

● I work at great depths.

● I plunge headfirst into everything I do.

● I do not get weekends or public holidays off.

● I work in a damp environment.

● I work in a dark workplace that has poor ventilation.

● I work in high temperatures.

● My work exposes me to contagious diseases.

▶ *The reply:*
Dear Penis, after assessing your request and considering the arguments you have raised, the administration rejects your request for the following reasons:

- You do not work eight hours straight.

- You fall asleep after brief work periods.

- You do not always follow the orders of the management team.

- You do not stay in your designated area and are often seen visiting other locations.

- You must be stimulated in order to start working.

- You leave the workplace rather messy at the end of your shift.

- You don't always observe necessary safety regulations, such as wearing the correct protective clothing.

- You will retire well before you are 65.

- You are unable to work double shifts.

- You sometimes leave your designated work area before you have completed the assigned task.

- And if that were not all, you have repeatedly been seen entering and exiting the workplace carrying two suspicious-looking bags.

Sincerely, the Management

▶ When I went to London, I saw a man with a penis growing halfway up his leg. Apparently he was a Cockney.

▶ A man walks into a clock shop, whips out his knob and puts it on the counter.
    The girl behind the counter says, 'Excuse me, sir, this is a clock shop, not a cock shop.'

To which the man replies, 'That's OK, just put two hands and a face on this, then.'

▶ What is the difference between medium and rare? Six inches is medium, eight inches is rare.

▶ *Five reasons not to be a penis:*

• Your head is bald forever.

• You live between two nuts.

• An arsehole lives behind you.

• Your best mate's a c***.

• When you get excited, you get sick and then faint.

▶ A guy's busy whittling a piece of wood. He doesn't realise his zip's open, and he almost cuts off his dick.

His dick looks up and says, 'You know, we've had a lot of fist fights, but I never thought you'd pull a knife on me.'

▶ The anatomy lesson for the week was the way in which the body of a disabled person compensates for its deficiency. As an example, the professor showed a slide of a man with no legs whose arms and shoulders had consequently become hugely muscled. 'Your assignment,' he instructed a pretty medical student, 'is to find someone who has compensated for a physical disability and to report on it for the class.'

After class the student went into the bar next door, and what should she catch sight of but a hunchback nursing a beer at the bar. Screwing up her courage, she went over and told him about her assignment. 'If you don't mind my asking,' she said sweetly, 'is there some part of your anatomy which has compensated for your disability?'

'As a matter of fact there is,' said the hunchback. 'Come up to my place and I'll show you.'

When they got upstairs, he dropped his pants and revealed the biggest cock she had ever seen. Kneeling down, she couldn't resist touching it, then caressing it, then rubbing it against her face.

'For God's sake, don't blow it!' screamed the hunchback, jumping back. 'That's how I got the hump on my back.'

▶ What do you get when you cross a rooster with a flea? An itchy cock.

▶ When Keith first noticed that his penis was growing larger and staying erect longer, he was delighted, as was his wife. But after several weeks, his penis had grown to nearly 20 inches. Keith became quite concerned. He was having problems dressing, and even walking. So he and his wife went to see a prominent urologist. After an initial examination, the doctor explained to the couple that, though rare, Keith's condition could be fixed through corrective surgery.

'How long will he be on crutches?' the wife asked anxiously.

'Crutches? Why would he need crutches?' responded the surprised doctor.

'Well,' said the wife coldly, 'you're going to lengthen his legs, aren't you?'

▶ A white guy, a black guy and a Japanese guy are drinking in a bar together. They are about to leave, when they discover they have no money.

The bartender says, 'All three of you can leave if your dick sizes add up to more than 24 inches. The men agree, and the white guy unzips his jeans. His dick is seven inches. The black guy is next and he unzips his jeans. The black guy's dick is 16 inches. The Japanese guy goes next, and his dick is one inch.

The bartender says, 'I guess your dick sizes add up to 24 so you guys can go now.'

As they are walking out, the black guy says to the Japanese guy, 'Thank God you had a boner, otherwise we'd be in there forever.'

▶ What's the name of the fairy story about an uncircumcised troll? Rumpled Foreskin.

▶ An Italian man was in a bad car accident and after months of recovery he still has a problem. He has to have his penis amputated. He goes to see the doctor and the doctor reassures him that he can help him.

'First of all you have to pick a new penis,' says the doctor. The doctor picks up a box from his table and says, 'This is our six-inch standard model. It is dependable and will cost you only £6,000. It comes with a lifetime guarantee.'

The man says, 'OK, that's about right but I have a question. What's in the other box?'

'This is our ten-inch super model. Ten inches of muscle to please any women. But for this, you have to pay £10,000!'

The man says, 'That's the one I want. My wife will love me forever. But does it also come with a lifetime guarantee?'

'Yes.'

'Well, what's in that other box?'

The doctor picks up yet another box from his desk.

'This is our super deluxe model. It's 12 inches solid and will drive all the ladies wild. But if you want this much power, you have pay £12,000 for it!'

The man is decided: 'Doc, that's it, that's the one for me. I'll be the envy of everyone I know. But does it have a lifetime guarantee?'

'Yes, sir.'

Then the man says he has just one more question. 'Does it come in white?'

▶ A guy goes to the doctor and says, 'Doc, I've got a problem. My dick's square.'

Rubbish,' says the doctor. 'Give me a look.'

The guy undoes his pants and flops it out on the table.

'Amazing,' says the doctor. 'How did it happen?'

'Well, you see, Doc, I was helping a mate shift a fridge when he slipped and the fridge landed on my dick. I rushed into the workshop and put it in the vice, tried to squeeze it back to shape, but the bastard ended up square.'

The doctor reaches for his prescription pad and starts to write.

'What are you going to give me, Doc?' asks the guy.

'Nothing, I'm giving you three days off work to pull yourself round.'

▶ What do you call a man with a two-inch penis? Justin.

▶ What did the elephant say to the naked man? 'How do you breathe through something so small?'

▶ Why can't women read maps? Because only the male mind can comprehend the concept of one inch equals a mile.

▶ A young man goes to a doctor for a physical examination. When he gets into the room, the man strips for his exam. He has a dick the size of a little kid's little finger. A nurse standing in the room sees his little dick and begins to laugh hysterically.

The young man gives her a stern look and says, 'You shouldn't laugh, it's been swollen like that for two weeks now!'

▶ A woman is picked up by Dennis Rodman in a bar. They like each other and she goes back with him to his hotel room. He removes his shirt, revealing all his tattoos, and she sees that on his arm is one which reads 'Reebok'. She thinks that's a bit odd and asks him about it.

Dennis says, 'When I play basketball, the cameras pick up the tattoo and Reebok pays me for advertisement.'

A bit later, his pants are off and she sees 'Puma' tattooed on his leg. He gives the same explanation for the unusual tattoo.

Finally, the underwear comes off and she sees the word 'AIDS' tattooed on his penis. She jumps back with shock.

'I'm not going to do it with a guy who has AIDS!'

He says, 'It's cool, baby, in a minute it's going to say "ADIDAS".'

LAWYERS

▶ A lawyer is paid £950 in new bills but, on counting the money, he discovers that two notes have stuck together and he's been overpaid by £50. This leaves him with an ethical dilemma – should he tell his partner?

▶ A lawyer opens the door of his BMW. Another car speeds by and hits the door, ripping it off completely. When the police arrive, the lawyer is complaining bitterly. 'Officer, look what they've done to my car!' he whines.

'You lawyers are so materialistic, you make me sick,' replies the officer. 'You're so worried about your stupid car, you haven't even noticed your left arm was ripped off!'

'Oh my God!' replies the lawyer. 'Where's my Rolex?'

LEPERS

Did you hear what happened when the leper who ran into a screen door? He strained himself.

What's the difference between a leper and a tree? A tree has limbs.

What do you do when a female leper bats her eyes at you? Catch 'em and yell, 'You're OUT!'

Did you hear about the guy who picked up a leper at the gay bar? After he pulled it out, he got himself a nice piece of ass.

How do you make a skeleton? Put a leper in a wind tunnel.

Did you hear about the lepers against the bomb? They were already disarmed.

Never say to a leper, 'Give me some skin!' Worse, don't ask them to give you head.

Why did the hooker leave the leper colony? Business was dropping off.

▶ What does a leper say to the hooker? 'Keep the tip.'

▶ How many lepers does it take to screw in a lightbulb? Two. One to screw it in, and the other to give him a hand.

▶ Why have lepers got soft heads? So their friends can dip their chips in.

▶ Do you know why the Beatles never played at a leper colony? 'Lend me your ear and I'll sing you a song... '

▶ Hear about the leper who failed his driving test? He left his foot on the clutch.

▶ Why was the leper unable to talk? Cat had his tongue.

▶ Why was the leper kicked off the relay team? He lost the last leg.

▶ Why did the leper fast bowler retire? He threw his arm out.

▶ Why couldn't the leper tie his new running shoes? They cost him an arm and a leg.

▶ Why do lepers make such good neighbours? They're always willing to lend a hand.

▶ Why did the lepers lose the war? Because they were defeated from the start.

LESBIANS

▶ What's the difference between a lesbian and a Ritz biscuit? One's a snack cracker...

▶ What do you call a lesbian dinosaur? Lickalotopis.

▶ How can you tell she's a macho woman? She rolls her own tampons.

▶ What do you call two lesbians in a canoe? Fur traders.

▶ What do you call three lesbians in bed together? Ménage à twat.

▶ How can you tell a tough lesbian bar? Even the pool table has no balls.

▶ What did the two lesbian frogs say to each other? 'We do taste like chicken!'

▶ Did you hear the new and politically correct name for 'lesbian'?
It has been changed to 'vagitarian'.

▶ What do you call a woman with her tongue sticking out? A lesbian with a hard-on.

▶ What is the leading cause of death among lesbians? Hairballs.

▶ Did you hear they came out with a new lesbian shoe? They're called Dikes. They have an extra long tongue and only take one finger to get off.

▶ What do you call a load of lesbians on top of each other? A block of flaps.

▶ Have you heard about the new treatment doctors are prescribing depressed lesbians? It's called Tricoxagain.

▶ A lesbian goes to a gynaecologist and the gynaecologist says, 'I must say, this is the cleanest vagina I've seen in ages.'
    'Thanks,' says the lesbian. 'I have a woman in four times a week.'

▶ How many nails are used to make a lesbian's coffin? None – it's all tongue and groove.

▶ What do you get when you put 50 lesbians in a room with 50 Scousers? One hundred people that won't do dick.

▶ What does a lesbian have in common with a mechanic? Snap-on tools.

▶ Two lesbians walk into a house of ill repute. They ask for the youngest woman in the joint. The madam says that she will not allow the youngest girl any time with them.
    The lesbians make the demand again. 'We want the youngest girl here!'
    The madam says, 'No. I don't serve minors to lickers.'

▶ I just read about the 26-year-old lesbian public school teacher who has been jailed for having a sexual relationship with a student.
Does *Crimewatch* take requests for reconstructions?

▶ Watched this film called *Anal Lesbians* the other day. They spent the entire film going through the fridge labelling everything.

LIBRARY

▶ A woman walks into a library and asks for a book on euphemisms. So the librarian took her up the rear aisle and let her have it.

▶ Is a book on voyeurism a peeping tome?

LIMERICKS

▶ There was a young man from Calcutta
Who spent all his life in the gutta
Till the tropical heat
Got the best of his meat
And turned his cream to butta

▶ Mary had a little skirt
With splits right up the sides
And every time that Mary walked
The boys could see her thighs
Mary had another skirt
'Twas split right up the front
… but she didn't wear that one very often

▶ Mary had a little lamb
Her father shot it dead
Now it goes to school with her
Between two chunks of bread

▶ Mary's lamb had foot and mouth
The vet he came and shot it
But Mary's dad had shagged it first
And now her mother's got it

▶ Mary had a little lamb
She called it baby Abby
They burned it in a great big pit
Cos its mouth and feet were scabby

▶ Humpty Dumpty sat on a wall
Humpty Dumpty had a great fall
All the king's horses and all the king's men said, 'S*d him
He's only an egg'

▶ Georgie Porgy pudding and pie
Kissed the girls and made them cry
When the boys came out to play
He kissed them, too... cos he was funny that way

▶ Jack and Jill
Went up the hill
To have some hanky-panky
Silly Jill forgot her pill
And now there's little Franky

▶ Jack and Jill went up the hill
To fetch a roll of cheese
Jack came down with a smile on his face
And his trousers down to his knees

▶ Jack and Jill went up the hill
To fetch a pail of water
Jill came down with £25
And it wasn't for carrying water

▶ Little Miss Muffet
Sat on her tuffet
Eating sausage and chips
Along came a spider and sat down beside her
And she bashed the poor blighter to bits

▶ Mary had a little lamb
She also had a bear
I have often seen her little lamb
But have never seen her bare

▶ Jack be nimble, Jack be quick
Jack jumped over the candlestick
Dear oh dear, he should have jumped higher
Oh good gracious, great balls of fire

▶ Jack and Jill went up the hill
So Jack could lick Jill's fanny
Jack got a shock
And a mouthful of cock
As Jill's a bloody tranny

▶ There was a young maid from Darjeeling
 Who said she had no sexual feeling
 Till a sailor named Boris
 Just touched her clitoris
 And she had to be scraped from the ceiling

▶ There was a young maid from Nepal
 Who had practically no bush at all
 The reason she said
 Was on top of her bed
 Perched a thatch-eating yellow macaw

▶ Now little John James was a dork
 Who thought he'd been brought by the stork
 His pa wasn't better
 He bought a French letter
 And tested its strength with a fork

▶ This is the story of Judith Smiles
 Who went out one night on the tiles
 But she made a mistake
 With a sailor named Drake
 Who missed and punctured her piles

▶ A horny young lady named Lil
 Fucked a dynamite stick for a thrill
 They found her vagina
 In North Carolina
 And bits of her tits in Brazil

▶ There once was a man from Brighton
Who said to his girl, 'You're a tight one'
She said, 'Pardon my soul
But you're in the wrong hole
There's plenty of room in the right one'

▶ There once was a man from Kansas
Whose nuts were made out of brass
In stormy weather
He'd clack them together
And lightning shot out of his ass

▶ There once was a guy from El Doot
Who found seven huge warts on his root
He put acid on these
And now, when he pees
He's got to finger the thing like a flute

▶ There was a young man from Cape Horn
Who wished he had never been born
He wouldn't have been
If his father had seen
That the end of his condom was torn!

▶ A dirty old man from Dundee
Once ravished an ape in a tree
The result was most horrid
All arse and no forehead
Three balls and a purple goatee

▶ An accident really uncanny
   Befell an unfortunate granny
   She sat down in a chair
   While her false teeth were there
   And bit herself right in the fanny!

▶ There was a young lady at sea
   Who said, 'Gosh, how it hurts me to pee'
   'I see,' said the mate
   'That accounts for the state
   Of the captain, the purser and me'

▶ There was a young fellow from Kent
   Whose prong was so long that it bent
   So to save himself trouble
   He put in a double
   And instead of coming, he went

▶ I chase all the girls when I'm spunky
   A five day a week sexual junkie
   I tend not to stray
   On Tues- or Wednesday
   On those nights I spank my own monkey

▶ Beneath these rocks, lies Mary Cox
   To a thousand men she gave the pox
   She may be gone but not forgotten
   Her heart was good, but her box was rotten

▶ There was a young lady named Gloria
    Whose boyfriend said, 'May I explore ya?'
    She replied to the chap
    'I will draw you a map
    Of where others have been before ya'

▶ There was an old pirate named Bates
    Who was learning to rumba on skates
    He fell on his cutlass
    Which rendered him nutless
    And practically useless on dates

▶ A worried man from Liverpool
    Discovered red spots on his tool
    Said the doctor, a cynic
    'Get out of my clinic
    And wipe off the lipstick, you fool!'

▶ Breathed a tender young man from Australia
    'My darling, please let me unveilia
    And then, of my own
    If you'll kindly lie prone
    I'll endeavour, my sweet, to impalia'

▶ A shiftless young fellow from Kent
    Had his wife screw the landlord for rent
    But as they grew older
    The landlord grew colder
    And now they live in a tent

▶ The nipples of Sarah Sarong
   When excited are 12 inches long
   This embarrassed her lover
   Who was pained to discover
   She expected no less of his dong

▶ There was old guy named Lee
   Who was stung in the balls by a bee
   He made oodles of money
   By oozing pure honey
   Every time he attempted to pee

▶ She demanded I gave her affection
   Then opened her thighs for inspection
   I found her quite nice
   Till I noticed the lice
   And immediately lost my erection

▶ There was a young lady named Hall
   Who wore a newspaper dress to a ball
   The dress caught on fire
   And burned her entire
   Front page, sporting section and all

▶ There was a young man from Rangoon
   Whose farts could be heard to the moon
   When you'd least expect 'em
   They'd burst from his rectum
   With the force of a raging typhoon

▶ There was a young man from Wales
  Who lived on snot, shit and snails
  When he couldn't get these
  He lived off the cheese
  That he scraped from his dick with his nails

▶ There was a young man from Duluth
  Whose dick was shot off in his youth
  So he fucked with his nose
  And his fingers and toes
  And came through a hole in his tooth

▶ A squeamish young fellow named Brand
  Thought caressing his penis was grand
  But he viewed with distaste
  The gelatinous paste
  That it left in the palm of his hand

▶ There was a young lady from Cheam
  Who tried out a breast-growing cream
  She awoke in the night
  With a terrible fright
  Another had grown in between!

▶ There once was a man from Calcutta
  Who took a sly peep through a shutter
  But all he could see
  Was his wife's twitching knee
  And the arse of the man that was up her

▶ There once was a young man named Gene
Who invented a screwing machine
Concave and convex
It served either sex
And it played with itself in between

LOTTERY

▶ A wife arrived home flashing a new diamond ring.
'Where did you get that?' asked her husband suspiciously.

She said, 'My boss and I played the lottery and we won, so I bought the ring with my share of the winnings.'

A week later, she arrived home wearing a new Italian leather coat.
'Where did you get that?' asked her husband.

'My boss and I played the lottery, and guess what, we won again. So I bought the coat with my share of the winnings.'

Three weeks later, she arrived home driving a new Ferrari. 'Where did you get that?' asked the husband.

'My boss and I played the lottery, and you'll never believe it, but we won again. So I bought the car with my share of the winnings.'

That night she asked her husband to run her a nice warm bath, but when she went into the bathroom she found that the bath water was only a couple of inches deep. 'Why did you only run a little amount of water?' she asked.

'Well,' he mumbled sourly, 'we don't want you to get your lottery ticket wet, do we?'

▶ A woman walks into a bar and orders a bottle of champagne. She then pulls down her knickers and pours the contents all over her fanny.

The barman shouts, 'What did you do that for?'

She says, 'I just won the lottery and this is the only c**t I'm sharing it with.'

LOVE

▶ What's the difference between love, true love and showing off? Spitting, swallowing and gargling.

▶ What's the definition of 'Endless Love'? Ray Charles and Stevie Wonder playing tennis.

▶ 'Tis better to have loved a short woman... than never to have loved a tall.

▶ 'Darling,' murmured the girl to her boyfriend, 'when did you first realise that you were in love with me?'

   'Well, I suppose,' whispered the man tenderly, 'it was when I started getting angry with all the other guys in the office who said you were a lousy lay.'

LUMBERJACKS

▶ Why did the lumber truck stop? To let the lumber jack off.

MAFIA

▶ What do the Mafia and a pussy have in common? One slip of the tongue and you're in deep shit.

▶ Why do Mafia members hate Jehovah's Witnesses? They hate ALL witnesses.

MAKE-UP

▶ Why did the Avon lady walk funny? Her lipstick.

▶ Why do women pay more attention to their appearance than to improving their minds? Because most men are stupid, but very few are blind.

▶ Beauty comes from within. From within bottles, jars, tubes, compacts...

MANCUNIANS

▶ What do you call 20 Mancunians in a filing cabinet? Sorted!

MARRIAGE

▶ 'Sir, if you were my husband, I would poison your drink.'
  'Madam, if you were my wife, I would drink it.'
  – A conversation between Lady Astor and Winston Churchill

▶ A man studies his marriage certificate for hours until his wife asks, 'What are you doing?'
  He says, 'I can't find the expiry date.'

▶ Man and wife married for 20 years, and every time they make love the man insists on having the lights off, curtains closed and everything in complete darkness... His wife finally gets the hump with this and suddenly switches on the lights to see what he is hiding. She is shocked when she sees him using a dildo on her.

'After all these years, you wanna explain the dildo, you bastard?!' she shouts.

'Sure, honey... Right after you explain the kids.'

▶ *That's how fights start...*

● My wife and I were watching *Who Wants To Be A Millionaire* while we were in bed.

I turned to her and said, 'Do you want to have sex?'

'No,' she answered.

I then said, 'Is that your final answer?'

She didn't even look at me this time, simply saying, 'Yes.'

So I said, 'Then I'd like to phone a friend.'

And that's when the fight started...

● My wife and I were at her high school reunion, and she kept staring at a drunken man swigging his drink as he sat alone at a nearby table.

I asked her, 'Do you know him?'

'Yes,' she sighed. 'He's my old boyfriend... I understand he took to drinking right after we split up those many years ago, and I hear he hasn't been sober since.'

'My gosh!' I said. 'Who would think a person could go on celebrating that long?'

And then the fight started...

• When our lawnmower broke and wouldn't run, my wife kept hinting to me that I should get it fixed. But somehow I always had something else to take care of first – the shed, the boat, making beer. Always something more important to me. Finally she thought of a clever way to make her point. When I arrived home one day, I found her seated in the tall grass, busily snipping away with a tiny pair of sewing scissors. I watched silently for a short time and then went into the house. I was gone only a minute, and when I came out again I handed her a toothbrush.

I said, 'When you finish cutting the grass, you might as well sweep the driveway.'

The doctors say I will walk again, but I will always have a limp.

• My wife sat down next to me as I was flipping channels.
She asked, 'What's on the TV?'
I said, 'Dust.'
And then the fight started...

• My wife was standing nude, looking in the bedroom mirror.
She was not happy with what she saw and said to me, 'I feel horrible; I look old, fat and ugly. I really need you to pay me a compliment.'
I replied, 'Your eyesight's damn near perfect.'
And then the fight started...

▶ Marriage is like a deck of cards. At first all you need is two hearts and a diamond. By the end you wish you had a fucking club and a spade.

▶ What is the definition of a wife? An attachment you screw on the bed to get the housework done.

▶ 'I can't take it anymore,' says a man to his friend. 'It's my wife. Every time we have an argument, she gets historical!'

'Don't you mean "hysterical"?' says his friend.

'No, I mean historical,' replies the man. 'Every argument we have, she'll go, "I still remember that time when you... "'

▶ A husband says to his wife, 'Honey, tell me something that will make me both happy and sad at the same time.'

The wife replies, 'You have the biggest dick of all your friends.'

▶ Wife to husband: 'I need a new dress.'

Husband: 'What's wrong with the dress you've got?'

Wife: 'It's too long and the veil keeps getting in my eyes.'

▶ FOR SALE BY OWNER:

Complete set of *Encyclopaedia Britannica*. Forty-five volumes. Excellent condition. £300 or best offer. No longer needed. Got married last weekend. Wife knows fucking everything.

▶ Wife to husband: 'Let's go out and have some fun tonight!'

Husband: 'OK, but if you get home before I do, leave the hall light on.'

▶ Wife to husband: 'My mother says I should never have married you. She says you're effeminate.'

Husband: 'Compared to her, everyone is.'

▶ Wife to husband: 'When I married you, you said you had an ocean-going yacht!'

Husband: 'Shut up and row.'

▶ Wife to husband: 'You certainly made a fool of yourself last night. I just hope nobody realised you were sober.'

▶ Harry is strolling through a cemetery, when he comes across a man weeping over a grave. 'Why did you have to go?' sobs the man. 'Why? Why?'

Harry stops to offer some words of comfort. 'I'm so sorry for your loss,' he says. 'Is that your wife's grave?'

'No,' sniffles the man. 'It belongs to her first husband.'

▶ A wife tries to explain the purchase of some expensive underwear to her husband. 'After all, dear,' she says, 'You wouldn't expect to find fine perfume in a cheap bottle, would you?'

'No,' replies her husband, 'And I wouldn't expect to find gift-wrapping on a dead beaver.'

▶ My wife keeps telling me I shouldn't piss in the bath – or if I really have to, I should at least wait till she gets out.

▶ My wife is temperamental. Fifty per cent temper and 50 per cent mental.

▶ I like to watch my wedding video running backwards so I can watch myself walking out of the church a free man.

▶ The marriage got off to a bad start during the wedding service. The vicar said, 'You may now kiss the bride.'

And she said, 'Not now. I've got a headache.'

▶ My wife has old Dyson's syndrome. She makes a constant whining noise and doesn't suck anymore.

▶ An Asian marriage broker has been given the job of finding a bride for an impoverished middle-aged groom. The broker warns the man's parents that he's not much of a catch so they'll have to make do with whatever brides are available. However, when the girl is presented, the man's parents are appalled.

'Look at her,' whispers the father to the mother. 'She has knock knees, cross eyes, a moustache, a huge wart and buck teeth.'

'There's no need to whisper,' says the broker. 'She's deaf, too.'

▶ Two women were talking.

'I suspect my husband used to visit hookers before we met.'

'Why do you say that?'

'One night we were just playing around downstairs. He picked me up and headed for the bedroom.'

'So what happened?'

'Well, I giggled and said, "Should I struggle?" And he replied, "I don't know. Does that cost extra?"'

▶ What does 'WIFE' stand for? Washing, Ironing, Fucking, Etc.

▶ *Playboy* is coming out with a new magazine for men who are married. Every month the centrefold is the exact same woman.

▶ What's the difference between a girlfriend and a wife? About 20 to 30 kilos!

▶ How do you know your wife's dead? Sex is the same but the dishes pile up in the kitchen.

▶ Marriage is a three-ring circus. An engagement ring, a wedding ring and suffer-ring.

▶ Why do married men hang strobe lights from their bedroom ceilings? To create the optical illusion that their wives are moving during sex.

▶ An old man goes to the wizard to ask him if he can remove a curse he has been living with for the last 40 years.

The wizard says, 'Maybe, but you will have to tell me the exact words that were used to put the curse on you.'

The old man says without hesitation, 'I now pronounce you man and wife.'

▶ Adam and Eve had an ideal marriage. He didn't have to hear about all the men she could have married, and she didn't have to hear about the way his mother cooked.

▶ When a husband's words are sharp, it may be from trying to get them in edgeways.

▶ My ex was a heart surgeon. She ripped my heart out.

▶ I've just been given two weeks to live. The wife's gone away for a fortnight.

▶ A dietician was addressing a large audience in London. 'The material we put into our stomachs is enough to have killed most of us sitting here, years ago. Red meat is awful. Soft drinks erode your stomach lining. Chinese food is loaded with MSG. Vegetables can be disastrous to some and none of us realise the long-term harm caused by the germs in our drinking water. But there is one thing that is the most dangerous of all and we all have eaten or will eat it. Can anyone here tell me what food it is that causes the most grief and suffering for years after eating it?'

A 75-year-old man in the front row stood up and said, 'Wedding cake.'

▶ My wife told me I should be more affectionate. So I got two girlfriends.

▶ A man, getting along in years, finds that he is unable to perform sexually. He finally goes to his doctor, who tries a few things, but nothing seems to work. Finally, as a last hope, the doctor refers him to an African medicine man.

The medicine man says, 'I can cure this.' With that said, he throws a white powder into a flame, and there is a flash with billowing blue smoke. Then he says, 'This is powerful healing but you can only use it once a year. All you have to do is say "One, two, three" and it shall rise for as long as you wish!'

The man then asks, 'What happens when it's over, and I don't want to continue?'

The medicine man replies, 'When your partner can take no more sex and is completely raddled, all she has to say is "One, two, three, four," and it will then go down. But be warned, the pork sword will not rise again for another year.'

The old gent rushes home, anxious to try out his new powers. That night he showers, shaves and smothers himself in aftershave. He slides into bed, cuddles up to his wife, says, 'One, two, three,' and suddenly he has the most gigantic stiffy ever, just as the medicine man promised.

His wife turns over and asks, 'What did you say "One, two, three" for?'

▶ Paddy takes his new wife home on his wedding night.

She lies on the bed, spread-eagled and naked, and says, 'Paddy.... you know what I want?'

'Yeah... the whole bloody bed by the looks of it!'

▶ How do most men define marriage? A very expensive way to get your laundry done for free.

▶ A guy on his wedding night is about to get it on with his newlywed for the first time in their hotel. They start to undress and he says, 'God, I never realised that your tits were this small.' The wife gets all upset and understandably throws him out.

While he is sitting outside the room, another guy comes down the corridor. The first man says, 'Hey, what happened?'

'Well, I saw my wife naked for the first time tonight and all I said was, "Oh, I never knew your arse was that big," and she just threw me out, just like that.'

Just then a third guy, also on his wedding night like the first two guys, comes storming out into the hall.

'Hey, did you put your foot in it as well?' ask the two men already outside.

'No,' says the third guy, 'but I bloody well could have.'

▶ My wife sent me a card saying 'Get better soon' today. I'm not ill, I'm just crap at sex.

▶ 'I will' is the shortest sentence in the English language. 'I do' is the longest.

▶ A woman sits down next to an attractive man on a bus. She says, 'You look just like my fourth husband.'

The man replies, 'Your FOURTH husband? How many times have you been married?'

'Three,' the woman replies.

▶ I love being married. It's so great to find that one special person you want to annoy for the rest of your life.

Marriage changes passion... suddenly you're in bed with a relative.

I just got back from a pleasure trip – I drove my wife to the airport.

My wife and I were happy for 20 years... then we met.

One woman says to another, 'Isn't your wedding ring on the wrong finger?'

The other woman replies, 'Why, yes, it is. I married the wrong man.'

After a quarrel, a husband said to his wife, 'You know, I was a fool when I married you.'

She replied, 'Yes dear, but I was in love and didn't notice.'

Man is incomplete until he is married. Then he is finished.

Just think, if it weren't for marriage, men would go through life thinking they had no faults at all.

'I was married by a judge. I should have asked for a jury' – Groucho Marx

Marriage is not a word; it's a sentence.

▶ Make love, not war. Hell, do both – get married!

▶ 'Congratulations, my boy!' said the uncle. 'I'm sure you'll look back and remember today as the happiest day of your life.'
  'But I'm not getting married until tomorrow,' the groom protested.
  'I know,' replied the uncle. 'That's what I mean.'

▶ The only difference between marriage and prison is that at least prisoners occasionally get to finish a sentence.

▶ I didn't get married until I was 37. By then I had done all the things I wanted to do, seen all the things I wanted to see, been to all the places I wished to visit. But I didn't know what real happiness was until I got married. Then it was too late.

▶ The secret to successful investing for retirement is to keep your first wife.

▶ A successful man is one who makes more money than his wife can spend. A successful woman is one who can find such a man.

▶ To be happy with a man, you must understand him a lot and love him a little. To be happy with a woman, you must love her a lot and not try to understand her at all.

▶ Any married man should forget his mistakes. There's no use in two people remembering the same thing.

▶ A woman has the last word in any argument. Anything a man says after that is the beginning of a new argument.

I married my wife for her looks, but not the ones she's been giving me lately.

If love is blind and marriage is an institution, then marriage is an Institution for the Blind.

▶ Marriage: five minutes to get in and a lifetime to get out of.

I married Miss Right. I just didn't know her first name was 'Always'.

What's the difference between a boyfriend and a husband? About 20 to 30 minutes!

Why do men die before their wives? They want to.

Why do married men gain weight while single men don't? A single man goes to the refrigerator, sees nothing that he wants and goes to bed. A married man goes to bed, sees nothing he wants and goes to the refrigerator.

It's not true that married men live longer than single men... It only seems longer.

Scientists have discovered a food to diminish a woman's sex drive by 90 per cent. It's called wedding cake.

▶ 'Instead of getting married again, I'm going to find a woman I don't like and give her a house.' – Lewis Grizzard

▶ Three women were sitting around talking about their sex lives.

The first said, 'I think my husband's like a championship golfer. He's spent the last ten years perfecting his stroke.'

The second woman said, 'My husband's like a racing driver. Every time we get into bed, he gives me several hundred exciting laps.'

The third woman was silent until she was asked, 'Tell us about your husband.'

She thought for a moment and said, 'My husband's like an Olympic gold-medal-winning quarter-miler.'

'How so?'

'He's got his time down to under 40 seconds.'

▶ Three blokes are talking in the pub. Two of them are talking about the amount of control they have over their wives, while the third bloke remains quiet.

After a while one of the first two turns to the third and says, 'Well, what about you? What sort of control do you have over your wife?'

The man says, 'I'll tell you. Just the other night my wife came to me on her hands and knees.'

The first two blokes are amazed.

'What happened then?' they ask.

'She said, "GET OUT FROM UNDER THE BED AND FIGHT LIKE A MAN!"'

MASTURBATION

▶ What do a Rubik's Cube and a penis have in common? The longer you play with them, the harder they get.

▶ What's the difference between a girl in church and a girl in the bath? One has hope in her soul...

▶ My uncle was jailed for his beliefs. He believed you could wank on the bus.

▶ Who's the world's greatest athlete? The guy who finishes first and third in a masturbation contest.

▶ A man is driving home late one night and is feeling quite aroused. As he is passing a pumpkin patch, he thinks to himself, 'You know, a pumpkin is soft and squishy inside, and there is no one around here for miles.'

He pulls over to the side of the road, picks out a nice juicy-looking pumpkin, cuts the appropriate size hole in it and begins to slake his erotic desires.

Soon, he is really into it, and doesn't notice the police car pulling up.

The cop walks over and says, 'Excuse me, sir, but do you realise that you are screwing a pumpkin?'

The man looks at the cop in complete horror and then down at the pumpkin he is holding between his hands.

Thinking fast, he says to the cop, 'A pumpkin? Damn! Is it midnight already?'

▶ Where can you get the best masturbation toys? Clit 'R' Us.

▶ A waitress walks up to the table of three Japanese men at a restaurant. When she gets to the table, the waitress notices that the three men are furiously masturbating.

She asks, 'What the hell are you perverts doing?', to which one of the men replies, 'We all berry hungry!'

She responds, 'But why are you whacking off?' One of the three says, 'Because menu say "first come, first served"!'

▶ Little Johnny had become a real nuisance while his father tried to concentrate on his Saturday afternoon poker game with friends and relatives. His father tried every way possible to get Johnny to occupy himself – television, ice cream, homework, video games – but the youngster insisted on running back and forth behind the players and calling out the cards they held. The other players became so annoyed that they threatened to quit the game and all go home.

At this point, the boy's uncle stood up, took Johnny by the hand and led him out of the room. The uncle soon returned back to the poker table without Johnny, and without comment the game resumed.

For the rest of the afternoon, little Johnny was nowhere to be seen and the card players continued without any further interruptions.

After the poker game ended, the father asked Johnny's uncle, 'What in the world did you say to Johnny? I haven't heard a peep from him all day!'

'Not much,' the boy's uncle replied. 'I just showed him how to masturbate.'

▶ This guy goes to Amsterdam to video a presentation. While staying in his hotel, he finds the porno channel on the telly. After a flash of inspiration he sets up the camera in front of the screen and tapes a whole hour of the hardcore proceedings. On arriving home, he tells his best friend about his trip and lends him the video tape. The following morning his friend returns the tape and says, 'Did you watch this tape?'

'No, I saw the original.'

'I think you better watch it yourself before you lend it out again.'

The guy did as he was advised. He immediately noticed with horror that he had omitted to take into account the reflective nature of the television screen.

▶ A guy was on a business trip and he's staying in this fancy hotel. When he goes up to his room, there's a sign near the bed that says: 'Try our Oriental massage'. So he rings down to the reception and tells the clerk that he'd like to try one of these massages. About ten minutes later this Japanese lady comes up and starts giving him a massage.

He's lying on his stomach and getting pretty horny, he gets a huge boner. She tells him to turn over and when he does, she sees his cock standing to attention. So she giggles and says, 'Ahh, you want wanky!'

He says, 'Oooh, yes!'

So she runs off into the bathroom and he lies on the bed waiting. A few minutes later she sticks her head out from behind the door and says, 'You finished yet?'

▶ A newly married couple returned to their house after being on honeymoon.

'Care to go upstairs and have a bop?' the husband asked.

'Shhhh!' said the bride, 'all the neighbours will know what we're about to do. These walls are paper thin. In the future, we'll have to ask each other in code. For example, how about asking, "Have you left the washing machine door open" instead?'

So the following night, the husband asked, 'I don't suppose you left the washing machine door open, did you?'

'No, I definitely shut it,' replied the wife, who rolled over and fell asleep.

When she woke up, however, she was feeling a little amorous herself and she nudged her husband and said, 'I think I did leave the washing machine door open after all. Would you like to do some washing?'

'No thanks,' said the husband. 'It was only a small load so I did it by hand.'

▶ A wino said to his buddy, 'I'll never forget the first time I turned to drink as a substitute for women.'

'What happened?'

'I got my dick stuck in the neck of the bottle.'

▶ The pope decides to go on tour so that he can speak to people all over the world. He wakes up one morning in his hotel room with a huge boner. He carefully looks around the whole room to make sure that nobody is there. After making sure that the room is clear, he begins to jerk off, but after a while a reporter bursts into his room and snaps his picture.

The pope says, 'Please, sir, you can't publish this picture, I'll be ruined! I'll tell you what, I'll give you $2,000 for your camera with that film in it.'

'OK,' the reporter says.

Later that day, while touring the city and taking pictures with his new camera, the pope starts talking to a local priest.

The priest compliments him on his new camera and asks what he paid for it.

'$2,000,' the pope replies.

'$2,000!' gasps the priest. 'Your holiness, they must have seen you coming!'

▶ Because his son wasn't the brightest kid in the world, old hillbilly Joe took him to the outhouse one day to teach him how to urinate properly. 'Now you lissen good, Jim Bob, cuz here's whatcha gotta do.

'One: Take out your penie-pipe.

'Two: Pull back the foreskin.

'Three: Pee.

'Four: Push back your foreskin.

'Five: Put your equipment back.'

The boy said he understood, but the next day while he was working at his still, Joe's wife came running over.

'Oh, Joe, Joe, come quick! Jim Bob went ta piss an' won't come out of the outhouse!'

'Tarnation, whut's he doin' in there?' Joe said.

'I dunno. He jess keeps sayin' "Two-four, two-four, two-four... "'

▶ You masturbate too much if you can change hands without missing a stroke.

▶ What's the ultimate in rejection? When you're masturbating, your hand falls asleep.

▶ If a guy breaks his left hand, how's his sex life? It's all right.

▶ What do you call a guy who sits in the balcony at a porno flick? A tier jerker.

▶ Did you hear about the guy that climbed to the top of the Empire State Building to masturbate? Police didn't know whether to arrest him for indecent exposure or for hijacking.

▶ What happened when the armless guy attempted masturbation? He was stumped.

▶ How is a medieval masturbator like an ocean wave? They're both pounding serfs.

▶ What is the female equivalent to 'pocket pool'? Playing the slots.

▶ Why do preachers masturbate? Because God helps those who help themselves.

▶ What's a masturbator's favourite holiday? Palm Sunday.

▶ Why does Dr Pepper come in a bottle? Because his wife died.

▶ A young man was shipwrecked on a remote island. Although he had plenty of food and water, there was nothing for him to do except play with himself. After many years, that became so monotonous that he couldn't even get an erection. Now, completely without any happiness, he started to lose his sanity. One morning, as he is lying on the beach, he thinks he sees a ship in the distance. He quickly starts a fire, then throws wet seaweed on top until smoke is billowing high in the air. The ship starts to come his way!

He gets all excited and thinks, 'Finally! I'm going to be saved! The first thing I want is to take a long, hot shower. Then they're going to give me some clothes and I'm going to go upstairs and have a nice dinner. I will find a nice lady to dance with, then I will take to her cabin and we can kiss and I can fondle her body. She'll start to take off her clothes and she'll be wearing red silk panties!' At this, he starts to get an erection. He slips his hand into his shorts, grabs his pecker and yells, 'Ha ha ha! I lied about the ship!'

▶ A sex therapist was advising a dysfunctional male patient on the release that could be obtained through masturbation. 'Oh, but I do get pleasure from my organ,' he replied. 'I frequently grasp my penis and hold it tight. It's a habit with me.'

'Well, it's a habit you'll have to shake,' said the therapist.

▶ My next-door neighbour was at a club the other night with her boyfriend, when the topic came around to masturbation. We noticed that there were all kinds of terms for men doing it, but there weren't any euphemistic phrases for women doing the same thing. We asked my neighbour what she called it.

Giving a scornful look at her boyfriend, she muttered, 'Finishing the job!'

▶ Ann and Sophie, both in their 50s, are having lunch, when Sophie, looking very serious, says, 'Ann, it's mine and Harry's 25th wedding anniversary next month, and I would really like to give him something special. I've never given him a hand job and I know how desperately he wants one but, Ann, I don't know how to give one... what should I do?'

Ann takes her friend aside and says, 'Go and get yourself a ketchup bottle. You have a month to practise.'

One month later, on their anniversary, while Sophie and Harry are in bed, Sophie tells Harry that she has a special present for him and when he finds out it's a hand job, he becomes hard with anticipation.

Sophie takes his penis and grips it with one hand and says, 'Here goes... I hope you like it.'

Sophie then takes her other hand and smacks the end of his penis with the palm of her hand three times.

▶ Pete had passed his 29th birthday and was still not married, so his father found him a nice girl, whom he married. Less than a month later, his father caught him masturbating in the garden shed.

'What's this?' he said. 'I thought you'd stop doing that once you got married.'

'But Dad,' answered the son, 'the poor girl's not used to it. Her arms get tired.'

▶ The minister, all fired up because of recent problems of infidelity, shouted out, 'I want everyone who has been he-ing and she-ing to stand up!'

Half of his congregation stood up.

He then shouted out, 'I want everyone who has been he-ing and he-ing to stand up!'

A couple of men stood up.

He then shouted out, 'I want everyone who has been she-ing and she-ing to stand up!'

Several women stood up. The minister looked over his congregation and noticed that everyone was standing except Little Johnny.

The minister shouted out, 'Brothers and sisters, look at Little Johnny – can he be the only one without sin? Little Johnny, stand up... I guess you are the only one here who isn't preoccupied with sex and committing sins. What do you have to say?'

Little Johnny replied, 'Reverend, you ain't said nothing about me-ing and me-ing!'

▶ Little Johnny is sleeping in bed, when his mother comes along and says, 'Rise and shine, Johnny, time to wake up.'

Johnny replies, like any normal kid, 'Five more minutes, Mum.'

Little Johnny's mother decides to give Johnny five more minutes, so she goes down the stairs and starts cooking breakfast.

Five minutes later Johnny comes down the stairs and is crying uncontrollably.

'What's wrong, Johnny?' asks Johnny's mother.

'I had a wet dream last night,' Johnny replies. His mother is surprised, but keeps her composure.

'That's nothing to cry over, is it, Johnny?' she says.

'Of course it bloody is,' says Johnny. 'Now whenever anyone asks me what the first thing I said after my first orgasm is, I'll have to tell them "Five more minutes, Mum!"'

▶ A bloke got his sleeping pills mixed up with his Viagra. He ended up having 40 wanks.

▶ What's the difference between purple and pink? The grip.

▶ I watched intently as the 'other' woman slowly peeled off my girlfriend's panties and stared closely as she delicately inserted her fingers into my girlfriend's pussy.

Naturally, I undid my trousers and started wanking.

Midwives, eh! Got no sense of humour at all.

▶ If a woman is uncomfortable watching a man wank, should she:
a) Get to know me better?
b) Stop being such a prude?
or
c) Find another seat on the bus?

▶ What do you call a herd of cows masturbating? Beef strokin' off.

▶ A man goes to the doctor and says, 'Doctor, you've got to help me. My dick's gone orange.'

The sceptical doctor pauses to think and asks the man to drop his pants so he can check.

Sure enough, the chap's dick is orange. The doctor tells the man, 'This is very strange. Sometimes things like this are caused by a lot of stress in a person's life.'

Probing as to the causes of possible stress, the doctor asks, 'How are things going at work?'

The man replies that he was fired about six weeks ago and the doctor tells him that this must be the cause of the stress.

The man responds, 'No. The boss was a real arse, I had to work 20 to 30 hours of overtime every week and I had no say in anything that was happening. I found a new job a couple of weeks ago where I can set my own hours, I'm getting paid double what I got on the old job and the boss is really great.'

So the doctor rules work stress out as the reason.

He asks the man, 'How's your home life?'

The man says, 'Well, I got divorced about eight months ago.'

The doctor reasons that this has got to be the reason for all of the patient's stress.

But the man says, 'No. For years, all I listened to was nag, nag, nag. God, am I glad to be rid of that old bitch.'

So the doctor takes a few minutes to think a little longer. He enquires, 'Do you have any hobbies or a social life?'

The guy replies, 'No, not really. Most nights I sit at home, watch porno films and eat Cheesy Wotsits.'

▶ A man goes to the doctor and says, 'I have a problem. After I masturbate, I start to sing "You'll Never Walk Alone".'

The doc says, 'Don't worry, lots of wankers sing that.'

▶ A man went to see the nurse this morning for his annual check-up.

She told him, 'You have to stop wanking.'

He said, 'Why?'

She said, 'Because I'm trying to examine you.'

▶ A wealthy hospital benefactor was visiting the hospital, when, during her tour, she spotted a male patient masturbating. 'Oh my God!' screamed the woman. 'That's disgraceful! Why is he doing that?'

The doctor leading the tour explained, 'I'm very sorry you had to see that but he has has a very serious condition. His testicles fill with semen so rapidly that he has to do that five times a day or they'll explode and he'll die within minutes.'

'Oh well, in that case I suppose it's OK,' said the benefactor. But in the very next room she saw a lovely young nurse performing oral sex on another male patient. Again the woman screamed, 'Oh my God! How can that ever be justified?'

'Same illness, private patient!'

▶ A woman had come to see her shrink. When he began using sexual terms, she interrupted.

'Wait, what is a phallic symbol?'

'A phallic symbol,' explained the doctor, 'represents the phallus.'

'What's a phallus?' asked the woman.

'Well,' said the analyst, 'the best way to explain it is to show you.' He stood up, unzipped his fly and took out his penis. 'This is a phallus.'

'Oh,' said the girl. 'It's like a prick, only smaller.'

▶ What's the most sensitive part of your body when you're wanking? Your ears, listening for footsteps.

▶ It's spring, and the baby bear comes out of his cave. His knees are wobbling; he's a wreck. He's skin and bones, with big circles under his eyes.

His mother says, 'Junior! Did you hibernate all winter like you were supposed to?'

He says, 'Hibernate? Shit! I thought you said masturbate!'

▶ *Synonyms for masturbation for men:*

• Auditioning the hand puppet

• Badgering the witness

• Blueball baseball

• Choking the bald guy 'til he pukes

• Committing mass spermicide

• Decongesting the weasel

• Escorting the one-eyed postal worker out of his denim cell

• Fishing for zipper trout

• Freeing the hostages

• Getting your palm red

• Giving yourself a low five

• Having a staff meeting

- Making the llama spit

- Million sperm march

- Performing diagnostics on your man tool

- Playing pocket polo with Agent Johnson

- Playing the stand-up organ

- Pulling the single serving soup dispenser

- Romancing the bone

- Running in single-user mode

- Sanding the obelisk

- Taking little Elvis to Graceland

- Test-firing the meat missile

- White-water wristing

▶ *Synonyms for masturbation for women:*

- Brushing your afro

- Checking for squirrels

- Cleaning your fur coat

- Diggin' the stench trench

- Doing the two-finger slot rumba

- Feeding the bearded clam

- Fishing for cumpliments

- Fishing for mackerel

- Going to and from the Batcave

- Making your own gravy

- Ménage à moi

- Muffin buffin'

- Opening the bottom drawer

- Paddling the pink canoe

- Playing the clitar

- Romancing thy own

- Rubbin' Hood

- Strumming the big open C

- Working out at the Y

▶ A man who was in the Air Force had just spent a year tour unaccompanied to Alaska. The first night he got home, he exclaimed to his wife, 'Darling, I want you to know that I haven't wasted all this time alone. Instead, I've mastered the art of mind over matter. Just watch this!'

And with that, he dropped his trousers and pants and stood before her in the altogether.

'Now watch,' he said. Next he said, 'Dick, ten-HUT!'

And with that, his dick sprang to full erection. Then he said, 'Dick, at EASE!'

And his dick deflated again.

'Wow, that was amazing,' said his wife. 'Do you mind if I bring our next-door neighbour over to see this? It's really something else!'

The man responded that he didn't mind at all, since he was proud of what he had accomplished. So the wife went next door and came back with a delicious-looking woman who got the man's full attention. After a brief pause to take her in, he said, 'Now watch this.' Then he said 'Dick, ten-HUT!' And the dick sprang to life.

Then it was, 'Dick, at EASE!'

But nothing happened. So the man again said, 'Dick, at EASE!'

But still nothing happened. So the man then said, 'For the last time, you son-of-a-bitch, I said AT EASE!'

Still nothing. The man, embarrassed, ran off to the bathroom. His wife made excuses for him and then joined her husband in the bathroom, where she found him masturbating.

'What in the world are you doing?' she asked.

The man replied, 'I'm giving this son-of-a-bitch a dishonourable discharge!'

▶ What do you call a man who cries when he masturbates? A tear-jerker.

MEDICAL

▶ First, I got angina pectoris and then arteriosclerosis. Just as I was recovering from these, I got tuberculosis, double pneumonia and phthisis. Then they gave me hypodermics.

Appendicitis was followed by tonsillectomy. These gave way to aphasia and hypertrophic cirrhosis.

I completely lost my memory for a while. I know I had diabetes and acute ingestion, besides gastritis, rheumatism, lumbago and neuritis.

I don't know how I pulled through it. It was the hardest spelling test I've ever had.

▶ I bought a suppository from Ikea. I had to put it up myself.

▶ I read a book about the digestive system. The ending was shit.

▶ One of my nipples is a different colour to the other two. Is this normal?

▶ At a naval barracks the enlisted men were being given their shots prior to going overseas. One lad, having received his series of injections, asked for a glass of water.

'What's the matter, mate?' asked the sick bay attendant. 'Do you feel pain?'

'No, just want to see if I'm still watertight.'

▶ What's the worst part about getting a lung transplant? The first couple of times you cough, it's not your phlegm...

MICE

▶ Why do mice have such tiny balls? Because so few of them can dance.

▶ A mouse was sitting in a bar having a drink, when a beautiful female giraffe came in and sat down at the end of the bar. The mouse looked over at her and ordered her a drink. Soon he had moved down beside her and ordered her another drink. After a third round, the bartender looked up and they were leaving the bar together.

The next day the mouse limped into the bar, barely crawled up on the bar stool and sat there gasping for air. His whiskers were bent and broken, tail was crooked and patches of hair were falling out.

The bartender took one look and said, 'How did it go last night?'

The mouse said, 'Man, that was the best sex I ever had.'

The bartender asked, 'Why do you look so bad?'

The mouse replied, 'Between the "Kiss me, screw me, kiss me, screw me", I must have run 20 miles!'

▶ Japanese authorities have banned all animal movements after several sofabeds were found nibbled in Tokyo. It is thought this may be an outbreak of the dreaded Futon Mouse disease.

▶ What did the mouse say when they gave him Viagra? 'Here, pussy, pussy, pussy!'

▶ A man goes into a bar. A mouse jumps out of his pocket.

The bartender says, 'Nice mouse!'

The man says, 'No ordinary mouse, though – this little feller talks!'

The bartender says, 'Oh yeah, what about?'

The man says, 'See that woman at the end of the bar – the mouse will tell me what colour panties she has on.'

The bartender says, 'Really? This I gotta see.'

The man points to the woman and says to the mouse, 'Mouse, woman!'

The mouse runs down, sees the woman's panties from the floor, comes back and says, 'Pink.'

'Wow,' the bartender says. 'Will he do that for me?'

The man says, 'Sure.'

The bartender sees a woman sitting at a table, points to her and says, 'Mouse: woman!'

The mouse runs out, comes tearing back and bounces off the bar into the bartender's pocket, shaking like a leaf.

The bartender says, 'What's wrong with you?'

The mouse says, 'I taught I taw a puddy tat!'

MID-LIFE CRISIS

▶ Why don't men have mid-life crises? They stay stuck in adolescence.

MISSIONARIES

▶ A missionary was sent to live with a primitive native tribe that lived in the depths of the jungle. He spent several years with the people, during which time he taught them English and how to read and write. He also taught them the Christian ways of the white man, and one thing that he stressed in particular was the evil of sexual sin, namely no adultery and no fornication. One day, the wife of one of the tribe's noblemen gave birth to a child. But to everyone's horror, the child was white. Not surprisingly, this caused a veritable stir in the village.

The chief sent for the missionary and said, 'You have taught us the evils of sexual sin, but here is a black woman who gives birth to a white child. You are the only white man who has been in the village for many years. What is the explanation?'

The missionary said, 'No, my good man, you are mistaken. This is a natural occurrence, what we English call an albino. Nature does this on some occasions. For example, look at that flock of sheep. They are all white except among them, look, there is one black sheep.'

The chief thought it over for a moment, called the missionary forwards, and whispered in his ear, 'OK. Tell you what. You don't say anything about the black sheep, and I won't say anything about the white child.'

▶ There was a woman who spent some months serving God in Kenya. On her final visit to a remote township she attended a medical clinic. As the Maasai women there began to sing together, she found herself deeply moved by their hauntingly beautiful harmonies. She wanted to always remember this moment and try to share it with friends when she arrived home.

With tears flowing down her cheeks, she turned to her friend and asked, 'Can you please tell me the translation of the words to this song?'

Her friend looked at her and solemnly replied, 'If you boil the water, you won't get dysentery.'

MONEY

▶ A customs agent stopped an elderly man who had just emigrated to England and asked him to open his two suitcases.

In the first suitcase, the agent found over a million pounds in £10 notes. 'Excuse me, sir,' he asked, 'where did you get all this money?'

'Well, I'll tell you,' said the old man. 'I love England. God bless the Queen. For many years I travelled all around the world and stopped off at all of the public toilets in all the major cities; I went to New York, I went to Berlin, I went to Madrid, to Moscow, to Paris, everywhere. As soon as I arrived, I went into all the cubicles where the men were peeing and I said to them, "Give me £10 for England or I'll cut off your testicles with my knife."'

'That's quite a story,' the customs agent said. 'What's in the second suitcase?'

'Well, you know,' said the old man, shaking his head, 'not everyone likes to give... '

▶ How much does a grand piano cost? £1,000.

▶ *Expense account:*

1 Jan. Ad for female secretary £5.

2 Jan. Flowers for new secretary £7.50.

6 Jan. Week's salary for secretary £225.

9 Jan. Roses for secretary £25.

10 Jan. Chocolates for wife £4.50.

12 Jan. Lunch with secretary £35.

13 Jan. Week's salary for secretary £300.

16 Jan. Theatre tickets for self and secretary £75.

19 Jan. Pot plant for wife £2.50.

20 Jan. Virginia's salary £375.

23 Jan. Champagne and dinner for 'Ginny' £160.

25 Jan. Doctor for stupid secretary £1,500.

25 Jan. Fur coat for wife £6,800.

27 Jan. Ad for male secretary £5.

▶ Why is a launderette a bad place for a man to pick up women? Women who can't even afford a washing machine will never be able to support you.

▶ A couple had been married for over 40 years but with the husband in serious financial trouble, he told his wife that he was thinking of committing suicide.

'Don't worry, honey,' she said reassuringly. 'We're not as hard up as you think because right from the start of our marriage I've been putting aside £2 every time we had sex. Our savings have now grown to over £100,000!'

'Oh, that's wonderful!' he exclaimed. 'What an amazing woman you are! And what an ingenious idea. I'm only sorry now that I didn't give you all my business!'

▶ A government spokesman has confirmed that in order to meet the conditions for joining the Euro, the phrase 'spending a penny' is not to be used after 31 December 2011. From this date the correct terminology will be 'euronating'.

▶ We were so poor, we couldn't get rid of the roaches in our house because they paid half the rent.

▶ We were so poor, we had to go to KFC to lick other people's fingers.

▶ Our house was so small, if we got a large pizza we had to go outside to eat it.

▶ The tax auditor has just read the story of Cinderella to his four-year-old daughter for the first time. The little girl is fascinated by the story, especially the part where the pumpkin turns into a golden coach.

'Daddy,' she says. 'When the pumpkin turned into a golden coach, would that be classed as income or a long-term capital gain?'

▶ I wouldn't say Harry was mean, but last Christmas Eve he fired a pistol in the garden and told the kids Santa had committed suicide.

▶ My uncle is very mean. I went round the other day and found him stripping the wallpaper. He wasn't redecorating; he was moving.

▶ He was so mean he used to give his children £1 each instead of an evening meal, then charged them £2 for breakfast.

MOTHERS

▶ What's pink and wrinkled and hangs out your pants? Your mum.

▶ 'Mummy, Mummy, are you sure this is how to learn to swim?'
  'Shut up and get back in the sack!'

▶ What do you call a woman who puts her diaphragm in crooked? Mother.

▶ A little boy is found crying in Tescos. The security guard says, 'Are you lost?'
  The little sobbing boy replies that he is.
  'What's your mummy like?'
  The little boy looks up and says, 'Big cocks and Bacardi Breezers.'

▶ *Mother's Day cards you'll never see:*

• I love you when you're happy
  I love you when you're sad

I love you though you told me
The milkman is my dad

- Roses are red
  My childhood was blue
  Get out of my cellar
  Your rent is past due

- The cards in the store
  Were just too full of sex
  But I thought, 'What the hell'
  Love, Oedipus Rex

- There once was a woman named Mother
  Who always did favour my brother
  But now that he's dead, Mother senses with dread
  That *her* nursing home's worse than the others

- You stood up to my father's kin, their many threats of extortion
  Thanks for having me, Mother dear, instead of an abortion

- Dear Mum, in your Mother's Day card
  Is a question that you may find hard:
  If Dad went astray, if he left, as you say,
  Who's that buried in the backyard?

- When I was born, you became a mum
  And gave me lots of joy and lovin'
  But now, I need to come back home
  I've got my own bun in the oven

- For my (almost) fifth stepmother:
  Congrats to you, my almost-mum
  You've nearly won the war
  Unlike all the other tramps
  Dad picks up in the bar!

- I'm going to Denmark, Mother dear
  For some changes of which you'll learn
  You always wanted a little girl
  Well, you'll have one when I return

- You've lovingly looked after me since I was just a baby
  So now I don't resent the fact that both my mums are ladies

- I think of you, dear Mother, as I'm in my cell, alone
  And miss the way you always made our crack house a crack home

- You probably won't even listen
  You may still think, 'How *could* he?'
  But no card's as heartfelt as this 'un
  Best wishes, Soon-Yi and Woody

▶ I remember when my mum would tuck me in. She really wanted a daughter.

MUSICIANS AND MUSIC

▶ A man walks into the doctor's office and says, 'Doctor, I haven't had a bowel movement in a week!'

The doctor gives him a prescription for a mild laxative and tells him, 'If it doesn't work, let me know.'

A week later the man is back: 'Doc, still no movement!'

The doctor says, 'Hmm, I guess you need something stronger,' and prescribes a powerful laxative.

Still another week later the poor guy is back: 'Doc, STILL nothing!'

The doctor, worried, says, 'We'd better get some more information about you to try to figure out what's going on. What do you do for a living?'

'I'm a musician.'

The doctor looks up and says, 'Well, that's it! Here's £10. Go and get something to eat!'

▶ The Beach Boys walk into a bar.
'Round?'
'Round?'
'Get a round.'
'I get a round?'
'Get a round.... '

▶ Did you hear about the man who bought a Casio keyboard that would only play Wagner? It was a Nazi synthesizer.

▶ What's the difference between Michael Jackson and Manchester United? Manchester United can still play Giggs.

▶ What's the difference between a Spice Girls video and a porn video? The porn video has better music.

▶ What do you call five dogs with no balls? The Spice Girls.

▶ What is 30 feet long, has ten teeth and smells of piss? The front row at a Des O'Connor concert.

▶ Went to a karaoke bar last night and discovered they didn't play any '70s music. At first I was afraid... I was petrified.

▶ Did you hear about the new band Prevention? They're going to be better than the Cure.

▶ I'm in a band called Stuck in the Departure Lounge! Check us out!

▶ How do Geordies listen to music? On a Why iPod.

▶ Have you heard of the band called Paper? They cover rock.

▶ Scientists managed to build a robot that walked 14 miles unaided this week.
The Proclaimers were unimpressed.

▶ A man walks into an extremely posh restaurant, sits down and waves the waiter over. 'I want to see the cocksucking motherfucking boss now!'
   Naturally the waiter is a bit taken aback and says, 'Would you please refrain from using that kind of language in here, sir. I'll get the manager as soon as I can.'
   When the manager comes over, the bloke greets him with, 'Are you the chicken fucking manager of this bastarding joint?'
   'Yes, sir, I am but I would prefer it if you did not use that kind of language in this restaurant. There are respectable guests dining here.'
   The bloke retorts, 'Screw you, anus features. Where's the fucking piano?'

The manager is a bit puzzled and asks the man to explain himself.

'You stupid smelly dickhead, are you fucking deaf or what? Where's the twatting piano?'

'Ah,' says the manager, 'you've come about the pianist job we advertised in the paper.'

'Too fucking right,' comes the reply.

The manager takes him over to the piano but begs him not to speak into the microphone. 'Can you play any blues?'

The bloke starts to play the most beautiful blues the manager has ever heard. 'That's superb,' he gasps. 'What's it called?'

'I want to shag your missus on the sofa but the springs keep hurting my knob end.'

The manager is a little perturbed. 'Hmmm.... well, do you know any jazz?'

The man plays the most melancholy piece of jazz the manager has ever heard.

'What's it called?'

'I wanked over the washing machine but my bollocks got caught in the powder drawer.'

The manager is now a tad embarrassed. 'Well, do you know any romantic ballads?'

The bloke plays the most heart-wrenching melody ever.

'That was fantastic,' crooned the manager. 'What's that one called?' – immediately wishing that he hadn't asked.

'Shagging sheep under the stars with the moonlight shining on my hairy ring piece.'

The manager finds the pianist's language totally repulsive but he is so moved by his music that he hires him on condition that he never introduces his songs. He agrees, and the arrangement goes swimmingly for a couple of weeks, until one night when the pianist sneaks off for a wank. He nips off to the staff toilets, grits his teeth and starts buffing his banana. Just as he is coming, he hears the manager shouting, 'Where the fuck is that pianist?' So he whips up his trousers and returns to the piano and starts to play some more tunes.

After a couple of minutes, a woman approaches him and whispers, 'Do you know your bollocks and knob are hanging out of your trousers dribbling come all over your shoes?'

'Know it?' replies the pianist. 'I fucking wrote it!'

▶ What was Beethoven's favourite fruit? BA-NA-NA-NAAAAA!

▶ Shot through the heart, and you're to blame.
You give the Archery World Championships a bad name.

▶ In the jungle, a group of explorers hear distant drumming. Their native bearers suddenly seem very afraid. The expedition's leader asks them, 'What's going on?'

A native bearer says, 'Very bad when drumming stops.'

So the leader asks, 'Why, what happens then?'

The bearer explains, 'Bass solo starts.'

▶ Did you hear about the drummer that was so depressed over his bad sense of time that he ran out and jumped behind a train?

NAMES

▶ What do Catherine the Great, Attila the Hun and Bozo the Clown have in common?
Same middle name.

▶ Judge: 'You say you're petitioning for a legal name change?'
  Leon: 'Yes, your honour.'
  Judge: (looking at petition) 'I can see why, your name is Mr... Leon Shitferbrains, is it?'
  Leon: 'Yes, your honour.'
  Judge: 'And what do you want to change your name to, Mr Shitferbrains?'
  Leon: 'Melvin, your honour.'

▶ What do you call a Russian with three testicles? Houdji Nikabollokov.

▶ A young man called directory assistance. 'Hello, operator, I would like the telephone number for Mary Jones in Phoenix, Arizona.'
  'There are multiple listings for Mary Jones in Phoenix,' the operator replied. 'Do you have a street name?'
  The young man hesitated, and then said, 'Well, most people call me "Ice Man".'

NECROPHILIA

▶ I wouldn't be caught dead with a necrophiliac.

▶ I went to see a sick friend in hospital earlier. I found him in the morgue masturbating.

▶ A ship sank and there were only five survivors – four men and one woman. They were washed up on a desert island, where they set about building shelter and finding food. After a few weeks the natural urges of the men started to take hold, so with the agreement of the woman they decided that each could have the right to have sex with her for a week at a time. This worked well for a few years – the men and the woman were satisfied with the arrangement. Then the woman died. The men took it badly – the first month was awful, the second even worse and the third month was almost unbearable. By the fourth month they couldn't take any more – so they buried her.

▶ Two necrophiliacs work in a morgue, and one of them tells the other one, 'You should have seen this woman they brought in last week. They pulled her out of the water after she'd been there for three weeks. Man, I'm tellin' you, she had a clitoris just like a pickle.'

'What,' the other asks, 'green?'

'No,' says the first, 'sour.'

▶ What's a necrophiliac's biggest complaint about sex? They just kinda lay there.

▶ A salesman stopped at an isolated farmhouse to see if he could get a bed for the night.

'Sure', said the farmer, 'but you must share the bed with my daughter and you mustn't bother her.' The man agreed and went upstairs. As he slipped into bed, he felt the body of the farmer's daughter next to him.

The next morning he went to pay the farmer for his night's stay. 'It will be £2 as you had to share,' said the farmer.

'Your daughter was very cold,' said the salesman, handing over the money.

'Yes,' replied the farmer, 'we're going to bury her today.'

▶ Necrophilia: That uncontrollable urge to crack open a cold one.

NEIGHBOURS

▶ Exhausted from a long day at work, a businessman returned home to find his wife in bed with his neighbour. 'That's it!' shouted the man. 'If you're screwing my wife, I'm going next door to sleep with yours.'

'Go ahead,' replied the man. 'The rest will do you good!'

NEW SLANG AND DEFINITIONS

▶ AEROPLANE BLONDE: One who has bleached/dyed her hair but still has a 'black box'.

▶ AUSSIE KISS: Similar to a French kiss, but given down under.

▶ BEER COAT: The invisible but warm coat worn when walking home after a booze session at three in the morning.

▶ BEER COMPASS: The invisible device that ensures your safe arrival home after a session, even though you're too pissed to remember where you live, how you get there and where you've come from.

▶ BEER SCOOTER: The ability to get home after a night out on the booze and not remember it, i.e., 'I don't even remember getting home last night. I must have caught the beer scooter.'

▶ BOBFOC: Body Off *Baywatch*, Face Off *Crimewatch*.

▶ BRITNEY SPEARS: Modern slang for 'beers', e.g., 'Couple of Britneys, please.'

▶ BUDGIE'S TONGUE: The female erection.

▶ DOUBLE-BASS: A sexual position in which the man enters the woman from behind and then fiddles with the woman's nipples with one hand and her Budgie's Tongue with the other. (The position is similar to that used when playing a double bass instrument, but the sound produced is slightly different.)

▶ ETCH-A-SKETCH: Trying to draw a smile on a woman's face by twiddling both of her nipples simultaneously.

▶ GOING FOR A McSHIT: Entering a fast-food restaurant with no intention of buying food; you're just going to the bog. If challenged by a pimply staff member, your declaration to them that you'll buy their food afterwards is a McShit with Lies.

▶ GREYHOUND: A very short skirt, only an inch from the hare.

▶ HAND-TO-GLAND COMBAT: A vigorous masturbation session.

IGNORANUS: A person who's both stupid and an arsehole.

MILLENNIUM DOMES: The contents of a Wonderbra, i.e., extremely impressive when viewed from the outside, but there's actually nothing in there worth seeing.

MONKEY BATH: A bath so ho that when lowering yourself in, you go 'Oo! Oo! Oo! Aa! Aa! Aa!'

▶ MUMBLER: An attractive girl in tight shorts or jeans, etc. You can see the 'lips' moving but can't quite make out what they're saying.

MYSTERY BUS: The bus that arrives at the pub on Friday night while you're in the toilet after your tenth pint and whisks away all the unattractive people so the pub is suddenly packed with stunners when you come back in.

NELSON MANDELA: Rhyming slang for 'Stella'.

OSTEOPORNOSIS: A degenerate disease.

PICASSO ARSE: A woman whose knickers are too small for her, so she looks like she's got four buttocks.

REINTARNATION: Coming back to life as a hillbilly.

SALAD DODGER: An excellent phrase for an overweight person.

SALMON DAY: The experience of spending an entire day swimming upstream only to get screwed and die.

▶ TART FUEL: Bottled alcopops, e.g. Hooch, regularly consumed by young women.

▶ TESTICULATING: Waving your arms around and talking bollocks.

▶ TITANIC: A lady who goes down first time out.

▶ TODGER DODGER: A lesbian.

▶ WANK SEANCE: During a masturbation session, the eerie feeling that you're being watched with disgust by your dead relatives.

▶ BIGAMIST: A fog over Italy.

▶ CONDOM: An item to be worn on every conceivable occasion.

▶ COPULATE: What an Italian police chief says to a constable who doesn't get to work on time.

▶ MINE SHAFT: What a German calls his penis.

▶ CLITERATURE: Pornography,

▶ RED RIDING HOOD: A Russian condom.

▶ SITTING PRETTY: Sitting Bull's gay brother.

▶ SPECIMEN: An Italian spaceman.

▶ SELF-DECEPTION: Faking orgasm during masturbation.

▶ MISTRESS: Something between the mister and a mattress.

NEWLYWEDS

▶ Two newlyweds turn up at a hotel and ask for the honeymoon suite. The receptionist checks the computer and asks, 'Do you have any reservations?'
  'Yeah,' replies the bride. 'I'm not sure about taking it up the arse... '

▶ Five weeks after her wedding a new bride called her sister. 'Oh, Tracey,' she said, 'Dave and I had the most awful fight last night.'
  'Oh, don't worry,' replied her sister, 'it's not as bad as you think. All couples have to have their first fight sometime.'
  'I suppose you're right,' the new bride sighed, 'but what am I going to do with the body?'

▶ How do you know when your honeymoon is over? When he no longer smiles as he scrapes the burned toast.

▶ Leaving their wedding ceremony, a young honeymoon couple hailed a taxi to take them to their country hotel. The driver wasn't sure how to get there and said he'd ask for directions when they got nearer their destination. Meanwhile the newlyweds started getting really passionate in the back seat. Seeing a fork in the road, the driver said, 'I take the next turn, right?'
  'No way,' panted the groom. 'Get your own, this one's all mine.'

▶ A newly married couple were in their honeymoon suite on their wedding night. As they undressed for bed, the husband, who was a big man, tossed his pants to his bride and said, 'Here, put these on.' She put them on and the waist was twice the size of her body.

'I can't wear your pants,' she said.

'That's right,' said the husband, 'And don't forget it. I'm the man who wears the pants in this family.'

With that, she flipped him her knickers and said, 'Try these on.' He tried them on and found he could only get them on as far as his kneecap.

He said, 'Hell, I can't get into your knickers.'

She replied, 'That's right, and that's the way it's going to stay until your attitude changes.'

▶ A hotel busboy looked through the keyhole of the honeymoon suite and exclaimed, 'Wowie!'

A maid heard him and pushed him out of the way for a look. She said, 'Oh my God!'

Just then the maitre d' walked down the hall and moved her out of the way. He took a look and said, 'I can't believe he complained about a hair in his soup last night!'

▶ On the night before his wedding, the shy young man thought he ought to ask his father what was expected of him in the bedroom.

'What exactly do I have to do?' he asked tentatively.

'Well, son,' said his father. 'You remember what you used to play with as a teenager? All you do is stick that where your wife pees.'

So the following night the young man threw his Action Man down the toilet.

NEWSPAPERS

▶ What's pink and hard in the morning? *The Financial Times* crossword.

▶ How many newspapers can a woman hold between her legs? One Post, two Globes and many Times.

NOISE

▶ There was a pregnant silence, followed by a lot of little silences.

▶ What is the noisiest thing in the world? Two skeletons screwing on a tin roof.

NUDISM

▶ A farmer was so concerned about drivers speeding down the country lane where he lived and endangering his sheep that he asked the police to put up a sign. So they put up a 'Slow' sign, but it had no effect. Then they erected a 'Hazard ahead' sign, but that had no effect, either. Finally they tried a 'Children crossing' sign, but still the motorists failed to reduce their speed.

As a last resort, the farmer asked the police if he could put up his own sign. The police agreed, and when an officer called on the farmer a week later to see whether there had been any improvement, he was amazed to see the traffic crawling slowly along the lane. Then he noticed the farmer's handmade sign by the roadside. It read: 'Nudist colony'.

▶ A woman was having an affair while her husband was out at work. One day she was in bed with her boyfriend, when she heard her husband's car pull into the driveway. 'Quick!' she shouted to her boyfriend. 'Grab your clothes and jump out the window. My husband is home early!'

The boyfriend looked out the window and said, 'I can't jump! It's raining like crazy out there and I'm naked!'

'I don't care,' she insisted. 'If my husband catches us, he'll kill the pair of us.' So the boyfriend grabbed his clothes and jumped from the bedroom window. When he landed, he found himself in the middle of a group of marathon runners. Hoping to blend in even though he was naked, he started running alongside them, carrying his clothes over his arm.

One of the runners asked, 'Do you always run in the nude?'

Thinking on his feet, the boyfriend replied breathlessly, 'Yes, always. It feels so free having the air blow over my skin while I'm running.'

'Do you always run carrying your clothes on your arm?' queried another athlete.

'Oh, yes,' panted the boyfriend. 'That way I can get dressed at the end of the run, get in my car and just go straight home without a shower.'

'And,' persisted the athlete, 'do you always wear a condom when you run?'

'Only if it's raining.'

▶ Did you hear about the flasher who was thinking of retiring? He decided to stick it out for one more year!

NUNS

▶ Why don't gang members ever become nuns? Because they find it difficult to say 'Superior' after the word 'Mother'.

▶ Two ship captains were sitting at the bar one night getting good and drunk, when one turned to the other and said, 'You know what gets me, though, is these damn sailors! Oh sure, they're fine for the first few weeks, but on those three-month trips at sea they start getting pretty hard up. With all the whacking off going on, it's a wonder any work is getting done, and it's making a mess all over the ship. I don't know what to do!'

The other captain smiles knowingly at his companion. 'Oldest trick in the book. You take the crew and divide them into two teams, then you buy about 50 barrels and put them on the ship. You tell the crew that the team that fills the most barrels wins a bag of gold.'

'Well, that's a great way to keep the ship clean, but then I'm out a bag of gold every trip!'

'Not so,' replied the other captain. 'After you get back to port, take all the barrels together and sell them to the wax factory to make into candles. You make a tidy profit every time.'

The captain pondered this and the next day he took his friend's advice and divided the crew, bought a bunch of barrels and set off to sea. Before long, the crew took to the new system and began filling barrel after barrel. When they finally reached port, the captain sold the barrels for a huge profit.

'This is great,' thought the captain. 'Before long, I'll be able to buy a new boat!'

This went on, voyage after voyage. Then one day, the ship happened back to that very first port. Coming down the gangplank, the captain was surprised to see the cops waiting for him. As they slapped the cuffs on him, the captain cried out, 'What's the meaning of this?!'

'You sick bastard,' replied the cop. 'Remember all those barrels you sold to the candle factory last time you passed through town?'

'Sure,' said the captain. 'What about 'em?'

'Well, they made them into candles, sold them to the convent and now all the nuns are pregnant!'

▶ Two nuns decide they're going to sneak out of the convent and have a real night on the town. They hit all the bars and dance clubs and decide they've finally got to head back to the convent.

To enter the convent's grounds, they have to crawl under some barbed wire. The nuns start crawling under the wire on their bellies.

As they're crawling under the wire, the first nun turns to the second and says, 'I feel like a marine.'

The second replies, 'Yeah, me too, but where can you find one this time of night?'

▶ Three nuns were killed in a car crash. They went to heaven, only to find a sign on the gates which said, 'Sorry – closed for rebuilding.'

Uncertain about what to do next, they knocked on the gates and St Peter answered. 'What are you doing here?' he asked. 'We're closed until Monday.'

'But what are we supposed to do until then?' chorused the nuns.

'I tell you what,' replied St Peter. 'What I'm going to do is to send you back to earth for the weekend as whoever you want to be and then we'll accept you into heaven in a few days' time. How's that for a deal?'

The nuns all nodded in agreement.

'OK, who do you want to be?' St Peter asked the first nun.

'Tonight, Peter, I'm going to be Mother Teresa because she led such a selfless, devoted life.'

The second nun said, 'I'd like to go back as Joan of Arc as she was a martyr and an inspiration to so many.'

The third nun said, 'I'd like to be Alice Kapipelean.'

St Peter looked confused, 'Who?'

'Alice Kapipelean,' the nun replied.

'I'm sorry, sister,' said St Peter, 'but there is no record of any Alice Kapipelean having lived on earth.'

'That's where you're wrong,' said the nun, producing a newspaper cutting. 'Here, read this. There's your proof!'

St Peter glanced at the article and said, 'No, no, sister. You've misread it. The article says the Alaska Pipeline was laid by 500 men in six months.'

▶ A guy was in New York on a business trip and decided to head to a local bar for a drink. Standing outside the bar was a nun holding a tin cup. As the man threw a few bucks into her cup, the nun launched into a long tirade about the evils of alcohol. She went on and on about how alcohol was tearing apart the fabric of society and how it was the root of all the city's problems. Slightly pissed off at having to listen to this, the guy said, 'Listen, sister, I work hard for my money and sometimes at the end of a long day I like a drink or two. That doesn't make me a bad person. I have a wife I idolise and two wonderful kids at home. I provide for my family, I volunteer my time to several local service clubs and I contribute regularly to various charities. Yet you stand here and condemn me just because I drink the occasional glass of Scotch!'

The nun was slightly taken aback and replied, 'I see your point, my son, and I apologise if I offended you but the alcohol is such a powerful demon that all who consume it are doomed... '

'Look, there you go again,' said the man. 'How can you make such a sweeping statement? Have you ever even TRIED alcohol?'

'Of course not!' gasped the nun. 'The evil alcohol has never touched my lips.'

'Do you really think that one glass of booze can change you from a devout nun to some kind of evil degenerate?'

'Well, I really don't know... '

'I'll tell you what, come into the bar with me and I'll buy you a drink. One drink. I'll prove to you that "evil" is not inside the glass, it's inside the person.'

'Oh, I could never be seen going into such a den of iniquity, it's out of the question. However, your comment about evil residing in the person rather than the glass is quite intriguing. I must admit you've aroused a curiosity in me.'

'Well, let's go inside and settle this.'

'No, my son, I could never enter such a place... but how about this. Take my tin cup with you and fill it with this "Scotch" you mentioned. Bring it out to me and I'll try it.'

'You're on!' said the guy.

The nun removed all the change and handed him the tin cup. He went into the bar and said to the bartender, 'Two Scotch on the rocks, and could you put one of them in this tin cup, please?'

The bartender sighed and said, 'Is that bloody nun out there again!'

▶ How do you get a nun pregnant? Dress her up as an altar boy.

▶ A nun goes to a doctor because she thinks she has pubic lice. She says to the doctor, 'Doctor, I think I have crabs, but I don't understand how I got them because I've never had sex before!'

So the doctor says, 'Well, let's take a look.'

The nun pulls down her pants, pulls down her underwear and fruit flies come flying out of her vagina.

The doctor says, 'Sister, you don't have crabs. Those are fruit flies. Your cherry's rotten!'

▶ The year's new intake of novices were getting their initial medical inspection from the convent doctor, when he noticed something different about one of the older girls. The kindly practitioner went immediately to the Mother Superior and informed her, 'Mother Superior, you have amongst the new girls one with an incredibly rare deformity: she has been blessed with two fannies.'

'Good gracious,' exclaimed the Mother Superior, 'will she be able to lead a normal life?'

'Of course,' the good doctor replied, 'especially as she is to be a nun, no one will ever notice. However, I should like it very much if you would allow me to consult with my professional colleagues and ask them to come and look at her.'

'Of course you may,' said the Mother Superior and off he went.

Three weeks later the convent medic returned with his professional colleagues and asked to see the affected nun. 'I'm afraid you can't,' said the Mother Superior. 'We had to get rid of her.'

'Why?' asked the doctor.

'We couldn't stand her holier-than-thou attitude,' was the reply.

▶ Why do nuns go around in pairs? So that one nun sees that the other nun gets nun.

▶ What did the liberal Mother Superior say? 'I have no objection to you getting a little bit from the monks across the way, but don't get into the habit.'

▶ A nun gave birth to a baby without anybody knowing about it. She was in two minds as to whether she should tell the Mother Superior about it. She eventually decided to tell her, so she took the baby and went to the

Mother Superior's room. Arriving there, she found the Mother sound asleep with her legs astride. Seeing a solution to her problem, she carefully placed the baby between the Mother's legs and left.

The next morning the Mother woke up and found the baby there and exclaimed, 'Damn, you can't even trust the altar candles these days.'

▶ A novice nun in the convent is asked to hold the fort while the Mother Superior is away and is given special instructions to look after an ailing old monk who is spending his last days there. On her return the Mother Superior asks, 'How is the old monk?' The novice says that on the first day soon after she had taken in his food she had seen a large lump under his habit and asked what it was. He had replied that it was the key to heaven and that she had the keyhole. He had unlocked the door to heaven several times since then. 'The old bastard,' replies the Mother Superior, 'he told me it was Gabriel's horn.'

▶ A novice in a convent garden is frightening pigeons from newly planted seeds by waving her hands and shouting, 'Fuck off!' to the birds.

Mother Superior is aghast and runs quickly to the little nun. 'Sshhhhhh!' says the Mother Superior. 'That's not the way to do it. You must just say, "Shoo shoo" and they'll fuck off by themselves.'

▶ What do you call one nun in a blender? Bloody Mary.

▶ What do you call two nuns in a blender? Twisted sister.

▶ What is the definition of suspicion? A nun doing press-ups in a cucumber field.

▶ What is the definition of innocence? A nun working in a condom factory, thinking she's making sleeping bags for mice.

▶ Three nuns who had recently died were on their way to heaven. At the Pearly Gates they were met by St Peter. Around the gates there was a collection of lights and bells. St Peter stopped them and told them that they would each have to answer a question before they could enter through the Pearly Gates.

St Peter: 'What were the names of the two people in the Garden of Eden?'

The first nun said: 'Adam and Eve.' The lights flashed, the bells rang and in she went through the Pearly Gates.

St Peter: 'What did Adam eat from the forbidden tree?'

The second nun said: 'An apple.' The lights flashed, the bells rang and in she went through the Pearly Gates.

And finally it came the turn of the last nun.

St Peter: 'What was the first thing Eve said to Adam?'

After a few minutes' thought, she said, 'Gosh, that's a hard one!' The lights flashed, the bells rang and in she went through the Pearly Gates.

▶ What do you call a nun who walks in her sleep? A roaming Catholic.

▶ What do you call a nun with a sex change operation? A tran-sister.

▶ Mother Superior: 'Sister Maria, if you walk through town at night, and you're accosted by a man with bad intentions, what would you do?'

Sister Maria: 'I would lift my habit, Mother Superior.'

Mother Superior: (shocked) 'And what would you do next?'

Sister Maria: 'I would tell him to drop his pants.'

Mother Superior: (even more shocked) 'And what then?'

Sister Maria: 'I would run away. I can run much faster with my habit up than he can with his pants down.'

▶ A nun and a priest were travelling across the desert and realised halfway across that the camel they were using for transportation was about to die. They set up a makeshift camp, hoping someone would come to their rescue, but to no avail. Soon the camel died. After several days they agreed that they were not going to be rescued. They prayed a lot, and they discussed their predicament in great depth.

Finally the priest said to the nun, 'You know, sister, I am about to die, and there's always been one thing I've wanted here on earth – to see a woman naked. Would you mind taking off your clothes so I can look at you?' The nun thought about his request for several seconds and then agreed to take off her clothes.

As she was doing so, she remarked, 'Well, Father, now that I think about it, I've never seen a man naked, either. Would you mind taking off your clothes, too?'

With little hesitation, the priest also stripped. Suddenly the nun exclaimed, 'Father! What is that little thing hanging between your legs?'

The priest patiently answered, 'That, my child, is a gift from God. If I put it in you, it creates a new life.'

'Well,' responded the nun, 'forget about me. Stick it in the camel!'

▶ Two nuns in a bath. The first one says, 'Where's the soap?'; the second one replies, 'Yes, it does, doesn't it?'

▶ A group of nuns were travelling in a car when it got a flat. They got out and tried to change it, but being rather unworldly didn't know how to do it. Luckily, a truck came along and the driver offered to change it for them. They gladly accepted. As the trucker jacked up the car, it slipped from the jack.

'Son of a bitch!' he yelled.

The eldest nun said to him, 'That is not nice language. We understand that you are upset, but you mustn't use such language.'

'Sorry, sister,' he said, and tried again. Again it slipped, this time almost mashing his fingers. 'Son of a bitch!' he yelled again.

'Please, don't use such language. If changing our tyre is causing you to do so, it would be better if you didn't help us.'

'But I get so upset, and it just comes out.'

'Well,' said the nun, 'say something else when you get upset, something like "Sweet Jesus, help me".'

So the trucker tried to jack up the car again. Again it slipped. He started to say, 'So...' but he corrected himself and said, 'Sweet Jesus, help me.'

At that, the car just lifted up into the air by itself. The nuns looked at the car and said, 'Son of a bitch!'

▶ A nun gets on a bus and sits behind the driver. She says to the bus driver she is very ill and wants to experience sex before she dies. The bus driver agrees to accommodate her, but the nun explains that she can't have sex with anyone who is married as that would be a sin. The bus driver says no problem, he is not married. The nun says she also has to die a virgin, so she will have to take it in the arse. The bus driver agrees again. Being the only two on the bus, they go to the back of the bus and take care of business.

When they are done, and he has resumed driving, he says, 'Sister, I have a confession to make. I am married and have three children'.

The nun replies, 'That's OK. I have a confession, too. My name is Dave, and I am on my way to a fancy-dress party.'

▶ Did you hear the one about the man who opened a dry-cleaning business next door to the convent? He knocked on the door and asked the Mother Superior if she had any dirty habits.

▶ A nun is driving her car through some very lonely countryside. The car breaks down and she notices there is no petrol left. So she walks to the nearest filling station. But of course, being a nun, she is a little unworldly, and she forgets to take along a canister for the petrol. The nice man at the filling station has no canister, either. He thinks for a while, then he hands her a chamber pot full of petrol. The nun walks back to her car and starts pouring the petrol into the tank.

A passing car stops, and the driver looks out and says, 'Sister, I wish I had your faith!'

▶ A man is in hospital recovering from an operation, when a nun walks into his room. She is there to cheer up the sick and lame. They start talking, and she asks about his life. He talks about his wife and their 13 children.

'My, my,' says the nun, '13 children. A good and proper Catholic family. God is very proud of you.'

'I'm sorry, sister,' he says, 'I am not Catholic, I'm Baptist.'

'Baptist?' she replies. 'You sex maniac!'

▶ Two nuns are riding bicycles down a cobbled street, and one turns to the other and says, 'Do you know, I've never come this way before.'

NURSES

▶ How can you tell which is the head nurse? The one with the dirty knees.

▶ An old man was in hospital. Lying in bed, he leaned over to the pretty young nurse attending to him and whispered in her ear, 'Give us a kiss, luv!'

'No!' replied the nurse.

'Oh, go on!' said the man.

'No!' replied the nurse again.

'Please!' begged the old man. 'Just a quick peck on the cheek?'

'For the last time, no!' said the nurse. 'I shouldn't even be wanking you off!'

▶ Did you hear about the army nurse who went to bed eating popcorn? She woke up with a kernel between her legs.

NYMPHOMANIA

▶ A woman went to the doctor and said, 'Doctor, I think I'm becoming a nymphomaniac.'

'Why don't you lie down and tell me about it?' he quickly replied.

▶ 'Mummy, Mummy! What's a nymphomaniac?'

'Shut up and help me get Grandma off the doorknob.'

▶ A man fell asleep on the beach one day and the wind came up and blew sand all over him until he was covered with only his big toe sticking out. A nympho was walking down the beach and saw the toe sticking up, she pulled down her bikini bottom and squatted over the toe. She humped away till she was satisfied, pulled up her drawers and left. The guy woke up, brushed the sand away and left, not knowing what happened.

The next day his foot itched like hell, and had a sore on it. He went to the doctor and after an exam the doc told him he had syphilis of the big toe.

'Syphilis of the big toe?' he enquired. 'Isn't that rare?'

The doc said, 'Yes, but if you think that's rare, I had a woman in here this morning with athlete's twat.'

▶ How do you know you're leading a sad life? When a nymphomaniac tells you, 'Let's just be friends.'

ODOURS

▶ A woman visits her doctor. The doctor asks her, 'Well, what can I do for you, madam?' The patient blushes and the doctor says, 'You can discuss any matter with me, everything is strictly confidential.'

So the patient says, 'My husband complains that my pussy smells bad. Is there a cure for this?'

'Sure,' the doctor says, 'it can be a fungus, or a little infection, nothing unusual. Please undress and lay down, so I can examine you and prescribe a treatment.'

The woman undresses, gets up on the table and, with her legs spread, waits until the doctor attends her. He comes in, walks towards her, starts gasping for air, covers his mouth and nose with his hand and runs out of the office. After a minute or so, he enters again, covering his mouth and nose with one hand and a seven-foot wooden stick with an iron hook on it in the other hand.

'Aaaaaaaaaaaaargh, what are you going to do to me?' shouts the patient.

'Nothing,' says the doctor, 'I'm just going to open the roof window a little.'

▶ A woman asked her husband to go to the video shop and rent *Scent of a Woman.* He came back with *A Fish Called Wanda.*

▶ What's the worst smell in the world? A kipper's pussy.

▶ A man was in the lift with a woman when he turned to her and said, 'Can I smell your fanny?'

'No, you cannot,' she snapped.

'Oh, it must be your feet, then,' he said.

▶ A woman went to the doctor complaining of body odour.

'Do you wash?' the doctor asked the rank woman.

'Oh, yes,' she answered. 'Each morning, I start at my head and wash down as far as possible. Then, I start at my feet and wash up as far up as possible.'

'Well, then,' the medic concluded, 'go home and wash possible.'

▶ Why do women pierce their belly button? It's a place to hang their air freshener.

▶ A man and a woman are driving along, when they see a wounded skunk on the side of the road. They stop; the woman gets out, picks it up and brings it into the car. She says, 'Look, it's shivering, it must be cold. What should I do?'

He says, 'Put it between your legs.'

She says, 'What about the smell?'

He says, 'Hold its nose.'

▶ A New England cabbie picked up a woman passenger late at night. She was very drunk and flopped in the front seat next to him, hitching up her short skirt to give him a good view of her pussy.

'Where to, lady?' he asked, trying to avert his gaze.

Wrapping an arm around his neck and opening her legs even wider, she whispered, 'I want you to go where it smells.'

He said, 'Lady, there's no way I'm taking you to Pittsburgh at this time of night!'

OLD AGE

▶ Three old men were discussing their lives. 'I'm still a once-a-night man,' said the first.

'I can manage it twice a night still,' said the second.

'My wife will tell you, I'm still a five-times-a-night man,' said the third, 'but then she would tell you it's my fault for drinking so many cups of tea before bed.'

▶ Be nice to your kids. They'll be choosing your nursing home.

▶ A woman was towelling off in front of the mirror, when she noticed a few grey pubic hairs. She bent down and said to her pussy, 'I know you haven't been getting much lately... but I didn't know you were so worried about it!'

▶ Grandmother says to her young grandson, 'Be a love and help your gran put this suppository in.'

'Course I will, Gran,' replies the young boy.

She bends over, pulls her knickers down and spreads her legs.

The grandson says, 'Do I put it in the brown hole or feed it to the turkey?'

▶ Twin sisters in St Luke's Nursing Home were turning 100 years old. The editor of the local newspaper told a photographer to get over there and take pictures of them.

One of the twins was hard of hearing and the other could hear quite well. Once the photographer arrived, he asked the sisters to sit on the sofa.

The deaf sister said to her twin, 'WHAT DID HE SAY?'

'WE GOTTA SIT OVER THERE ON THE SOFA!' said the other.

'Now get a little closer together,' said the photographer.

Again: 'WHAT DID HE SAY?'

'HE SAYS SQUEEZE TOGETHER A LITTLE.'

So they wiggled up close to each other. 'Just hold on for a bit longer, I've got to focus a little,' said the photographer.

Yet again: 'WHAT DID HE SAY?'

'HE SAYS HE'S GONNA FOCUS!'

With a big grin, the deaf twin shouted out, 'OH MY! BOTH OF US?'

▶ In our 20s we don't care what the world thinks of us. In our 30s we worry about what the world thinks of us. By our 40s we realise that nobody actually gives a damn about us.

▶ An old lady is at her husband's funeral. She tells her granddaughter that throughout their married life they had enjoyed physical relations each and every Sunday morning in time to the church bells.

'Maybe he was getting a bit old for that sort of thing,' says the granddaughter.

'Nonsense,' replies the old lady. 'If it hadn't been for that ice-cream van, he'd be alive today.'

▶ An old man goes to his doctor and says, 'Can you give me something to lower my sex drive?'

The doctor replies, 'I would have thought at your age it's all in the mind.'

'It is,' agrees the old man. 'That's why I want it lower.'

▶ An old man wakes up in the middle of the night and finds that his pecker is as hard as a rock for the first time in years. He wakes his wife and shows her his erection. 'Look at that?' he exclaims happily. 'What do you think we ought to do with it?'

His wife replies, 'Well, seeing as you've got all the wrinkles out, now might be a good time to wash it.'

▶ Two old ladies are discussing their dead husbands. 'Tell me,' says one. 'Did you have mutual orgasms?'

'No,' says the other. 'I think we were with the Prudential.'

▶ Eighty-eight-year-old Vern and 82-year-old Mildred became very close to each other at their nursing home.

Although they didn't have sex, every night Mildred would go to Vern's room and they would lie in bed and watch TV while she held his privates.

One night Mildred went into Vern's room and found another resident of the nursing home, Edith, in Vern's bed, watching TV and holding his privates.

'Vern!' Mildred cried. 'Is she prettier than me?'

Vern replied, 'NO!'

'Does she have a better personality?'

Vern replied, 'NO!'

'Then please tell me what does Edith have that I don't?'

'Parkinson's,' Vern replied.

▶ An 85-year-old man went to his doctor to get a sperm count. The doctor gave the man a glass jar and said, 'Take this jar home and bring back a semen sample tomorrow.' The next day the 85-year-old man reappeared at the doctor's office and gave him the jar, which was as clean and empty as on the previous day.

The doctor asked what happened and the man explained, 'Well, Doc, it's like this. First I tried with my right hand, but nothing. Then I tried with my left hand, but still nothing. Then I asked my wife for help. She tried with her right hand, then her left, still nothing. She tried with her mouth, first with her teeth in, then with her teeth out, and still nothing. We even called up Arleen, the lady next door, and she tried, too, first with both hands, then an armpit and she even tried squeezing it between her knees, but still nothing.'

The doctor was shocked: 'You asked your neighbour?'

The old man replied, 'Yep, no matter what we tried, we still couldn't get the bloody jar open.'

▶ My grandparents are called Pearl and Dean. But I prefer to call them Grandma and Grand-pa pa-pa pa-pa pa pa-paaaa...

▶ Did you hear about the old lady who died at the shops from the big C? It's known as 'ostcutter' now.

▶ I found my first grey pubic hair the other day. It was in a kebab.

▶ Two elderly women were eating breakfast in a restaurant one morning. Ethel noticed something funny about Mabel's ear and she said, 'Mabel, did you know you've got a suppository in your left ear?'

Mabel answered, 'I have a suppository?' She pulled it out and stared at it. Then she said, 'Ethel, I'm glad you saw this thing. Now I think I know where my hearing aid is.'

▶ Two old ladies were rocking in their chairs on the nursing home porch.

One says, 'Martha, do you remember the minuet?'

Martha answers, 'Heck, I don't even remember the ones I slept with.'

▶ The body of a dead pensioner has been found dumped at a council recycling centre.

That's disgusting! The signs clearly say: Paper, metal and glass only.

▶ I was driving past my gran's house today and saw 11 pints of milk on her doorstep.

I thought, 'She must be thirsty today.'

▶ I was stood at the cash machine and there was a little old lady struggling to see the screen.

She said to me, 'Can you check my balance?'

So I pushed her over.

▶ Two old men were talking. 'I was thinking about myself this morning and I couldn't believe just how things have got worse now that I'm old. I'm living with osteoporosis and my kidneys are so bad that I have to have regular dialysis. I have terrible circulation in my feet and can't feel my toes. I've survived a triple-heart bypass operation and had both my hips replaced. I'm losing the sight in my right eye and my hearing is terrible. I've got a new left knee and the other one is deteriorating.

'And that's not all. I'm sure I'm suffering from senile dementia – I can't remember whether I'm 73 or 79. I'm also sure I'm suffering from senile dementia – I can't remember whether I'm 73 or 79.

'But I continue to survive, at a price! As a result of the 50 daily medications I take to live from day to day, I suffer from diarrhoea, wind, dizziness and sometimes even blackouts. But, thank God, I still have my driver's licence.'

▶ Ninety-one per cent of people over 60 believe that we show less respect to others than we did in the past. Silly old fuckers.

▶ What's 100 yards long and smells of piss? The Post Office queue on Thursday mornings.

▶ A family was supposed to stay the night at a hotel, but there was a screw-up with the rooms, so Grandpa had to sleep in the same bed as the 15-year-old grandson.

In the middle of the night Grandpa woke up and shouted, 'Quick! Get me a woman, fast!'

The grandson moaned, 'Please, Grandpa, calm down. First, it's three o'clock in the morning, and you'll never find a woman at this hour. Second, you're 82 years old and third, that's MY dick you're holding... not yours.'

▶ I was driving on the motorway last week when I noticed a sign that said: 'Turn-off – 500 metres.' Sure enough, 500 metres later, on the side of the road, was my granny with no knickers, lifting up her dress.

▶ Two medical students were walking along the street, when they saw an old man walking with his legs spread apart.

One of the students said to his friend: 'I'm sure he has Petry Syndrome. Those people walk just like that.'

The other student said: 'No, I don't think so. The old man surely has Zovitzki Syndrome. He walks just as we learned in class.'

Since they couldn't agree, they decided to ask the old man. They approached the old man and one of the students said to him: 'We're medical students and couldn't help but notice the way you walk, but we couldn't agree on the syndrome you might have. Could you tell us what it is?'

The old man said: 'I'll tell you, but first tell me what you think.'

One of the students said: 'I think it's Petry Syndrome.'

The old man said: 'You thought... but you're wrong.'

Then the other student said: 'I think you have Zovitzki Syndrome.'

The old man said: 'You thought... but you're wrong.'

So they asked him: 'Well, what do you have?'

And the old man said: 'I thought it was a fart... but I was wrong.'

▶ Doctor Jones is known throughout London as one of the best consultants on arthritis. He always has a waiting room full of people who need his advice and specialist treatment. One day an elderly lady slowly struggles into his waiting room. She is completely bent over and leans heavily on her stick. A chair is found for her. Eventually, her turn comes to go into Doctor Jones's office.

Fifteen minutes later, to everyone's surprise, she comes briskly out of his room walking almost upright. She is holding her head high and has a smile on her face. A woman in the waiting room says to her, 'It's unbelievable, a miracle even. You walk in bent in half and now you walk out erect. What a fantastic doctor he is. Tell me, what did Doctor Jones do to you?'

'Miracle?' replies the old lady. 'He just gave me a longer walking stick.'

▶ An elderly gentleman went to the local chemist and asked the pharmacist for Viagra. The pharmacist said, 'That's no problem. How many do you want?'

The man answered, 'Just a few, maybe four, but cut each one in four pieces.'

The pharmacist said, 'That won't do you any good.'

The elderly gentleman said, 'That's all right. I don't need them for sex anymore as I am 83 years old. I just want it to stick out far enough so I don't pee on my shoes.'

▶ An old couple go to a private doctor and ask him to watch them have sex and tell them if he sees them doing anything wrong. So they proceed to have sex in front of him. While they are getting dressed afterwards, the doctor says, 'Well, I don't see anything wrong.'

A week later they come again and ask the doctor to watch to see if they are doing anything wrong. They have sex and again the doctor says, 'Well, I still don't see anything wrong.'

This goes on for weeks. The doctor eventually feels he has to ask why they keep coming.

The old man says, 'If we go to her house, her husband will catch us. If we go to my house, my wife will catch us. A hotel costs 50 quid. Here it's £35, and BUPA pays half!'

▶ After playing bridge together for many years, two old ladies had got to know each other pretty well. Then one day, during a game of cards, one lady suddenly looked up at the other and said, 'I realise we've known each other for many years but for the life of me I can't remember your name. Would you mind telling me it again?'

There was silence for a couple of minutes, and then the other lady replied, 'How quickly do you need to know?'

▶ Two old men were talking. One said, 'I'm 83 and full of aches and pains. How about you?'

The other replied, 'Oh, I feel just like a newborn baby.'

'Really?'

'Yeah, no hair, no teeth and I think I just wet my pants.'

▶ Keith was soon to be 80 years old and his friends didn't know what to buy him. His wife had died some years ago and he did not go out very often, at least, not with the opposite sex. In the end, they came to the conclusion that Keith needed a bit of female comfort, so they hired a call girl. She knocked on his door.

When Keith answered, she said to him, 'Happy birthday to you, darling. I've come to offer you super sex.'

He replied, 'If it's all right with you, I'll have the soup.'

ORGANIC

▶ A wife asked her husband to buy her some organic vegetables. He went to his local supermarket but couldn't find any of the shelves. So he asked one of the male employees for help. 'These vegetables are for my wife – have they been sprayed with any poisonous chemicals?'

'No,' replied the employee, 'you'll have to do that yourself.'

OSAMA BIN LADEN

▶ A group of Osama Bin Laden's Taliban soldiers were marching down a track in Afghanistan, when they heard an American voice call out from behind a sand dune, 'One Marine is better than ten Taliban!' Bin Laden quickly dispatched ten of his finest soldiers over the sand, whereupon there was a fierce gun battle, followed by silence. An American voice then called out, 'One Marine is better than 100 Taliban!' The furious Bin Laden immediately sent his next best 100 soldiers over the dune. A battle raged for ten minutes, followed by silence. An American voice then called out, 'One Marine is better than 1,000 Taliban!' Enraged, Bin Laden mustered 1,000 fighters and sent them over the dune. There was a huge battle, lasting for more than an hour, followed by silence. Eventually one wounded Taliban fighter crawled back over the dune and, with his dying words, told Bin Laden, 'Don't send any more. It's a trap. There's actually two of them.'

▶ Newsflash: 'The FBI recently announced a failed operation to capture the regional head of Al Qaeda in Ibiza.' Unfortunately, 'Osama Bin Larging It' got away.

▶ A recent report from the government stated that 'terrorists in Britain are ready to strike at any moment.' Not only do we have to live in constant fear of these people, we've got to listen to them complain about their work conditions, too. What is the world coming to?

▶ Since singer Susan Boyle has been on TV, there's been a marked drop in suicide bombings.
Apparently, a lot of the terrorists didn't realise what a virgin looks like.

▶ Little Melissa comes home from first grade and tells her father that they learned about the history of Valentine's Day. 'Since Valentine's Day is for a Christian saint and we're Jewish,' she asks, 'will God get mad at me for giving someone a Valentine?'

Melissa's father thinks a bit, then says, 'No, I don't think God would get mad. Who do you want to give a Valentine to?'

'Osama Bin Laden,' she says.

'Why Osama Bin Laden?' her father asks in shock.

'Well,' she says, 'I thought that if a little American Jewish girl could have enough love to give Osama a Valentine, he might start to think that maybe we're not all bad, and maybe start loving people a little bit. And if other kids saw what I did and sent Valentines to Osama, he'd love everyone a lot. And then he'd start going all over the place to tell everyone how much he loved them and how he didn't hate anyone anymore.'

Her father's heart swells and he looks at his daughter with newfound pride. 'Melissa, that's the most wonderful thing I've ever heard.'

'I know,' Melissa says, 'and once that gets him out in the open, the army could blow the hell out of him.'

▶ A bloke walks into a cocktail bar and asks for an Osama Bin Laden.
The bartender replies, 'Never heard of that one, what's in it?'
The bloke says, 'Three shots and a splash of water'.

▶ Osama Bin Laden is in the ocean. How ironic. Once again, surrounded by seals...

▶ Coincidentally, an anagram of Osama Bin Laden is 'Lob da man in sea'.

Starbucks have announced they are introducing a new coffee. It's called Osama Bin Latte – dark bodied with a white frothy head and two shots in it.

There's a load of Taliban standing in a cave discussing their security. 'The British army have been infiltrating our organisation,' says the leader. 'Therefore we must be extra vigilant and increase our security.' They all nod and agree. The leader carries on, 'The first patrol tonight will be Omar Abdul Ishim and Dave Smith.'

How do you play Taliban bingo? B-52... F-16... B-1...

How is the Taliban like Fred Flintstone? Both may look out their windows and see Rubble.

What do the Taliban and General Custer have in common? They both want to know where those Tomahawks are coming from.

Why doesn't the Taliban have drivers' ed and sex ed classes on the same day? Because the camels can't handle it.

Osama Bin Laden phoned President Bush and said, 'Mr President, I called you because I had this incredible dream last night. I could see all of America, and it was beautiful, and on top of every building, there was a beautiful banner.'
Bush asked angrily, 'And what was on the banner?'
Osama responded, 'It said Allah is God, and God is Allah.'
Bush said, 'You know, Osama, I'm really glad you called, because last night I had a dream, too. I could see all of Kabul, and it was even more

beautiful than before the Russian occupation. It had been completely rebuilt, and on every building there was also a beautiful banner.'

Bin Laden said, 'What was on the banner?'

Bush replied, 'I really don't know. I don't read Hebrew.'

▶ Bush got a coded message from Osama. It read: 370HSSV-0773H. Bush was stumped and sent for the CIA. The CIA was stumped, too, so it went to the NSA. The NSA couldn't solve it, either, so they asked Bill Clinton. He suggested turning it upside down.

▶ Did you hear that it is twice as easy to train Iraqi fighter pilots? You only have to teach them to take off.

▶ One of the Glasgow bombers Singed Majeep is complaining that all he gets in hospital to eat is haggis, neeps and tatties. What the heck does he expect in the burns unit?

▶ There's been another incident in Glasgow, with 24 people killed when two bunk beds collapsed. Police are investigating an al Ikea sleeper ring.

OUTER SPACE

▶ What's the difference between a man and ET? ET phoned home.

▶ Why haven't they sent a woman to the moon yet? It doesn't need cleaning.

▶ Why is duct tape like 'The Force'? It has a light side and a dark side, and it holds the universe together.

PAIN

▶ One day a man went to the dentist to get a tooth pulled. When the dentist told him he needed to give him some anaesthetic, he refused. The dentist told him this again and he refused, saying, 'I have experienced the two worst pains in the world so I don't need anaesthetic.'

So the dentist pulled the tooth and the man just sat there and didn't even flinch. When this was done, the dentist said to the man, 'What were those pains?'

The man said, 'The first happened while I was out hunting, I squatted down to take a shit and my balls got caught in a bear trap'.

The dentist asks him what the second one was and the man said, 'When I reached the end of the chain.'

PARANOIA

▶ My doctor reckons I'm paranoid. He didn't say it, but I know he's thinking it.

PARROTS

▶ A woman had a parrot that she took with her everywhere she went. She would even take the parrot to the clubs with her when she went dancing and drinking on Saturday nights.

Whenever the woman went onto the dance floor, the parrot would yell, 'The roof, the roof, the roof is on fire, we don't need no water, let the muthafukkah burn! Burn muthafukkah burn!' The crowd on the dance floor would always cheer and shout in appreciation when the parrot yelled. This would make the parrot yell even more, and of course make the crowd go wild. This would go on all night long, every time the parrot went out.

One Sunday morning the woman took the parrot to church with her. When the choir started to sing, the parrot yelled, 'The roof, the roof, the roof is on fire, we don't need no water, let the muthafukkah burn! Burn muthafukkah burn!'

Embarrassed, she corrected the parrot, 'No, you don't say that here!'

The parrot looked around and asked, 'Why not? These are the same muthafukkahs that was at the club last night!'

▶ What would you get if you mixed a parrot with a Rottweiler? Who knows? But if it starts to talk, you better listen!

▶ A rather large lady had saved her money for a long time to be able to afford a cruise on a ship to the Bahamas. When she gets settled in her cabin, she goes to the dining room for her first meal on board, and is invited to sit at the captain's table.

As she is seated at the table, a mimicking voice behind her loudly squawks, 'Aawwk, lady! How's your hole?'

Totally embarrassed, she turns to see a parrot on his perch behind her. She says to the steward, 'Will you please get rid of that foul-mouthed beast?'

The steward replies, 'I can't, madam, that is the captain's parrot, which he dearly loves.'

As the meal progresses, the bird continues to harass the lady with his loud squawks, 'Aawwk, lady! How's your hole?'

The embarrassed woman finally retires to her cabin and goes into a restless sleep.

In the middle of the night the ship gets into distress and sinks, and the lady finds herself floating in the ocean on a chest. As daylight breaks the next morning, the lady hears this loud squawk behind her, 'Aawwk, lady! How's your hole?'

The lady turns around to see the parrot floating on some debris and she replies, 'Aah, shut up!'

The parrot says, 'Aawwk, mine, too! Must be the salt water!'

▶ Three nuns passed every day through a street that led them from the church to the convent. They noticed a parrot that stood at the entrance of a big residential house. Every time they passed in front of that house, the bird would pronounce three sequential colours.

One day, they heard, 'Yellow, blue, black.' One of the nuns noticed that those colours perfectly matched the colours of their underwear. She mentioned her discovery to the other two nuns, but both were reluctant to believe that could be possible.

The next day, they all wore black underwear and passed in front of the house, and very precisely the parrot said, 'Black, black, black.'

Hearing that, the three nuns were astonished. One of the nuns said, 'Girls, tomorrow we are going to trick that bird.' She recommended that the next day, none of them should be wearing any underwear under their vestments.

Respecting their agreement, the next day they wore no underwear, and proceeded to pass in front of the parrot's house. They peeked at the bird, who looked a bit puzzled. He swung back and forth on the cane he was perched on.

Then, after a while, the parrot spoke: 'Straight, straight, curly!'

▶ A man is selling three parrots. A guy who wants to buy a parrot approaches him and asks, 'How much are your parrots?'

The salesman answers, 'The first one is £1,000.'

'What does he know?'

'He knows 10,000 words and 500 sentences and is able to solve mathematical equations.'

'How about the second one?'

'The second parrot costs £5,000.'

'What does he know?'

'He knows 100,000 words and 10,000 sentences, is able to solve mathematical equations and can create computer programs.'

'Then what is the price for the third one?'

'This one costs £20,000.'

'Really?' says the excited buyer. 'What does he know?'

'This one knows absolutely nothing but the two others always call him "Boss".'

▶ A man strolls into the paint section of a DIY store and walks up to the assistant.

'I'd like a pint of canary-coloured paint,' he says.

'Certainly,' says the assistant. 'Mind if I ask why you need it?'

'My parakeet,' says the man. 'See, I want to enter him in a canary contest. He sings so sweetly that I know he's sure to win.'

'Well, you can't do that, sir!' the assistant says. 'The chemicals in the paint will almost certainly kill the poor thing!'

'No, they won't,' the man replies.

'Listen, buddy, I'll bet you ten bucks your parakeet dies if you try to paint him.'

'You're on!' says the man.

Two days later the man comes back looking very sheepish and puts ten bucks on the counter in front of the clerk.

'So the paint killed your bird?'

'Indirectly,' the man says. 'He seemed to handle the paint OK, but he didn't survive the sanding between coats.'

▶ A honeymooning couple purchased a talking parrot on their vacation and took it to their room, but the bridegroom became annoyed with the bird when it kept up a running commentary on his lovemaking skills. Finally he threw a towel over the cage and threatened to give the bird to the zoo if it didn't stay quiet.

Early the next morning, packing to return home, they couldn't close a large suitcase.

'You get on top and I'll try,' the groom instructed. But that didn't work.

The new bride figured they must need more weight on top of the suitcase to shut it. 'Darling, YOU get on top and I'll try.' Still no success.

Finally the annoyed groom said, 'Look, let's both get on top.'

At that point the parrot used his beak to pull the towel off the cage and said, 'Zoo or no zoo, I just have to see this!'

▶ A lady's dishwasher stops working so she calls a repairman. Since she has to go to work the next day, she tells him, 'I'll leave the key under the mat. Fix the dishwasher, leave the bill on the table and I'll post you the money. Oh, by the way, don't worry about my Rottweiler, he won't bother you. But, whatever you do, do NOT, under ANY circumstances, talk to my parrot!'

When the repairman arrives at the house the next day, he discovers the biggest and meanest Rottweiler he has ever seen. But just as she said, the dog just lies there on the carpet watching the repairman go about his business.

The parrot, however, drives him nuts the whole time with his incessant yelling, cursing and name-calling.

Finally the repairman can't contain himself any longer and yells, 'Shut up, you stupid ugly bird!'

And the parrot says, 'Get him, Spike!'

▶ A man buys a parrot cheap at the pet shop. When he gets home, he discovers why it was cheap – the parrot swears like a sailor. He can swear for five minutes straight without repeating himself. Trouble is, the guy who owns him is a quiet, conservative type, and this bird's foul mouth is driving him crazy. One day, it gets to be too much. The guy grabs the bird by the throat, shakes him hard and yells, 'QUIT IT!' But this just makes the bird mad and he swears more than ever. The guy gets mad and locks the bird in a kitchen cabinet. This really aggravates the bird and he claws and scratches, and when the guy finally lets him out, the bird cuts loose with a stream of vulgarities that would make a veteran sailor blush. At this point, the guy is so mad that he throws the bird into the freezer. For the first few seconds there is a terrible din. The bird kicks and claws and thrashes. Then it suddenly gets very, very quiet. At first the guy just waits, but then he starts to think that the bird may be hurt. After a couple of minutes of silence, he's worried enough to open the freezer door.

The bird calmly climbs onto the man's outstretched arm and says, 'Awfully sorry about the trouble I gave you. I'll do my best to improve my vocabulary from now on.' The man is astounded. He can't understand the transformation that has come over the parrot. Then the parrot says, 'By the way, what did that chicken do to you?'

▶ A woman gets up, puts up the shades, takes the cover off the parrot's cage, makes a coffee and has a cigarette. Suddenly the phone rings: her boyfriend is coming over. She puts out the cigarette, pulls down the shades, puts the cover back on the parrot's cage and gets back into bed.

The parrot, from under the cloth, then squawks, 'Well, that was a short bloody day!'

PENGUINS

▶ A penguin is driving through Arizona, when he notices the oil-pressure light is on. He gets out to look and sees oil dripping out of the motor. He drives to the nearest town and stops at the first petrol station.

After dropping the car off, the penguin goes for a walk around town. He sees an ice-cream shop and, being a penguin in Arizona, decides that something cold would really hit the spot.

He gets a big dish of vanilla ice cream and sits down to eat. Having no hands, he makes a real mess trying to eat with his little flippers.

After finishing his ice cream, he goes back to the garage and asks the mechanic if he's found the problem.

The mechanic looks up from the engine and says, 'It looks like you've blown a seal.'

'No, no,' the penguin replies, wiping his mouth. 'It's just ice cream.'

PERIODS AND PMT

▶ Why do women stop menstruating in their 50s? Cos they need the blood for their varicose veins.

▶ What's the difference between tampons and cowboy hats? Cowboy hats are for arseholes.

▶ What's the best thing about fingering a gypsy on her period? You get your palm red for free.

▶ What relieves period pain? Ear plugs.

▶ What's red and blue with a long string? A Smurfette with her period.

▶ How do you know when a Barbie has her period? All your Tic-Tacs are gone.

▶ How do you piss off a female archaeologist? Give her a used tampon and ask her what period it comes from.

▶ Have you heard about the new radio station in town? It's called WPMS... Every month they give you three weeks of the blues and then one week of ragtime.

▶ Have you heard about the new Tampax with bells and tinsel? They're for the Christmas period.

▶ How can you tell when a woman is having a bad day? She has her tampon behind her ear, and she can't find her cigarette.

▶ Why did the army send so many women with PMT to Iraq? Because they fought like animals and retained water for four days.

▶ Did you hear about the new Greek tampon? It's called Abzorba the Leak.

▶ It said on the news today that Barack Obama is enjoying a 'honeymoon period' with the American people. Enjoying? My new wife had one of them, and it ruined the whole trip.

▶ Why do tampons have strings? So you can floss after using them.

PEST CONTROL

▶ A woman was having an affair with an inspector from a pest-control company. One afternoon they were having sex, when her husband arrived home unexpectedly.

'Quick, she said to her lover. 'Into the wardrobe!'

When the husband reached the bedroom, he spotted two drinking glasses on the table and immediately became suspicious. He started searching the room and eventually discovered the man in the wardrobe.

'Who are you?' asked the husband.

'I'm an inspector from Bugzap,' replied the lover.

'What are you doing in there, then?' asked the husband.

'I'm investigating a complaint regarding an infestation of moths.'

'And where are your clothes?'

The lover looked down at his naked body and said, 'Those little bastards!'

PHONES

▶ A man walks into a bar and sits down. He starts dialling numbers on his hand, like a phone, and talking into it. The barman walks over and tells him that this is a very rough neighbourhood and he doesn't need any trouble.

The man replies, 'You don't understand; I'm very hi-tech. I had a phone installed in my hand because I was tired of carrying my mobile.'

So the barman asks him to prove it.

The man dials up a number and hands his hand to the barman. The barman talks into the hand and carries on a conversation.

'That's incredible,' says the barman. 'I would never have believed it!'

'Yeah,' said the guy, 'I'm really very hi-tech. I can keep in touch with my work, my wife, you name it! By the way, where are the toilets?'

The barman directs him to the toilets. The man goes in and ten minutes go by and he still hasn't come out. Fearing the worst given the rough neighbourhood, the barman goes into the toilets.

The man is spread-eagled against the wall, his pants are pulled down and he has a roll of toilet paper up his bum.

'Oh my God!' said the barman. 'Did they rob you? How much did they get?'

The man turns and says, 'No, no, I'm just waiting for a fax!'

PIGS

▶ A farmer was worried that none of his pigs were getting pregnant, so he called a vet and asked what he should do if he wanted more pigs. The vet told him he should try artificial insemination. Unclear on what the vet meant by artificial insemination, the farmer decided it must mean he had to impregnate the pigs himself, so he loaded the pigs in his truck, drove down to the woods and shagged them all.

The next day he called the vet again, and asked how he would know if the pigs were pregnant. The vet told him that if pregnant, they would be lying down rolling in the mud. But when the farmer looked out the window not even one pig was lying down. So he loaded them up in his truck again, drove them to the woods and shagged them again.

To his dismay, the next morning, they were all still standing. So again he loaded the pigs into his truck, drove them to the woods and shagged them for the third time.

By the next morning the farmer was so tired, he asked his wife to hop out of bed and look out the window to see what the pigs are doing.

She said, 'Hmmm, that's weird! They are all in the truck and one of them is blowing the horn.'

PILOTS

▶ A famous French wartime pilot named Pierre was having dinner with a brunette, and when they finished they headed to a hotel where he called room service and asked for a bottle of red wine. When it arrived, he put some red wine on the woman's lips and began kissing her passionately.

'What is the red wine for?' she panted.

The pilot replied suavely, 'For when Pierre the famous fighter pilot has red meat, he has red wine.'

'Ooooh!' she sighed, and they carried on.

A few minutes of heavy kissing later, he reached for the phone and ordered a bottle of white wine. When it arrived, he splashed it on her chest and began kissing her breasts.

'What is the white wine for?' she gasped.

The pilot replied suavely, 'For when Pierre the famous fighter pilot has white meat, he has white wine.'

'Ooooh!' she groaned.

Soon he worked his way down to her pussy, pulled out a can of lighter fluid and a match, sprinkled it on her muff and set fire to it.

'Aaagh! Why the fuck did you do that?' she screamed.

The pilot replied proudly, 'For when Pierre the famous fighter pilot goes down, he goes down in flames!'

▶ What did the kamikaze pilot instructor say to his students? 'Watch closely. I'm only going to do this once.'

PLASTIC SURGERY

▶ A man decides to have a facelift for his birthday. He spends £5,000 and feels really good about the result. On his way home, he stops at a newsagent and buys a newspaper. Before leaving he says to the newsagent, 'I hope you don't mind me asking, but how old do you think I am?'

'About 35,' says the newsagent.

'I'm actually 47,' the man says, feeling really happy. After that he goes into McDonald's for lunch, and asks the order-taker the same question, to which the reply is, 'Oh, you look about 29.'

'I am actually 47!' This makes him feel really good.

While standing at the bus stop, he asks an old woman the same question.

She replies, 'I am 85 years old and my eyesight is going. But when I was young there was a sure way of telling a man's age. If I put my hand down your pants and play with your balls for ten minutes I will be able to tell your exact age.'

As there is no one around, the man thinks, 'What the hell,' and let her slip her hand down his pants. Ten minutes later the old lady says, 'OK, it's done. You are 47.'

Stunned, the man says, 'That was brilliant! How did you do that?'

'I was behind you in McDonald's,' replies the old lady.

▶ Two women were having lunch together, and discussing the merits of cosmetic surgery.

The first woman says, 'I need to be honest with you – I'm getting a boob job.'

The second woman says, 'Oh, that's nothing, I'm thinking of having my arsehole bleached!'

To which the first replies, 'Whoa, I just can't picture your husband as a blond.'

▶ Two plastic surgeons are talking about their recent operations, and one mentions that he grafted tits onto a sailor's back some time ago.

'Was it successful?' asks the other.

'Incredibly!' says the first. 'I did it on a percentage basis, and if his arsehole holds out, we'll be millionaires pretty soon.'

POLICE

▶ A policeman tries to pull over a man for speeding, but he tries to outrun him. Finally the guy gives up and pulls over. The now pissed off policeman walks up and yells at the man, 'What's the big idea?'

'Last week my wife ran off with a cop,' the man says, 'and I was afraid he was trying to give her back!'

'Off you go,' says the officer.

▶ Police have finally admitted they got it wrong in the shooting of Jean Charles de Menezes. It was his naughty brother Dennis they were after.

▶ I'm going to go rob a bank tomorrow. I plan on dressing up in a clown wig and make up and only wearing a thong and nipple tassels. I'll carry a goat and a can of fluorescent paint in one arm and, while in the bank, I'm going to fuck the goat and throw the paint over the walls, all the time ripping up pages of a phonebook and swearing my head off. After getting the money, I'll take a shit on the floor and piss everywhere. I then will escape in a van shaped like a giant pink cock.

Let's see *Crimewatch* stage a reconstruction of that.

▶ Police are on the lookout for a cross-eyed burglar. They have stated: 'If you see him peering in your front window, please warn the people next door.'

▶ What do you call two hookers who testify on behalf of their pimp? Support hos.

▶ A US cop catches an illegal alien by the Mexican border.

'Sorry,' he says. 'You know the law; you've got to go back.'

The Mexican pleads with him, 'No, señor, I must stay in de USA! Pleeeze!'

The cop says, 'OK. Tell you what, I'll let you stay if you can use the words green, pink and yellow in a sentence.'

The Mexican thinks, then says, 'Hokay. The phone, it went green, green, green... I pink it up and sez "Yellow?"'

PORN

▶ Did you hear about the male porn star who was sacked from his job as a petrol pump attendant? He kept putting the pump in the car, then pulling it out and spraying all over the bonnet.

▶ *Least popular porn websites:*

- www.beergut-chicks.com

- www.fully-clothed-middle-aged-housewives-doing-laundry.com

- www.36-24-88.com

- www.your-mum-naked.com

- www.GordonBrownBedroomCam.com

- www.your-granny-in-the-nude.com

- www.NaughtyAmishAnkles.com

- www.bodymodifications.com/lbobbitt

- www.goldengirls-goldenshowers.com

- www.dead-sluts.com

- www.colonic-irrigation-for-the-chronically-obese.com

▶ What do a ninja warrior and a softcore porn star have in common?
No one sees them coming.

POVERTY

▶ I came from a very poor family. One Christmas, my dad gave me an empty box and told me it was an Action Man deserter kit.

PREGNANCY

▶ A girl walked up to the information desk in her local hospital and said, 'I need to see the upturn, please.'

'I think you mean the intern, don't you?' asked the nurse on duty.

'Yes,' said the girl. 'I want to have a contamination.'

'Don't you mean examination?' the nurse questioned her again.

'Well, I want to go to the fraternity ward, anyway.'

'I'm sure you mean the maternity ward.'

To which the girl replied, 'Upturn, intern; contamination, examination; fraternity, maternity.... What's the difference? All I know is I haven't demonstrated in two months, and I think I'm stagnant.'

▶ EPT (early pregnancy test) colour codes explained:

Blue means not pregnant.

Pink means pregnant.

Brown means you had it in the wrong hole.

▶ An old woman on the beach walked up to a man with a rather large belly who was sunbathing. She said, 'If that belly was on a woman, I'd say she was pregnant!'

The man replied, 'It was, and she is!'

▶ 'Doctor,' said the husband, 'I've got nine kids and the wife's expecting again. How do I stop the stork?'

The doctor replied, 'Shoot it in the air!'

▶ A young girl had not been feeling well and went to her family doctor.

'Young lady,' said the doctor, 'you're pregnant.'

'But that can't be. The only men I've been with are nudists and in our colony we practise sex only with our eyes.'

'Well, my dear,' said the doctor, 'someone in that colony is cockeyed.'

▶ A Glasgow woman dials 999 and requests an ambulance. The operator enquires as to the nature of the emergency and the woman replies that she is pregnant.

'Madam, you can't have an ambulance simply because you are pregnant,' replies the operator.

'Aye, I know,' says the woman, 'but ma watters hae broke!'

'Oh, right, well, that's a different matter,' says the operator. 'Where are you ringing from?'

Woman replies, 'Frae ma fanny tae ma feet!'

▶ How did Burger King get Dairy Queen pregnant? He forgot to wrap his whopper.

▶ What's the worst thing a woman can get on her 30th wedding anniversary? Morning sickness.

▶ A man speaks frantically into the phone: 'My wife is pregnant, and her contractions are only two minutes apart!'

'Is this her first child?' the doctor queries.

'No, you idiot!' the man shouts. 'This is her husband!'

PREMATURE EJACULATION

▶ 'Doctor, doctor, I suffer from premature ejaculation. Can you help me?'

'No, but I can introduce you to a woman with a short attention span!'

▶ Can a guy get a girl pregnant without physical contact? It's a long shot.

▶ I went to a Premature Ejaculation Anonymous meeting the other day, but nobody was there. I think I came too early.

▶ A man was having problems with premature ejaculation. This was affecting marital relations with his wife, so he decided to go to the doctor. He asked the doctor what he could do to cure his problem.

In response the doctor said, 'When you feel the urge to ejaculate, try startling yourself.'

On the way home the man went to a sports store and bought himself a starter pistol. All excited to try out this suggestion, he ran home to his wife. When he got home, he was surprised and delighted to find his wife in bed, already naked. So horny and keen to try out his new 'system', he didn't think twice and leaped on board.

After a few minutes' slap and tickle, they found themselves in the '69' position. Sure enough, only moments later the man felt the sudden urge to come. Following doctor's orders, he grabbed the starter pistol off the bedside table and fired it.

The next day, the man went back to the doctor. The doctor asked, 'How did it go?'

The man answered, 'Just great. When I fired the pistol, my wife shat on my face, bit three inches off my dick and my neighbour came out of the closet naked, with his hands in the air.'

▶ Two guys are in a strip joint, one sitting in front of the other. A woman comes on stage and starts stripping.

The guy in back, Paul, says, 'Oh yeah! Oh yeah!'

The first guy turns around and says, 'Hey Paul, shut up!'

Then two women come out and start stripping. Paul, once again, starts, 'Yeah baby... mmmm... yeah!'

Once again the guy in front turns around and tells Paul to be quiet.

Then three women come out and start stripping. Paul is silent.

The guy in front says, 'Hey, Paul, where's all your excitement now?'

Paul says, 'All over your back!'

PRIESTS

▶ A doctor starts having an affair with a much younger woman. Before too long, she becomes pregnant and they don't know what to do. They won't consider abortion and don't want to give the baby up for adoption. But the doctor's not going to leave his wife, and the young woman can't stand the thought of taking care of the child alone.

Several months later, just about the time she is going to give birth, a priest goes into the hospital for a prostate gland operation. The doctor says to his mistress, 'I know what we'll do. After I've operated on the priest, I'll give the baby to him and tell him it was a miracle.'

'Do you think it will work?' she asks the doctor.

'It's worth a try,' he says.

So the doctor delivers the baby and then operates on the priest. After the operation, he goes in to the priest and says, 'Father, you won't believe this.'

'What?' says the priest. 'What happened?'

'You gave birth to a child.'

'But that's impossible!'

'I just did the operation,' insists the doctor. 'It's a miracle! Here's your baby.'

About 15 years go by, and the priest realises that he must tell his son the truth. One day he sits the boy down and says, 'Son, I have something to tell you. I'm not your father.'

The son says, 'What do you mean, you're not my father?'

The priest replies, 'I'm your mother. The archbishop is your father.'

▶ What's the difference between a pimple and a priest? A pimple waits till you're about 15 till it comes on your face.

▶ Is murdering a priest classed as a white collar crime?

▶ Mary Clancy goes up to Father O'Grady after his Sunday morning service and she's in tears.

He says, 'So what's bothering you, Mary, my dear child?'

She says, 'Oh, Father, I've got terrible news. My husband passed away last night.'

The priest says, 'Oh, Mary, that's terrible. Tell me, Mary, did he have any last requests?'

She says, 'That he did, Father. '

The priest says, 'What did he ask you, Mary?'

She says, 'He said, "Please, Mary, put down that feckin' gun... "'

▶ A 12-year-old boy gets hit by a car at a busy junction. A woman witnesses the entire event and runs over to the boy, who's lying on the ground in a pool of blood.

She gently cradles the boy's head in her arms and whispers, 'Do you need a priest?'

The boy moans, 'How can you think of sex at a time like this?'

▶ What do you give the paedophile who has everything? Another parish.

▶ A preacher wanted to earn money for the building expansion programme of his church. He had heard there was big money in horse racing, so he decided to purchase a horse and enter him in the races. However, at the local auction the going price for horses was too steep and the preacher ended up buying a donkey. The preacher figured that as he had the donkey, he might as well enter it in the race.

The next day the donkey came in third. The racing form's headline the following day read: 'Preacher's ass shows.'

The preacher was so pleased with his donkey that he entered him the next day also. The donkey won. The newspaper's headline read: 'Preacher's ass out in front.'

The bishop was so upset with this type of publicity that he ordered the preacher not to enter the donkey in the races anymore. Then the headline read: 'Bishop scratches preacher's ass.' This was too much for the bishop, and he ordered the preacher to get rid of the donkey.

The preacher decided to give the animal to a nearby convent. Next day's headline read: 'Nuns have best ass in town.' The bishop fainted! He informed the nuns to get rid of the animal.

So they sold it to a farmer for £10. Next day the paper read: 'Nun peddles ass for ten bucks.'

They buried the bishop the next day. The paper read: 'Too much ass responsible for bishop's death.'

▶ An old priest was getting fed up with the number of people in his parish who were confessing to adultery. One Sunday in the pulpit, he announced, 'If I hear one more person confess to adultery, I'm quitting!'

Since he was so popular, the parishioners came up with a code word to avoid incurring his wrath; anyone who had committed adultery would say they had 'fallen'. The arrangement appeared to satisfy the old priest right up until his death.

His young replacement soon settled into parish life and visited the mayor to express his concern about safety in the town. 'You have to do something about the pavements,' the new priest told the mayor. 'When people come into the confessional, they keep talking about having fallen.' The mayor began to laugh, realising that nobody had told the new priest about the code word. Before the mayor could explain, the priest shook an accusing finger at him and said, 'I don't know what you're laughing about. Your wife has fallen three times already this week!'

PRISONS

▶ Who is the only man, weighing over 11 stone, who has ridden a Derby winner since 1945? Lester Piggott's cellmate.

▶ My dad told me, 'Son, never open the cellar door!' But I couldn't resist. I opened it and saw things I'd never seen before: grass, sky, trees...

▶ Did you hear about the combine harvester killings? The main suspect was baled.

▶ I remember the year my uncle went to prison for forgery. It was around the same time I stopped getting birthday cards from Pamela Anderson.

▶ These two men were cellmates in prison for nine years. One day Larry said to Joe, 'You know, it's been a long time since we had some sex so you ought to let me screw you.'

Joe replied, 'Are you crazy?!'

Larry went on to say, 'I promise you that it won't hurt and we'll flip a coin and see who screws who first.'

So, Joe thought about it for a minute and agreed. They flipped a coin and Larry won. Still having strong reservations, Joe asked, 'How will you tell if it hurts or not?'

Larry told Joe, 'If it hurts, you start making animal noises, and I'll stop. But if it feels good, start singing.'

Larry started the insertion and Joe screamed, 'Moooooooo... Moooooo... Mooooon River!'

PROCRASTINATION

▶ My mother always told me I wouldn't amount to anything because I procrastinate. I said, 'Just wait.'

PROCTOLOGISTS

▶ What car does a proctologist drive? A brown Probe.

▶ A student wants to be a really good proctologist, so he decides to go down to the morgue after lectures and practise a little. The first man he uncovers has a cork up his arse. He thinks, 'This is a little strange,' so he pulls it out and music starts playing '... On the road again, just can't wait to get on the road again...'

The student really freaks out! He runs to fetch the pathologist and drags him to the table. 'Look!' he says, and pulls the cork out again. '... On the road again... '

The pathologist is totally unimpressed. 'So what?' he says.

'Isn't that the most amazing thing you've ever seen?' the student asks.

'Are you joking?' says the pathologist. 'Any arsehole can sing country music!'

▶ What's a Pokemon? A Jamaican proctologist.

PROSTHETICS

▶ I once went out with a girl with a wooden leg. I had to break it off.

▶ I was at a bar, I asked a girl to dance and every time I twirled her around, she got two inches taller.

I said, 'What's going on?'

She said, 'You're unscrewing my wooden leg.'

▶ A severed foot is the ultimate stocking stuffer.

PROSTITUTES

▶ A counsellor was helping a husband and wife through some marital difficulties. He called the husband into his office and said, 'I've questioned both you and your wife about how often you have sex, and I wonder if you could explain the answers. You said once a week, but your wife said several times a night.'

'That's right,' replied the husband, 'and that's the way it will be until the mortgage is paid off.'

▶ I met this blind prostitute the other night; you've got to hand it to her.

▶ How are a lawyer and a prostitute different? The prostitute stops fucking you after you're dead.

▶ After a whirlwind romance, a woman and an older millionaire decide to get married. The woman is worried that they don't know enough about each other, but the millionaire believes it will be more fun to discover each other in wedlock. On their honeymoon the millionaire leaps from the diving board of their hotel pool and executes a perfect dive. 'I used to be a diving champion when I was younger,' he tells his wife. 'Y'see, I told you it would be fun getting to know each other this way.' The woman agrees, then gets in the pool and does 50 lengths in a row.

'Wow,' says her husband. 'I'll bet you used to be some sort of Olympic endurance swimmer.'

'No,' replies his wife. 'I was a whore in Venice who used to work both sides of the canal.'

▶ One day, after striking gold in Alaska, a lonesome miner came down from the mountains and walked into a saloon in the nearest town. 'I'm lookin' for the meanest, roughest and toughest whore in the Yukon!' he said to the bartender.

'Well, we got her!' replied the barkeep. 'She's upstairs in the second room on the right.'

The miner handed the bartender a gold nugget to pay for the whore and two beers.

He grabbed the bottles, stomped up the stairs, kicked open the second door on the right and yelled, 'I'm lookin' for the meanest, roughest and toughest whore in the Yukon!'

The woman inside the room looked at the miner and said, 'You found her!'
Then she stripped naked, bent over and grabbed her ankles.

'How do you know I want to do it in that position?' asked the miner.

'I don't,' replied the whore, 'but I thought you might like to open those
beers first.'

▶ A family of prostitutes are talking. The daughter says, 'I got £50 for a
blowjob today.'

The mother says, 'In my day it was £5.

'The grandmother says, 'In my day we were just glad for the warm drink.'

▶ A man walked up to a prostitute in the street and agreed a price. When
they got to the hotel room, he began masturbating.

The prostitute asked him what he was doing and the man replied, 'You
didn't think you were going to get the easy one, did you?'

▶ I slept with one of those high-class prostitutes the other week. I'm not
happy, though: the bitch gave me lobsters.

▶ What do you call a prostitute in a wheelchair? Park and ride.

▶ A guy went into a whorehouse and said he wanted the best blowjob
money could buy. The madam said it would cost £150, and told him to go
upstairs to a room. A few minutes later, the hooker came in and proceeded
to suck him off. Afterwards, she reached under the bed, pulled out a jar
and spat in it. The guy enjoyed the whole experience so much that he paid
another £150 for a repeat performance.

The hooker happily gave him another blowjob. Afterwards, she again
pulled out the jar and spat in it. Intrigued, he asked her what the jar
was for.

She said, 'I have a bet with the girl across the hall. Whoever fills up their jar first gets to drink them both.'

▶ If a firefighter's business can go up in smoke, and a plumber's business can go down the drain, can a prostitute get laid off?

▶ Did you hear about the prostitute who was into bondage? She was strapped for cash.

▶ Two friends were talking. One says, 'You and I use the same call girl and I've discovered she is charging you, an accountant, twice as much as she charges me. Aren't you angry?'

'No,' replies the other. 'I use the double entry system.'

▶ Did you hear about the male prostitute who got leprosy? He did OK until his business fell off.

▶ What do you call a Serbian prostitute? Slobodan Mycokubitch.

▶ A tourist approached a prostitute in the back streets of Soho in London.

'How much?' he asked.

'It'll cost you 20 quid,' replied the tart.

'American Express?' he enquired.

'You can go as fast as you like,' she said.

▶ What do a farmer and a pimp have in common? Both need a hoe to stay in business.

▶ Two prostitutes were talking. The first one said, 'Last night I made £500 and I feel like a bottle of champagne.'

'Well, last night I made £5,000,' said the second, 'and I feel like a pot of glue!'

PSYCHIATRY AND PSYCHOANALYSIS

▶ The psychiatrist was interviewing a first-time patient. 'You say you're here,' he said, 'because your family is worried about your taste in socks?'

'That's correct,' muttered the patient. 'I like wool socks.'

'But that's perfectly normal,' replied the doctor. 'Many people prefer wool socks to those made from cotton or acrylic. In fact, I myself like wool socks.'

'You DO?' exclaimed the man. 'With oil and vinegar or just a squeeze of lemon?'

▶ I went to the local library for a book. I asked the lady for a book on Psycho the Rapist. She said, 'I think it's pronounced Psychotherapist.'

▶ One day on the psychiatric ward a nurse walks into a patient's room and sees him pretending to drive a car, with his hands at ten and two.

The nurse asks him, 'Charlie, what are you doing?'

Charlie replies, 'Can't talk right now, I'm driving to Edinburgh!'

The nurse wishes him a good trip and leaves the room.

The next day the nurse enters Charlie's room, just as he stops driving his imaginary car and she asks, 'Well, Charlie, how was your trip?'

Charlie says, 'I'm exhausted, I just got into Edinburgh and I need some rest.'

'That's great,' replies the nurse. 'I'm glad you had a safe trip.'

The nurse leaves Charlie's room, then goes across the hall into another patient's room and finds Ed sitting on his bed masturbating vigorously. Startled but smiling, she asks, 'Ed, what do you think you're doing?'

To which Ed replies, 'Sshhh, I'm shagging Charlie's wife while he's in Edinburgh.'

▶ When the new patient was settled comfortably on the couch, the psychiatrist began his therapy session.

'I'm not aware of your problem,' the doctor said. 'So perhaps, you should start at the very beginning.'

'Of course,' replied the patient. 'In the beginning, I created the heavens and the earth... '

▶ Why is psychoanalysis quicker for men than for women? When it's time to go back to his childhood, he's already there.

▶ A man goes to the psychiatrist's office and says, 'Doc, you gotta help me. I'm 38 years old and I still wet my bed.'

The psychiatrist said, 'My good man, that is merely an acting out of a retarded ego development and a rejection of adult responsibilities. We can stop you from wetting your bed in two ways. The first is psychoanalysis; five visits a week, £50 a visit.'

The guy says, 'What's the second way?'

The doctor replies, 'Rubber shorts, £2 a pair.'

PUBS

▶ How do you know when a pub is rough? When the first question in the quiz is, 'What the fuck are YOU looking at?'

▶ My girlfriend was in the Blacksmith's Arms. So I clobbered him with a horseshoe.

▶ I was meeting a friend at a bar and as I went in, I noticed two pretty girls looking at me.

'Nine,' I heard one whisper as I passed.

Feeling pleased with myself, I swaggered over to my buddy and told him a girl had just rated me as nine out of ten.

'I don't want to ruin it for you,' he said, 'but when I walked in they were speaking German.'

▶ A bloke strolls into a pub and walks up the wall, across the ceiling, back down the other wall, then over to the bar, where he orders two whiskies. He drinks them, walks up the wall, across the ceiling, back down the other wall and out the door.

'That's strange,' says a punter to the barman.

'I know,' the barman replies. 'He normally orders a pint.'

PUBES

▶ What's got 400 legs and no pubic hair? The front row of a JLS concert.

▶ What's black and triangular? Kate's bush.

▶ What do parsley and pubic hair have in common? Push it aside and keep on eating...

▶ What do you call an adolescent rabbit? A pubic hare.

RABBITS

▶ Why do bunnies have soft sex? They have cotton balls.

▶ Did you hear about the man who broke into a pet shop and stole a rabbit? He made a run for it.

▶ Two rabbits were being chased by a pack of wolves. The wolves chased the rabbits into a thicket. After a few minutes, one rabbit turned to the other and said, 'Well, do you want to make a run for it or stay here a few days and outnumber them?'

▶ An angora rabbit decides he wants good sex, so he goes to an animal brothel. There, he asks the madam, who is a fox, for a suitable female.

'For you, I got this nice little squirrel,' says the fox.

'No, better give me a boa constrictor snake,' replies the rabbit.

'But a boa will eat a little angora rabbit like you alive!' says the fox.

'Never mind, just give me the woman – I want a big, long, cold boa snake,' answers the rabbit.

So he is taken to this incredible boa female. Seeing the little rabbit, the snake swallows it in a second. But, because it's an angora rabbit, the boa, with its stomach irritated by the fur, spits the little animal out so violently that the rabbit lands two kilometres away.

Stunned, the rabbit slowly gets on his feet, with a huge happy smile on his face, and proudly says to himself, 'Oh, boy, what a blowjob!'

▶ Once upon a time, in a nice little forest, there lived an orphaned bunny and an orphaned snake. By surprising coincidence both were blind from birth. One day, the bunny was hopping through the forest, and the snake was slithering through the forest, when the bunny tripped over the snake and fell down. This, of course, knocked the snake about quite a bit.

'Oh, my,' said the bunny, 'I'm terribly sorry. I didn't mean to hurt you. I've been blind since birth so I can't see where I'm going. In fact, since I'm an orphan, I don't even know what I am.'

'It's quite OK,' replied the snake. 'Actually, my story is much the same as yours. I too have been blind since birth, and also never knew my mother. Tell you what, maybe I could slither all over you, and work out what you are, so at least you'll have that going for you.'

'Oh, that would be wonderful,' replied the bunny.

So the snake slithered all over the bunny, and said, 'Well, you're covered with soft fur; you have really long ears, your nose twitches and you have a soft cottony tail. I'd say that you must be a bunny rabbit.'

'Oh, thank you! Thank you!' cried the bunny in obvious excitement. The bunny suggested to the snake, 'Maybe I could feel you all over with my paw and help you the same way you've helped me.' So the bunny felt the snake all over and remarked, 'Well, you're scaly and smooth, and you have a forked tongue, no backbone and no balls. I'd say you must be either an accountant, or possibly someone else in senior management.'

▶ Two rabbits and a hedgehog are standing by the side of a road one day, when the hedgehog says to the rabbits, 'Tell me, how do you rabbits manage to cross the road safely when we always seem to get splattered by a car?'

'Well, that's easy,' says one of the rabbits. 'All you have to do is first make sure nothing is coming either way, then make your way across, keeping a lookout for any cars. If you see a car coming towards you, turn and face it and stare at the driver. Then just as the car gets close to you, roll yourself up into a ball and the car will go over you with the wheels either side of you, then carry on to the other side of the road.'

'Brilliant,' says the hedgehog, 'I'll try that now.'

So the hedgehog looks both ways, nothing coming, so off he goes across the road, keeping a lookout for any cars.

Just over halfway across, he sees a car coming towards him, so he does exactly as the rabbits told him – he turns round and faces the car, stares at the driver and just as the car gets close, he curls up into a ball.

SPLAT!!!!

The car squashes the poor little sod in the middle of the road.

On the side of the road the two rabbits have just witnessed what has happened.

One rabbit says to the other, 'Damn! That was unlucky – that's the first time I've ever seen a Reliant Robin come down this road.'

▶ A little girl walked into a pet shop and asked in the sweetest little lisp, 'Excuthe me, mithter. Do you keep widdle wabbits?'

As the shopkeeper's heart melted, he got down on his knees to her level and asked, 'Do you want a widdle white wabbit or a thoft and fuwwy bwack wabbit or maybe one like this cute widdle bwown wabbit over there?'

The little girl leaned forwards and said in a quiet voice, 'I don't fink my pet python weally gives a thit.'

▶ When the ark's door was closed, Noah called a meeting with all the animals.

'Listen up!' Noah said. 'There will be NO sex on this trip. All of you males take off your penis and hand it in to my sons. I will sit over there and write you a receipt. After we see land, you can get your penis back.'

After about a week Mr Rabbit stormed into his wife's cage and was very excited. 'Quick!' he said. 'Get on my shoulders and look out the window to see if there is any land out there!'

Mrs Rabbit got onto his shoulders, looked out the window and said, 'Sorry, no land yet.'

'Damn!' exclaimed Mr Rabbit.

This went on every day, until Mrs Rabbit got fed up with him. Mrs Rabbit asked, 'What is the matter with you? You know it will rain for 40 days and nights. Only after the water has drained will we be able to see land. But why are you acting so excited every day?'

'Look!' said Mr Rabbit with a sly expression, as he held out a piece of paper, 'I GOT THE HORSE'S RECEIPT!'

RACING DRIVERS

▶ What's big and hairy and drives a Ferrari? Michael Chewbacca.

REDNECKS

▶ *Signs that you might be a redneck:*

- Your wife's hairdo was once ruined by a ceiling fan.

- You've been married three times and still have the same in-laws.

- You can't get married to your sweetheart because there's a law against it.

- You think loading a dishwasher means getting your wife drunk.

- Your toilet paper has numbers on it.

- You think Dom Perignon is a Mafia boss.

- You think a woman who is 'out of your league' bowls on a different night.

▶ Have you seen the redneck version of *Star Wars*? It ends with the line: 'Luke, I am your father – and your uncle.'

RELIGION

▶ Mrs Murphy and Mrs Cohen had lived next door to one another for over 40 years, and over the years became firm friends. The day came when each went into a retirement home of their respective religions: Mrs Murphy to the Catholic home and Mrs Cohen to the Jewish one. After a few weeks Mrs Murphy decided to visit her old friend to see how she was getting on. When she arrived, she was greeted by Mrs Cohen, who seemed very happy – she went on and on about the wonderful food, the wonderful facility and the wonderful carers. She then said, 'And that's not all. You know the best thing is that I now have a boyfriend.'

Mrs Murphy said, 'That's wonderful. Tell me what you do.'

Mrs Cohen said, 'After lunch we go up to my room and sit on the edge of my bed. I let him touch me on the top and then down below and then we sing Jewish songs. And how is it with you, Mrs Murphy?'

Mrs Murphy said it was also wonderful at her new facility and that she also had a boyfriend.

Mrs Cohen said, 'That's wonderful. So what do you do?'

'We also go up to my room after lunch and sit on the edge of my bed. I let him touch me on top and then let him touch me down below.'

Mrs Cohen said, 'And then what do you do?'

Mrs Murphy replied, 'Since we don't know any Jewish songs, we shag!'

▶ 'I've taken so many cold showers,' said the monk, 'that whenever it rains, I get a hard-on.'

▶ Religion is man's quest for assurance that he won't be dead when he will be.

▶ A mother is preparing pancakes for her sons – Kevin, five, and Ryan, three. The boys begin to argue over who gets the first pancake and their mother sees the opportunity for a moral lesson. 'If Jesus were sitting here,' she says, 'He would say, "Let my brother have the first pancake. I can wait."'

Kevin turns to his brother and says, 'OK, Ryan. You be Jesus.'

▶ Little Johnny comes home from school and says, 'Dad, today we found out what God's name is. He's called Harold.'

'Harold?' replies his father. 'What gave you that idea?'

'It said so in the poem,' replies Johnny. 'Our Lord who art in heaven. Harold be thy name.'

▶ At the Last Supper, Jesus stands and declares he'll turn the water into wine.

'No, you don't,' shouts Judas. 'Put in 20 shekels like everyone else.'

▶ Our priest is very liberal. He likes to show he's as imperfect as the rest of us. Halfway through confession, he often pulls back the screen so we can see him puffing on his crack pipe.

▶ A man attended a Billy Graham crusade. When the very emotional sermon was over, Reverend Graham asked those who'd been moved by the Lord to come forwards. The man had really been taken by the sermon and came forwards to shake hands with Graham. When the man got to the Reverend, Graham held his hands up, grabbed the microphone, stopped the music and waved for silence.

'My dear man, who put those clothes on your body?'

The man replied, 'The Lord did!'

'AMEN!' shouted the congregation.

'My good man, who put food on your table?'

'The good Lord did, Reverend!' the man shouted.

'AMEN! Hallelujah!' the crowd roared in response.

'My good fellow, who put that smile on your face and a rosy look to your cheeks?'

'Reverend, it was the Lord!'

'PRAISE GOD!' the crowd cheered.

Reverend Graham again raised his hands and called for silence. 'Now, kind sir, what did the devil ever do for you?'

The man thought for a second. 'Nothing. Fuck him.'

▶ I took my car in for a service yesterday. You should have seen the look on the minister's face.

▶ It's a pity Jeremy Kyle was not around in biblical times. Then we could find out who really was the father of Jesus.

▶ I've got the body of a god. Unfortunately, it's Buddha.

▶ A blind man, deaf man and a lame man went on a pilgrimage to a healing spring.

The blind man washed his eyes with water from the spring and exclaimed, 'I can see! I can see!'

The deaf man washed his ears with the spring water and exclaimed, 'I can hear! I can hear!'

The lame man drove his wheelchair into the water and out the other side. yelling, 'I got new tyres! I got new tyres!'

▶ *World religions:*

• Atheism – Shit happens.

• Hare Krishna – Shit happens rama dama ding dong.

• Hinduism – This shit happened before.

• Islam – If shit happens, take a hostage.

• Zen – What is the sound of shit happening?

• Buddhism – When shit happens, is it really shit?

• Confucianism – Confucius say, 'Shit happens'.

• Seventh Day Adventist – Shit happens on Saturdays.

• Protestantism – Shit won't happen if I work harder.

• Catholicism – If shit happens, I deserve it.

• Jehovah's Witness – Knock knock, shit happens.

• Unitarian – What is this shit?

- Judaism – Why does shit always happen to me?

- Mormon – Shit happens again and again and again.

- Rastafarian – Let's smoke this shit.

▶ The pope had become very ill and was taken to many doctors, all of whom could not figure out how to cure him. Finally he was brought to an old physician, who stated that he could figure it out. After about an hour's examination, he came out and told the cardinals that he knew what was wrong. He said that the bad news was that it was a rare disorder of the testicles. He said that the goods news was that all the pope had to do to be cured was to have sex. Well, this was not good news to the cardinals, who argued about it at length. Finally they went to the pope with the doctor and explained the situation.

After some thought, the pope stated, 'I agree, but under four conditions.'

The cardinals were amazed and there was quite an uproar. Over all of the noise there arose a single voice that asked, 'And what are the four conditions?' The room stilled. There was a long pause...

The pope replied, 'First, the girl must be blind, so that she cannot see with whom she is having sex. Second, she must be deaf, so that she cannot hear with whom she is having sex. Third, she must be dumb so that if somehow she figures out with whom she is having sex, she can tell no one.'

After another long pause a voice arose and asked, 'And the fourth condition?'

'Big tits,' replied the pope.

▶ An English monk goes to God, and says, 'Lord, we need to learn the meaning of patience, the meaning of eternity, how to sit for hours and not feel guilty.'

And God says, 'Certainly, my son, here you are. The rules of cricket.'

▶ What would have happened if it had been three wise women instead of three wise men?

They would have asked directions, arrived on time, helped deliver the baby, cleaned the stable, made a casserole and brought practical gifts. But what would they have said as they left?

'Did you see the sandals Mary was wearing with that gown?'

'That baby doesn't look anything like Joseph!'

'Virgin, my arse! I knew her in school!'

'Can you believe that they let all of those disgusting animals in there!'

'I heard that Joseph isn't even working right now!'

'And that donkey they are riding has seen better days, too!'

'Want to bet on how long it will take until you get your casserole dish back?'

▶ Jesus and St Paul are sitting in heaven, talking about the pollution on earth and wondering what can be done about mankind's filthy ways. Jesus says he's going to pop down to Skegness to see the situation for himself, and Paul agrees to join him. When they get there, Jesus asks what the huge metal pipe is for. Paul tells him it's used to take human waste out to sea, where the muck kills dolphins, so Jesus decides to take action and strides across the waves. Walking alongside, Paul is soon knee-deep in filthy water, while Jesus scoots along on top of the sea. Ever hopeful of some help, he slogs on, and Jesus keeps walking on water... but soon the water is up to Paul's chin.

'Master,' he calls, 'I will follow you anywhere, but I'm up to my neck in shitty water and I think I'm going to drown.'

At this Jesus stops walking and looks at Paul. 'Well,' he says, 'why don't you just walk on the pipe like me, you silly prick?'

▶ After Moses and God were finished with their talk up on Mount Sinai, Moses finished with this one last question.

'OK, let me get this straight – the Arabs get all that oil and we have to cut the ends of our dicks off, right?'

'That's right.'

'And WE'RE the "chosen people"?'

▶ This fellow comes to confession. 'Father,' he said, 'forgive me, for I have sinned.'

The priest asked, 'What did you do, my son?'

'I lusted,' the fellow replied.

'Tell me about it,' the priest said.

The fellow then related his story. 'Father, I am a delivery man for UPS. Yesterday I was making a delivery in the affluent section of the city. When I rang the bell, the door opened and there stood the most beautiful woman I have ever seen. She had long blonde hair and eyes like emeralds. She was dressed in a sheer dressing gown that showed her perfect figure. And she asked if I would like to come in.'

'And what did you do, my son?' asked the priest.

'Father, I did not go in the house but I lusted. Oh, how I lusted,' replied the man.

'Your sin has been forgiven,' replied the priest. 'You will get your reward in heaven, my son.'

'A reward, father? What do you think my reward might be?' the fellow asked.

The priest replied, 'I think a bale of hay would be appropriate, you jackass.'

▶ A window cleaner goes to a monastery looking for work. The chief abbot tells him to clean all the windows except the top three, so the window cleaner cleans all the windows for years and years, until curiosity gets the better of him and he puts his ladder up against the first of the three windows. He looks in and sees 12 monks with their robes up and their cocks lying on a table, with a mouse running around on top of the table.

The window cleaner goes down the ladder, moves to the second window and looks in. There is this beautiful woman and a monk in bed fucking like mad.

The window cleaner goes down the ladder and puts it up against the third window. He looks in and sees a monk tied up, stripped to the waist, being flogged.

He goes down the ladder and when he gets to the bottom, the chief abbot is waiting for him. The window cleaner says, 'Look, I know you're going to sack me, but please, at least tell me what is going on.'

'Well,' says the abbot, 'in the first window you saw a competition to see which is the lucky monk – wherever the mouse stops is the lucky monk. And in the second window you saw a monk with the prize.'

'But what about the third window?' the window cleaner asks.

'Well,' says the abbot, 'that monk was caught with a piece of cheese in his foreskin.'

▶ One day while the pope was eating his breakfast, one of his assistants came running up to him.

Out of breath, he panted, 'I've got good news and bad news. Which do you want first?'

The pope, being good-natured and all, replied, 'If I hear something good and of value, I think I could take anything that's bad. So, let me hear the good news first.'

The assistant then said, 'OK, here goes. The good news is God is on the phone for you!'

'Great, I've been waiting to talk to him for years!' the pope exclaimed excitedly. Then the pope enquired, 'If God is on the phone, what possibly could be the bad news?'

'Well,' the assistant stammered. 'He's calling from Mecca.'

RESTAURANTS

▶ A man goes into a restaurant and orders a starter. The waitress brings him a bowl of soup but the man notices she has her thumb stuck in it. When the soup is finished, the waitress suggests beef stew as a main course. The man agrees but when she brings the stew to the table, he notices she has her thumb stuck it that, too. Once the stew is finished, the waitress suggests hot apple pie as a dessert. The man agrees, but again, the waitress brings him his plate with her thumb stuck in his food.

'Look,' says the man, 'I wasn't going to mention it, but every time you bring food to my table you've got your thumb stuck in it.'

'Sorry,' says the waitress. 'But my thumb's got an infection. My doctor says I have to keep it in a warm, moist place.'

'Well, why not stick it up your arse!' says the man.

The waitress replies, 'Where d'you think I've been putting it when I'm in the kitchen?'

▶ A customer is ordering food in an Indian restaurant. 'Waiter, what's this chicken tarka?'

The waiter replies, 'It's the same as chicken tikka, but it's a little 'otter.'

▶ It's a very authentic Spanish restaurant. They bring you a glass of water, then warn you not to drink it.

▶ We were eating in an open-air café, when it started raining really heavily. It took us an hour and a half to finish our soup.

▶ I found a café that serves chicken dinners for 50 pence. You sit down and they bring you a plate of bird seed.

▶ 'Waiter! There's a fly in my soup!'
  'That's not a fly, that's a vitamin Bee.'

▶ A tourist goes into a restaurant in Madrid and sees a dish called 'cajones' on the menu. The man asks the waiter what a 'cajone' is.

The waiter replies, 'They are the testicles of a fighting bull that has died in the arena.'

The man looks a bit squeamish at this news but decides to give them a try. He orders them and finds they taste really good.

Next day he returns to the restaurant and, again, orders cajones. However, when they arrive, he finds the cajones are the size of small walnuts, not the huge juicy testicles he had yesterday. He calls the waiter over, 'What's the meaning of this?' he says. 'These cajones are tiny. What sort of bull had these?'

'The bull didn't have those,' replies the waiter. 'The bull doesn't always lose.'

▶ An Irishman, a Mexican and a redneck are doing construction work on a tall building. They're eating lunch, when the Irishman says, 'Corned beef and cabbage! If I get corned beef and cabbage one more time, I'm going to jump off this building.'

The Mexican opens his lunch box and exclaims, 'Burritos again! If I get burritos one more time, I'm going to jump, too.'

The redneck opens his lunch and says, 'Bologna again. If I get a bologna sandwich one more time, I'm jumping off as well.'

Next day the Irishman opens his lunch box, sees corned beef and cabbage and jumps to his death. The Mexican opens his lunch, sees a burrito and jumps as well. The redneck opens his lunch, sees bologna and jumps with them.

At the funeral, the Irishman's wife is weeping, 'If I'd known how tired he was of corned beef and cabbage, I never would have given it to him!'

The Mexican's wife weeps, saying, 'I didn't realise he hated burritos so much.'

The women turn to the redneck's wife. 'Hey, don't look at me,' she says. 'He made his own lunch.'

▶ Harry keeps a record of everything he eats. It's called a tie.

▶ I always take my wife to the finest restaurants. One day I might let her inside one.

ROMANTIC VERSE

▶ Love may be beautiful, love may be bliss
But I only slept with you because I was pissed

▶ I thought that I could love no other
Until, that is, I met your brother

▶ Roses are red, violets are blue, sugar is sweet, and so are you
But the roses are wilting, the violets are dead, the sugar bowl's empty,
and so is your head

▶ Of loving beauty, you float with grace
If only you could hide your face

▶ Kind, intelligent, loving and hot
This describes everything you are not

▶ I want to feel your sweet embrace
But don't take that paper bag off of your face

▶ I love your smile, your face and your eyes
Damn, I'm good at telling lies!

▶ My darling, my lover, my beautiful wife
Marrying you screwed up my life

▶ I see your face when I am dreaming
That's why I always wake up screaming

▶ My love, you take my breath away
What have you stepped in to smell this way?

▶ My feelings for you no words can tell
Except for maybe 'go to hell'

▶ What inspired this amorous rhyme?
Two parts vodka, one part lime

ROYALTY

▶ Kate confides in the Queen and says, 'Every time I suck William's cock, I get acid indigestion.'

The Queen considers this for a moment and replies, 'Have you tried Andrew's?'

▶ The King of Jordan visits London and is invited to dinner with the Queen. The servants bring out the first course and start dishing it out. 'No soup for me,' says the King of Jordan. 'It makes me fart.' Silence falls over the room. Everyone is horrified. 'What's the matter with you all?' asks the King, patting his belly. 'Don't you think I'm fart enough already?'

▶ On the day of the wedding, Sophie was getting dressed, surrounded by all her family, and she suddenly realised she had forgotten to get any shoes. Panic ensued until her sister remembered she had a pair of white shoes from her wedding, so she lent them to Sophie for the day.

Unfortunately, they were too small and by the time the festivities were over, Sophie's feet were in agony. When she and Edward withdrew to their room, the only thing she could think about was getting her shoes off.

The rest of the royal family crowded round the door to the bedroom and they heard what they expected: grunts, straining noises and the occasional muffled scream. Eventually they heard Edward say, 'God, that was tight.'

'There,' whispered the Queen. 'I told you she was a virgin.'

Then, to their surprise, they heard Edward say, 'Right. Now for the other one.'

More grunting and straining followed, and at last Edward said, 'My God! That was even tighter!'

'That's my boy,' said the Duke. 'Once a sailor, always a sailor.'

▶ Prince Phillip and the Queen are dining in one of London's top restaurants. The waiter comes over and asks what Phillip would like to order.

'I'll have two rare steaks, my good fellow.'

Waiter: 'Does sir mean two bloody steaks?'

Phillip: 'Yes, quite right, old chap, two bloody steaks.'

Queen: 'And plenty of fucking chips!'

▶ Prince Charles arrived at Hartlepool on an official visit. When he got out of the car, the mayor was surprised to see that Charles had a red animal skin on his head, with a bushy tail hanging down the back. Keeping a straight face, he asked the prince what the headgear was for.

Prince Charles said, 'Oh, Mummy told me to wear it. When she asked, at breakfast, where I was going today, I told her Hartlepool. She said, "Oh, wear the fox hat!"'

▶ Camilla Parker Bowles bought Prince Charles a bookmark for Christmas. It was to stop him bending the pages over.

▶ A group of American tourists were visiting Windsor Castle, which is situated directly in the flight path of Heathrow Airport. While they were admiring the castle walls, a plane flew overhead at a relatively low altitude, making a tremendous amount of noise. One of the American tourists complained, 'Why the heck did they build the castle so close to the airport?'

▶ The Queen was visiting a hospital and she stopped by one of the beds to speak to the man lying there.

'What is wrong with you, sir?' she asked the man.

'I got a wart on my balls,' he replied, much to the astonishment of the nurses. One of the nurses immediately rushed over to him.

'You can't say that to the Queen!' the nurse shouted.

'Well, what should I have said, then?' replied the man.

'Something like you have a bruise on your back, or a cut on your arm, or a graze on your knee. Anything but "I have a wart on my balls!"' answered the nurse.

Two months later, Princess Anne is visiting the same hospital and just happens to pass the same bed, with the same man in it.

'What is wrong with you, sir?' asked the princess.

'Er.... I have a bruise on my back,' replied the man.

'Oh,' the Princess answered, 'I'm so glad to hear that your balls are better... I'll tell the Queen.'

▶ Three London surgeons were playing golf together and discussing surgeries they had performed. One of them said, 'I'm the best surgeon in London. A concert pianist lost seven fingers in an accident, I reattached them and eight months later he performed a private concert for the Queen.'

One of the others said, 'That's nothing. A young man lost an arm and both legs in an accident, I reattached them and two years later he won a gold medal in field events in the Olympics.'

The third surgeon said, 'You are amateurs. Several years ago a woman was high on cocaine and marijuana and she rode a horse head on to a train travelling 80 miles an hour. All I had left to work with was the horse's blond mane and a big arse. Now she's the Duchess of Cornwall.'

▶ On a visit to London, an Australian applied for a job as a royal footman. Armed with his references from his previous job, he went along to the interview, where he was asked to drop his trousers. Seeing the Australian's puzzled expression, the interviewer explained, 'Don't worry, it's merely a formality. You see, footmen are often required to wear kilts when accompanying the Queen to Balmoral, so we like to examine the knees of applicants to check for any unsightly scars.'

The Aussie duly dropped his trousers to allow his knees to be inspected.

'Excellent,' said the interviewer. 'Now could you show me your testimonials?'

Thirty seconds later, the Aussie found himself lying in the corridor, nursing a black eye.

'Strewth,' he said, picking himself up and dusting himself down. 'I reckon I'd have got that job if I'd known the lingo a little better.'

▶ Long ago, a king and his court jester were marooned on a desert island. The king immediately began missing the sexual gratification that his position of power had commanded. By the end of the third day, he was complaining loudly to the jester about the lack of sexual release. By the end of the week, he was at his wit's end.

RUSSIAN JOKES

▶ A Russian tsar's birthday arrived, and when he woke up, he saw a message written in piss on the heavy snow from the night before: 'A happy birthday to you, my master', signed 'Ivan, your loyal servant'.

The tsar called Ivan and said, 'It was nice of you to remember my birthday, but how the heck did you did it? You are illiterate.'

The servant responded, 'Oh, it was simple. I was pissing in the snow and your wife was holding my dick!'

▶ Russian nuclear scientists are instructed to NEVER wear loose boxer shorts because – the authorities explain – 'Chernobyl fallout'.

SADDAM HUSSEIN

▶ What did Saddam Hussein say when he came out of his hole? 'Did I beat David Blaine?'

▶ Why is Saddam Hussein afraid to have sex with a girl? Because when he opens her legs, he'll see bush.

SAILORS

▶ What do you call an 80-year-old impotent sailor? A salt with a dead weapon.

▶ Who first sailed around the world single-handed? Captain Hook.

▶ What's this?

```
        R
       R R
      R R R
     R R R R
```

A pirate eye chart.

▶ A sailor was talking about the last time he was on leave. 'So it was the first fuckin' leave in six fuckin' months. I dropped off my fuckin' uniform at the fuckin' Y, went to a fuckin' bar and picked up a fuckin' broad. I took her to a fuckin' hotel, laid her out on the fuckin' bed and had sexual intercourse.'

SALESMEN

▶ A disgruntled-looking man walks into a second-hand car showroom and approaches the salesman. 'Do you remember the car you sold me last week?' he asks.

'Yes,' says the salesman.

'Could you go through your sales patter again,' asks the man. 'Only I'm starting to get discouraged.'

▶ Used car salesmen aren't in it for the money. They just like lying to strangers.

▶ He was such a great salesman, he could sell underarm deodorant to the Venus de Milo.

▶ An estate agent is trying to sell a very old man a new home.

'It would be a marvellous investment,' says the agent.

'You've got to be joking,' says the old man. 'At my age I don't even buy green bananas.'

S&M

▶ Sue and Sally meet at their 30-year class reunion, and they haven't seen each other since graduation. They begin to talk and bring each other up to date. The conversation covers their husbands, children and homes, and finally gets around to their sex lives.

Sue says, 'It's OK. We get it on every week or so but it's no big adventure. How's yours?'

Sally replies, 'It's just great, ever since we got into S&M.'

Sue is aghast. 'Really, Sally, I never would have guessed that you would go for that.'

'Oh, sure,' says Sally. 'He snores while I masturbate.'

▶ A man was sitting in a bar looking depressed, when a woman approached and asked him what's wrong. He told her sadly that his girlfriend just left him and, after some pressuring, admitted that it was because he was just too kinky for her.

'What a coincidence!' exclaimed the woman. 'My boyfriend just left me for the same reason.'

The two hit it off and, after a few drinks, decided to go back to her place as it was nearest. The woman left the man alone in the living room and disappeared into the bedroom. After ten minutes she reappeared dressed in full leather and chains, with whip and ball gag in hand, only to see the man about to leave.

'Where are you going?' she asked. 'I thought you were kinky.'

'I am,' he replied. 'I shagged your cat and just took a shit in your purse. I'm off home now.'

SCHOOL

▶ My son was sent home from school for swearing. I said to him, 'What did you say?'

He replied, 'I used the C word.'

I said, 'That wasn't clever, was it?'

'No,' he said. 'It was c**t.'

▶ On my first day of school my parents dropped me off at the wrong nursery. There I was... surrounded by trees and bushes.

▶ Ninety-two per cent of cross-eyed teachers have difficulty controlling their pupils.

▶ Teacher draws a penis on the board, then asks, 'Does anyone know what this is?'

Little Johnny says, 'My dad has two of them, a small one for weeing and a big one for cleaning the babysitter's teeth.'

▶ When we were kids, my sister always said she'd go down in history. Looking back, that's probably why she got such good marks.

▶ I went to a school reunion the other day. Sadly all my friends had become so fat and old no one could recognise me.

▶ I went to a really posh school. In fact, the school was so posh that the gym was called James.

▶ *What school reports really mean:*

• A born leader – Runs a protection pack

• Easy-going – Bone idle

• Making good progress – Slightly less awful than last year

• Friendly – Never shuts up

• Helpful – A creep

• Reliable – Informs on his friends

• Expresses himself confidently – A rude bastard

• Enjoys physical education – A bully

• Does not accept authority easily – Dad is in prison

• Often appears tired – Insomniac telly addict

• A rather solitary child – He stinks and has no friends

• Popular in the playground – Sells porn

▶ Teacher says to little Johnny, 'For the last two years you have been bringing me a big bag of raisins every week – why have you stopped?'
   Little Johnny says, 'My rabbit's dead, miss.'

▶ A man is in a queue at Tesco and sees this busty blonde staring at him. He can't believe she is staring at him, then she starts waving.
   'Excuse me, do I know you?' he asks.
   'Yes, I think you are the father of one of my kids,' she says.
   The man thinks back and remembers his one act of infedelity and says,

'Fucking hell, are you the bird I shagged on my stag do, while your mate whipped me and your other mate stuck a brush up my arse?'

'No,' she replies, 'I am your son's English teacher.'

▶ In response to the government's new education initiative, it is proposed that students will have to pass a test to be promoted to the next grade level. The new test will be called the 'First Arithmetic and Reading Test', or FART. All students who cannot pass a FART in the second grade will be retested in grades three, four and five until they are capable of passing a FART.

If a student does not successfully FART by grade five, that student shall be placed in a separate English programme known as the 'Special Masters Easy Learning Language', or SMELL.

If, with this increased SMELL programme, the student cannot pass the required FART test, he or she can still graduate to middle school by taking another course in 'Comprehensive Reading and Arithmetic Preparation', or CRAP. If by age 14, the student cannot FART, SMELL or CRAP, he or she can earn promotion in an intensive one-week seminar known as the 'Preparatory Reading for Unprepared Nationally Exempted Students', or PRUNES.

It is the opinion of the School Inspectorate that an intensive week of PRUNES will enable any student to FART, SMELL or CRAP. And in the long term, this revised education initiative should help 'clear the air'.

▶ One day when the teacher walked to the blackboard, she noticed someone had written the word 'penis' in tiny letters. She turned around and scanned the class, looking for the guilty face. Finding none, she quickly erased it and began her class.

The next day she went into the room and she saw, in larger letters, the word 'penis' again on the blackboard. Again, she looked around in vain for the culprit, but found none, so she proceeded with the day's lesson.

475

Every morning for about a week, she went into the classroom and found the same word written on the board, and each day it was written in larger letters.

Finally, one day, she walked in, expecting to be greeted by the same word on the board, but instead found the words: 'The more you rub it, the bigger it gets!'

▶ Students in London protesting about higher tuition fees are complaining of police brutality and heavy tactics being used in order for them to disperse. Police are believed to be using boxes of soap and job adverts.

▶ How do you teach a blonde maths? Add a bed, subtract her knickers, divide her legs, enter your square root, leave your solution and hope she doesn't multiply!

▶ I recently lost my job as a teacher. I got caught shagging the ugliest teacher in the whole school. Gross Miss Conduct.

▶ A class was given some homework. They had to write an essay on what they would do if they had won a fortune on the lottery.

The next day, while the homework was being handed in, a lad gave the teacher a blank piece of paper.

'What's this?' asked the teacher. 'Your essay was meant to say what you would do if you won the lottery.'

'It explains exactly,' he replied. 'I'd do absolutely fuck all.'

▶ My wife is getting concerned about our kids schooling. There is too much drinking, drugs and violence. She says if I don't stop, I can't home school them anymore.

▶ I kept on getting into trouble at school for handing my homework in late, so I bought a book of excuses. Unfortunately, the dog ate it.

SCOTS

▶ One misty Scottish morning a man was driving down from Wick to Inverness. Suddenly out of the mist, a huge red-haired man stepped into the middle of the road. The man was about six foot three and built like a brick shithouse. He had a huge red beard and despite the wind, mist and near-freezing temperatures, was only wearing his kilt and a tweed shirt. At the roadside there also stood a young woman. She was absolutely beautiful. The car driver's attention was dragged from the girl when the Highlander opened the car door and dragged him from the seat onto the road.

'Right, you!' he shouted. 'I want you to masturbate.'

'But... ' stammered the driver.

'Now... or I'll bloody kill you,' said the man.

So the driver turned his back on the girl, dropped his trousers and started to jerk off. Thinking of the girl on the roadside, this only took a few seconds.

'Right,' said the Highlander, 'do it again!'

'But... ' said the driver.

'Now... '

So the driver did it again.

'Right, do it again,' demanded the Highlander. This went on for nearly two hours. The driver had cramps in both arms and had rubbed himself raw. Despite the mist and wind, he had collapsed in a sweating, gibbering heap on the ground, unable to walk. 'Do it again,' said the Highlander.

'I just can't anymore – you'll just have to kill me,' whimpered the man.

The Highlander looked down at the pathetic heap slumped on the roadside. 'All right,' he said, 'NOW you can give my daughter a lift to Inverness.'

▶ The Glasgow Royal Infirmary are fully supporting the new bill on embryo research. Asked by religious groups and other concerned parties if they wouldn't be concerned about creating horrific mutations and how they would handle the human/animal genetic material left over from these experiments, a spokesman for the hospital said: 'Nae bother! As long as it's deep fried in batter, they'll eat anything round here.'

▶ Angus was only five feet tall. He reckoned it was due to his diet as a child – condensed milk and shortbread.

SCOUSERS

▶ What do you call a Scouser in a university? Caretaker.

▶ There are so many boarded-up houses in Liverpool that the window cleaner goes round with a sander.

▶ Why did audiences scream so loudly at Beatles concerts? The shock of seeing four Scousers working.

▶ A Scouser inadvertently goes into a gay bar for a beer. He sits at the bar supping his pint, when one gay gentleman decides to chance his luck. He approaches the Scouser and whispers something into his ear, whereupon the Liverpudlian turns around in complete disgust and horror and proceeds to punch the living hell out of the homosexual, fist after fist, beating him out the door, kicking him across the pub car park, relentlessly punching and stamping until the victim lies comatose. The Scouser then dusts himself down and calmly returns to his pint at the bar, while the horrified staff and clientele stand silent and motionless. Eventually, the barman plucks up the courage to ask what happened.

'Bloody hell, mate. What on earth did he whisper to you?'

Scouser, 'Dunno, something about a job.'

▶ An Irishman, an Aussie and a Scouser are in a bar and spot Jesus drinking on his own. They each send him a drink over and he sips each one slowly.

When he's finished, he walks over to the Irishman and shakes his hand and thanks him for the Guinness. 'Stone me, my arthritis has gone!'

Jesus then thanks the Aussie for the Fosters. 'Strewth, mate, my bad back's cured!'

Jesus then approaches the Scouser, who runs away screaming, 'Bugger off, you git – I'm on disability benefit.'

▶ My Scouser cousin's girlfriend had a baby today. They're so proud of him. He's the only one in the family who's been inside for less than nine months.

▶ Police have cordoned off an area in Croxteth after sightings of an unidentified, never seen before, circular object. Turns out it's a tax disc.

▶ What's the difference between a cow and a tragedy? A Scouser wouldn't know how to milk a cow.

▶ I was round Liverpool the other day, when some Scousers started squaring up to us.

'Pretend we're the police,' my mate whispered to me.

They kicked the shit out of me before I even got to the chorus!

▶ One thousand scousers were asked if they thought Britain should change its currency – 99 per cent said no, they were happy with the giro.

SEALS

▶ A baby seal walks into a bar and asks for a whisky.

The barman asks, 'What sort?'

The seal says, 'Anything but a Canadian Club.'

SEX

▶ Doug meets Bill at the bar for their usual after-work drink. Bill is sitting there looking somewhat depressed.

Doug asks, 'What's wrong, pal?'

Bill replies, 'Well, I finally succeeded in talking my girlfriend into a threesome.'

'Wow, lucky you. But why the long face?' Doug remarks.

Bill sighs and says, 'Yeah, well, as the threesome entered into its second hour of hot and heavy action, it dawned on me that I really should have specified that I wanted to be one of the three.'

▶ I was making love to this girl and she started crying. I said, 'Are you going to hate yourself in the morning?'

She said, 'No, I hate myself now.'

▶ A very naive sailor is in a bar in London. He meets a wild girl, and she takes him upstairs. She takes off her skirt and her panties. He looks between her legs and he says, 'What's that?'

She says, 'It's my lower mouth.'

He says, 'What do you mean, your lower mouth?'

She says, 'Just what I said, it's my lower mouth. It's got a moustache... It's got lips... '

He asks, 'Has it got a tongue in it?'

She says, 'Not yet... '

▶ A guy has been asking the prettiest girl in town for a date and finally she agrees to go out with him. He takes her to a nice restaurant and buys her a fancy dinner with expensive wine. On the way home, he pulls over to the side of the road in a secluded spot. They start necking and he's getting pretty excited. He starts to reach under her skirt and she stops him, saying she's a virgin and wants to stay that way.

'Well, OK,' he says. 'How about a blowjob?'

'Yuck!' she screams. 'I'm not putting that thing in my mouth!'

He says, 'Well, then, how about a hand job?'

'I've never done that,' she says. 'What do I have to do?'

'Well,' he answers, 'remember when you were a kid and you used to shake up a Coke bottle and spray your brother with it?' She nods. 'Well, it's just like that.'

So, he pulls it out and she grabs hold of it and starts shaking it. A few seconds later, his head flops back on the headrest, his eyes close, snot starts to run out of his nose, wax blows out of his ear and he screams out in pain.

'What's wrong?!' she cries out.

'Take your thumb off the end!'

▶ What do a tightrope walker and a young man getting head off his granny have in common?
Neither look down.

▶ Have you heard about the new mint-flavoured birth control pill for women that they take immediately before sex? They're called 'Predickamints'.

▶ The delivery driver had just carried a large sack of potatoes up six flights of stairs.

'That will be seven quid, lady,' he said.

Smiling, the woman let her robe slip open. 'Wouldn't you like some of this instead?' she said.

'I'll have to see my partner,' said the driver. 'Already this morning we have screwed away ten cases of bananas, 20 kilograms of tomatoes and seven sacks of potatoes.'

▶ One night I managed to make love for an hour and five minutes. It was when they put the clocks forwards.

▶ What do a woman and Kentucky Fried Chicken have in common? By the time you're finished with the breast and thighs, all you have left is the greasy box to put your bone in.

▶ Wife comes home to find the old man shagging the dog in the front room.

'My God, Henry!' she screams. 'I know you've had other women but this time you've gone too far!'

'You may be right,' he says. 'I think I'm stuck.'

▶ A husband and wife were having marital problems. They decided the solution was to spice up their sex life, so they bought a waterbed. Unfortunately, it didn't work. They just started drifting apart.

▶ What's the definition of eternity? The time between when you come and she leaves.

▶ What is a 6.9? A 69 interrupted by a period.

▶ Definition of a bastard: a guy who makes love to a woman all night with a four-inch dick, then kisses her goodbye in the morning with a six-inch tongue.

▶ What is the definition of indefinitely? Well, when your balls are slapping against the back of her arse, I'd say you're in definitely.

▶ Paramedics rescued a 40-year-old man who got his manhood stuck in the vacuum cleaner. The man told authorities his relationship with his vacuum cleaner was purely sexual – he didn't want any attachments.

▶ What's the best way to get into a sleeping bag? Wake her up first.

▶ What do rhubarb and cocks have in common? Both are long, thin, covered in skin, pink in the middle and go in tarts.

Who says men can't multi-task? I can shag my girlfriend and think about her sister at the same time.

My girlfriend coyly asked me if I've got any fantasies.
I said, 'I've got a couple of Terry Pratchett books.'

My ex-wife was so cold that when you spread her legs, a little white light came on.

Sex is like hacking. You get in, you get out and you hope you didn't leave something behind that can be traced back to you.

Why is a woman's pussy like a warm toilet seat? They both feel good, but you wonder who was there before you.

A married couple slept in twin beds. One night just as they were settling down to sleep, he called across to her, 'My little honey bunch, I'm lonely.' Taking the hint, she got out of her bed and crossed to his, but on the way she tripped on the rug and fell flat on her face.
Concerned, he enquired, 'Oh, did my little honey-woney fall on her nosey-wosey?'
After they had passionate sex, she got up to return to her own bed, but on the way back she again tripped on the rug and fell flat on her face. He glanced at her and said, 'Clumsy bitch!'

Sex is like software: for everyone who pays for it, there are hundreds getting it free.

▶ Just as he was leaving for work, the man's wife told him that there was a leak in the plumbing. He told her to call a plumber and have it fixed. When he got to work, he gave her a call and asked, 'Has the plumber come yet?'

She replied, 'Not quite, but I have him breathing hard.'

▶ A woman with three vaginas goes to the doctor about her embarrassing problem to ask for some help. The doctor takes a look down below and asks her to jump up on the table. She spreads her legs apart and the doctor proceeds to sew up two of the holes, leaving the middle one open. The woman asks, 'Am I cured?', and the doctor replies, 'No, but it'll stop you getting shagged left right and centre'

▶ How can you tell if you're making love to a teacher, a nurse or an airline stewardess?

A teacher says, 'We've got to do this over and over again till we get it right.'

A nurse says, 'Hold still, this won't hurt a bit.'

And an airline stewardess says, 'Put this over your mouth and nose and breathe normally.'

▶ Why did God give women multiple orgasms? So they can moan when they're happy, too.

SEX – ANAL

▶ What's the difference between oral sex and anal sex? Oral sex makes your day, anal sex makes your hole weak.

▶ I used to go out with an English teacher, but she dumped me. She didn't approve of my improper use of the colon.

▶ Two couples have gone away for the weekend. The two guys, Jack and Bill, decide to try to persuade their wives to do a bit of partner swapping for the night. After several drinks they succeed.

Jack knows it's that time of the month for his wife and the thought of Bill not knowing this makes him smile. The guys agree that when they sit around the breakfast table the following morning, they will tap their teaspoons on the side of their coffee mug the number of times that they did it with each other's wives.

The next morning they are all at the breakfast table, slightly hungover and quite uncomfortable, when Jack proudly taps his teaspoon three times against his coffee mug.

After a brief moment of thinking, Bill takes his teaspoon and taps it once on the strawberry jam and three times on the peanut butter.

▶ What's the difference between a microwave cooker and anal sex? Microwaves don't brown the meat.

▶ Why do women have two holes so close together? In case you miss.

▶ The funeral parlour called an 85-year-old widow to tell her that her 90-year-old husband had died with such a massive erection that they could not close the lid of the coffin. They had never seen such seen such a big knob.

'Well,' she said, 'cut it off as close to his body as you can, then put it up his arse.'

The next day the whole family arrived at the funeral home to pay their respects and the widow kneeled down near her departed husband and noticed there was a tear coming down his cheek. She leaned over and whispered in his ear, 'I told you it hurt, you old bastard!'

▶ A couple want to have a bash at anal sex, but the woman decides to play it safe and seek medical advice first.

'Anal sex is perfectly safe,' says her doctor, 'as long as you take it slowly at first and use plenty of lubricant. And you take care not to get pregnant, of course.'

'What?' says the woman incredulously. 'You can get pregnant from anal sex?'

'Certainly,' replies the doctor. 'Where do you think Spurs fans come from?'

SEX EDUCATION

▶ Little Johnny comes home from school and says to his dad, 'At school the boys were talking about pussy. What is pussy?'

His dad goes up to his bedroom, rummages through his sock drawer and gets a copy of *Penthouse* magazine out. He brings it downstairs, opens it, draws a circle and says, 'There, that's it, everything in that circle. That's a pussy.'

Johnny nods, then says, 'They were also talking about a bitch. What's a bitch?'

'Everything outside that circle!'

▶ At school one day, the teacher was trying to approach the topic of sex education and asked her students if they'd ever seen anything that was related to sex education on TV. Mary raised her hand and said she had seen a movie about women having babies. 'Great,' said the teacher, 'that's very important.'

Then Judy raised her hand and told the teacher she had seen a TV show about people getting married. 'Well, that has to do with it, too,' said the teacher.

Then Johnny raised his hand and said he had seen a western where some Indians came riding over the hill and John Wayne shot them all. The teacher said, 'Well, Johnny, that really doesn't have anything to do with sex education.'

'Yes it does,' said Johnny. 'It taught those Indians not to fuck with John Wayne.'

▶ A cop is patrolling Lover's Lane, when he sees the strangest thing. A young teenage couple is sitting in a car, the guy in the front and the girl in the back. The guy is reading a magazine and the girl appears to be knitting. He stops the patrol car and walks over to knock on the young man's window. He rolls the window down.

'Yes, officer?'

'I have to ask you, what are you doing?'

'Well, sir, I am reading a magazine.'

'What about the young lady in the back seat?'

The young man turns to look behind him. 'Well, I think she is knitting a pullover sweater.'

'How old are you, young man?' the officer asks.

'I am 18, officer.'

'And the girl?'

The young man looks at his watch. 'Well, she'll be 16 in 11 minutes.'

▶ Did you hear about when they made KY Jelly millennium-compliant? It allowed you to safely insert four digits in your date.

SEX – GOOD

▶ The sex was so good that even the neighbours had a cigarette.

▶ Why do men get their great ideas in bed? Because they're plugged into a genius!

▶ There's a new sex position out, it's called the plumber. You both stay in all day, and no one comes!

▶ A husband and wife were in the bathroom getting ready to go to work, when the husband looked at his wife and said, 'I gotta have you!'
   He backed her up against the bathroom door, ripped her knickers off and gave her one there and then. When he finished, he started putting his clothes on and saw his wife still writhing around against the door
   'What's wrong? Didn't you come? Do you want more?'
   His wife said, 'No, no, it's not that. I'm just trying to get the doorknob out of my arsehole!'

SEX – LACK OF

▶ Sex is like air – it's not important unless you aren't getting any.

▶ A man came home from work one day to find his wife on the front porch with her bags packed. 'Just where the heck do you think you're going?' said the man.

'I'm going to Las Vegas,' said the wife. 'I just found out I can get £400 a night for what I give you for free!'

The man said, 'Wait a minute!', and then ran inside the house only to come back a few minutes later with his suitcases in hand.

'Where the heck are you going?' said the wife.

The man said, 'I want to see how you're gonna live on £800 a year!'

▶ Shag: funny word, isn't it? To a smoker, it's a type of tobacco; to an American, it's a type of dance; to an ornithologist, it's a bird; and, to you, it's just a remote possibility.

SEX – ORAL

▶ A woman was in a coma. Two nurses were in her room giving her a sponge bath.

One of them was washing her private area and noticed that there was a response on the monitor when she touched her between the legs. They went to her husband in the waiting room and explained what happened, telling him, 'Crazy as this sounds, maybe a little oral sex will do the trick and bring her out of the coma.'

The husband was sceptical, but they assured him that they'd close the curtains for privacy. He finally agreed and went into his wife's room.

After a few minutes, the woman's monitor flatlined: no pulse, no heart rate. The nurses ran into the room.

'What happened?'

The husband shrugged. 'I guess she choked.'

▶ What's the speed limit of sex? Sixty-eight, because at 69 you have to turn around.

▶ While making love, a man says: 'Darling, let's do 68!'
  'Sixty-eight? What's that?'
  'You do it to me and I'll owe you one.'

▶ When does a Cub Scout become a Boy Scout? When he eats his first Brownie.

▶ There was a promiscuous young couple making out in the back seat of a car. Temperatures were rising and things were getting pretty intense, and finally the girl gasped, 'Oh darling, darling, kiss me where it smells.'
  So he drove her to Hull.

▶ What do women and spaghetti have in common? They both wiggle when you eat them.

▶ At a news conference, a journalist said to a politician, 'Your assistant said publicly that you have a small penis. Would you please comment on this?'
  'The truth is,' he replied, 'my assistant has a big mouth.'

▶ Three guys are arrested in an adult bookstore and appear before the judge. He asks the first guy to stand.
  'What is your name?' he asks.
  'John,' the guy answers.
  'And why were you arrested?' the judge asks.
  'I was by the magazine rack holding a big fat cigar and blowing smoke,' he answers.

The judge doesn't see anything wrong with that, so he dismisses the guy and calls up the next one.

'What's your name?' he asks.

'John,' the guy answers.

'Why were you arrested?' the judge asks.

'I was by the magazine rack holding a big fat cigar and blowing smoke,' he answers.

Again, the judge sees nothing offensive. 'This so-called adult store is begining to sound more like a smoking club,' he thinks. So he dismisses the charge and calls up the next guy.

'What's your name? No, wait, let me guess – John,' he says.

'No,' says the guy. 'My name is Smoke.'

▶ A woman, getting married for the fourth time, goes to a bridal shop and asks for a white dress.

'You can't wear white,' the sales clerk reminds her, 'you've been married three times already.'

'Of course I can, I'm a virgin!' says the bride.

'Impossible,' says the sales clerk.

'Unfortunately not,' the bride explains. 'My first husband was a psychologist. All he wanted to do was talk about it. My second husband was a gynaecologist. All he wanted to do was look at it. My third husband was a stamp collector... God, I miss him.'

▶ Bill and Ben the Flowerpot Men are sat in the garden one evening.

Bill says: 'Flobalobbablob.'

Ben says: 'If you loved me, you'd swallow.'

▶ Why is being in the military like a blowjob? The closer you get to discharge, the better you feel.

▶ How can you tell if you eat pussy well? You wake up in the morning with a face like a glazed doughnut and a beard like an unwashed paintbrush.

▶ A mother is in the kitchen making dinner for her family, when her daughter walks in.

'Mummy, where do babies come from?'

The mother thinks for a few seconds and says, 'Well, dear, Mummy and Daddy fall in love and get married. One night they go into their bedroom, they kiss and hug and have sex.'

The daughter looks puzzled, so the mother continues, 'That means the daddy puts his penis in the mummy's vagina. That's how you get a baby, darling.'

The child seems to understand. 'Oh, I see, but the other night when I came into your room you had Daddy's penis in your mouth. What do you get when you do that?'

'Jewellery, my dear. Jewellery.'

▶ What's the difference between a penis and a bonus? Your wife will blow your bonus.

▶ Back in the good ole days in Texas, when stagecoaches and the like were popular, there were three people in a stagecoach one day: a true red-blooded born-and-raised Texas gentleman, a tenderfoot city slicker from back east and a beautiful and well-endowed Texas lady.

The city slicker kept eyeing the lady, and finally he leaned forwards and said, 'Lady, I'll give you $10 for a blowjob.'

The Texas gentleman looked appalled, pulled out his pistol and killed the city slicker on the spot.

The lady gasped and said, 'Thank you, suh, for defendin' mah honour!'

Whereupon the Texan holstered his gun and said, 'Your honour, hell! No tenderfoot from back east is gonna raise the price of a woman in Texas!'

▶ What's the difference between an airship and 365 blowjobs? One's a good year, the other's an excellent year.

▶ What's the similarity between lobster thermidor and a blowjob? You only ever get them when you're on holiday.

▶ What is a woman's idea of a perfect lover? A man with a nine-inch tongue who can breathe through his ears.

▶ Why does a bride smile when she walks up the aisle? She knows she's given her last blowjob.

▶ Why did God give men penises? So they'd always have at least one way to shut a woman up.

▶ What comes after 69? Mouthwash.

▶ A man goes to a party and gets so totally drunk that he passes out. He wakes up the next day and discovers two lines around his penis. There's a red one and a brown one. He goes to the doctor, who takes samples of both lines. A few days later the doctor asks him to come back in. The man arrives and the doctor says, 'There's good news and bad news. The good news is the red was lipstick. But the brown is the bad news.'

The guy asks, 'Why, what was it?'

'It was chewing tobacco.'

▶ A daily newspaper surveyed its male readers to see what exactly each enjoyed from having oral sex performed on them. Seven per cent said they most enjoyed the physical sensations. Five per cent confessed that their chief enjoyment came from the sense of domination. A staggering 88 per cent said that they really enjoyed the peace and quiet.

▶ Why do women have foreheads? So that men have somewhere to kiss after they've given them a blowjob.

▶ How do you know who gives good blowjobs? Word of mouth.

▶ If the dove is the bird of peace, what's the bird of true love? The swallow.

▶ A young chav was walking through town, when a girl came up to him and whispered, 'Blowjob, £5.'

Confused, the boy ignored her and walked on.

When he got home, he decided to ask his sister what it meant, 'What's a blowjob?'

'£5, same as in town,' replied his sister.

▶ Why don't guys like to perform oral sex on a woman the morning after sex? Have you ever tried pulling apart a grilled cheese sandwich?

▶ What's the difference between your paycheque and your cock? You don't have to beg your wife to blow your paycheque.

Why do men pay more for car insurance? Women don't get blowjobs while they're driving.

A guy came home late and very drunk. His wife was waiting for him.
'You've been kissing someone, haven't you?' she barked.
'No,' he protested.
'Then explain the lipstick on your shirt,' she shouted.
'That's easy,' he said. 'I used my shirt to wipe my dick.'

When his date asked him to perform cunnilingus on her, Keith's smooth answer was, 'Only if I get a miner's lamp and a canary.' The relationship didn't last too long after that.

How does a guy know if he has a high sperm count? If the girl has to chew before she swallows.

'Hey girls, do you wanna go turkey shootin?'
'OK.'
'Good. You gobble, I'll shoot.'

The answer: A cockrobin.
The question: 'What are you putting in my mouth, Batman?'

SEX OUTDOORS

A man takes a lady out to dinner for the first time. Later they go on to a show. The evening is a huge success and as he drops her at her door he says, 'I have had a lovely time. You looked so beautiful, you remind me of a beautiful rambling rose. May I call on you tomorrow?' She agrees and a date is made.

The next night he knocks on her door and when she opens it she slaps him hard across the face. He is stunned. 'What was that for?' he asks.

She says, 'I looked up rambling rose in the encyclopaedia last night and it said: "Not well suited to bedding but is excellent for rooting up against a garden wall".'

SHARKS

▶ One day two brothers, Bill and Bob, decided to go out diving for seafood. After filling the first sack, Bill took it back to shore to grab a replacement, but while Bob was left alone out at sea, he suddenly spotted a shark swimming towards him.

Bob frantically called out to his brother, 'Bill, help me! There's a shark heading straight for me!'

Bill called back, 'OK, I'm coming, bro.'

Bob was freaking out as the shark swam right up to him and bit off his left leg. Again he called out to Bill, who was still at the shoreline.

'Bill, come and help me, the shark's bitten off one of my legs!'

Bill yelled back, 'Hold on, bro, I'm coming.'

Bob tried to stay calm and wait for his brother, but then the shark bit off his left arm. He shouted to Bill, 'Hurry up! Come and help me! The shark has bitten off my arm and my leg!'

Bill called back, 'Hold on, I'm coming.'

Then the shark bit off Bob's right leg. Bob screamed, 'Bill, you have to come and save me! The shark has bitten off both my legs and an arm!'

Bill called back, 'Just wait, I'm coming.'

The shark then bit off Bob's other arm. Now he had no arms or legs.

Bill finally arrived to save him. 'Come on, bro,' he said, 'get on my back and I'll swim you back to shore.'

When they finally made it back to the shore, Bill said with an exhausted sigh, 'I feel fucked.'

Bill replied, 'Well, I had to hold on somehow!'

▶ Marine biology researchers have developed a new method to fend off shark attacks. If you are diving and approached by a shark, they recommend that you swim towards it aggressively and punch it in the nose as hard as possible. If this doesn't work, beat the shark with your stump.

SHEEP

▶ A New Zealander is walking along the road with a sheep under each arm. He meets another New Zealander, who asks, 'You shearin', mate?'

The first man replies, 'Naw, they're all mine.'

▶ A group of cowboys were branding some cattle. While they were away, the cook saw a sheep tied to a post. Thinking it was for that night's dinner, he slaughtered the sheep and cooked it.

That night after dinner the cowboys were all sulking and ignoring the cook. He pulled one aside and asked, 'Did I screw up the cooking?'

'No,' the cowboy replied, 'you cooked up the screwing.'

▶ Why is a sheep better than a woman? A sheep doesn't care if you shag her sister.

▶ A flock of sheep decided to go down the local on a bender because they were depressed by foot and mouth disease. By closing time they were all slaughtered.

▶ How do shepherds practise safe sex? By putting a big X on the sheep that kick!

▶ What is the worst thing about having sex with a sheep? Breaking its neck when you try to kiss it.

SHELLFISH

▶ Far away in the tropical waters of the Caribbean, two prawns were swimming around in the sea – one called Justin and the other called Christian. The prawns were constantly being harassed and threatened by sharks that patrolled the area. One day Justin said to Christian, 'I'm bored and frustrated at being a prawn. I wish I was a shark, then I wouldn't have any worries about being eaten.'

Suddenly, a mysterious cod appeared and said, 'Your wish is granted,' and lo and behold, Justin turned into a shark.

Horrified, Christian immediately swam away, afraid of being eaten by his old mate.

Time went on and Justin found himself becoming bored and lonely as a shark. All his old mates simply swam away whenever he came close to them. Justin didn't realise that his new menacing appearance was the cause of his sad plight.

While out swimming alone one day, he saw the mysterious cod again and couldn't believe his luck. Justin figured that the fish could change him back into a prawn. He begged the cod to change him back and lo and behold, he is turned back into a prawn. With tears of joy in his tiny little eyes, Justin swam back to his friends and bought them all a cocktail.

Looking around the gathering at the reef, he searched for his old pal. 'Where's Christian?' he asked.

'He's at home, distraught that his best friend changed sides to the enemy and became a shark,' came the reply.

Eager to put things right again and end the mutual pain and torture, he set off to Christian's house.

As he opened the coral gate, the memories came flooding back. He banged on the door and shouted, 'It's me, Justin, your old friend, come out and see me again.'

Christian replied, 'No way, man, you'll eat me. You're a shark, the enemy, and I'll not be tricked.'

Justin cried back, 'No, I'm not. That was the old me. I've changed. I've found Cod. I'm a prawn again, Christian!'

SHERLOCK HOLMES

▶ One evening, Dr Watson paid an unexpected call on Holmes.

'Is he expecting you?' asked the housekeeper.

'No,' said Watson, 'but I just need to speak with him for a minute.'

'I don't know what he's up to,' said the housekeeper, 'but he left very strict instructions not to be disturbed until nine o'clock.'

'I'll wait downstairs in the library,' replied Watson.

A few minutes later, Watson heard the unmistakable sound of girlish laughter coming from the detective's bedroom, followed by shrieks of excitement from Holmes.

As nine o'clock approached, Watson could hardly contain his curiosity. Finally, Holmes came down the stairs, accompanied by a pretty dark-haired young girl in a school blazer and check skirt.

As soon as she left, the good doctor cried out, 'Holmes, just what kind of schoolgirl was that?'

'Elementary, my dear Watson.'

▶ One day Sherlock Holmes and Watson sat down to enjoy their favourite lunch of fish and chips. Just as they were about to tuck in, Holmes suddenly stood up and shouted, 'Watson, stand up!'

Confused, Watson stood up.

'Watson! Drop your trousers!' he barked.

Worried, Watson loosened his belt and dropped his trousers.

'Watson! Bend over!' Holmes ordered.

Watson bent over.

Holmes then plucked the wedge of lemon from Watson's plate and shoved it straight up Watson's arse.

Watson screamed, 'In God's name, Holmes, what on earth are you doing?'

To which Holmes calmly replied, 'A lemon-entry, my dear Watson... a lemon-entry... '

▶ 'I say, Watson. All this cocaine has made me rather constipated.'

'No shit, Sherlock.'

▶ Sherlock Holmes was sent to heaven to find Adam and Eve. He came back within a day and said he had found them.

Watson: 'How did you find them so quickly?'

Sherlock: 'Elementary, my dear Watson, they were the only ones that didn't have belly buttons!'

SHIPWRECKED

▶ A guy, a pig and a dog were the only survivors of a terrible shipwreck, as a result of which they found themselves stranded on a desert island. After being there for a few weeks, they got into a ritual of going to the beach every evening to watch the sun go down. One particular evening, the sky was red with beautiful cirrus clouds, and the breeze was warm and gentle. It was a perfect night for love. In such a romantic atmosphere, that pig gradually started looking better and better, and soon the guy rolled towards the pig and put his arm around it.

The dog was not happy with this and growled fiercely at the guy, until he removed his arm from the pig. Over the ensuing weeks, the trio continued to enjoy the sunsets together, but there was no further cuddling. Then there was another shipwreck, and this time the sole survivor was a beautiful young woman. Slowly they nursed her back to health and she was eventually introduced to their evening beach ritual. It was another beautiful evening, red sky, cirrus clouds, warm gentle breeze, perfect for romance, the four of them lying there. The guy started getting 'those' ideas again, so he leaned over towards the girl and said, 'Er, would you mind taking the dog for a walk?'

SHOPPING

▶ Marks and Spencer has announced they are in financial trouble. They have merged with Poundstretcher. They will now be known as Stretch Marks.

▶ Ordered some stuff online the other day and I used my donor card instead of my debit card.
Cost me an arm and a leg.

▶ A bloke went into a record shop and asked, 'Do you have anything by The Doors?'
 The assistant said, 'Yes, a fire extinguisher and a bucket of sand.'

▶ Marks and Spencer's new advert states that it wouldn't be Christmas without M&S.
They're right, too. It'd be Chrita.

▶ *What not to say in an Ann Summers' shop:*

● 'Does this come in children's sizes?'

● 'No thanks – just sniffing.'

● 'I'll be in the changing room going blind.'

● 'Mum will love this.'

● 'Oh, the size doesn't matter. She's inflatable.'

● 'Will you model this for me?'

▶ Two friends went to Pincus the tailor for new suits. 'Listen, Pincus,' one said, 'the last suits you made for us were sort of grey. We want black suits, the darkest black cloth that we can get.'
 'See this cloth?' Pincus said, fingering a roll of fabric. 'This is the stuff they make nuns' habits from. There ain't no blacker cloth.'
 A few weeks later, the two men were walking down the street in their

new suits, when they passed two nuns. Impulsively, one of the men went up to the nuns and matched his suit against their habits. Becoming angry, he muttered something to his friend and they both walked off.

'What did that man want?' one nun asked the other.

'I don't know,' she replied. 'He looked at my garment, said something in Latin and left.'

'What did he say?'

'He said, "Pincus Fucktus".'

SIGNS

▶ *Lost in translation – real signs from around the world:*

- Bangkok temple: IT IS FORBIDDEN TO ENTER A WOMAN, EVEN A FOREIGNER, IF DRESSED AS A MAN.

- Cocktail lounge, Norway: LADIES ARE REQUESTED NOT TO HAVE CHILDREN IN THE BAR.

- Doctor's office, Rome: SPECIALIST IN WOMEN AND OTHER DISEASES.

- Dry cleaners, Bangkok: DROP YOUR TROUSERS HERE FOR THE BEST RESULTS.

- Nairobi restaurant: CUSTOMERS WHO FIND OUR WAITRESSES RUDE OUGHT TO SEE THE MANAGER.

- Athi River highway (main road to Mombasa, leaving Nairobi): TAKE NOTICE: WHEN THIS SIGN IS UNDER WATER, THIS ROAD IS IMPASSABLE.

- Kencom poster: ARE YOU AN ADULT THAT CANNOT READ? IF SO, WE CAN HELP.

- Cemetery: PERSONS ARE PROHIBITED FROM PICKING FLOWERS FROM ANY BUT THEIR OWN GRAVES.

- Tokyo hotel's regulations: GUESTS ARE REQUESTED NOT TO SMOKE OR DO OTHER DISGUSTING BEHAVIOURS IN BED.

- Swiss restaurant menu: OUR WINES LEAVE YOU NOTHING TO HOPE FOR.

- Tokyo bar: SPECIAL COCKTAILS FOR THE LADIES WITH NUTS.

- Yugoslavia hotel: THE FLATTENING OF UNDERWEAR WITH PLEASURE IS THE JOB OF THE CHAMBERMAID.

- Japan hotel: YOU ARE INVITED TO TAKE ADVANTAGE OF THE CHAMBERMAID.

- Lobby of Moscow hotel: YOU ARE WELCOME TO VISIT THE CEMETERY WHERE FAMOUS RUSSIAN AND SOVIET COMPOSERS, ARTISTS AND WRITERS ARE BURIED DAILY EXCEPT THURSDAY.

- Sign in Germany's Black Forest: IT IS STRICTLY FORBIDDEN ON OUR BLACK FOREST CAMPING SITE THAT PEOPLE OF DIFFERENT SEX, FOR INSTANCE, MEN AND WOMEN, LIVE TOGETHER IN ONE TENT UNLESS THEY ARE MARRIED WITH EACH OTHER FOR THIS PURPOSE.

- Zurich hotel: BECAUSE OF THE IMPROPRIETY OF ENTERTAINING GUESTS OF THE OPPOSITE SEX IN THE BEDROOM, IT IS SUGGESTED THAT THE LOBBY BE USED FOR THIS PURPOSE.

- Rome laundry: LADIES, LEAVE YOUR CLOTHES HERE AND SPEND THE AFTERNOON HAVING A GOOD TIME.

SIN

What is the difference between a sin and shame? It's a sin to stick it in and a shame to take it out.

For sale:
One glove. Genuine reason for sale: Caught shoplifting in Saudi Arabia.

SINGERS

What do you call a 1950s French cabaret singer with Tourette's Syndrome? Edith Pissoff.

Did you hear Cher is joining the Spice Girls? They're going to call her Old Spice.

Mick Hucknall was arrested for having sex with an underaged rabbit last night. Apparently he was holding back the ears and the bunny was too tight to mention.

Paul McCartney is still depressed about his marriage breakdown with Heather Mills. He said yesterday, 'She's a wonderful woman and I can't imagine anyone else filling her shoe.'

Interviewer: 'So, Sir Paul, would you go down on one knee again?'
Paul McCartney: 'I'd prefer it if you called her Heather.'

What had three legs and lived on a farm? The McCartneys.

▶ It's a very sad world we live in when Paul McCartney and his wife are facing divorce and all anyone wants to do is make jokes about her false leg. Personally, I think it's prosthetic.

▶ The Beatles have reformed and brought out a new album. It's mostly just drum and bass.

SKODAS

▶ What's the difference between a Jehovah's Witness and a Skoda? You can shut the door on a Jehovah's Witness.

▶ What's the difference between a Skoda and a tampon? The tampon comes with its own tow rope.

▶ What's the difference between being caught inside Kylie Minogue's bra and being caught inside a Skoda? You feel a bigger tit in a Skoda.

▶ A boy is walking along the road, when a car pulls up alongside him.
  'If you get in my car,' says the driver, 'I'll give you a bag of sweets.' The boy ignores him. 'OK,' says the driver. 'Get in my car and you can have two bags of sweets and £5.'
  The boy ignores him. The driver says, 'Listen, if you'll just get in the car, I'll give you all the sweets you want and £20.'
  The boy turns to the driver and says, 'Dad, for the last time, I'm not getting into that Skoda.'

▶ A lady went to a car dealer to buy a Skoda, only to be told that due to new EU regulations she had to provide an account of her medical history before she could purchase the car. Mildly irritated, she complied, and returned the following day with the required information. The salesman read through her documents but said, 'Sorry, madam, you can't buy a Skoda.'

'Why on earth not?' she asked.

'Because,' said the salesman, 'it says here that you've had a hysterectomy, and you have to be a complete c**t to buy a Skoda.'

SKYDIVING

▶ Why do female skydivers wear jockstraps? So they don't whistle on the way down.

SLEEP

▶ If you go to bed eight hours before you have to wake up, and your wife wants to have an hour of sex, how much sleep will you get? Seven hours, 59 minutes. Who cares what she wants.

▶ What's soft and warm when you go to bed, but hard and stiff when you wake up? Vomit.

SLUGS AND SNAILS

▶ What did the slug say to the snail? *'Big Issue?'*

▶ Why don't snails go faster if you pull their shells off? Because it makes them sluggish.

▶ How is a snail's life taken? With a pinch of salt.

SNOW

▶ Why did Frosty the Snowman pull down his pants? He heard the snow blower coming.

▶ Why does it take longer to build a blond snowman? Because you have to hollow out the head.

SPERM

▶ Why does it take one million sperm to fertilise one egg? They don't stop for directions.

▶ What's white and wiggles across a disco floor? *Come Dancing*.

▶ What's white and shoots across the sky? The coming of the Lord.

▶ What's white and sticky and found on the gents' wall? George Michael's latest release.

▶ Overcome: the one who sleeps on the wet spot.

▶ What's the similarity between illegal immigrants and sperm? Thousands of the buggers get in but only one of 'em works.

▶ I've tried to help childless couples by making anonymous donations of my sperm. However, I've now been told I should really be doing this through a clinic and not straight through their letterboxes.

▶ A man has just jacked off and is staring at the sperm in his hand thoughtfully. He thinks, 'You could have been a great person. Perhaps a scientist, a bestselling author, even the prime minister.' He then raises his hand and licks it clean. 'Guess I'll give you another chance.'

▶ A man wearing a balaclava comes into a sperm bank wielding a shotgun. He shouts to the lady at the desk, 'Open the fucking safe!'

The lady replies with, 'Sir, this is a sperm bank.'

The man yells even louder, 'Just grab the damn sperm and drink it!'

Lady: 'Please... '

Man: 'DO IT!'

So the lady takes one and drinks it. The man then commands her to do it again. She does. Then the man takes off his mask.

The woman is surprised to see it is her husband.

Her husband lays down the shotgun and says, 'Now that wasn't so fucking hard, was it?'

SPIDERS

▶ Why do black widow spiders kill their males after mating? To stop the snoring before it starts.

▶ What's worse than spiders on your piano? Crabs on your organ.

SPORTS

▶ The depressing thing about tennis is that no matter how much I play, I'll never be as good as a wall. I played a wall once. They're fucking relentless.

▶ Why do mountain climbers rope themselves together? To prevent the sensible ones from going home.

▶ The local bookstore had this huge display with a sign advertising 'Newly translated from the original French: 37 mating positions'. The book was already wrapped in plain brown wrapper and I just had to buy one.

Once safely at home and alone, I opened it and found that I had just purchased an expensive book about chess.

▶ A woman weightlifter goes to the doctor and says, 'I've been taking steroids, and now I've grown a cock.'

'Anabolic,' says the doctor.

'No,' she replies. 'Just a cock.'

▶ Two men are standing at the bar of a country club.

One says: 'I'm a country member.'

Other one says: 'Yes, I remember.'

▶ After examining a 3,000-year-old mummy, an archaeologist announces that it's the body of a man who died of a heart attack.

'How can you tell?' asks one of his students.

'I examined a piece of parchment found in the mummy's hand,' replies the archaeologist. 'It was a betting slip that said "5,000 on Goliath".'

▶ Boris Johnson is rehearsing his speech for the 2012 Olympic Games. He begins his remarks with, 'Oh,oh,oh,oh,oh.'

Immediately his speech writer rushes over to the lectern and whispers in the mayor's ear, 'Mr Mayor, those are the Olympic rings. Your speech is underneath.'

▶ I shot someone with a starting gun. I've been charged with race crimes.

▶ *Rude golf phrases:*

- 'Look at the size of his putter.'

- 'Oh, dang, my shaft's all bent.'

- 'After 18 holes, I can barely walk.'

- 'My hands are so sweaty, I can't get a good grip.'

- 'Lift your head and spread your legs.'

- 'You have a nice stroke, but your follow-through leaves a lot to be desired.'

- 'Just turn your back and drop it.'

- 'Hold up. I've got to wash my balls.'

- 'Damn, I missed the hole again.'

STATISTICS

▶ Incompetence is officially at its lowest level since records were lost.

▶ I'll stop at nothing to avoid using negative numbers.

STDS

▶ What's the difference between love and herpes? Love doesn't last forever.

▶ How can you tell if a crab is an insomniac? It only sleeps in snatches.

▶ What is the difference between a clever midget and a venereal disease? One is a cunning runt, and the other is a...

▶ What happens when you kiss a canary? You get chirpes. It can't be tweeted because it's a canarial disease.

▶ An enormous funeral wound its way through the streets of the town and in every way no sign of sorrow had been stinted, right down to the open cars filled with flowers. A bystander, who had been away from the neighbourhood for a while, nudged a neighbour. 'Who died?' he whispered.
'Big Angelo's girlfriend,' said the other.
'Big Angelo's girlfriend? But she was so young! What did she die of?'
'Gonorrhea.'
'Gonorrhea! But that's impossible. No one dies of gonorrhea.'
'You do when you give it to Big Angelo.'

▶ If they bring shrimps home on shrimp boats, fish home on fish boats and clams home on clam boats, what do they bring crabs home on? The captain's dinghy.

▶ A worried father telephoned his family doctor and said that he was afraid that his teenage son had come down with VD. 'He says he hasn't had sex with anyone but the maid, so it has to be her.'

'Don't worry so much,' advised the doctor. 'These things happen.'

'I know, Doctor,' said the father, 'but I have to admit that I've been sleeping with the maid also. I seem to have the same symptoms.'

'That's unfortunate.'

'Not only that, I think I've passed it to my wife.'

'Oh God,' said the doc. 'That means we all have it.'

▶ A young couple were making passionate love in his van and suddenly the girl, being a bit on the kinky side, yells out, 'Oh lover, whip me! Please whip me!'

Well, the guy, not wanting to pass up an opportunity like that but unsure what to do as he has no whips around, gets an inspired flash, opens one window, snaps the antenna off his van and proceeds to whip the girl until they both collapse in sado-masochistic ecstasy.

Almost a week later the girl notices that the welts she sustained are beginning to fester a bit and goes to her doctor. The doctor takes one look at the wounds and exclaims, 'Extraordinary! It appears you've got a bad case of "van-aerial" disease!'

▶ A businessman returns from Thailand. After a few days he notices a strange growth on his penis. He goes to see his doctor, who says, 'You've been screwing around in the East – it's very common there. I'm afraid there is no cure. We'll have to cut it off.'

The man panics but reasons that if it is common in the East, they must know how to cure it. So he goes back and sees a doctor in Thailand.

The Thai doctor examines him and says, 'You've been having intercourse in my country. This is a very common problem here. Did you see any other doctors?'

The man replies, 'Yes, in England.'

The Thai doctor says, 'I bet they told you it had to be cut off.'

The man answers, 'Yes!'

The doctor smiles and nods. 'That is not correct. It will fall off by itself.'

▶ Why did God invent yeast infections? So women know what it feels like to live with an annoying c***.

STEVIE WONDER

▶ A friend of Stevie Wonder's bought him a cheese grater for his birthday. A few weeks later, the friend met up with Stevie and asked him whether he liked his present.

'Hey, man!' replied Stevie. 'That was the most violent book I've ever read!'

▶ Why are Stevie Wonder's legs always wet? Because his dog is blind, too.

▶ What is the name of Stevie Wonder's favourite book? *Around the Block in 80 Days.*

▶ I just found out Stevie Wonder is married. This shocked me – I didn't think he was seeing anyone.

▶ What's the fastest thing on land? Stevie Wonder's speedboat!

▶ Stevie Wonder and Jack Nicklaus were in a bar. Jack turned to Stevie and asked, 'How is the singing career going?'

'Great, said Stevie. 'The latest album has gone into the top ten and I'm setting off on a world tour next month. How's the golf?'

'Not too bad,' replied Jack. 'I don't play as much as I used to, but I still make a bit of money. I had some problems with my swing, but I think I've got that sorted now.'

Stevie nodded. 'I always find that when my swing goes wrong, I need to stop playing for a while and think about it. Then the next time I play it seems to be all right.'

'You play golf?' said Jack, surprised.

'Yeah, I've been playing for years,' replied Stevie.

'But I thought you were blind,' said Jack. 'How can you play golf if you're blind?'

'I've got a system,' explained Stevie. 'I get my caddie to stand in the middle of the fairway, and he calls to me. I listen for the sound of his voice and I play the ball towards him. Then when I get to where the ball lands, the caddie moves to the green or further down the fairway and again I play the ball towards his voice.'

'But how do you putt?' asked Jack.

'Well,' said Stevie, 'I get my caddie to lean down in front of the hole and call to me with his head on the ground, and I just play the ball to the sound of his voice.'

'What's your handicap?' asked Jack.

Stevie replied, 'I play off scratch.'

Jack was amazed and said to Stevie, 'We must play a game sometime.'

Stevie said, 'Well, people don't take me seriously, so I only play for money. And I never play for less than $100,000 a hole.'

Jack thought about it for a moment before saying, 'OK, I'm up for that. When would you like to play?'

Stevie said, 'I don't mind. Any night next week is OK with me.'

SUICIDE

▶ A blonde walked into the doctor's office with a hole in her hand. The doctor told her that he had to report all gunshot wounds, and this was an obvious gunshot wound.

The blonde said, 'Well, to be honest with you, I was trying to commit suicide, and first I stuck the gun in my mouth, but then I thought, wait a minute, I just had all that bridgework done, and I don't want to ruin it, so I pointed the gun between my eyes, and then thought, wait a minute, I got a nose job not too long ago, and I don't want to ruin it! Then I pointed the gun at my heart and thought, wait a minute, I just had these boobs done, and I don't want to ruin them. So then I stuck the gun in my ear and thought, wait a minute, this is going to be loud... '

▶ Bruce was driving over Sydney Harbour Bridge, when he spotted his girlfriend Sheila about to throw herself off. Bruce slammed on the brakes and yelled, 'Sheila, what the hell d'ya think you're doing?'

Sheila turned around with a tear in her eye and said, 'G'day, Bruce. You got me pregnant and so now I'm gonna kill myself.'

Bruce got a lump in his throat when he heard this. 'Strewth, Sheila,' he said, 'not only are you a great shag, but you're a real sport, too.' Then he drove off.

▶ Major Charles Ingram, who was convicted of trying to cheat the *Who Wants To Be a Millionaire* TV programme out of a million pounds, has committed suicide. The producers of the show have offered to pay most of the funeral expenses, but not for the coffin.

SUNBATHING

▶ Jackie wants an all-over suntan but is not quite sure how to go about it, so she says to Keith her husband, 'Do you think I should go sunbathing in the nude in the back garden?'

'Yeah, why not?' says Keith. 'Go for it.'

'But what if the neighbours see me naked, what will they think?'

'That I married you for your money.'

SWIMMING

▶ Why does a squirrel swim on its back? To keep its nuts dry.

▶ On vacation, a little boy asked his mother, 'Can I go swimming in the sea?'

'No, darling, you can't,' she replied. 'The sea's way too rough, there's a dangerous offshore current and this stretch of coastline is supposed to be plagued with jellyfish and sharks.'

'But Daddy's gone swimming in the sea,' protested the boy.

'I know,' said the mother. 'But Daddy has excellent life insurance.'

TATTOOS

▶ A girlfriend told her boyfriend to prove his love for her by getting her name, Wendy, tattooed on his penis. He agreed, and when erect it spelled out her name in full, but when it was limp it just said 'Wy'. They went away for a holiday to the Caribbean, and while there decided to go on the nudist beach. There the husband saw a black guy with 'Wy' on his penis as well.

'You must have a girlfriend called Wendy, too,' said the boyfriend.

'No, mine says: "Welcome to Jamaica man have a nice day".'

▶ An America soldier is wounded and lying dying in Iraq. He croaks to a passing nurse, 'I wish I could kiss the old Stars and Stripes one last time before I go.'

The nurse is touched by his simple patriotism and leans over his bed. 'Soldier, I have a tattoo of the American flag on my ass. You may kiss that if you want.'

The soldier weakly nods, so the nurse slips off her panties and presents her ass for the soldier to kiss. He raises his head to kiss the tattoo, then falls back onto his pillow. He gestures for the nurse to come closer. She leans over and he whispers in her ear, 'I want to show my respect to our president, too. Turn around so I can kiss Bush.'

TAX INSPECTORS

▶ At the end of the tax year, the Tax Office sent an inspector to audit the books of a synagogue. While he was checking the books, he turned to he rabbi and said, 'I notice you buy a lot of candles. What do you do with the candle drippings?'

'Good question,' noted the rabbi. 'We save them up and send them back to the candlemakers, and every now and then they send us a free box of candles.'

'Oh,' replied the auditor, somewhat disappointed that his unusual question had a practical answer. But on he went, in his obnoxious way, 'What about all these matzo purchases? What do you do with the crumbs?'

'Ah, yes,' replied the rabbi, realising that the inspector was trying to trap him with an unanswerable question. 'We collect them and send them back to the manufacturers, and every now and then they send a free box of matzo balls.'

'I see,' replied the auditor, thinking hard about how he could fluster the know-it-all rabbi. 'Well, rabbi,' he went on, 'what do you do with all the leftover foreskins from the circumcisions you perform?'

'Here, too, we do not waste,' answered the rabbi. 'What we do is save up all the foreskins and send them to the Tax Office, and about once a year they send us a complete dick.'

▶ A man from the Inland Revenue knocked on the front door of a house. A small boy answered. 'Is your mum in?'

'Yeah, she's in the backyard screwing the goat,' he replied.

The man was horrified. 'Son, it's not nice to make up stories like that!'

The boy said, 'I'm not making it up. If you don't believe me, come through and I'll show you.'

So the taxman followed the boy to the back of the house and, sure enough, through the window he could see a woman screwing a goat. Disgusted, he turned to the boy and said, 'Doesn't that bother you?'

The boy replied, 'Naaaaaaaaaah!'

TEENAGERS

▶ Did you hear about the adolescent girlfriend with acne? She had a cracking pair of zits.

▶ A man passed out in a dead faint as he came out of his front door and someone dialled 999. When the ambulance men arrived, they helped him regain consciousness and asked if he knew what caused him to faint.

'It was enough to make anybody faint,' he said. 'My son asked me for the keys to the garage, and instead of driving the car out, he came out with the lawnmower.'

▶ Why is Spiderman like adolescence? One day a teenage guy wakes up with muscles, hair in new places and the ability to spray white sticky goo around the house.

▶ Teenagers today drink twice as much as they did ten years ago. To be fair, though, they were only aged between three and nine ten years ago.

▶ What's brown and hides in the attic? The diarrhoea of Anne Frank.

▶ How did the teenager know he had bad acne? His dog called him Spot.

TESTICLES

▶ A little girl walks in on her naked father. Intrigued, she points to his balls and asks, 'Daddy, what are those?'

'These,' replies her father, 'are the apples of life'.

Puzzled with this explanation, the little girl wanders off to find her mum and tells her what Daddy said.

'Well, dear,' says her mother, 'they might be apples, but did he tell you about the dead branch they're hanging off?'

▶ A man goes to the doctor and says, 'Doctor, I've got one ball bigger than the other.'

'Rest them on the table and I'll have a look,' says the doctor.

Using two hands and struggling, the man heaves a huge bollock onto the table top.

The doctor examines it and says, 'It's actually not unusual to have one testicle larger than the other.'

'Could you give me a hand with the other one?' says the man.

▶ Have you heard about the guy with no dick? He went home and gave his wife a good bollocking.

THANKSGIVING

▶ What would happen if the Pilgrims had killed cats instead of turkeys? There'd be pussy to eat every Thanksgiving.

THEFT

▶ A man noticed that his credit card had been stolen but didn't report it. The thief was spending less than his wife.

TOILET

▶ A railway worker was writhing on the floor on the station platform in obvious agony. A concerned crowd gathered round him. 'What can we do to help? Do you need an ambulance?' they asked.

  'No, it's all right' he replied. 'I'm desperate for a shit, but I don't start work for another ten minutes.'

▶ I'm in serious trouble. I got caught urinating in the shower this morning.
It seems they frown on that at B&Q.

▶ Every man has, at some stage while taking a pee, pulled the lever halfway through, then raced against the flush.

▶ What do a toilet and a woman have in common? Without the hole in the middle, they aren't good for shit.

▶ I got a job at a paperless office. Everything was great until I needed a shit.

▶ Why do men whistle when they're sitting on the toilet? Because it helps them remember which end they need to wipe.

▶ Why don't they have any toilet paper in KFC? Because it's finger-licking good!

▶ A man was sitting in the men's cubicle of a motorway service station, when he heard a voice coming from the next cubicle.

  'Hi, how are you?' asked the voice.

Embarrassed at the sudden intrusion, the man replied hesitantly,
'Er... yeah... OK, I guess.'

'And what are youp to?' asked the voice from next door.

The man really didn't know what to say. 'Pretty much the same as you,
I guess,' he eventually replied.

Then the voice spoke again. 'Look, I'll have to call you back. There's some
idiot in the cubicle next door answering all the questions I'm asking you!'

▶ Why was Tigger's head in the toilet? He was looking for pooh!

▶ What's the biggest advantage of speed-reading? You can take a shit in
half the time.

▶ A guy found a magic lamp and, naturally, rubbed it. The genie popped
out and said, 'I'll grant you any wish you want.'

The guy thought and thought and finally gave his answer. 'I want to be
hard all the time and get all the ass I want.'

'As you wish,' the genie replied.

So the genie turned him into a toilet seat.

▶ *Refined toilet graffiti:*

- Harriet Smythe-Blenkinsop performs quality sexual favours

- Your mother and father are of the same genetic background

- Last night you enjoyed carnal pleasures with your sister

- Your intelligence quota is dubious at best

- For a moderate fee i believe your mother would fellate me

- You look upon your dog with lust

- I am persuaded you have the odour of faecal matter upon you

- I partook in intercourse with your sister's derriere

- The acne on your face spreads throughout your nether regions

- The people of France know not the joys of deodorant

- A hamster is superior in intelligence to your mother

- For an evening of sordid delights involving both sadism and masochism, please ring Mary at 212.555.5555

- Your sexually promiscuous mother can be found in the phonebook under 'whore'

- Your father's proclivities lead him to engage in relations with livestock

TONY BLAIR

▶ Tony Blair gave the half-time team talk at a football match. But nobody believed him when he warned that the opponents could mount a serious attack in the next 45 minutes.

▶ Bill Clinton, George W Bush and Tony Blair all died in a plane crash and went to heaven. First God asked Clinton about his beliefs.

Clinton replied, 'I am a strong believer in freedom of choice for people.'

'Those are admirable principles,' said God. 'Come and sit at my right.'

Then God asked Bush for his views. Bush answered, 'I believe in freeing countries from tyrannical regimes.'

'Noble sentiments,' said God. 'Come and sit at my left hand.'

Finally God turned to Blair, who was staring at him indignantly. 'What's the matter, Tony?' asked God.

Blair replied, 'You're sitting in my bloody chair!'

TORTOISES

▶ Two small boys – Tommy and George – were playing with their pet tortoises in the garden. Tommy boasted that his tortoise was the faster, so they agreed to have a race to the garden wall. George's tortoise lumbered away, but Tommy's just sat there in its shell.

'You're going to lose! You're going to lose!' laughed George as his pet headed off up the garden.

'No, I'm not!' yelled Tommy. And with that he picked up his tortoise and hurled it at the wall.

TOYS

▶ Why did Raggedy Anne get thrown out of the toy box? Because she kept sitting on Pinocchio's face, moaning, 'Lie to me!'

▶ What's the last thing Tickle Me Elmo receives before he leaves the factory? Two test tickles.

TRAMPS

▶ Bob is walking home, when he sees a tramp begging for change. Feeling a bit sorry for the man, he gives him some change and begins to walk off.

'Thank you,' says the homeless man. 'It used to be so good for me but look at me now.'

'What do you mean?' asks Bob.

The tramp replies, 'I was a multi-millionaire, I had bank accounts all across the world with millions in them. I had investments, bonds, stocks, shares and all sorts.'

'What happened, where did it go wrong?'

The tramp replies, 'I forgot my mother's maiden name.'

▶ Two tramps stagger into a bar. 'Let's have a Guinness,' says one. 'They say it puts lead in your pencil.'

'All right,' replies his friend, 'but I haven't got anybody to write to.'

▶ A tramp was in front of a judge. The judge says to him, 'You've been brought here for drinking.'

The tramp says, 'OK, let's get started.'

▶ Two tramps were sitting talking. The first started bragging, 'Today was the best day ever! I found a brand new pack of fags just sitting on the ground. So you know what I did? I sat and smoked every last one of them – had the best day ever!'

The second tramp just laughed. 'That's nothing. Today I was walking along the railway tracks when I found a girl lying on them. You know what I did? I shagged her all day long. It was my best day ever!'

The first tramp sneered, 'No way did you do it all day long!'

'OK,' conceded the second tramp, 'but it was for a good few hours – best day of my life!'

'So,' persisted the first tramp, 'did she give you a blowjob?'

'No,' replied the second tramp.

'Huh! How could you possibly be screwing this girl for hours, and she didn't even give you a blowjob?'

'How could she?' protested the second tramp. 'She didn't have a head!'

▶ One night, two starving tramps are walking through an alley, when one of them sees a dead cat. He runs over, sits down and starts to eat the cat, tearing the meat from its limbs.

He says to the other tramp, 'Hey, I know you're hungry, too. Why don't you eat some of this cat?'

'Hell no!' replies the second tramp. 'That cat's been dead for days; he's all stiff and cold and all!'

The first tramp says, 'OK, suit yourself,' and continues to eat everything, skin, muscle, guts, all but the skeleton.

A few hours later, as they are walking down the street, the first tramp says, 'Oh, I don't feel so good. I think there might have been something wrong with that cat.' And just then, he pukes up a huge puddle of rotten cat flesh and guts with stomach bile mixed in, all half-digested and looking like mush.

The second tramp sits down next to the puddle and says, 'Now you're talking! It's been months since I had a WARM meal!'

▶ Two tramps walk past a church and start to read the gravestones.
The first tramp says, 'Bloody hell – this bloke was 182!'

'Oh yeah?' says the other. 'What was his name?'

'Miles, from London.'

TRANSVESTITES

▶ Define transvestite: a man who likes to eat, drink and be Mary!

▶ Two blokes were out walking home from work one afternoon. 'Shit,' said the first bloke, 'as soon as I get home, I'm gonna rip the wife's knickers off!'
'What's the rush?' his mate asked.
'The bloody elastic in the legs is killing me,' the bloke replied.

▶ I met this wonderful girl today. We had so much in common. We both liked football, beer, pub food and she even laughed at my offensive jokes.
So I took her back to my place and she sat me down and stripped totally naked.
And it was at this point I saw we had something else in common.

▶ Why don't blondes wear miniskirts in San Francisco? Because their balls hang down below their hemlines.

▶ A guy is hiking up a mountain, when he sees a girl standing at the edge of a cliff, crying.
'Hey,' he says, 'if you're going to jump, how about giving me a blowjob before you do it?'
'My life's been nothing but crap,' says the girl. 'So I might as well.'
After the girl's done, the guy says, 'Wow, that was great! Why are you so depressed, anyway?'
The girl replies, 'My family disowned me for dressing like a woman.'

▶ What's the biggest crime committed by transvestites? Male fraud.

TRAVEL

▶ It was a perfect summer's day, and a guy was driving along the motorway to a scenic lake where he intended on spending the afternoon fishing. About an hour from his destination, he spotted a man dressed from head to toe in red standing by the side of the motorway and gesturing him to stop. The fisherman pulled over, wound down his window and asked, 'How can I help you?'

'I am the red arsehole of the asphalt,' replied the man in red. 'You got anything to eat?'

Blessed with a generous spirit on such a beautiful day, the fisherman handed the man one of his sandwiches before resuming his journey. A few miles down the road, he noticed a man dressed all in yellow standing by the side of the road and beckoning him to stop. Mildly irritated by a second interruption to his progress, the fisherman called out, 'What do you want?'

'I am the yellow arsehole of the asphalt,' replied the man in yellow. 'Got anything to drink?'

The fisherman handed him a can of Coke and quickly drove off. Not wanting to lose any more time, he put his foot down in an attempt to reach the lake by lunchtime, but a few miles further down the road he saw a guy dressed all in blue standing by the side of the road, gesturing him to stop.

Frustrated at yet another delay, the fisherman pulled over, wound down the window and yelled, 'Let me guess, you're the blue arsehole of the asphalt. What the hell do you want?'

The man in blue replied, 'Driver's licence and registration, please.'

▶ White van man to pedestrian: 'S'cuse me, mate, does yow know if there's a B&Q in Wolverhampton?'

Pedestrian: 'Sorry, mate, I don't, but I knows there's two Ds in Dudley.'

▶ Three passengers are on a train discussing why the train company is losing money.

'Bad management,' says one.

'Too many staff,' says another.

'Not enough investment,' says the third.

Then they hear the ticket inspector coming and all run to hide in the toilets.

▶ An explorer is telling his friends about a new tribe he's discovered in Africa – the Fukawe. 'They're pygmies,' explains the explorer. 'But unlike most pygmies, who live in the forests, these fellows live in the tall grasses of the plains.'

'And what does the name of the tribe mean?' asks one of his friends.

'I'm not sure,' replies the explorer. 'But when I found them wandering through the six-foot grass, virtually the first thing they said to me was, "We're the Fukawe."'

▶ I asked my grandmother for 'something Cuban' for my birthday, and she got me a Che Guevara shirt. Clothes, but no cigar.

▶ Two friends had agreed to meet at a resort for a weekend of fishing. The first arrived on Friday evening, as scheduled, but his fishing buddy never showed up. Finally, about lunchtime the next day, the late fisherman arrived beaten and bandaged.

When asked what the hell had happened, the wounded man replied, 'The last thing I remember is stopping at the motorway rest stop and spotting a parked car with what appeared to be people in the back seat, so I stuck my head through the window and asked, "Hey, just how far is The Olde Log Inn?"'

▶ What events follow the famous Running of the Bulls? The Soiling of the Pants and the Burying of the Idiots.

▶ Mr Johns from the USA goes to Israel to visit all the holy places there.

On his tour he came by the Sea of Galilee and saw a man on a small boat with a sign: 'Sea of Galilee Tours.'

He asked the man, 'How much for a tour?'

The man said, 'Three hundred and eighty Shekels.'

'What? Why so much?'

'Well, sir,' said the man, 'you know that the Lord Jesus walked on these waters.'

'Yeah,' said Mr Johns, 'with prices like that, I'm not bloody surprised!'

▶ The Tube carriage was packed. It was rush hour, and many people were forced to stand. One particularly cramped woman turned to the man behind her and said, 'Sir, if you don't stop poking me with your thing, I'm going to the police!'

'I don't know what you're talking about, miss – that's just my pay packet in my pocket.'

'Oh really,' she spat. 'Then you must have some job, because that's the fifth raise you've had in the last half hour!'

▶ A travelling salesman finds himself stranded in the tiniest town in Australia. He knocks on the door of a little hotel.

'Sorry, we don't have a spare room,' says the manager, 'but you're welcome to share with a little red-headed schoolteacher, if that's OK.'

'Oh, that'll be great,' says the salesman, grinning from ear to ear. 'And don't worry, I'll be a real gentleman.'

'Just as well,' says the manager. 'So will the little red-headed schoolteacher.'

TV

▶ What do Americans call a TV set that goes for five years without need of repair? An import.

▶ What do you call a Tellytubby that's been burgled? Tubby.

TWINS

▶ A man was in the urinal of a pub, when he heard an argument coming from the cubicle.

'Get lost, will you?' said one voice.

'No, it's my turn,' said the other.

'But you had it earlier.'

'Let me have it, you bastard.'

'No way, I'm not finished.'

Back in the pub the man relayed the conversation to the barman.

The barman replied, 'Oh, don't worry, it's just those Siamese twins having a wank.'

▶ Two young guys, Phil and John, were sleeping with the same girl, so when she fell pregnant there was no way of knowing which was the father. Not wishing to be burdened with responsibility, they paid for her to have the baby out of town, but then months went by without any news.

Eventually Phil phoned the girl. The following day he phoned John. 'There's good and bad news,' said Phil. 'The good news is, she's fine and had twins.'

'What's the bad news?' asked John.

Phil said, 'Mine died.'

UGLY

▶ A doctor examines a woman and takes her husband aside. 'I don't want to alarm you,' he says, 'but I don't like the way your wife looks.'

'Me neither, Doctor,' says the husband. 'But she's a great cook and real good with the kids.'

▶ He was an ugly baby. His mother only started to get morning sickness after he was born.

▶ He was so ugly, when he was a baby his mother left him on the steps of a police station – then went and handed herself in.

▶ The camera always caught her worst side – her outside.

▶ They broke the mould when they made him. In fact, I think they might have broken the mould before they made him.

UNDERWEAR

▶ Why do witches never wear any underwear? So they can get a better grip on the broom.

▶ Why was the bikini invented? To separate the meat section from the dairy section.

▶ Why do women wear black underwear? They're in mourning for the stiff they buried the night before.

▶ Harry has invented a bra for middle-aged women. He calls it the 'sheep dog' because it rounds them up and points them in the right direction.

▶ Have you heard about the pants called harvest festivals? All is safely gathered in.

▶ What do you get when you cross a brassiere with Texas? Playtex.

▶ What's white, smells and can be found in panties? Clitty litter.

▶ Why was the washing machine laughing? Because it was taking the piss out of the undies.

▶ A woman sends her clothing out to the Chinese laundry. When it comes back, there are still stains in her panties. The next week she encloses a note to the cleaner: 'Use more soap on panties'.

This goes on for several weeks, with the woman sending the same note to the laundry. Finally the cleaner responds with a note: 'Use more paper on arse.'

▶ A very flat-chested woman finally decided she needed a bra and set out to the shops in search of one in her size. She entered an upscale department store and approached the saleslady in lingerie. 'Do you have a size 28AAAA bra?'

The assistant haughtily replied in the negative, so she left the store and proceeded to another department store, where she was rebuffed in much the same manner.

After a third try at another department store in the mall, she had become disgusted. Leaving the mall, she drove to Marks and Spencer. Marching up to the sales desk, she unbuttoned and threw open her blouse, yelling, 'Do you have anything for this?'

The lady looked closely at her and replied, 'Have you tried Clearasil?'

▶ Do you know why they call it the Wonderbra? When you take it off, you wonder where her tits went.

▶ One day a girl, who is wearing a skirt, goes out to play with her friends. She goes to the park and meets a boy. They talk about climbing trees, and the boy encourages the girl to climb the tree. The girls climbs up and the boy just stands there and looks up to the girl's knickers.

When the girl goes home she tells her mum about what happened. Her mum scolds her, tells her she must watch out for boys and that she mustn't show them her knickers on any account. The next day the girl goes to the park, again wearing a skirt, and meets the same boy. And again he asks her to climb the tree and again she does.

When she gets home she tells her mum what happened. Her mother gets very cross and starts shouting that she told the girl that she mustn't let boys see her knickers.

'But I didn't let him see,' replies the girl proudly. 'Today I didn't wear any pants!'

▶ How many animals can you get into a pair of tights? Ten little piggies, two calves, one beaver, one ass, one pussy, thousands of hares and a dead fish no one can ever find.

VALENTINE'S DAY

▶ Last year, on Valentine's Day, my fiancée of five years bought me a lottery ticket and I won £6.2 million. I wonder what she's doing nowadays?

▶ I gave blood today. I know it's not the best gift to give my wife for Valentine's Day, but it came from the heart.

▶ Valentine's Day: blowjob tax.

▶ It's been two days now and I'm frantically trying to find the guy who sent my wife her only Valentine's card to put him in hospital.
The bloke seriously needs immediate psychiatric help.

VASECTOMY

▶ A man went to his doctor and said, 'I'm thinking of having a vasectomy.'
  'That's a pretty big decision,' said the doctor. 'Have you talked it over with your family?'
  'Yes,' replied the man. 'They're in favour, 15 to two.'

▶ Two men both have 9.00 a.m. appointments at a vasectomy clinic. A nurse greets the two men, tells them she has to prep them for surgery and takes them to a private room. She asks the first man to take off his clothes and sit on an exam table, which he does. She then takes his manhood in one hand and begins to masturbate him.
  'Whoa!' he says. 'What's going on here?' She replies that it is all

standard procedure to ensure that he has no blockages. The man says to himself, 'How bad can it be?' So he allows the nurse to finish her task.

Once done, the nurse tells him to sit down and repeats the instructions to the second man. When he is up on the exam table, the nurse licks her lips and begins to perform fellatio on him.

Upon seeing this, the first man interrupts, 'Hey, what's this? I get a wank, and he gets a blowjob. That's not fair.'

The nurse looks up at the first man and says, 'Sorry, but that's the difference between the NHS and BUPA!'

▶ What's the definition of macho? Jogging home from your own vasectomy.

VENTRILOQUISM

▶ How can a woman scare a gynaecologist? By becoming a ventriloquist.

VEGETARIANS AND VEGANS

▶ What do you call a vegetarian with diarrhoea? A salad shooter.

▶ Why did the tofu cross the road? To prove he wasn't chicken.

▶ How many vegans does it take to change a lightbulb? Two; one to change it and one to check for animal ingredients.

▶ Why does vegan cheese taste bad? It hasn't been tested on mice.

▶ What did one vegetarian spy say to the other vegetarian spy? We have to stop meating like this.

▶ What do you call a vegetarian who goes back to eating meat? Someone who lost their veginity!

▶ What do you call a militant vegan? Lactose intolerant.

▶ What do vegan zombies eat? Graiinnnzzzz.

▶ What's a vegan's favourite chat-up line? 'If I said you had the body of an all-natural, organic-living, animal-loving, environment-nurturing, whale-saving sex machine, would you hold it against me? Please?'

▶ Why did the vegan cross the road? Because she was protesting for the chicken, man!

▶ A couple heard that their vegetarian son was coming home from university for Thanksgiving.
'Kill the fatted zucchini, Martha! Our prodigal son is returning.'

▶ I follow a strict vegan diet. I eat only vegans.

▶ Man: 'Do you serve vegans here?'
Waiter: 'Of course. How would you like them cooked?'

▶ If vegetarians eat vegetables, what do humanitarians eat?

▶ Nine out of ten cannibals agree – vegetarians taste better!

▶ A vivisector is having a nightmare: lying on a cold steel table, he's going numb as a giant rat approaches with a large knife.

The rat says, 'We are going to need those kidneys, my friend.'

'Wait!' shouts the vivisector. 'I understand that I'm going to die, but just tell me, is it for the good of humanity?'

'Something like that,' the rat tells him with a smirk. 'It's for the good of two manatees.'

▶ How many vegetarians does it take to eat a cow? One if nobody's looking.

▶ I didn't fight my way to the top of the food chain to be a vegetarian!

▶ A husband and wife were sitting around talking about their hard day at work and the wife was complaining that she needed to be more assertive to get anywhere, etc., when her husband told her, 'You know what the problem is, don't you? It's a dog eat dog world out there, and you're a vegetarian!'

▶ What do you call a vegan guy who likes to pleasure himself?
A non-dairy creamer.

▶ A young vegan couple decided to spice up their life so they bought The Joy of Sex.' A friend later asked them if the book had helped.

Disgusted, the lady replied, 'We didn't know what we were getting into. That book goes against everything we believe.'

The friend, a bit surprised, asked them if they were against free sexual expression.

'No,' said the man, 'but you wouldn't believe what they want us to put in our mouths!'

▶ Why do vegans give good head? Because they are used to eating nuts.

VETS

▶ A vet walks into a library and asks for a book called *The Immortal Dog*. The librarian hands him the book and says, 'Great book, you won't be able to put it down.'

VIAGRA

▶ Did you hear about the Viagra nasal spray? It's for dickheads.

▶ What do DisneyWorld and Viagra have in common? They both make you wait an hour for a two-minute ride.

▶ Harry picks up his Viagra prescription at the pharmacy. Eager to try it out, he takes one as soon as he gets home and anxiously waits for his wife to get home from work. In his excitement, he leaves the open package on the table and his parrot gobbles down all of the pills. Seeing the results and panicking, Harry grabs the parrot and sticks him in the freezer to cool off.

Unfortunately, Harry's Viagra kicks in just as his wife walks through the door and hours pass before he remembers the parrot. He rushes to look in the freezer, fearing the worst, but finds the bird breathing heavily, dripping with sweat and totally exhausted.

'What happened?' exclaims Harry. 'You've been in there for hours, yet you're not only alive, you're sweating like crazy.'

Panting, the parrot says, 'Listen, pal, have you ever tried to prise apart the legs of a frozen chicken?'

▶ The government has just announced the new generic names for Viagra. After careful discussion they have decided on Mycoxafloppin. Also considered were Mycoxafailin, Mydixadrupin, Mydixarizin, Dixafix and, of course, Ibepokin.

▶ A woman asks her husband if he'd like some breakfast: bacon, eggs, perhaps a slice of toast? Grapefruit with coffee to follow?

He declines. 'It's this Viagra,' he says, 'it's really taken the edge off my appetite.'

At lunchtime, she asks if he would like something. A bowl of homemade soup, maybe, with a cheese sandwich? Perhaps a plate of snacks and a glass of milk?

He declines. 'It's this Viagra,' he says. 'It's really taken the edge off my appetite.'

Come teatime, she asks if he wants anything to eat. She'll go to the café and buy him a burger. Maybe a steak and cheese pie? Pizza? Or a tasty stir-fry that would only take a couple of minutes?

He declines. 'It's this Viagra,' he says, 'it's really taken the edge off my appetite.'

'Well,' she says, 'would you mind getting off me? I'm starving!'

▶ A middle-aged man went to his doctor and asked for a prescription of the strongest Viagra available because he had got two young nymphomaniacs staying at his house for the weekend. Later that week he went back to the doctor and asked for painkillers.

'What's the problem?' asked the doctor. 'Is your penis in that much pain?'

'No,' said the man. 'It's for my wrists – the girls never showed up.'

▶ Concerned about his failing manhood, a farmer went to the local doctor for help. The doctor gave him a small container of Viagra and told him to take no more than one a day. Back home, the farmer thought he'd try the medication on his stud horse first. The horse swallowed the pill, jumped out of his stall, kicked a side of the barn over and ran off down the road. 'Those pills are too strong for me,' the farmer thought, and poured the rest into his well.

Later, when the doctor came to check on him, the farmer told how he had disposed of the medication.

'Heavens!' exclaimed the doctor. 'You haven't drunk any of the well water, have you?'

'No,' said the farmer. 'We can't get the pump handle down.'

▶ A bus driver is prescribed Viagra by his doctor and visits the pharmacist, who fills the prescription. Home is a good hour away so the bus driver quickly downs one of the little blue pills. When he gets home, he doesn't even have to tell his wife with words. That twinkle in his eye speaks volumes. They tear off each other's clothes and are quickly in bed. He manages to 'rise to the occasion' three times. Three times! He expects his wife to be delighted, but instead she seems rather sad.

'What's wrong, dear?' he asks.

'I think your job is taking over every aspect of your life and it's doing you in,' she sighs.

'What do you mean?' he says.

'I mean, even our sex life is like the bus service. Nothing for ages, and then three come all at once!'

▶ Have you tried the new hot beverage, Viagraccino? One cup and you're up all night.

▶ Did you hear about the man who took a course of Viagra along with some iron tablets? Now his cock always points north.

▶ Did you hear about the consignment of Viagra pills stolen from a warehouse? Police are on the lookout for hardened criminals.

▶ A man goes to a doctor and, twitching with shame and nerves, finally manages to stutter, 'Doctor, I have a sexual performance problem. Can you help me?'

'Oh, that's not a problem for us men anymore!' announces the proud physician. 'They just came out with this new wonder drug, Viagra – that does the trick! You take some pills and your problems are history!'

So the doctor gives the man a prescription and sends him on his way.

A couple of months later, the doctor runs into his patient on the street. 'Doctor, Doctor!' exclaims the man excitedly. 'I've got to thank you! This drug is a miracle! It's wonderful!'

'Well, I'm glad to hear that,' says the pleased physician. 'What does your wife think about it?'

'Wife? I haven't been home yet!'

VIBRATORS

▶ What did the banana say to the vibrator? 'Why are you shaking? It's me she's going to eat.'

▶ How do you know if a woman used a vibrator when she was pregnant? The child stutters.

▶ On his first day working in a sex shop, a young man was left alone for the afternoon while his boss went out. The man was nervous about dealing with customers' questions, but his boss assured him he would be fine.

The first customer was an elderly white lady. 'How much for the white vibrator?' she asked.

'£30,' he replied.

'How much for the black one?'

'Same price, £30.'

'Right,' she said, 'I think I'll take the black one; I've never had a black one before.' And she paid the money and left.

Shortly afterwards an elderly black woman came in. 'How much for the black vibrator?' she asked.

'£30,' he replied.

'How much for the white one?'

'Same price, £30.'

'Right,' she said. 'Hmmm, I think I'll take the white one; I've never had a white one before.' And she paid the money and left.

An hour later a young blonde woman came in and asked, 'How much are your vibrators?'

'£30 for the white one and £30 for the black one,' he replied.

'Hmmm' she said. 'And how much for the tartan one on the shelf?'

The young man replied, 'Well, that is a very special vibrator and will cost you £250.'

The blonde thought for a moment and said, 'OK, I'll take the tartan one; I've never had a tartan one before.' And she paid the money and left.

Finally his boss returned. 'How did you get on today?' he asked.

'Great,' the young man replied. 'I sold one black vibrator and one white vibrator, and I sold your thermos for £250!'

▶ What do you get when you cross a vibrator with an anteater? An armadildo.

▶ A farmer in Devon has successfully grown a field of dildos. Unfortunately, he's having trouble with squatters.

VIOLENCE

▶ Some yob attacked me down the local park tonight with a bat. I was really impressed at how well he'd trained it.

▶ A farmer comes home from the fields early and sees a light on in his bedroom. Suspecting foul play, he grabs his shotgun and creeps up the stairs. He bursts into the bedroom and finds one of his farmhands naked, in bed with his wife.

The farmhand stands up and shouts, 'Don't shoot! For God's sake give me a chance!'

The farmer aims his gun and says, 'OK, I'll give you a chance – now swing 'em!'

▶ I've just been threatened by an agoraphobic skinhead.

He said, 'Oi you! Inside!'

VIRGINITY

▶ What do you call an Afghan virgin? Never Bin Laid On.

▶ What do you call a virgin on a waterbed? A cherry float.

▶ What do you say to a virgin when she sneezes? Goes-in-tight.

▶ In a crowded pub, all of a sudden the cute little thing on the stool began to cry.

The barman asked, 'What's the trouble, sweetheart?'

She sobbed, 'I'm a virgin, and my boyfriend won't have anything to do with me because I'm inexperienced. What should I do?'

Three men and a lesbian were killed in the rush.

▶ In a tiny village lived an old maid. In spite of her old age, she was still a virgin. She was very proud of it. She knew her last days were getting closer, so she told the local undertaker that she wanted the following inscription on her tombstone: 'Born as a virgin, lived as a virgin, died as a virgin.'

Not long after, the old maid died peacefully, and the undertaker told his men what the lady had said. The men went to carve it in, but the lazy no-goods thought the inscription to be unnecessarily long.

They simply wrote: 'Returned unopened.'

▶ A family are driving behind a garbage truck, when a dildo flies out and thumps against the windscreen. Embarrassed, and to spare her young daughter's innocence, the mother turns around and says, 'Don't worry; that was an insect.'

To which her daughter replies, 'I'm surprised it could get off the ground with a cock like that.'

WAYNE ROONEY

It's great to see Wayne Rooney back on form. At long last he's broken his prostitute drought.

Wayne Rooney's international teammates have rallied round his betrayed wife, Coleen. John Terry is already said to have offered to pop round any time.

There was good and bad news for Wayne Rooney on the front of Tuesday's *Daily Mirror*. On the downside, a second girl is about to do a kiss-and-tell on him. On the upside, he's really looking forwards to that free Gregg's Steak Bake.

Fabio Capello is worried Wayne Rooney's got the wrong end of the stick about England's latest qualifier. He told the striker to stay at home but Rooney said he wasn't going to miss out on the chance of a Swiss roll.

Coleen wasn't that keen on sex with Wayne Rooney anyway. She said it was ogre-rated.

▶ Coleen says their marriage is ruined. In fact, it's completely Shreked.

What's the difference between Wayne Rooney and Shrek? Shrek can save the day.

Rooney has released a statement to the media, reading: 'Who says I couldn't score in a brothel now, eh?'

▶ How can you tell the Rooneys apart? One's dirty, the other's Coleen.

▶ Wayne Rooney's been told to take a long look at himself in the mirror. Like that's going to cheer him up.

▶ This isn't quite what Sir Alex had in mind when he told Wayne to start banging them in again.

▶ Some of Wayne Rooney's sponsors are sticking by him. Spokesmen from Durex, Yellow Pages and Travelodge insisted he'd done absolutely nothing wrong.

▶ Coleen will have Rooney followed everywhere from now on. It's the WAG tailing the dog.

▶ No one is saying Wayne Rooney's obsessed with sex, but he's been asking teammates if Swiss cheese is the one with the holes in it.

▶ Poor Wayne Rooney. He hired a stripper from the Yellow Pages and someone came round and took off all his wallpaper.

▶ *Shrek 4*'s plot line is going to be interesting now, isn't it?

▶ Wayne Rooney's been arrested for shoplifting a packet of Cherry Bakewells. He explained to police that he'd promised Coleen never to pay for another tart again.

WEATHER

▶ What do you get if you cross a hurricane and a tsunami? Katrina and the Waves.

▶ Some people can tell the time by looking at the sun, but I've never been able to see the numbers.

WELSH JOKES

▶ How does a Welshman find a sheep in tall grass? Very satisfying.

▶ Notice outside London theatre: 'The part of the Welshman has been filled. The Dai is cast.'

▶ Did you hear the price of lamb in Wales has just gone up? It's now £4.95 per hour.

▶ The Welsh have just discovered two new uses for sheep. Meat and wool.

▶ Little Ifor's father was livid when he walked around the back of the house only to find his son with his pants down and balls deep in his prize ewe. 'You had better explain yourself right now!' yelled the dad.

Little Ifor thought for a minute and replied, 'Well, Dad, it ain't love... but it ain't baaaaaaaaaad, either.'

▶ A researcher is conducting a survey into sheep shagging. First of all, he visits a Cornish farmer. 'So, Farmer Jethro, how do you shag your sheep?'

'Well, oi takes the hind legs of the sheep and puts them down my wellie boot and takes the front legs of the sheep and puts them over a wall.'

'That's very interesting,' replies the researcher.

He then interviews a Midlands farmer. 'So, Farmer Smith, how do you shag your sheep?'

'Well, I take the hind legs of the sheep and put them down my wellie boots and take the front legs of the sheep and put them over a wall.'

'That's very interesting,' replies the researcher. 'That's how they do it in Cornwall, too.'

Then he interviews a farmer from Wales. 'So, Farmer Jones, how do you shag your sheep?'

'Well, I do it lying up against a wall.'

'Against a wall?' replies the researcher. 'Don't you put their legs down your wellies like everyone else?'

'What?' says the farmer. 'And miss out on all the kissing?'

WHALES

▶ Willie the Whale and his whale girlfriend, Monica, are swimming happily through the ocean, when they come upon a boat. On seeing the boat, Willie says, 'Hey, I've got a great idea! Let's swim up under that boat and blow out really hard through our blowholes!'

Monica says, 'Oh, I don't know... '

'Come on, it'll be fun – come on, just this once!' says Willie.

Monica agrees and they swim up under the boat and blow out, capsizing the boat and sending hapless sailors into the water.

As they are swimming away, Willie says, 'Wow, that was fun, wasn't it? Hey! I've got another idea! Let's swim back there and eat all the sailors!'

To which Monica, exasperated, replies, 'Look, I agreed to the blowjob, but I'm not swallowing any seamen.'

WHAT IS... ?

▶ What's the difference between a genealogist and a gynaecologist? The genealogist looks up trees; the gynaecologist looks up bushes.

▶ What was Dick van Dyke's real name? Penis van Lesbian.

▶ What was the name of the Scottish dentist? Phil McCavity.

▶ What's green and smells? Hulk's fart.

▶ What's green and walks through walls? Casper the friendly cabbage.

▶ What's 12 feet long and smells of lavender and stale wee? A line dance at an old people's home.

WIDOWS

▶ Two widows were talking.
  'Rose has just buried her fifth husband,' said the first.
  'That's the way it goes,' said the other. 'Some of us can't find a husband; others have husbands to burn.'

▶ A love-starved widow was so desperate that she went to a local newspaper office and enquired about putting an advertisement in the Lonely Hearts column.

'Well, madam,' the assistant said, 'we charge a minimum of £1 per insertion.'

'You don't say!' said the widow. 'Well, then, here's £20 and to hell with the advertisement!'

WISDOM

▶ Good news rarely comes in a brown envelope.

▶ Rummaging in an overgrown garden will always turn up a bouncy ball.

▶ You never know where to look when eating a banana.

▶ You've never quite sure whether it's OK to eat green crisps.

▶ Despite constant warnings, you have never met anybody who's had their arm broken by a swan.

▶ Nobody ever dares make Cup-a-soup in a bowl.

▶ Always remember you're unique – just like everyone else.

▶ Always try to read stuff that will make you look good if you die in the middle of it.

▶ The number of people watching you is directly proportional to the stupidity of your action.

▶ *Advice to women:*

• WHAT KIND OF MAN MAKES THE BEST LOVER? Unfortunately, many men who seem attractive on the surface are actually strongly homosexual, often without even knowing it. Men with lean waists, overdeveloped chests and arms and clean skin are actually subconsciously obsessed by male bodies. You should stay far away from men who are, or look like, athletes or rock stars and men who feel compelled to dress in fancy suits with clean shirts and polished shoes. These 'men' often have a compulsion to spend money on sumptuous meals, taxis and expensive trinkets to compensate for their affliction. Experienced, self-confident lovers – the kind you want – don't need to alter the natural contours of their bodies. They are content with slender arms, relaxed chests and waists with a comfortable amount of flesh, which can come in handy during moments of intimacy (why do you think they call them 'love handles'?).

One other tip: Married men can be depended on not to cause embarrassing rumours about you at home or school. Men on short business trips are discreet, grateful and particularly driven by passion. Look for them!

• HOW 'BIG' SHOULD A MAN BE? Don't be shy. It's an important question, and one surrounded by confusion. The average man's penis is two and a half to three inches long. Men substantially larger than this must often undergo painful surgery to cure their condition. In thickness, the average man is somewhat larger than a ballpoint pen.

- HOW 'LONG' SHOULD A MAN LAST? Some men can prolong the sex act beyond the once-imponderable 30-second barrier; intercourse with an experienced man can go on for up to 45 seconds. Once in a long while, you'll find a man who can 'last' as long as a minute. Whatever you do, don't let your girlfriends know you've landed one of these desirable '60-second wonders'.

- HOW DO I KNOW IF I'M HAVING AN ORGASM? The female orgasm is a sensation that's very hard to put into words, but most fulfilled, experienced women agree that it 'feels like something inside of you'. When a man's penis is inside your vagina, mouth or buttocks, that is an orgasm. You'll find a really skilled lover applies the same techniques to love as a gourmet does to a meal; he 'leaves a little something on your plate'. When, after intercourse, you feel a vague sensation that there could be 'more to come', that 'vaguely unsatisfied' feeling, then you can be sure you've experienced a sexually memorable adventure.

- WHAT IS A MULTIPLE ORGASM? There is no such thing.

- WHAT ABOUT ORAL SEX? This is one of the most significant differences between the sexes. If you look at pictures of a man and a woman, you'll see that a man's penis fits naturally into a woman's mouth. On the other hand, a man's mouth does not naturally fit into a woman's vagina. Thus, a woman orally stimulating a man is performing a 'natural' act. But a man seeking to put his mouth on or near your vagina is committing an 'unnatural' act (why do you think they call the vagina your 'private parts'?).

- WHAT IS AFTERPLAY? Men have ways of expressing their satisfaction. His satisfied sigh, followed by a deep, consuming sleep, is a sure sign that he and you are 'Good in Bed'. Another example of male 'afterplay' is his turning on a football or basketball game immediately after climax. Many women find a particularly satisfying post-coital experience in going into the kitchen and bringing a nice, cold beer for the man, along with a light snack, sandwich, potato chips and dip, to help her love put back depleted calories.

- WHAT IS IMPOTENCE? Impotence is what happens when a girl fails to stimulate her man properly. This can happen when her figure is not perfect, or when she tries to talk with him for too long before getting into bed with him. If this happens, you can help by turning on a sports event on TV or getting your man a sandwich. Another really good 'foreplay' technique is to invite a really good-looking girl friend over, and do whatever he asks, to him or to each other, while he watches.

- HOW CAN I KEEP THE MYSTERY ALIVE? One good way to keep things from becoming routine is to vary your dress. Garter belts, black mesh stockings, leather or rubber suits will all help get your man's attention. Also, don't keep playing 'one on one'. Invite your more attractive and energetic girlfriends over to take part. Another technique, and we think the best, is to use anonymous names. Have your lover call himself 'Mr Smith'. Don't let him tell you where he lives, or his home telephone number. You'll find it lends an air of real 'mystery' to the affair.

- HOW CAN I MEET REAL MEN? When looking for the ideal man – about 25 to 50, married, on a business trip, with enough flab to assure you of his masculinity – go to a local about 8.30 at night. Look around the bar, then, when you've found your man, unbutton the top three or four buttons on your blouse, wink at him, walk over and whisper in his ear, 'You're a hunk, can I buy you a drink?' This is a real conversation icebreaker and things will naturally progress from here.

- SOME OTHER IMPORTANT QUESTIONS:

Q: If I get pregnant, how do I know who the father is?

A: There is absolutely no way to tell.

Q: What's the best way to keep my teeth and skin looking healthy and shiny?

A: One of the best and most frequently neglected substances is semen. The more you can somehow get on your teeth and skin, the better you'll look.

Q: What are some 'loving nicknames' we can use?

A: You should always call him 'Mr Smith'. You can also call him 'King Kong', 'Master' or 'stud'. Men often call their favourite lovers 'Hey you' or 'Bitch'.

Q: Where should a man take me?

A: Because so many homosexual men like to take their 'dates' out for 'fancy' meals, look for the man who will send you out to KFC or McDonald's for a 'snack'.

WORK

▶ I'm against strikes, but I don't know how to show it.

▶ In the beginning was the plan.

And then came the assumptions.

And the assumptions were without form.

And the plan was completely without substance.

And the darkness was upon the face of the workers.

And they spoke among themselves saying, 'It is a crock of shit, and it stinketh.'

And the workers went unto their supervisors, and sayeth, 'It is a pail of dung, and none can abide the odour thereof.'

And the supervisors went unto their managers and sayeth unto them, 'It is a container of excrement, and it is very strong, such that none can abide it.'

And the managers went unto the directors and sayeth, 'It is a vessel of fertiliser, and none can abide its strength.'

And the directors spoke amongst themselves, saying one to another, 'It contains that which aids plant growth, and is very strong.'

And the directors went unto the vice presidents and sayeth to them, 'It promotes growth, and is very powerful.'

And the vice presidents went unto the president, and sayeth unto him, 'This new plan will actively promote growth and efficiency of this company, and certain areas in particular.'

And the president looked upon the plan and saw that it was good.

And the plan became policy.

And this is how shit happens.

▶ Advice for office managers: keep the sexual harassment complaint forms in the bottom drawer, then when she goes to get one out you'll get a great view of her arse.

▶ What does it mean when the flag at the Post Office is flying at half mast? They're hiring.

▶ A man telephones his office and says, 'Sorry, I can't come into work today, I'm sick.'

'How sick are you?' asks his boss.

'Well,' he replies, 'I'm in bed with my sister and her dog.'

▶ A bloke goes for the job of cook on a ship. The geezer who is interviewing asks, 'Can you fry eggs?'

'Can I fry eggs! I've worked in some of the top hotels in England,' replies the bloke. 'Give me half a dozen.'

So he's given six eggs which he starts to juggle with. After a minute of brilliant juggling, he throws the eggs one by one over his shoulder towards the frying pan, which is behind him. Each egg hits the side of the pan, cracks open and the shell falls into the bin below and the eggs slide unbroken into the frying pan.

'That's amazing,' says the interviewer, 'but it must have been a fluke.'

'A fluke! Give me a dozen,' says the bloke. He then proceeds to do even more elaborate juggling and repeat the finale so there's now 18 unbroken eggs sizzling in the frying pan.

'Well, then, do I get the job?'

'No, you piss about too much!'

▶ I wish my brother would learn a trade so I would know what kind of work he's out of.

▶ My brother was a lifeguard in a car wash.

▶ The only thing worse than being unemployed is having a job.

▶ I got a job as a historian, but I realised there was no future in it.

▶ Two men go to sign on for unemployment benefit after being laid off at a factory. The first man goes for an interview and tells the employment clerk that he was a panty stitcher. He's given £150 a week in benefits and goes off. The second man goes in and tells the clerk he was a diesel fitter. He's given £200 a week and goes off.

Later the two men are in the pub and the panty stitcher finds that the diesel fitter is getting £50 more than he is. Outraged, he goes to the unemployment office to complain.

'Why should a diesel fitter get more than a panty stitcher?' he shouts.

The clerk replies, 'It's a new grant given to skilled workers. Engineers like diesel fitters are eligible.'

'He wasn't an engineer!' says the panty stitcher. 'He was in quality control. After I'd stitched a pair of panties, I'd give them to him. If he could pull them over his arse, he'd say, "Yeah, diesel fitter."'

A clean desk is a sign of a cluttered desk drawer.

Avoid employing unlucky people – throw half the CVs in the bin without reading them.

Doing a job right the first time gets the job done. Doing the job wrong 14 times gives you job security.

How do I set a laser printer to stun?

I thought at one point I could see the light at the end of the tunnel – turned out to be some bastard with a torch bringing me more work.

Monday is an awful way to spend one seventh of your life.

Never put off until tomorrow what you can avoid altogether.

Never be afraid to try something new. Remember, amateurs built the ark. Professionals built the *Titanic*.

▶ Never do today that which will become someone else's responsibility tomorrow.

▶ Plagiarism saves time.

▶ Working here is a bit like being a mushroom. You're kept in the dark and have shit thrown over you from a great height.

▶ My father came home and told us he'd been fired. His company had replaced him with a machine that was able to do everything he could, but do it much, much better. The tragic thing was my mother went out and bought one, too.

YO MOMMA

▶ Yo momma so ugly, her shadow quit.

▶ Yo momma so fat, she downloads cheats for Wii Fit.

▶ Yo momma so poor, I saw her chasing the garbage truck with a shopping list.

▶ Yo momma so hairy, when you were born you almost died from rug burn.

▶ Yo momma like a stop sign: she's on every corner.

Yo momma so fat, she wears a real horse on her Polo shirt.

Yo momma so poor, she DJs for the ice-cream van.

Yo momma so fat, she puts tampons in with a bazooka.

Yo momma like a revolving door: everyone gets a turn.

Yo momma like a bus: 50 pence and she's ready to ride!

Yo momma so fat, she needs two husbands just to give her a hug.

Yo momma like a bus: guys climb on and off her all day long.

Yo momma like a bubble gum machine: 25 pence a blow.

Yo momma so poor, I saw her walking down the street kicking a can. I said, 'What you doing, Mrs Johnson?' She said, 'Moving.'

Yo momma like a shotgun: give her a cock and she blows.

Yo momma so old, she was alive when the Dead Sea was just ill.

▶ Yo momma like a refrigerator: everyone puts their meat in!

▶ Yo momma like a golf course: everyone gets a hole in one!

▶ Yo momma pussy so dry, the crabs carry canteens.

▶ Yo momma so nasty, when your daddy ate her pussy he got food poisoning.

▶ Yo momma like a race car: she's always burning rubber.

▶ Yo momma so hairy, the only language she speaks is wookiee.

YORKSHIRE MEN

▶ Two old Yorkshire men were walking through the park on a hot summer's day, when they saw a girl sunbathing nude. The only thing hiding her modesty was a roofing tile from a local building site, placed strategically between her legs.

'I'll be buggered, Alf,' said one. 'Times have changed. I can remember when they used to be thatched.'

ZEBRAS

▶ A zebra living on the African plains is depressed. All his life he has been troubled because he wasn't sure whether he was white with black stripes or black with white stripes. Finally the uncertainty forces him to pray to God, in order to answer his question. He kneels down, looks up to the heavens and says, 'Dear God, please put me out of my misery. Please let me know whether I am a white zebra with black stripes or a black zebra with white stripes.'

The skies clear and a booming voice replies, 'You are what you are.'

The little zebra is puzzled by this answer and goes to see his wise old friend, the giraffe. He tells the giraffe precisely what his question was and what the answer was. 'I'm still no wiser,' he says to the giraffe.

'But,' says the giraffe, 'the answer was very clear – you are a white zebra with black stripes. If you had been a black zebra with white stripes, then God would have said, "You is what you is."'

ZOOS

▶ What's a shiatsu? A zoo with no animals.

▶ What's the difference between a European zoo and a Chinese zoo? In a European zoo there's a sign by the cage with the animal's name and description. In a Chinese zoo there's a sign by the cage with the animal's name and cooking methods.

▶ I was thinking of starting up a small zoo, so I wrote a letter to London Zoo: 'Dear sir, I'm starting up a zoo, please send me two mongooses.'

I thought that didn't sound right, so I tried again: 'Dear sir, I'm starting up a small zoo, please send me two mongeese.'

Nope, that still didn't sound right. 'Dear sir, I'm starting up a small zoo, please send me two mongi.'

'Ahh, sod it,' I thought. 'Dear Sir, I'm starting up a small zoo, please send me a mongoose. P.S. Send me another one.'